Birds of the British Isles

Birds of the British Isles

Edited by Jim Flegg

CAXTON

Acknowledgements

Contributing authors John H Barrett · John Burton · William Condry · Mike Everett · Chris Feare · Jim Flegg · Eric Hardy · Roger Lovegrove Nigel Matthews · Chris Mead · Robert Morgan Malcolm Ogilvie · Robert Spencer

Photo credits Heather Angel 15(T), 17(BL), 25(B), 76(B), 92, 96, 110(B), 111, 121(T), 124(T),133, 134(main), 138, 142(T), 158, 167(T), 186, 192(T), 195(T), 200, 208, 244, 264(T), 278(M):Aquila Photographics/GG Bates 41(M), 61(B); GG & IM Bates 198(B); JB Blossom 147(B),149(T); AJ Bond 152(T); PT Castell 146(T,M), 198(M); A W Cundall 116(B); NR Foster 30(B), 31(B), 55(B), 228; NW Harwood 82, 260(TL); EA Janes 220(T), 238(T), 278(T); R Kennedy 104; H Kinloch 24; MHV Lane 151(TL); W Lankinen 91, 147(T), 149(B), 234; JLawton-Roberts 189; T Leach 219(T); AT Moffett 178(M), 282(B), 298(T), 304(T), 314(B); RG Powvey 118; CJ Smale 185(B), 283(B); E Soothill 178(B); EK Thompson 79(B); MC Wilkes 21(T,B), 100, 114, 253, 267, 308(B), 312(T): Ian Beames 2, 26(T,B), 42, 53, 70, 97,109, 112(B), 140, 154(B), 156, 278(B), 283(M), 289: Richard Bilharry 38, 40: Biofotos/BM Rogers 22-3(T), 229: Frank Blackburn 62, 194, 249, 263: Kevin Carlson 244(inset): JPA Clare 68, 137(B): Bruce Coleman Ltd/E Breeze-Jones 144; J Burton 32, 187, 238(B), 262(M); B Coleman 273; S Dalton 204, 212, 214, 222, 251(T), 285; AJ Deane 88(T), 231; F Erize 60(B); CB Frith 185(T); D Green 20, 209; P Helo 46, 49(B); U Hirsch 183; P Hughes 105; G Langsbury 99, 164, 215; L Lee Rue 111, 48(B); L Lee Rue IV, 142(B); SC Porter 257, 303; A Purcell 59; H Reinhard 36, 50, 58, 74-5, 76(T), 108, 245, 269(T); R Tidman 113(B); NTomalin 232; J Van Wormer 48(T); P Ward 112(M); R Wilmhurst 224; G Ziesler 86, 88(B): Adrian Davies 16(B): Martin Dohrn 16(T): Jim Flegg 202: Bob Gibbons Photography/B Gibbons 240(T); P Wilson 8, 22(M), 127(T), 252, 255(T), 297(M): Dennis Green 15(M), 18(T), 44, 45(T), 55(T), 71, 77(B), 81(B), 89, 90(B), 101, 107(B), 115(B), 117(T), 146(B), 148(BL,BR), 150, 151(TR), 153, 155(T), 157, 175, 179, 181(T), 182, 196(T), 203, 239, 240(B), 243(B), 254(B), 262(B), 266(T), 268(B), 282(T), 296, 297(B), 306(T), 311, 315(B), 316: Melvin Grey 77(T), 163, 184(B): Brian Hawkes 64, 98: E & D Hosking 66: M King & M Read/G Dore 152(B);M Read 124: Richard Mills 1, 13(B), 17(T,BR), 31(T), 93, 119, 126, 127(M), 174(TL),178(T), 225(B), 247(B), 250(T), 258(T), 271, 272(M): Pat Morris 18(BL,BR), 30(T), 78, 79(T), 95(B), 116(T), 184(M), 272(T): WJC Murray 216(M,B): NHPA/M & J Bain 173(B), 292(T); A Barnes 9(TR), 122(BR), 260(TR); 266(B), 274(T), 275, 310: GT Cambridge 162(M); L Campbell 154(M); DN Dalton 135, 177, 228, 248(inset), 276, 279, 305, 313; S Dalton 12, 15, 226, 265, 290; J Good 31(M), 41(T), 247(T), 258(B); F Greenaway 192(M); SJ Harris 55(M), 107(T), 127(B); B Hawkes 25(T), 35, 60(T), 103, 121(B), 165(T), 188, 196(B), 218, 220-1(T), 277, 302(B); R Hosking 243(T); EA Janes 208, 223, 294, 301(T); J Jeffery 236, 250(B), 300; RWS Knightsbridge 171(T); E Martomak 45(B); WJC Murray 180(T), 213, 301(B); J Sauvanet 307; P Scott 13(T), 102; JR Soothill 220(B): Nature Photographers Ltd/T Andrewartha 134(inset), 162(B); SC Bisserot 292(B); FV Blackburn 29, 52, 73, 87, 120, 130, 132(T), 206, 256, 299, 309; D Bonsall 192(B); K Carlson 43, 57(T,B), 94, 122(T), 174(B), 317(B); RJ Chandler 167(B); A Cleave 248; R Crane 80; AK Davies 28, 162(T), 195(B); RH Fisher 172; ME Gore 171(B), 199, 288(T); P Heard 241(B); MR Hill 233(T); J Hunt 123; D Hutton 128, 129(M); EA Janes 260(B), 268(T), 269(B), 280, 281; C & J Knights 302(T); CK Mylne 30(M). 33(T), 49(T); O Newman 106, 145, 201; WS Paton 23(M), 41(B), 54, 83, 113(M), 190; N Picozzi 196(M); D Sewell 75,174(TR); D Smith 23(B), 61(T), 155(B), 160, 227(M), 235; P Sterry 81(T), 143, 159, 161, 176; EK Thompson 9(TL), 90(T); R Tidman 8(T), 14, 117(B), 165(B), 166, 197(T), 219(B), 283(T), 306(B), 312(B), 314(T); M Walker 181(B): Naturfoto/S Christoffersen 132(B); B Gensbøl 27(B); Jacana 63; Lüthen & Junge 137(T); Prestige Pictures/D Avon & T Tilford 33(B), 125, 133, 169, 170, 254(B), 255(B), 261, 315(T), 317(T): John Robinson 27(T), 122(BL), 129(B), 173(M), 180(B), 184(T), 207, 210, 211, 233(M,B), 241(M), 246, 264(B), 268(M), 274(B), 288(B), 291(T,B), 293, 295, 298(B), 304(B): Bryan Sage 6, 79(M): Phillipa Scott 84: D Sewell 110(T), 270: Roger Tidman 197(B): BS Turner 64-5(T), 65(B), 95(T), 142(M), 286: Universal Natural History Agency/A Goodger 225(T): Wildlife Services/M Leach 9(B), 107(M), 198(T), 308(T): MC Wilkes 227(B), 237.

Artists' credits Norman Arlott 51, 52-3, 62-3, 67, 68, 69, 94, 95, 98, 109, 131, 136, 187, 189, 191, 201, 202, 207, 210, 213, 215, 216, 217, 246, 251, 271, 272, 287, 289, 294, 300, 301: Russell Barnett 221(B): Wayne Ford 14, 15(B), 22, 39, 43, 44, 47, 59, 71, 72-3, 75, 79, 87, 88, 91, 112, 113, 115, 117(B), 119, 120, 123, 126, 127, 129, 132, 141, 145(T), 148, 151, 154, 158, 159, 161, 162, 165, 166, 170, 173, 185, 195, 199, 221(T), 223, 224-5, 227, 229, 232, 235, 254, 257, 259(birds), 262(birds), 263 (birds), 265(birds), 268, 275, 277, 279, 284, 291, 303, 307(birds), 310, 311(birds), 313(birds), 316 (birds): Will Giles 40: The Hayward Art Group 30, 210(map), 214(map), 245, 311(maps): Linden Artists/Tim Hayward 297: Kathryn Lunn 145(B): Orbis Publishing Ltd 99: Denys Ovenden 177: WS Paton 82: Sandra Pond 117(T), 259(B): Colin Salmon 13, 15(T), 34, 35, 56, 77, 101, 219, 229(map), 234, 256, 259(maps), 262(maps), 263(maps), 265(maps), 267, 274, 307(map), 313(map), 315(map): Ken Wood 106. Distribution map data courtesy of the B.T.O.

Material in this book previously appeared in *The Living Countryside*
© 1981, 1982, 1983, 1984 Eaglemoss Publications Limited and Orbis Publishing Limited.

First published in Great Britain by Orbis Publishing Limited, London 1984
© Orbis Publishing Limited 1984

This edition specially produced for CEEPI/Dealerfield Ltd in 1990

Printed in Czechoslovakia by Artia.

ISBN 0-907 305-41-5

52186

Contents

Introducing birds

Birds are beautiful and fascinating creatures. Not the least of their appeal is that they are so numerous and widespread, and far easier for most of us to see without difficulty than, say, mammals or even butterflies. Indeed, they are so ubiquitous that they may be difficult to get away from–should we of course wish to do that, since they contribute so much to the enrichment of our lives. Birds can be found in every conceivable habitat–the golden eagle soaring over the mountain top, the curlew on the moor, the yellowhammer on the farm, the jay deep in the wood, the blackbird in the garden and the house sparrow deep in the innermost heart of the grimy city are in each case just examples of the range of birds to be seen.

Thus birdwatching has the great advantage that it can be pursued with whatever degree of vigour one wishes. Should you so desire, then an expedition can be planned to one of the remoter habitats, and even in well-inhabited areas, remote habitats still do exist within reach of 'civilisation'. But to set against the additional pleasures of breaking new ground– pitting your endurance against a hard day's walking in the hills, for example, to see unusual birds–are the many advantages of what might be considered as mundane garden birdwatching. For the housebound, or those willing to use the house as a large hide, the confiding nature of birds allows them to be watched as they go about their daily business. Even viewed from the kitchen sink their squabbles at the bird table or frantic comings and goings to the nestbox can provide hours of enjoyment. Common birds some of them may be, but in close-up their lives reveal many interesting and even surprising facets of animal behaviour.

As the seasons change, so birds change with them. Spring brings back many of the songbirds that delight us in summer wood- lands, while the onset of autumn heralds the arrival of birds from Arctic breeding grounds. Rarely are these good songsters, but often–as with geese, ducks or waders flying in masses over coastal marshes or an estuary–they are visually more spectacular and thrilling.

Watching, marvelling at the beauty of plumage, or listening to the variety of songs, inevitably leads to other things. Like many hobbies, an increasing involvement fires an increasing interest. The starting point of birdwatching is normally just bird identifica- tion–something to do to enliven a long journey or just the daily walk to school or the station. But next, you want to watch them more closely (perhaps 'studied' would be a better term), and with developing knowledge comes the desire to know more about them– how do they run their daily lives? How far does a robin or a rook commute each day? Where do our migrants go, or come from? What structural adaptations–beaks and feet for example–do they have for their way of life? How long do birds live, and what are the major threats they face? How many eggs do they lay, and how many nestlings survive to become the next generation?

The pages which follow provide answers to just these questions–and others equally fascinating–as well as giving details of plumage and other information to help identification. For, following an introductory general section on bird classification, be- haviour and biology, highly readable and comprehensive accounts are given for over 125 popular common, unusual or interesting British species. The species are grouped in four categories–birds of prey, birds of fresh water, birds of coast and estuary, and songbirds and garden birds–which allow the lifestyles of birds with similar habits or habitats to be the better compared and contrasted.

Opposite: A colony of guillemots on Herma Ness, Unst.

Britain's birds classified

Few groups of animals are so immediately recognisable as the birds, but what are the differences which separate one bird order from another?

Above: A fulmar in flight. White sea-birds are not all closely related to gulls: the fulmar is one of the petrels, a primitive order of birds that are distinguished by their 'tube-noses'. The other white sea-bird on British and Irish coasts that is not related to gulls is the gannet, which belongs with the cormorant and shag in the order Pelecaniformes.

Below: This black-tailed godwit, on the other hand, does not look like a gull, but belongs to the same order as the gulls, the Charadriiformes. The 16 British families in this order include the Scolopidae family of long-legged waders, to which godwits belong, and the Laridae—the gulls and terns.

Modern bird classification is intended not only as a 'filing system' for easy reference—it is an attempt to show the natural relationships between groups of birds. As in all systems of classification, it can be depicted as a family tree. Like all family trees, the lineage of birds can be viewed from above—from the 'twigs' down the 'branches' to the 'trunk'—or from below, starting at the trunk and following its divisions into branches and then twigs. The twigs represent the various species of birds.

Of these two views, the one from the trunk upwards would in many ways be more satisfying. For if we had sufficient information, for example from fossils, we would be able to construct a classification that was perfectly faithful to evolution. Species, genera, families and orders would be purely natural ones and the taxonomist's work would be done for ever.

Unfortunately, the fossil record is far too full of gaps for this to be remotely possible. Thus bird classification has to depend heavily on the view from the top of the tree, arrang-

ing species, genera and families for the most part by what can be examined in a specimen today.

Confusing similarities Two important features are common to all birds: feathers and a pair of wings. These structures have resulted in a number of other common features that conform to the needs of an airborne life—such as lightweight bones, a flexible neck and a streamlined body. These adaptations so dominate the appearance of birds that, as a class, they are far more uniform than other well-known classes such as insects, mammals or reptiles. It follows that the features that distinguish one order of birds from another are often relatively minor. (Species, of course, can usually be distinguished most easily by their plumage patterns.)

The problem of classification into orders is increased, however, where, during the course of evolution, widely separate groups have developed, but which show much the same characteristics. This happens when various birds have a particular activity or habitat in common. The hobby, the swift and the swallow, for example, all live by fast flight, and in each species evolution has emphasized long, sickle-shaped wings with long primary feathers to achieve great speed. Other obvious features (beak and claws) quickly remove the hobby from this trio, but it takes an examination of, for example, the feet to place the swift and the swallow into different orders. The swift has all four toes pointing forward, while the swallow has three toes forward, one back. It is this relatively obscure feature that places swallows in the vast order of perching birds, the Passeriformes, while swifts are not even closely related—they belong with the hummingbirds of the New World, in the order Apodiformes.

Besides the sickle-shaped wings, many other examples can be cited of unrelated birds which have evolved to look alike. This is known as parallel evolution. Just as puzzling, on the other hand, can be the specialist species within an otherwise relatively uniform group. A good example of this is the peculiar beak of the crossbill, a pine-cone eater, compared with the pyramid-shaped beaks of the rest of the finch family.

The key features False clues apart, however, the majority of the features by which birds are told apart are clearly visible to the ordinary birdwatcher. For instance, the differences between the various ducks are clearly signalled–not only by the different plumage patterns but also by the detailed shape of the beak; and the same goes for the many finches. Birds of prey are distinguished from one another by their feet as well as by their colours. Bird ringers use the length and shape of the primary feathers to separate willow warblers from the similar-looking chiffchaffs, and taxonomists make wide use of the wing feathers in classification.

In certain cases taxonomists also use the skeletal anatomy, the nature of the palate, the shape of the syrinx (part of the windpipe), the layout of the intestinal loops in the gut, the length of the caecum (part of the gut) and many other internal features. Behavioural characters are sometimes used, although more attention is given to the details of physiology. In recent years, studies of blood plasma proteins, nucleic acids and egg-white proteins have joined the classical methods. In many cases the results of these exciting techniques support the established order, but in some cases they indicate that previous thinking may have been wrong.

The system unfolds If we look at the classification of birds–the class Aves–starting from the twigs of our tree, we find that there are about 8600 species of birds alive today in the world as a whole, grouped into about 170 families. Some families contain only one, or a few species, while others contain over 300.

The next level in the family tree is the order, which contains (normally) several families. Here the logic of the groupings may be more difficult for the birdwatcher, with his experience of the bird in the field, to understand. Gulls and terns, for example, which form the family Laridae, are placed by taxonomists in the order Charadriiformes. Some parts of the Charadriiformes seem to 'make sense', for its is natural to link the gulls and terns with the various wader families (oystercatchers, plovers, snipes, sandpipers and others) and with

Above: The barn owl is our only member of the family Tytonidae. All our other owls belong to the family Strigidae, placed in the owl order Strigiformes.

Right: A linnet perches beside its nest of young. The very act of perching is a clue to its membership of the vast order Passeriformes, which includes nearly half the bird species of Britain and Ireland. Although the name of this order means 'perching birds', it is easy to think of non-members that also perch–falcons, pigeons, owls and kingfishers–and of a few 'awkward' passerines that rarely perch, such as swallows and skylarks.

Below: The coot is a member of the order Gruiformes. Its fellow members in Britain and Ireland are the moorhen, the water rail and the corncrake. But the order derives its name from a Continental member, the crane (*Grus grus*).

the skuas. But the same order includes the auk family, including our razorbill, guillemot and puffin, which seem superficially to be vastly different. Another, even more unlikely, fellow member is the tropical family of the lily-trotters; these would seem more sensibly located with the other long-toed birds, such as the moorhen and water rail, which are in the order Gruiformes. Nevertheless, the members of each family placed into a particular order have sufficient features in common for taxonomists to have grouped them in this way.

Most orders contain only a handful of families, though the Charadriiformes, as we have seen, is something of an exception with its 16 families. But the greatest exception of all is the last order in the list, the Passeriformes. This is an enormous order containing about half the bird species existing at present. Its gigantic range embraces wrens, birds of paradise, New World and Old World warblers, flycatchers, thrushes, pipits, tits, starlings, crows, finches, buntings and many others–altogether some 67 families.

2 Great crested grebe

3 Storm petrel

4 Cormorant

1 Black-throated diver

Bird classification

20 House sparrow

19 Green woodpecker

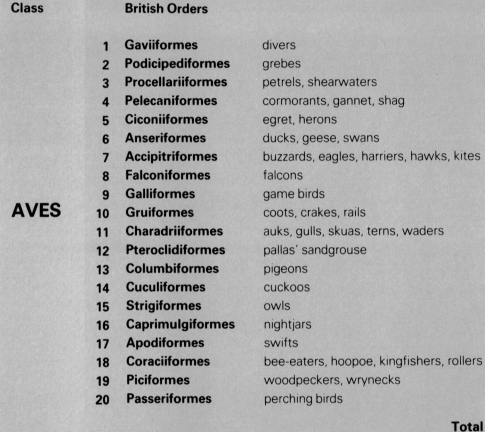

Class		British Orders	
	1	Gaviiformes	divers
	2	Podicipediformes	grebes
	3	Procellariiformes	petrels, shearwaters
	4	Pelecaniformes	cormorants, gannet, shag
	5	Ciconiiformes	egret, herons
	6	Anseriformes	ducks, geese, swans
	7	Accipitriformes	buzzards, eagles, harriers, hawks, kites
	8	Falconiformes	falcons
	9	Galliformes	game birds
AVES	10	Gruiformes	coots, crakes, rails
	11	Charadriiformes	auks, gulls, skuas, terns, waders
	12	Pteroclidiformes	pallas' sandgrouse
	13	Columbiformes	pigeons
	14	Cuculiformes	cuckoos
	15	Strigiformes	owls
	16	Caprimulgiformes	nightjars
	17	Apodiformes	swifts
	18	Coraciiformes	bee-eaters, hoopoe, kingfishers, rollers
	19	Piciformes	woodpeckers, wrynecks
	20	Passeriformes	perching birds

Total

18 Kingfisher

17 Swift

16 Nightjar

15 Tawny owl

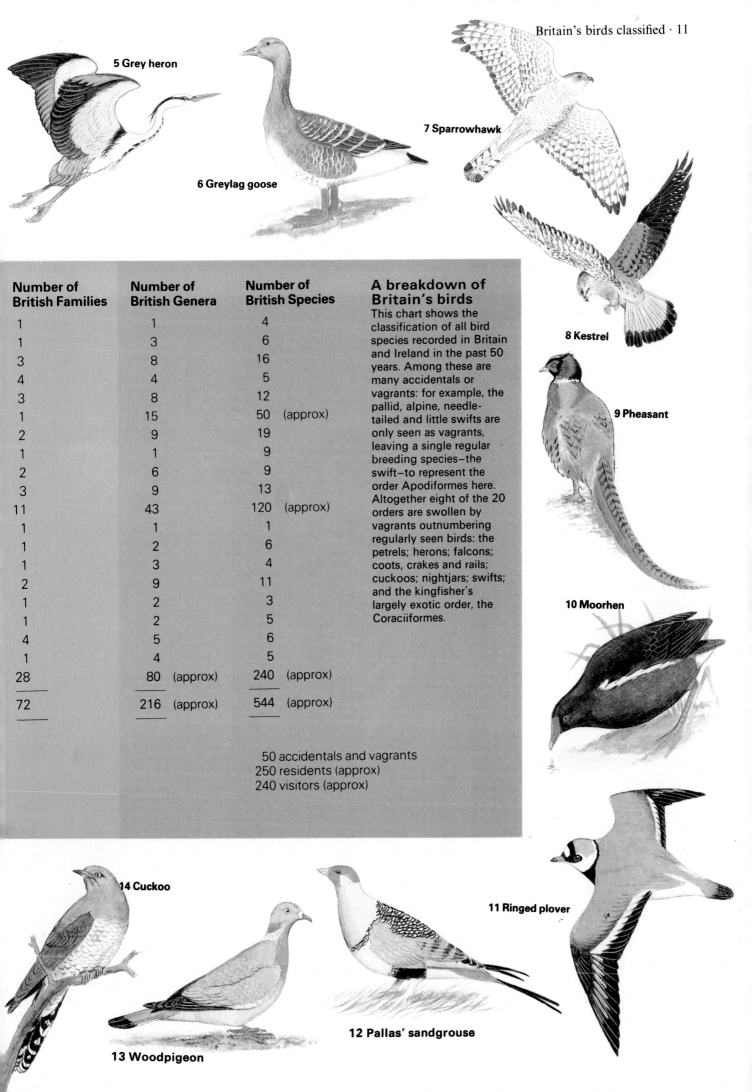

5 Grey heron

6 Greylag goose

7 Sparrowhawk

8 Kestrel

9 Pheasant

10 Moorhen

A breakdown of Britain's birds

This chart shows the classification of all bird species recorded in Britain and Ireland in the past 50 years. Among these are many accidentals or vagrants: for example, the pallid, alpine, needle-tailed and little swifts are only seen as vagrants, leaving a single regular breeding species–the swift–to represent the order Apodiformes here. Altogether eight of the 20 orders are swollen by vagrants outnumbering regularly seen birds: the petrels; herons; falcons; coots, crakes and rails; cuckoos; nightjars; swifts; and the kingfisher's largely exotic order, the Coraciiformes.

Number of British Families	Number of British Genera	Number of British Species
1	1	4
1	3	6
3	8	16
4	4	5
3	8	12
1	15	50 (approx)
2	9	19
1	1	9
2	6	9
3	9	13
11	43	120 (approx)
1	1	1
1	2	6
1	3	4
2	9	11
1	2	3
1	2	5
4	5	6
1	4	5
28	80 (approx)	240 (approx)
72	216 (approx)	544 (approx)

50 accidentals and vagrants
250 residents (approx)
240 visitors (approx)

11 Ringed plover

12 Pallas' sandgrouse

13 Woodpigeon

14 Cuckoo

Bird flight

Birds have perfected their powers of flight over aeons of evolution. The result is a series of brilliant wing designs: some that give high speed, some that allow easy control, and others that provide a useful, all-round range of flying skills.

If numbers of species are a worthwhile guide, birds – with over 8000 species that fly compared with 4000 non-flying mammal species – are arguably the most successful class of vertebrates today. Their success is due in large part to the powers of movement, and thus the wide choice of habitat, that flight allows.

How flight works The mechanical problem concerned with flight is how to lift a weight clear of the ground, keep it airborne for a practical time and propel it forwards at the same time. For this, an upward force (lift) and a forward force (propulsion) are required.

A glance at the wing cross-section of a model aircraft shows the solution to this problem. Rounded and thicker at the front than at the slender 'trailing edge', shallowly convex above and concave below, this is called an aerofoil section. Move an aerofoil section forwards through the air, and it causes air to flow in such a way across its surfaces as to produce lift. The discovery of the aerofoil section enabled man to fly: birds have used it for aeons. The inner portion of a bird's wing, which is anatomically equivalent to the human forearm, has a classic aerofoil section.

The next requirement is propulsion. For this, birds rely on the beating of their wings, powered by the breast muscles (the pectorals) which are highly developed. Propulsion is provided by the outer part of the wing, from the angle (where the front edge bends) to the tip. This part is anatomically equivalent to the human hand, from wrist to fingertips. The ten or twelve long, strong feathers at the end of the wing (the flight feathers) are vitally important and merit their technical name 'primaries'.

Variable geometry The vast majority of aircraft have wings and tail securely fixed in position, and only the provision of flaps and ailerons allows their shape to be altered so that the aircraft is manoeuvrable. Some of the most sophisticated modern fighter planes are famed for their 'variable geometry' but this merely allows the wings to swing in and out from the fuselage. It is easy to see, therefore, how much more manoeuvrable birds are than aircraft, with an almost infinite variety of positions, not just of the wings and tail, but of the parts of the wings and often of the individual feathers.

Take-off and landing To complete their manoeuvrability, birds have to be able to take off and land at will. Many survive precisely

Above: Freedom of the air enables these snow geese to choose the best places for feeding and roosting. With advantages like this, birds as a class have evolved twice as many species as mammals.

Opposite: A great tit in flight, showing the outstretched primaries.

Below: A bird the size of a heron needs large wings which it flaps slowly and laboriously.

because they can do this at a split second's notice, escaping the ever present danger of attacking predators. Taking off requires the maximum output of propelling force (thrust) that the bird is capable of producing.

The smaller species are capable of exerting sufficient effort to lift themselves off the ground with no preliminary 'run'. Heavier birds, on the other hand, have to survive without the ability to respond to danger by an instant take-off. Large waterbirds, such as swans and the great northern diver, attain safety by spending much of their time on the open water, far away from the predators on dry land. Their take-off is so difficult that they often have to 'run' some distance across the water surface, and can only occupy stretches of water large enough to allow space for this long take-off.

To land, birds need to 'spill' the lift that their wings and tails have been providing during flight. One way to lose lift is to raise the tail, thus steering into a descent towards the landing place. To halt their flight, birds rear up in mid-air to an upright posture as

How an aerofoil works

lift is created by pressures resulting from the air flow

reduced air pressure

air flow

increased air pressure pushes wing upwards

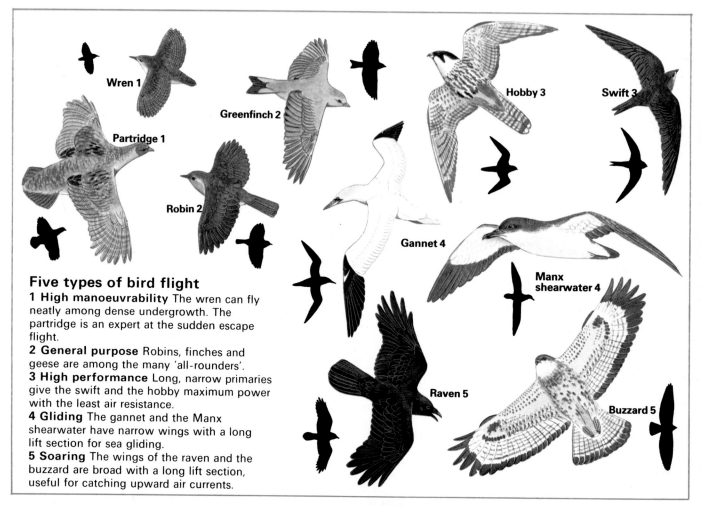

Five types of bird flight

1 High manoeuvrability The wren can fly neatly among dense undergrowth. The partridge is an expert at the sudden escape flight.

2 General purpose Robins, finches and geese are among the many 'all-rounders'.

3 High performance Long, narrow primaries give the swift and the hobby maximum power with the least air resistance.

4 Gliding The gannet and the Manx shearwater have narrow wings with a long lift section for sea gliding.

5 Soaring The wings of the raven and the buzzard are broad with a long lift section, useful for catching upward air currents.

Above: Brent geese have a 'general purpose' wing layout, but improve their flight efficiency by means of a cunning use of the V pattern. The bird at the front creates turbulence in its wake with the beating of its wings; this turbulence gives extra lift to the birds flying on either flank behind. The lead bird is usually an old and powerful female, who may change places with another as she becomes tired. The less powerful flyers, including youngsters, stay in the arms of the V.

they approach the selected spot. This tilts the wings until they are nearly in a vertical plane, so that they can act as 'brakes', or even beat against the direction of flight. The tail is lowered, also acting as a brake against forward movement.

The hard impact of landing is absorbed by flexible legs and strong muscles, which are attached to the most rigid part of the bird's skeleton – the pelvis, which is fused on to the lower spine for added strength.

Many shapes of wings In the course of evolution, families of birds have developed the capability of flight in a number of different ways to suit the various modes of life they have adopted.

First, there are naturally many birds without a specialised form of flight and these have a 'general purpose' wing layout. In this layout, the lift and power sections of the wing are roughly of equal length. The wing is twice as long as it is wide. Garden birds such as the greenfinch and the robin fit into this category. So, too, do larger birds like geese.

If the 'general purpose' category is placed in the middle of a range of flight styles, one of the extremes on the scale would be 'high manoeuvrability'. Birds in this category have wings with lift and power sections of equal length, but the wing is much rounder in appearance, rather than long, for it is almost as broad at its base as it is long from base to tip. Examples include the game birds, which need fast and almost vertical take-off to escape predators, and birds of thick cover, such as the tiny wren. This wing pattern provides strong propulsion, but the high manoeuvrability results from the broad wing area.

The other extreme consists of the birds that specialise in extra-efficient flight. Among these species, flight is developed to the highest standards of performance. For maximum speed, their wings do not have the same proportions as those of the other categories of birds. The power section of the wing (the primary feathers) is much longer than the lift section – in some cases by as much as a factor of four – and the wing is long and thin.

Above: The black primaries of the gannet clearly show the proportions of the wing layout: the white lift section is longer, a good gliding characteristic.

Left: A female golden eagle soars effortlessly. The primary feathers are spread out to obtain maximum advantage from rising air currents; they are also specially shaped to reduce turbulence, helping the eagle to gain speed when gliding downwards, after soaring to its peak.

Exploiting wind power

The seabird takes a shallow downward glide across the wind, then turns into the wind and climbs steeply, until it resumes gliding in its original direction. It thus uses relative wind speeds to power both the climb and control the long, downward glide over the ocean.

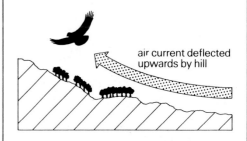

Upward air currents are used by ravens, eagles and buzzards. Typical soaring flight is in a slow, circling climb. The birds also exploit thermals, which are upward currents created when the sun's warmth causes air to rise.

The swift is an excellent example.

Two ways of gliding Gliding (in the case of birds) is flying without flapping wings. Two groups of birds are adapted for this type of flight: those that use wind power to travel over the sea (gliding in the common sense of the word) and those that not only glide but also exploit rising air currents to gain height (soaring).

The 'gliding' birds have extremely long and narrow wings, with a lift section either as long as the power section or longer. Most of them are oceanic birds, best exemplified by the albatrosses of the southern hemisphere but represented in British waters by the fulmar, the gannet and the Manx shearwater.

The 'soaring' birds use upcurrents at a ridge of hills or, in warm conditions, columns of rising air called thermals. In warmer countries these currents are the province of the vultures, but in Britain and Ireland the best examples of soaring flight are given by the raven, the buzzard and the golden eagle.

These birds are quite different in silhouette from the seagoing gliders: they too have a lift section as long as the power section or else even longer, but their wings are much broader. Further, the wingtips, rather than being pointed, have a broadly splayed 'fingered' appearance which helps to reduce turbulence. The birds flap slowly and laboriously into the air in wide circles, but once they catch the rising air they soar effortlessly.

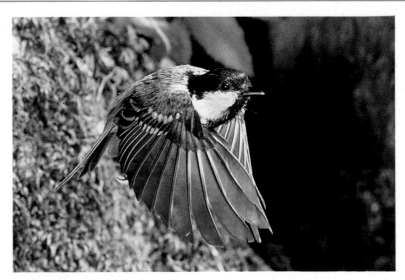

Rowing through the air

1 On the downstroke (above) the wings move forward and then, at the bottom of the stroke, push backwards. The feathers are held firmly together, presenting a flat, blade-like surface.
2 On the upstroke (right) the primary feathers twist, like the vanes of a Venetian blind, and thus open a slight space allowing air through; this reduces air resistance to the upstroke.

Territoriality

Several kinds of territory and territorial behaviour can be observed in the birds of Britain and Ireland, forming an exciting aspect of bird study.

A territory is a defended area: in discussing territories, the use of the word defence implies that someone will take your territory from you if you do not adequately defend it. Experiments with many species of birds have shown that there is indeed constant pressure on territories: when researchers captured and removed the territory holders, new occupants of the same species quickly replaced them, often in hours rather than days.

Social behaviour in birds contrasts with territoriality, for sociality involves flocking, colonial breeding or the common ownership or use of a particular area. However, sociality and territoriality can be combined in the same species in various ways. For example, in the crow, pairs of breeding birds occupy territories, while non-breeding crows live in a flock nearby, often in an area that is unsuitable for breeding due to a shortage of nest sites. Should a crow territory fall vacant, it is quickly occupied by one of the members of the flock.

Territorial song With such pressure on territory holders, it is essential that they devote as much time as possible to securing their hold on their own plots. However, in many situations it is not possible for a territory holder to see all of his boundary from one vantage point, and he cannot therefore be on hand to see and drive away any marauder. Furthermore, it would take up far too much of his time and energy if he attempted to patrol the boundary with the constancy needed to keep out intruders. In fact, such constant vigilance is rendered unnecessary by a form of communication that works over long distances – song.

Song has several functions, of which mate attraction is perhaps the most obvious. But in an experiment where male great tits were

Above: A scene on the Grassholm gannetry, Wales. These are non-breeding birds that do not hold territories, but occupy a small area on the edge of the colony known as a 'club'. They include adults who have failed to secure a territory as well as immature birds such as the mottled sub-adult at the centre.

Below: The nesting colony at Grassholm. The nest sites are densely packed and vigorously defended, making a regular pattern.

removed, their territories were kept free of intruders for some time by playing tape recordings of great tit song over loudspeakers.

In other birds, the posture of the territory owner may be sufficient to signal to a potential settler that an area is already occupied. For example, starlings adopt a characteristic posture while singing, with the wings held slightly away from the body, the feathers of the crown and throat puffed out and the tail directed downwards, giving a 'hunch-backed' appearance. Starlings often adopt this posture while not singing, but while perched on an exposed song post within easy view of any bird looking for a territory.

At first sight, it appears strange that a bird looking for a place to settle should be deterred by a bird that is simply singing or displaying. When this system fails, however, and the intruder does try to stake a claim, the home-owner almost always wins the ensuing contests, whether these consist of threatening displays or physical combat.

It is not entirely clear why a male is usually victorious on his own territory. It may be because of his superior knowledge of the terrain. Whatever the advantage, the presence of a bird advertising that he is the landowner is often sufficient indication to an intruder that if he does attempt to settle, he will use up valuable time and energy in a conflict that he is unlikely to win.

Kinds of territory The kind of territory with

Above: Starlings going to roost at sunset. The birds live in flocks all year round, sometimes joining together in vast communities. The area over which the flock ranges in search of food is known as the home range. Since the birds nest in holes, which are naturally some distance apart, their breeding colonies have to be spread out over a large area. For this reason, starling colonies are not as obvious to view as those of rooks or seabirds.

Left: Part of a rookery, in tall trees by a motorway.

Below: The territorial song of the cock robin can be heard clearly all round his territory. This spares him a lot of the work of patrolling the boundary.

which most people are familiar is that of the garden blackbird. In this type, a breeding pair defends a plot of land of around one fifth of a hectare ($\frac{1}{2}$ acre) against other blackbirds. Within this territory, the pair feed and build their nest.

Breeding pairs of robins also vigorously defend a territory in the breeding season but, unlike blackbirds, robins become aggressively territorial again in the autumn. Now, however, males and females defend separate territories in which each individual feeds, and these autumn territories are smaller than those held by pairs in the spring.

Starlings and rooks, on the other hand, are far more social than robins and blackbirds. They stay in flocks during the breeding season, just as they flock at other times of year. It is readily apparent, from looking at a rookery, that rooks are social while nesting. The same applies to starlings, although their requirement for holes as nest sites leads to a somewhat greater dispersal of nests and their coloniality is less readily visible. Sociality has its limits, however, and around the nest

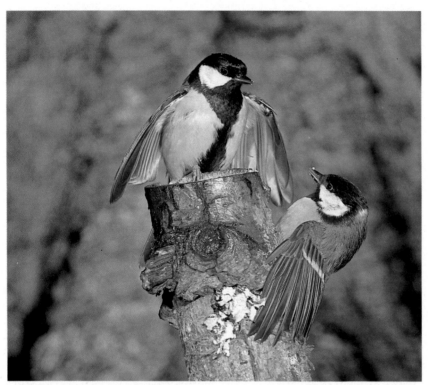

both species drive off intruders. In these species, the territory is therefore restricted to a small area around the nest. The birds are content to share their feeding grounds, and do not even defend them against birds of their own species from neighbouring colonies.

The area over which the breeding rooks and starlings travel in search of food is thus not a defended territory, and is known as a home range. A tiny nesting territory and an even larger home range, sometimes extending 100km (60 miles) from the nest, is typical of many seabirds, such as the gannet, kittiwake and guillemot. In the case of the guillemot, the defended area is limited to a small length of cliff ledge around the egg or chick, so that each narrow ledge looks from a distance like a line of black and white birds.

Territories with no nests In the breeding territories mentioned so far, the nest site has been a vital component. While this is the case for most British birds, there are exceptions. When shelduck return to their breeding grounds from the moulting areas to which

Above: This scene on a great tit territory illustrates two display postures at the same time. The male (on top of the stump) is displaying to his own mate, but in many species a similar posture is used in defence of a territory. Vanquished males adopt postures rather like the submission posture of his mate, with bowed head and trailing wings.

Below: Robins defend territories in winter as well as spring, as the two photographs clearly show. On the left, a territory holder confronts a stuffed robin that has been placed on his 'patch'. On the right, he triumphs over the intruder, of whom little can be seen but the upturned wooden base.

they migrate in autumn, they spend much of the winter in flocks. In late winter, however, they form pairs. These pairs are territorial and defend feeding sites on the muddy banks of estuaries.

The ownership of a territory is, as in other species, essential for breeding: but shelduck do not breed on their territory. They breed under cover of thick vegetation, or use rabbit burrows in dunes and sea walls, some distance from the feeding territory. During incubation, the feeding territory remains the centre of activity for the non-incubating male, and his mate leaves the nest about four times each day to feed on the territory.

In the case of ruff and black grouse, a small and vigorously defended territory is used neither for nesting nor for feeding, but only for display. Such display territories, or leks, are used by those males that have been able to obtain one in complex ritualised displays which become more and more intense when females are around. The females are attracted to the display territories by the activity of the males, and visit the territories to mate. The lekking area is generally on an open piece of ground, and while 20 or more males hold territories there, the females are attracted to some males more than others. As a result, most copulations are achieved by relatively few of the males. Presumably this polygamous mating system selects the 'best quality' males (a form of natural selection) to father the next generation.

Pied wagtails in winter Like the robin in autumn, some pied wagtails occupy individual territories in winter. These are simply feeding territories, and the occupation of one of these depends both on the individual's status and on how much food is available. Where food is predictably plentiful, high-ranking individual birds hold territories. A juvenile pied wagtail may be allowed to feed within the territory, and when it does it helps in territorial defence. Where food supplies are more transient or scarce, pied wagtails feed in flocks. Should the 'dependable' food supply fail, as when a river bank freezes, then the territory-holders vacate their plots, and join the flocks.

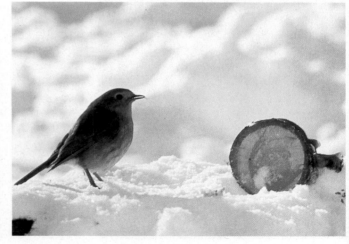

Types of territory

Birds are either solitary or communal nesters. Breeding territories vary from relatively large (eg blackbird) to very small (eg gannet). Similarly birds feed either alone or in flocks. Some solitary feeders (eg shelduck) defend feeding territories, while flocking birds use undefended areas. Pied wagtails are unusual because in winter they feed either in defended territories or in flocks, depending on conditions. The most unusual type is the lek territory (eg ruff): this is used for neither nesting nor feeding, but purely for display and mating.

- nest site
- defended breeding territory
- defended feeding territory
- defended display territory
- home range (non-defended area used for feeding)

Blackbird

Robin

Starling

Rook

Shelduck

Ruff

Pied wagtail in winter

Breeding strategies

Birds have an intriguing variety of egg colours, laying times, clutch sizes and nest designs, arising from the endless search for ways to ensure survival of the young.

A long way back in time, perhaps over 140 million years ago, the fossil record shows that the first truly bird-like creatures developed as an offshoot of the reptiles. Unlike mammals, birds continue to use the reptiles' method of reproduction—the fertilised ovum developing inside an egg that is incubated outside the body of the adult until it is ready to hatch.

It is not easy to assess whether laying eggs is a better or worse method of reproduction than the mammalian system, in which the young develop inside the mother until birth. Each method has shown its advantages and disadvantages, and as the 'egg method' has endured for over 100 million years, it must

be regarded as a success in evolutionary terms.

Eggs of all shades One striking feature of eggs is their intriguing range of colours and markings. Often it seems easy to attribute some advantage to the colouring–the black-speckled, sand-coloured eggs of terns or of the ringed plover, for example, are ideally camouflaged, for these birds nest on sand, among fragments of seaweed or on shingle beaches. The eggs of hole-nesting birds such as stock doves, woodpeckers and owls, are generally white: no doubt this helps the incubating bird to locate the eggs in the dark nest, and so avoid trampling on them. In addition, it seems natural that eggs so well

Above: An exceptionally large clutch of mallard eggs–the normal clutch has seven to eleven eggs. Large clutches help to compensate for losses caused by predators.

Opposite: A pair of bullfinches with their young. Both parents share in the task of feeding.

Below: A pair of reed warblers engaged in courtship feeding: this builds up the female's body reserves in preparation for breeding.

hidden need no colour camouflage. Birds that nest in crowded colonies need to recognise their own eggs, and this may be the explanation for the wide variety of ground shades (the basic colour of the egg) and black squiggles found on the eggs of guillemots in their cliff-ledge colonies.

There are, however, unexplained anomalies. For instance, each egg in every clutch laid by the red-backed shrike is a different colour: this has made them so attractive to egg collectors, from Victorian times to the present day, that the species has been plundered almost to extinction in England. Another anomaly is the dunnock: few birds are so well camouflaged as this species, its colours matching the undergrowth in which its nest is built. But once the sitting bird has flown what could be more glaringly conspicuous than the clutch of bright sky-blue eggs? Quite the opposite of being camouflaged, these must be positively eye-catching to predators such as jays and magpies.

Feeding for fitness For many birds, breeding success must depend heavily on the good physical condition of the pair. The whole breeding cycle must occur during a period when plenty of food is available. Well before the time for laying, the male needs plenty of food to give him the strength to perform his lively song and active display in order to attract a mate. He also needs all his strength to establish and hold a territory against rival claims.

The female must also get into first-class condition for the hardships of the breeding season. Courtship feeding, in which the male fetches caterpillars or other delicacies for his mate, has true practical importance: producing eggs requires a great deal of energy, and the female needs every scrap of food she can get. The female blue tit, for example, stores up so much food in her body that she increases in weight by half as much again during the fortnight before egg laying begins.

Nests of many kinds One advantage of laying eggs is that the mother does not have to carry heavy young within her body. But it gives rise to more problems in turn. First, eggs are fragile and need protection from break-

age. Secondly, they need correctly controlled warmth and insulation from the harshness of the weather. Besides this, the eggs, and in most cases the young, are static and may be vulnerable to a number of specialist or opportunist nest predators. Birds have derived solutions to all these problems from a single feature – the nest.

The simplest 'nests' are merely places where one or more eggs are laid directly on to the ground. The eggs may be protected by their own camouflage or by the sheer inaccessibility of the nest site – a cliff ledge for example. In some waders and many ducks and gulls, the art of nest building is a little more elaborate: nearby vegetation is gathered into a heap to help insulate the eggs and offer some protection against change in the water level. The grebes have a subtle variation of this method: their nests are 'rafts' of vegetation that float on the water, rising and falling with the water level, and moored in place with pliable stems of long foliage.

The cup-shaped nest built by most small and medium-sized birds offers protection in a variety of ways. The eggs naturally cluster

Left: Cuckoos practise a form of parasitism in their unique method of breeding. They do not build nests or look after their young, but lay their eggs into other birds' nests. The young cuckoo hatches first and ejects its potential 'brothers and sisters' from the nest. Here a dunnock is seen looking after a young cuckoo, thinking it is its own offspring. The commonest hosts are meadow pipits, dunnocks and reed warblers.

Opposite: Another unusual breeding method is practised by the short-eared owl: the owl lays its eggs at intervals of two days or more, and starts to incubate as soon as the first egg is laid. The eggs hatch at similar intervals, so that in a clutch of seven there may be a two-week difference in age between the oldest and the youngest chick. There is some flexibility in the size of the owl's brood, although it is achieved in a manner that we find distasteful: should the food supply diminish, the oldest may eat the youngest, and so on, until the family is reduced to a more viable size.

The helpless and the active young

Nidicolous (nest-loving) species of birds hatch naked, blind and helpless: these include most songbirds and some of the larger species, such as eagles.

Nidifugous (nest-fleeing) species hatch with eyes open and a covering of down, and can soon run and feed themselves; these include ducks, gulls and waders.

Blackbird

Common sandpiper

nidifugous

nidicolous

of a particular food supply. This bird has a highly specialised feeding technique, for it lives on the seeds of pine and other cone-bearing trees. These may mature at almost any time of year, and the crossbill is able to adjust its breeding time to coincide with the supply, so it is possible to see crossbills sitting on eggs in winter.

The nesting brood The nestling stage is a time of considerable risk. The young are noisy and inexperienced, and may easily draw the attention of a predator. Parent birds have to spend almost all the daylight hours in ceaseless attempts to keep the young well-fed. In consequence the young are vulnerable to cold weather, heavy rain or hailstorms.

Birds clearly take great pains through spring and summer, and the young have to undergo many hazards before the lucky few that survive fly away and join the adult population. Many eggs and young are lost in the process, so the breeding patterns may seem highly wasteful; but their success can be judged by the variety and the numbers of birds that surround us in their many different habitats.

together in the base of the cup, where they are well insulated from cold and partly hidden from the eyes of predators.

Even better protection from prying eyes is given by domed nests, more complex structures made by small birds such as wrens and long-tailed tits. Tree holes also give good all-round protection, and are used as nesting sites by many species of birds, including owls, woodpeckers and pied flycatchers. Wheatears are well concealed in their nests in cavities among rocks and in walls, as are puffins in their underground burrows.

Timing it right In the course of evolution, a number of patterns of breeding have arisen that specifically take advantage of certain circumstances. The blue tit and great tit populations in Britain are a case in point. The majority of these birds depend on winter moth caterpillars as a supply of food for their young. These caterpillars occur in enormous numbers, but only for a month or so in early summer. To take the best advantage of this annual event, the blue tit or great tit lays its eggs all in one clutch, between 5 and 16 in number. Laying is timed precisely so that the young will hatch and grow to their most demanding size when the caterpillars are fully grown.

In contrast to this, almost a literal case of 'all eggs in one basket', the majority of small and medium-sized garden birds produce two or three clutches, and may even lay more in a good summer. Their clutches are smaller, with only four to six eggs. This method allows them to exploit a moderate food supply throughout the summer, rather than a short-lived glut in June.

The crossbill has a variable breeding time which, like that of the tits, is linked to the time

Above: A ringed plover's nest, superbly camouflaged on the shingle—so well that you may not notice it even when you know it's there! This nest is no more than a place where eggs are laid directly on to the ground, but in some of these 'scrapes' the ringed plover may make a scant lining with a few strands of seaweed or other plants.

Right: The chaffinch conceals its eggs and brood within an elaborately constructed nest. The lichens that it uses to make the outer layers of the nest may also camouflage the nest if it is built on a branch that is also lichen-covered.

Nest sites

A bird's nest can be just a scrape in the ground or an intricately woven cup, but it must protect eggs and shelter young from predators and bad weather.

Nests are the places where birds lay their eggs. But nests are not exclusive to birds: reptiles, fish, various insects, worms and other animals all make structures called nests. All these creatures make a nest for one good reason – to protect its contents. Eggs are fragile and need protection from breakage; they need warmth to develop and must not be exposed to bad weather; the eggs (and the young emerging from them) are particularly vulnerable to predators and must be guarded by the nest's construction and concealment.

Although a bird's nest always contains the eggs, it may not always house the developing young. Most small song birds, and some larger birds such as crows, owls and birds of prey, hatch out naked, blind and helpless and remain in the nest until they are ready to fly. Ducks and waders, on the other hand, hatch with their eyes open, with a covering of down and well-developed legs, and can scamper about or swim as soon as they have dried off.

Early in spring, or even during winter with larger birds, the male establishes his territory. Usually, within that territory there will be a number of suitable nest sites. With some birds, like the wren, the male does the bulk of the construction work on several nests, before the pair finally settles on one and puts the finishing touches to it. In the same way, the male lapwing will make several scrapes (by shuffling his feet and belly to produce a

Above: The eggs of the oystercatcher – perfectly camouflaged against the pebbles on the beach – need no extra protection.

Opposite: The Slavonian grebe builds a floating raft of vegetation on which it lays its eggs – well away from predators.

Below: Nest and eggs of a red grouse; the long grass helps to hide the nest, but the eggs are protected mainly by the camouflage coloration of the hen.

saucer-shaped depression in the soil) before the final site is selected and a dried grass lining added.

With many other birds, it seems that the female plays the major role in selecting the actual site, and subsequently in building the nest. The male, however, does not idly watch his female dash back and forth with beakfuls of nesting material. He still has the vital job of guarding the territory, which demands continual alertness. The biological complexities of the breeding season become apparent: both birds must get themselves into the peak of condition – which means long hours of feeding – but at the same time territory must be secured and patrolled *and* the nest built.

Ground nests The simplest nests are those where the eggs are laid on the ground. Often, in such circumstances, protection from predators comes with the site; for example, guillemots nest on inaccessible sea cliff ledges. For others, such as the oystercatcher or ringed plover, birds which nest on a beach, the camouflage colours of the eggs provide the necessary concealment. Many wader nests look very simple – just scrapes in the ground – but they are in fact structured and in some cases ornamented; one nest contained over 1000 small pebbles, as well as twigs and pieces of shell.

Other waders, ducks and gulls make nests which are a further development of the simple

The basic structure of cup nests is the same, even when the size varies from the few centimeters in diameter of finches' nests to the one metre or more of those made by the heron and golden eagle. An outer framework of stout grasses, small roots, twigs or branches is lodged in a suitable tree fork or similar place. Gradually smaller and more flexible materials are tucked and woven into this structure, until the central cup is ready for lining. This nest is typical of the majority of perching birds – called passerines – which includes most small birds of farm, wood and garden. Where such birds extend their breeding range high up mountains or well to the north where there are few trees, similar nests are built on or close to the ground.

Domed nests are elaborations of the cup nest; additional protection is given by roofing over the structure and making a side entrance. Willow warblers build low-level grass nests of this type, while magpies construct high level, much bulkier versions. The most attractive examples are the long-tailed tits' cobweb-and-lichen, flask-shaped nests which are amazingly flexible to accommodate the

ground type. They gather dead vegetation, flotsam and jetsam into a mound and make a depression at its centre. The structures made by ducks and waders are usually at a low level, but the black-headed gull makes a built-up nest on the flat terrain of estuarine saltmarshes or moorland bogs, where the water level may rise suddenly and inundate low-lying eggs.

Game birds are also ground nesters and lay their eggs in grass-lined hollows. The hen protects her clutch from predators by her own camouflage colouring and will not budge from the nest unless it is absolutely necessary. Game birds do not have a strong scent, so predators like foxes find it hard to detect a red grouse or ptarmigan hen on a nest.

The floating nest is the next logical development. The little grebe's nest, loosely anchored to nearby vegetation, can rise and fall with the floodwaters and naturally survives far better than those of the coot or moorhen, which are fixed firmly in the reeds or on a low-hanging bough. For specialist swimmers like the grebes, which have legs set well back on a torpedo-shaped body, walking is awkward; floating nests are easier to get on and off.

Cup nests The cup is a practical shape for many purposes: the eggs cluster naturally in the bottom safe from disturbance and, if the nest is well constructed, safe too from the eyes of prying predators. Often the cup is lined with dried mud, fine grasses, moss, fur or feathers, which provide excellent insulation for the eggs; this also enables the incubating female to slip off occasionally to eat or drink. This insulation becomes more important when she has to help gather food for the young.

Above: Song thrush with young on nest. The cup shape of the nest stops the eggs rolling out and keeps the chicks safely in.

Right: Up to 12 chicks can be stuffed into the tiny, stifling, dome-shaped nest of the long-tailed tit. The nest is built of moss and cobwebs and is lined with countless feathers.

Nest boxes in the garden

One of the major problems for birdwatchers who wish to observe nesting behaviour is that birds try to make their nests as inconspicuous as possible. A nest box in your own garden gives you the opportunity to watch nesting birds at close quarters and in comfort. You can buy or make suitable boxes, or even put out an old kettle or an oil can.

Position the box high enough up a tree or the side of a house or shed so it is well out of reach of marauding cats (or children), but so that you still have a clear view. Make sure the box is not in direct sunlight or beating rain – you don't want the nestlings to overheat or drown. If you want to put up several boxes, position them at least 18m (60ft) apart, so different families do not disturb each other.

Once the box is in position, watch carefully to see which species of birds take an interest in it, and what nesting materials they use. The birds do not usually object if you want to look inside the box to check progress, but don't disturb a female sitting on eggs; watch for her to leave, then look but don't touch.

growing brood, and the better known dried leaf constructions of the wren. The male wren may build in any sort of crevice, from a tangle of ivy to an old jacket pocket in the garden shed.

Cavity nests Several birds, notably the owls, jackdaw and stock dove, nest in natural or man-made cavities such as hollow trees and church belfries. The house sparrow is a notable exploiter of cavities in buildings (although fully capable of building an untidy, domed nest outdoors). You might think these nests would be safer than other types, but this is not the case. The tit family are cavity nesters, but are vulnerable to attack from mice, woodpeckers and weasels.

Right: Suspended securely between reeds, the nest of the reed warbler is well hidden from predators and is so shaped that the eggs will not fall out even though the reeds sway in the wind.

Below: The great spotted woodpecker uses its strong beak like a hammer and chisel to excavate a nest hole high up the trunk of a tree where few predators will venture.

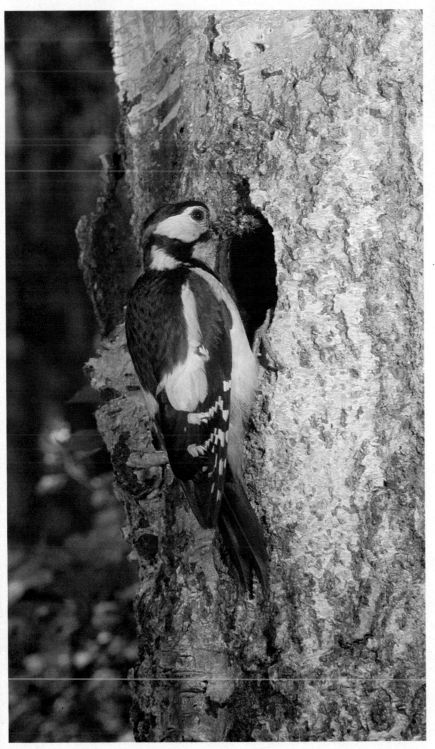

Other species, such as the woodpeckers, kingfisher and sand martin, excavate their own cavities in wood or the soil. Woodpeckers, which make a speciality of hammering and chiselling out nest cavities in tree trunks, are equipped with an extra pad of cartilage tissue situated just between the end of the beak and the nasal bone that acts as a shock-absorber, preventing the birds from developing a splitting headache.

Soil excavation is done with the feet and (sometimes) the beak. In sandy soils, some species produce metre-long tunnels ending in a nest chamber. The Manx shearwater and puffin – both seabirds – are also tunnel nesters. Both use natural rock crevices or oust rabbits from burrows in the cliff-top turf.

Suspended nests Perhaps the most sophisticated nests of all are the suspended ones. In the British Isles, the best examples are the woven mossy hammock nest of the tiny goldcrest and the basketwork nest of the reed warbler which incorporates supporting reed stems. This structure must withstand not only the movement of the reeds in high winds, but also (as the reed warbler is a common foster parent) the massive weight of a young cuckoo.

Exceptions to the rule In general terms it is possible to group nest types and relate them broadly to groups of birds and their habitats; but there are always exceptions. One example is the woodcock, which is a wader and would therefore be expected to nest on the seashore or in swampy moors and marshes; in fact it scrapes its nest on the ground in deep woodland. Another exception is the goldeneye – a duck, and therefore likely to nest on the ground beside water – which actually nests in holes in trees, often high above the ground.

Types of eggs

Eggs come in a splendid variety of shapes, sizes, colours, markings and clutch numbers— each adapted to meet specific survival needs. Egg-laying and incubation are equally varied.

Over the years collectors have stored the shells of eggs in cabinets for their marvellously varied colours. For some years now this activity has been illegal for almost all species. Despite this, undercover egg-collecting still continues, which is all the more tragic when you consider the fascination that the live egg offers.

Development of the shell During the egg's time in the female's oviduct a watery jelly egg-white (albumen) is deposited around the yolk. The albumen is itself surrounded by two soft, but relatively strong membranes, and finally by successive thin layers of a chalky (calcareous) deposit. These harden to form the protective shell. The two membranes both lie very close to the shell except at its broadest end where an air pocket, from which the hatching chick will eventually draw its first breaths, separates them.

The hard, porous shell is designed to protect the egg's contents from injury; the pores allow the passage of air for the developing embryo, but prevent the intrusion of water and other liquids, as well as the evaporation of the egg's liquid contents.

Egg-laying intervals Unevenly shaped eggs are often laid broad-end first, however painful that may seem; but evidence suggests that some birds lay theirs pointed-end first. Birds of many species lay eggs at daily intervals, usually early in the morning, until the final complement of eggs in the nest (clutch) is complete. In these cases incubation of the eggs by the parent begins when all, or almost all the eggs are laid. The result is that the nestlings are roughly the same size when they hatch, and are able to compete on equal terms with each other for the food brought by their parents, which is normally in plentiful supply.

However, some birds at the top of food pyramids, such as the tawny owl (see page 68), the kestrel (see page 64) and the heron lay their eggs at two day intervals, or even longer, and may begin incubation as soon as the first or second egg is laid. So, when all the young have hatched they are of unequal age and size. The apparent reason for this is that the birds have adapted their egg-laying to a variable and uncertain food supply.

In breeding seasons when there is a food shortage, only the oldest nestlings are strong enough to secure a sufficient share of the available food to fledge successfully, and the youngest die. If they were all the same size in times of food scarcity, then all would be in danger either of starving, or fledging in too weak a condition to survive the hazardous first few months of life on their own. In seasons when food is abundant, all the nestlings may fledge successfully. Conversely, if there is a dramatic drop in the food supply the parent bird may not breed at all.

How birds incubate The female, together with the male in some species, incubates the eggs by sitting on them and warming them with its body heat. This stimulates the embryo to grow. Many species have a feather-free area under their bodies, known as a brood patch. This patch allows the eggs direct contact with bare skin through which the incubating bird transfers heat from well-developed blood vessels. In those birds where incubation is shared by the sexes, such as the avocet (see page 189), the males may also have brood patches. Other species, including the gannet, use their fleshy feet to incubate eggs and therefore lack brood patches.

Incubation periods vary considerably according to the species. It takes 10 to 14 days for the eggs of most perching birds (passerines) to hatch, but rooks and other crows, for instance, take up to 19 days. Herons, ducks,

Many waders, such as the avocet and the lapwing (above), lay relatively large, pear-shaped eggs which do not roll away from the nest on the ground when left unattended. Usually four eggs are laid. The incubating parent arranges them so that the pointed ends are turned to the middle of the nest; this makes it easier to sit on them, and even less likely that they will roll away. Notice the 'egg-tooth' on the chick: this is a small extension on the upper bill which the developing bird uses to break out of the egg. It falls off shortly afterwards.

Opposite: A black-headed gull incubating its clutch of eggs.

auks and some birds of prey take 25 days, while gannets take 40 days, and petrels, including the fulmar and Manx shearwater, incubate for as long as 50 days.

You can sometimes spot an incubating bird turning the eggs: such behaviour is believed to ensure that the eggs receive an even amount of warmth; they are also positioned to make it easy for the young birds to hatch.

On the whole, those young birds which are most developed on hatching belong to species which have fairly long incubation periods. Thus newly hatched ducklings are active, covered in down and able to feed themselves right away; while passerine nestlings, which hatch after relatively short periods of incubation, are naked, blind, utterly helpless and entirely dependent upon their parents for food.

Emergence from the egg Whether the chicks inside the egg are downy or naked, they escape from the egg-shell either by chipping out a small hole or a line of weakness in it (depending upon the species) with an 'egg-tooth' – a small protruberance on the upper mandible which falls off afterwards. The break-out is completed by a series of convulsive stretching movements. The broken egg-shells, which could attract the unwelcome attention of predators, are then usually removed by the parents and dropped at a safe distance.

Clutch-sizes It is difficult to discover precisely what factors determine the characteristic clutch-sizes of different species. In those species whose young are hatched in a helpless condition and have to be fed by the parents, not only to the point of fledging but for some time afterwards, it seems obvious that the time and energy available for collecting sufficient food is crucial. Thus within these limits the parents rear the largest number of young for which they can provide adequate food, and the clutch-size has become adjusted accordingly. This is borne out by the fact that within particular species clutch-size tends to increase the further north the birds are because there are more daylight hours for the birds to collect food.

In some species with helpless young, such as tits and short-eared owls, the clutch-size

Above: The large, elongated pear-shaped egg of the guillemot would be easily blown off the bare cliff ledge on which it is laid — were it not for its shape, which causes it to roll round in a tight circle on its axis. Right: Grebes often cover their white eggs with decaying waterweed and this, together with the mud, stains them brown. So on shallow flats, where the eggs are exposed to view in the open nest, some camouflage is achieved.

Development within the egg

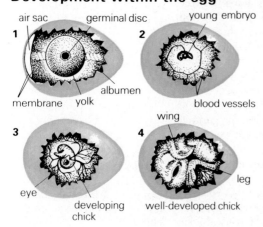

air sac · germinal disc

1

membrane · yolk · albumen

2 young embryo

blood vessels

3 eye

developing chick

4 wing

leg

well-developed chick

When freshly laid (**1**) the fertilised egg of a grey partridge (left) has already begun to develop. By the third day (**2**) the main blood vessels are visible. A week later the network of blood vessels is advanced (**3**) and the chick's eyes and legs are evident. Close to hatching (**4**) the chick begins to twist round. Right: The little tern is conspicuous against its open sandy nest, so it leaves its well-camouflaged eggs to avoid the gaze of predators.

can nevertheless vary from year to year, or location to location, according to fluctuations in their chief sources of food. Birds such as ducks and game-birds, whose offspring are more or less capable of fending for themselves on hatching, often lay very large clutches because the parents do not have to collect food for them. Of course, the ability of a sitting bird to cover the eggs in its nest comfortably is, in itself, an additional limiting factor, and probably influences egg-size too. It could also have something to do with the bird knowing when it has laid enough eggs; though precisely how it knows when to stop is not yet understood. Certainly more eggs are produced within the female's ovary than are required, but they are re-absorbed once the requisite clutch has been laid.

Eggs that suit the nest Birds' eggs vary in shape between the species as well as in size. The egg-shape is generally related to the type of nest or nest-site. The guillemot's eggs are pear shaped, an adaptation which prevents them falling off their precarious cliff ledge and smashing hundreds of feet below. The pear-shaped eggs of waders, and other birds which nest in a scrape in the ground, helps prevent them rolling away if left unguarded. The eggs of those birds which build cup-shaped nests, such as many song birds, or nest in holes or similar secure places, such as puffins, are often oval or spherical in shape as they are in no danger of rolling away.

Colours, spots and blotches The first birds' eggs were white like those of their distant reptilian ancestors, and many birds today still lay white eggs–the petrels, ducks, owls and woodpeckers in particular. In those species which nest in holes or burrows the white eggs are more easily seen in the darkness by the incubating bird and thus less likely to be broken.

Coloration (pigmentation) appears to have evolved in response to a need to protect the eggs from the prying eyes of predators. The pigments are deposited during the later stages of the formation of the shell in the oviduct. While basically similar, tints and markings show a good deal of individual variation both within the species and between eggs laid by the same female.

The eggs of species which lay in open nests or scrapes on the ground are marvellously and effectively camouflaged. Sometimes, as in the little tern for instance, they are almost indistinguishable from their surroundings. It may be difficult to understand what protection is achieved by the brightly coloured and conspicuously marked eggs of some song-birds, such as the song thrush or yellowhammer; but here it seems that the effect is disruptive: breaking up the outline of the eggs sufficiently, especially in the constantly moving, dappled sunshine and shadow thrown by the adjacent vegetation, to deceive the eyes of a less perceptive intruder. Such patterns also help birds in colonies recognise their own eggs.

Left: The tufted duck lays its dozen or so greenish-grey eggs in a depression in a grass tussock, hidden from any predator's view. Ducks' eggs are normally oval, but they cannot roll out of their nests which are cup-shaped. After the chicks have hatched the broken egg-shells are left in the nest. This is unusual, as most birds hide them to avoid predators.

Above: The chaffinch's eggs are bluish-white with red wine-coloured blotches. Four to five is the normal clutch. These eggs are well concealed and protected by the cup-shaped nest of lichens, moss and spiders' webs.
Right: The clutch of a song thrush's bright blue eggs, spotted with black, and nestled in a smooth mud cup of the compactly constructed nest, seem surprisingly poorly camouflaged against the mottled green and browns of the foliage.

Migration

Single migrations of over 6000 miles seem to us to be beyond the capabilities of such small birds as swallows and willow warblers. But billions of these birds make vast trips each year.

Those birds which migrate, rather than remain at home, do so for one simple reason – to find food. Birds which breed in the far north in summer come to spend winter in Britain because there is no food available in their Arctic breeding grounds. (In the Arctic tundra in summer there is a short-lived flush of insect life which, together with other sources of food, sustains the birds while they mate and raise young.) In the same way, there is not enough food in Britain in winter to supply most of our insect-eating birds. Such aerial species as swallows (see page 212), swifts (see page 215) and martins have almost no chance of finding flying insects to feed on during the winter. Similarly, the warblers and flycatchers that depend on arthropods which are plentiful during the warmer months, cannot rely on them being available during the winter. These birds therefore move south to winter in the tropics.

Perhaps the most interesting question is why do they ever return from their winter home – where there is plenty of food and nesting space? The answer is that there is a wide variety of local birds – including several species of swallow, for instance – that are specially adapted to a year-round existence in the tropics. There is no chance of a vast number of northern birds being able to breed and compete successfully for food in such a network of tropical species.

Above: Arctic terns are the longest distance migrants of all birds. Those that breed north of the Arctic circle spend winter close to the Antarctic pack ice and so experience continuous daylight for up to eight months of the year. Several Arctic terns from Europe have been reported from as far away as Australia.

Above: The observatory at Fair Isle in the Shetlands which sees an astonishingly large percentage of rare migratory birds from as far afield as North America and the Far East.

Left: A Heligoland trap at the Fair Isle Observatory. Such traps are derived from the traditional bird-catching methods in the remote island of Heligoland, and they have been used for the last 30 years. This trap is built in a gully, others may be located over areas with bushes where migrating birds gather naturally. Most Heligolands are about 3.5m (10ft) high and up to 17m (55ft) wide at the entrance.

Summer migrants
(birds that come to
Britain in summer.)
Swallows winter furthest
south in Africa. Route
northwards in spring just
east of southern route in
autumn.
Swifts in Britain only in
May, June and July.
Winter in Malawi.
Lesser whitethroats
winter in east Africa.
Intermediate fattening
area in northern Italy,
also call in on Nile Delta.
Whitethroats migrate
south-south-westerwards.
Autumn fattening area in
N-W Spain; winter in
Sahel region of W Africa.

Seabird and wader routes
(not illustrated).
Knots reach Britain from
Greenland and Canada.
Manx shearwaters
winter off Brazil.
Gannets migrate further
as juveniles than adults,
to tropics and
Mediterranean.
Ruffs from E Siberia to
Britain, winter in W
Africa, return via Italy.

To feed or fly away During the winter months, British birds have two options: sit it out or move southwards. If they remain they must either exploit a new food source, or a specialised feeding style which allows them to feed in the same way. In the first case, species like the blue and great tits feed during the winter on dormant insects and their eggs that are hidden in the bark of trees, or on different foods like the tor.s of peanuts fed to them by bird-lovers. In the second case, birds such as wrens and dunnocks remain here, feeding largely on the arthropods which they prize out from shelters in thick cover.

Network of routes The journeys that bird migrants make vary enormously. Many people think of bird migration as something which just concerns swallows from Europe reaching southern Africa; but this is only a minute part of the web of migration woven round the British Isles. Not only do our summer birds leave here to winter in warmer areas, but our islands also play host to millions of birds spending their winters with us. The geographical position of the British Isles on the western flank of Eurasia, with the warming influence of the Atlantic and the subtropical water brought north-east to our shores by the Gulf Stream, makes them a welcome refuge for many species of waterfowl which spend their summers in Siberia.

The distinction between migratory and sedentary species, is not clear-cut because there are continental populations of many resident British birds which are themselves migratory—some of them, like starlings and blackbirds, reaching Britain as winter visitors in large numbers.

Timetables of flights The timing of migration is crucial; in spring returning birds cannot afford to arrive too early. They would starve on arrival if their food supply was not available. On the other hand the individuals which arrive first, and manage to survive, are able to occupy the best territories.

In most bird species the males arrive first so that they can mark out territories and then attract the females to them. On the other hand some species, particularly ducks and geese, pair off in the winter quarters and migrate to the breeding grounds together. Sometimes the ducks which pair in the winter originate from very different areas but, once joined together, one will follow the other to unfamiliar territory. This phenomenon—called abmigration—accounts for some puzzling recoveries of ringed British-bred ducks in central Russia during the breeding season.

The main activity for most birds, which starts immediately they come to Britain in summer, is breeding. But for many birds this is followed by another crucial period—the annual moult—when they renew all their feathers. The timing of the autumn migration is also crucial: for the adult birds, the moult follows the busy breeding period, and for the young birds the autumn pre-migration period determines whether they will be able to build up their strength and survive.

Daylight trips Those birds that make their journey in daylight are called diurnal migrants. Generally the diurnal migrants make their trips in rather short bursts of a hundred or so miles at a time. Often their routes are greatly influenced by the local landscape, the birds funnelling through mountain passes or across short stretches of sea. In the British Isles the autumn flights of finches, meadow pipits and skylarks down the east coast, and the flights of geese up the mountain passes of Scotland, are an unforgettable sight.

These concentrations of diurnal migrants are responsible for the enormous congestion of soaring birds at the Straits of Gibraltar and the Bosphorus each autumn. Hundreds of thousands of white storks and birds of prey congregate at these places each year. Falsterbo, in southern Sweden, provides another concentration point for migrants moving southwards from Scandinavia. Britain is not endowed with such spectacular sites, but you may see high numbers of diurnal migrants at many south and east coast headlands during the autumn—Portland Bill and Selsey Bill, Beachy Head, Dungeness, Gibraltar Point and Spurn Head are all good vantage sites.

Night-flights Those bird migrants that travel at night—nocturnal migrants—are not always as easy to see when they migrate; but you can infer their movements by watching

Winter migrations

chaffinch
◻ autumn/spring route
redwing
◻ autumn route
◻ spring route

white-fronted goose
◻ autumn route
◻ spring route
wigeon
◻ spring route
◻ autumn route

Summer migrations

swift
spring/autumn route
swallow
spring route
autumn route

whitethroat
spring route
autumn route
lesser whitethroat
autumn route
spring route

any suitable area and recording the fluctuating numbers. This is particularly easy on offshore islands or coastal headlands where migrants that would never normally be seen in such barren areas may appear in large numbers. Bird observatories dotted around the country, have been operating for up to 30 years and carefully record the birds which pass through. Their records show what the common birds do each year as well as the activities of rare visitors.

In contrast to the short steps generally made by the diurnal species, nocturnal migrants may fly non-stop for more than three days – in some cases regularly for 80 or even 100 hours. With an air speed of about 25 miles per hour this means that many can fly 2500 miles in one stretch. The birds which do this, such as sedge warblers, store fat under their skin (subcutaneously) to use as fuel on their flight. They may well double their weight before migrating. Sedge warblers take off from southern England in the autumn weighing about 22g ($\frac{3}{4}$oz), fly for four days and land in Senegal, south of the Sahara, four days later weighing about 10g ($\frac{1}{4}$oz). Other species, like the closely related reed warbler, do not make such long single trips, but stop off on the west coast of Portugal to refuel.

How do they navigate? Such long journeys are not without their hazards. Even if the bird has fuelled up adequately it must still be able to find its way properly. Birds navigate by referring to the sun, stars (which implies some sort of in-built timing mechanism) as well as to the earth's magnetic field. They also rely on an inbuilt homing device to give an indication of direction. They have evolved their migratory routes simply because these routes work. It is certain that the newly hatched warbler, for instance, has within its genetic make-up

the information it needs to accomplish its migration.

Perhaps the one aspect that makes bird migration such a fascinating part of ornithology is the tremendously varied habitats that one individual bird visits and lives in during its year. For example, the Black-headed gulls which take bread from the tourists on Westminster embankment include individuals bred on marshes in Poland, Czechoslovakia and Scandinavia. The swallow nesting in your garage may have been feeding among the debris of a South African gold-mine last winter, and will have passed over the vast expanse of the Sahara during March.

Above: House martins congregate on telegraph wires, before migrating on the long trip to their wintering quarters in Africa. Our best known migrants, the swallows, also do this; and both species, which find ample supplies of insects to catch on the wing in summer, migrate in winter rather than attempt to exploit different food sources.

Birds of prey

The birds of prey have long had a special fascination for man. The owls, for example, are often associated with the supernatural–no doubt on account of the strange hoots and shrieks of the tawny and barn owls, their nocturnal habits, and their ghostly silent flight, often near churchyards. More often, they are synonymous with wisdom. This stems from ancient Athens, where the little owl was the city's symbol. *Athene*, the generic name of the little owl, has an obvious derivation from the goddess of Wisdom.

Other birds of prey, like the golden eagle, are renowned for their majestic size and power as hunters, and even today there remains much speculation and occasional fierce debate on the lifting power of a golden eagle: some arguing that it has the power to carry off prey the size of a red deer calf–an animal it could certainly kill even if it could not lift it. Hunting prowess also makes the peregrine falcon a well-known bird, despite the fact that it is really a scarce bird, and one from habitats rarely visited by most people. The very skills that the peregrine falcon displays in the speed and control of its hunting power-dive or stoop may be a major threat to its existence, since it is so popular for falconry.

Perhaps the birds of prey are held in rather inflated esteem: most of them (like all predators) are lazy, and many often feed on carrion rather than on prey secured after a hot-blooded hunting foray. And most, even birds as large as a buzzard, often feed on prey as mundane as an easily captured earthworm or beetle!

The owls dominate the night-time hunting scene, with ultra-acute sight and hearing, coupled with feathers adapted to silence their flight. Among the daytime birds of prey, the hunting techniques are varied and usually well suited to the habitat of the particular species. The golden eagle and the buzzard are soaring birds, watching and waiting on high, as is the peregrine falcon, cast in the role of the modern fighter-interceptor aircraft. At lower levels are the slower-moving harriers, quartering their rather featureless marsh or moor hunting grounds and dropping suddenly, from a few feet up, on to prey taken unawares. In woodland the long wings and associated speed of the falcons are useless, and so this is the habitat of the agile and manoeuvrable sparrowhawk, which is far better adapted to chases through the trees due to its rounded wing geometry. Wetlands are exploited by the osprey, one of the most cosmopolitan of birds, its feet and talons well adapted to hold the slippery fish for which it plunge-dives.

Even the kestrel, commonest and most widespread of the European birds of prey, and one that (like the tawny owl) has adapted well to urban life, must give the birdwatcher cause to marvel. Hovering, even into a stiff wind, it can keep its head rock-steady, stable enough to allow its supremely acute eyes to spot even a beetle moving several hundred feet below. As a group, the birds of prey show enormously detailed and varied adaptations to their ways of life, which are not only the secret of their success, but also the basis of their fascination to birdwatchers.

Opposite: This goshawk shows the all-seeing eye and powerful hooked beak typical of the birds of prey.

Golden eagle

For the birdwatcher there is no more magnificent sight than that of a golden eagle soaring in the sky, yet centuries of ignorance and persecution have brought this bird close to extinction.

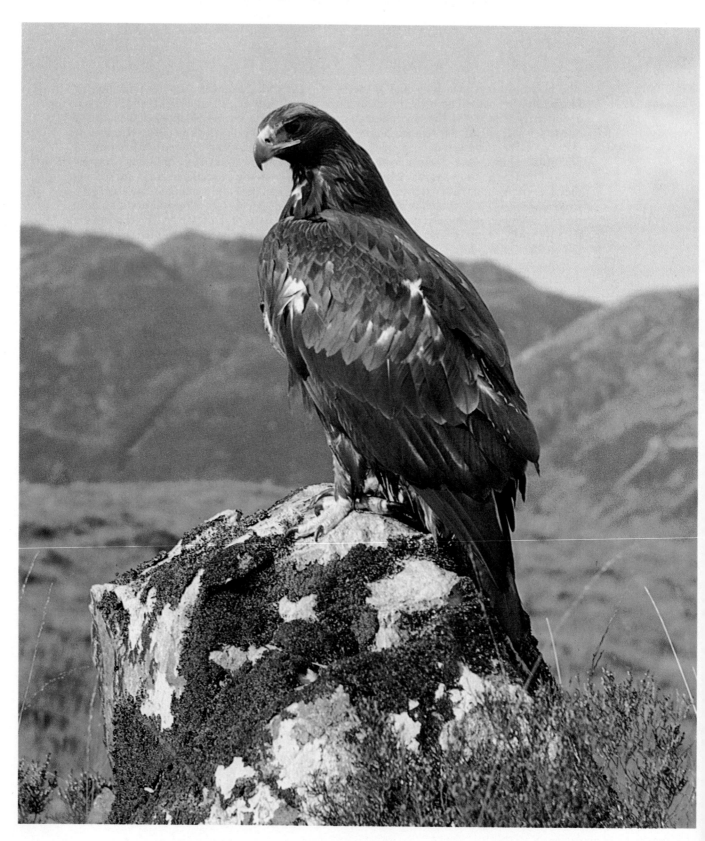

Golden eagles were once widely distributed throughout the mountainous regions of the British Isles, but over many years their numbers have steadily dwindled. Now they are essentially birds of the Scottish highlands and islands, with a few pairs nesting in the uplands of south-west Scotland and two pairs recently re-established in the Lake District.

The most reliable estimates put the size of our golden eagle population at 250 to 300 pairs. Their numbers were thought to be fairly stable, but recent evidence suggests that they may be declining slightly. Certainly there are suitable tracts of country where eagles are either scarce or absent altogether, and other areas where breeding success is poor. On the other hand, some areas have thriving local populations.

Despite its lack of numbers, the golden eagle is the most widespread large eagle in the world. It is found in all the main mountainous areas of Europe, from arctic Norway and Russia down to Spain. It has outposts in North Africa and occurs right across Asia, apart from the Indian sub-continent and south-east Asia. It is also found in the New World from Canada down to Mexico.

In all these areas it is primarily a mountain eagle or a bird of wide desolate upland plains, but in some areas it also occurs on rocky sea-cliffs, particularly in north-west Scotland and the Hebrides.

Golden nape Adult golden eagles are mostly brown, although there is a lot of variation between individuals, some birds looking quite dark while others are much paler. All adults have the rear crown and nape a pale straw-yellow—hence its English name. This feature may be difficult to see in the field, but on some birds it can be conspicuous and, in bright sunlight, may appear almost white. Another feature possessed by most adults is paler feathering on the shoulders and wing coverts (where the wing joins the body).

An immature eagle is usually much darker than an adult and has characteristic white patches on its wings. The tail is white with a black band at the end. These white markings disappear as the bird matures, and have virtually gone by the time it reaches the age of five, although breeding adults show traces of it for some time.

Look-alikes In this country the bird most likely to be confused with a golden eagle is the common buzzard. If the bird is not too far away then you can tell the two species apart by size: the golden eagle is much bigger. Otherwise, compare the underparts. Those of the buzzard have characteristic white and dark markings, whereas an adult golden eagle is plain brown and the young brown with white patches.

In poor light or from far away, shape is an important aid to identification. The golden eagle is longer in the wing, with a much more

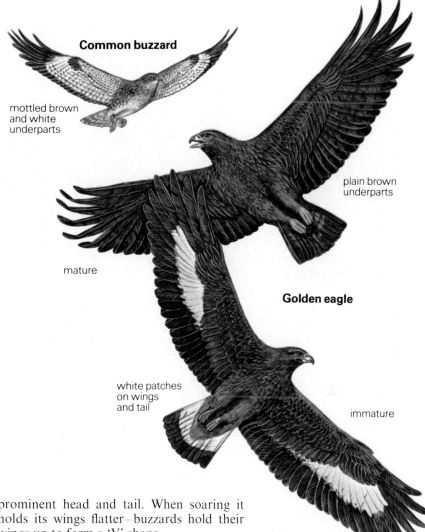

Common buzzard

mottled brown and white underparts

plain brown underparts

mature

Golden eagle

white patches on wings and tail

immature

prominent head and tail. When soaring it holds its wings flatter—buzzards hold their wings up to form a 'V' shape.

Hunting techniques Golden eagles are superb fliers, able to hunt in the wildest terrain and in all but the most ferocious of weather. They rarely rely on sheer speed or manoeuvrability when hunting. For these birds it is a much more painstaking business. The eagle flies low over the ground, patiently going back and forth, contouring along hill sides and across valleys, until it locates its prey, then killing with a swift pounce or a brief chase. The kill is achieved by means of its powerful feet and huge curved talons. The bill may be used to kill prey but is really designed for feeding with afterwards.

Quite often, a golden eagle hunts from a vantage point on a rock or some other lookout in the manner of many other birds of prey. It may even chase down and kill a flying bird, but this is rare. Without some height advantage to give it impetus a golden eagle is not at its best and a fit grouse can usually outfly it over a short distance.

Take-away food Eagles much prefer to carry their food away rather than eat it at the scene of the kill. This limits the size of the prey they attack. Golden eagles are immensely powerful birds, but there is still a lot of nonsense talked about their lifting powers. Much depends on the lift they can get from the wind and whether the ground slopes so

Above: The only species likely to be confused with the golden eagle is the buzzard. Close up, size alone separates the two birds, the golden eagle being half as big again. Further away, look for the contrasting light and dark markings on the underside of the buzzard. A mature golden eagle is plain brown beneath, whereas the immature bird has white markings on the wing and tail.

Opposite: A young golden eagle. Older birds develop the characteristic straw-yellow plumage on the nape. Notice the heavily feathered legs and powerful talons for killing.

Golden eagle (*Aquila chrysaetos*). Resident bird of prey, now confined mostly to the Scottish highlands and islands. The male is 75-90cm (30-35in) long; the female usually about 7.5cm (3in) longer.

Above: Golden eagles feed off a variety of prey, the most common being rabbits, hares, red grouse and capercaillie. Near the coast, seabirds are an important source of food. They also eat carrion to a much greater degree than is usually realised.

Below: When hunting, a golden eagle flies low over the ground, following the contours of hillsides along valleys and skirting hill tops in the hope of catching prey off guard.

they can take off downhill. Normally, however, under the most favourable circumstances they can lift only as much as their own weight – a large hare, say.

Nevertheless this still leaves the golden eagle with a wide choice of prey. Scottish birds can kill almost any small to medium-sized mammal or bird, from mice and sparrows up to capercaillies and young deer. Some of the more unusual kills include cats, dogs, fox cubs, squirrels and geese. But most of the prey taken consists of just a few species: rabbits and hares, and among birds, red grouse and ptarmigan. Eagles also feed on carrion, mainly sheep and red deer. This source of food may well be important in winter and in areas where prey is scarce.

Pairing and breeding By the time a golden eagle reaches the age of five it is ready to find a mate and breed. The pair then establishes a hunting ground, usually about 20 square miles in Scotland, though sometimes it can be as large as 30 square miles. Golden eagles are not territorial about their hunting grounds; adjacent areas often overlap.

Golden eagles pair for life and are largely sedentary, staying within their hunting grounds. Sometimes, however, an immature eagle may move in to replace a lost partner, or it may occupy a hunting ground singly or with another immature eagle.

eagle appears on horizon

flies low over scree and grass

hidden in dead ground

reappears over rock outcrop

surprises prey

In late winter, with the approach of the breeding season, the male performs a courtship display. This consists of a spectacular rising and falling sky-dance and is sometimes performed by the female as well.

Nest-building or repairs begin in March. An established pair usually has several nests and favourite sites: on cliffs or crags–not necessarily high up or inaccessible–or even in trees. Each year the pair either picks one of their nests and repairs it for the coming season, or it establishes a new nest.

The nest itself is built with branches and heather stems and lined with finer vegetation. Two eggs (sometimes one, rarely three) are laid in late March or early April and are incubated for about six weeks, mainly by the female.

The young chicks exhibit a curious phenomenon known as the 'Cain and Abel battle', in which the elder of the two chicks kills the younger one, usually within the first three weeks of life. This battle occurs in 80% of nests in which two eggs are laid. Why this happens and what its function is ornithologists do not yet know, and it is still the subject of much debate.

The young survivor stays in the nest for 10 to 11 weeks before fledging, after which it remains dependent on its parents for many weeks more.

Persecution Despite being protected by law our golden eagle population still faces many threats and its continued survival in this country is by no means assured. Unscrupulous egg-collectors still raid nests, and traditional haunts of the golden eagle are being disturbed by tourism and development. But the most serious threat comes from certain farmers and

Above: The eggs, usually two, are laid in late March or early April at intervals of three to four days. They are white, usually with brown or red blotches. Incubation is mostly by the female alone and takes about six weeks.

Right: During the first three weeks or so, the older chick is likely to attack and kill the younger one. In only one nest out of five where two eggs hatch do both young survive.

Below: The young golden eagle develops its feathers at around four to seven weeks and begins flying at about 10 to 11 weeks, though it remains dependent for many weeks more.

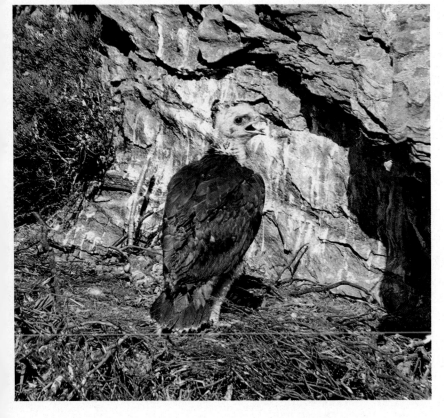

gamekeepers who believe, wrongly, that the golden eagle conflicts with their interests.

The problem arises because the golden eagle eats grouse and, occasionally, lamb. Grouse is an important part of the eagle's diet, but research shows that it eats only about 220-280g (8-10oz) of food a day. This is too insignificant an amount to affect seriously the quantity of grouse, yet some people are still ignorant enough to think that an eagle kills dozens of grouse a week.

The same sort of misconception occurs with eagles and lambs. Some eagles do kill lambs, but the numbers taken are tiny and never on a scale to do much serious damage, as is sometimes alleged. Most lambs eaten by golden eagles are taken as carrion, and there is never any shortage of dead lambs in the Scottish hills in spring.

Such prejudices mean that golden eagles are still being systematically persecuted by people who do not know the facts. The biggest problem facing conservationists in the highlands of Scotland today, at least where birds of prey are concerned, is trying to persuade people that golden eagles do far less damage than they think.

Common, rough-legged and honey buzzards

Buzzards, usually seen wheeling and soaring, gained an early reputation for laziness, although patient waiting is part of their efficient hunting strategy. They are not agile, relying mainly on a silent planing approach to catch their varied prey.

Three buzzards occur regularly in Britain, the common buzzard, the much scarcer rough-legged buzzard and the unrelated, but equally scarce, honey buzzard which is a similar sized bird to the other two but belongs to an entirely separate family.

The common buzzard (pictured left) is a familiar bird of prey in Wales, south-west England, the Lake District and Scotland, although it is absent from much of lowland England. It is the British bird which, perhaps, comes nearest to the familiar conception of what a bird of prey really looks like. One of the most obliging features, for the bird watcher, is that this bird is so conspicuous. Perched, it has a slightly hunched attitude, and its compact, robust features are clear; in flight, its broad wings, short tail and soaring habit, often with wings rigid and upturned, immediately proclaim it as a bird of prey. In sunny weather it spends much time in the air, wheeling and circling above woodland or open hillside, often calling loudly with a plaintive and characteristic mewing.

Although it is predominantly a brown plumaged bird, relieved only by the bright yellow of its feet, legs and cere (the fleshy covering at the base of the bill), individuals are very variable. The wings can be the whole range of colours from blackish brown through all shades of blotching and streaking to almost white in some birds.

In population terms the buzzard qualifies as a successful bird in the British Isles. There are 20-30,000 individuals, although they are by no means universally distributed. In upland areas where the buzzard is now concentrated numbers may be prodigious. Although buzzards are numerous in the south-west, slightly less so in the Lakes and Scotland, they are nowhere more numerous than in Wales. Here on a sunny day in April you may see up to 100 individuals in a day's travelling, with pairs breeding at intervals of half a mile or so. The densest buzzard population yet recorded was on Skomer Island where up to eight pairs have been noted on the 722 acres.

Diversity of habitat appears to be the key to the buzzard's success. Over extensive areas of

Rough-legged buzzard

legs feathered to toes

dark belly patch

Right: **Rough-legged buzzard** (*Buteo lagopus*), 55cm (22in) from beak to tail. Breeds in Scandinavia where it is at the mercy of fluctuating populations of small mammals for food.

Honey buzzard (light form)

bold bar at tip of tail

whitish tail with dark terminal band

soaring flight

broad rounded wings with upturned tips

Common buzzard

Left: **Honey buzzard** (*Pernis apivorus*), 58cm (23in) from beak to tail. Rare summer visitor in the extreme south. (Common buzzard also shown for plumage comparison).

Below: Some buzzards nest in crags or cliffs; pairs move to a new site annually.

mountain, moorland or forest numbers are relatively low, but in valleys where broken countryside is studded with trees and copses, old hedgerows and small fields, breeding pairs can be numerous. Here the variety of countryside and rough vegetation guarantees high numbers of the small mammals which form the bulk of their prey, and buzzards are in their ideal habitat.

Chequered history The buzzard has had a chequered history in the British Isles, intimately bound up with its relationship with man. The clearance of woodland by the Middle Ages opened up much suitable country and the bird was certainly common by the 15th century. Thomas Pennant, writing in 1776, regarded it then as the commonest hawk in Britain, although it was already suffering from lack of food because of vermin control. This campaign intensified throughout the 18th, 19th and early 20th centuries, latterly in the name of game preservation. By the First World War the buzzard was very rare; it was absent from lowland England and found only in the more mountainous western areas. With the rapid decline of gamekeeping at the outbreak of World War II the buzzard reoccupied some of its lost ground; and the slightly more enlightened attitudes since that time have enabled the recovery to continue, albeit within limits.

In the mid-1950s myxomatosis, which killed thousands of rabbits, had an instant effect on the buzzard with widespread decreases in breeding reported, especially in southern England. But within only a few years the numbers had readjusted to somewhat lower levels and then stabilised as those individuals which had exploited the plague populations of rabbits in some areas divers-

Common buzzard

Above and below: **Common buzzard** (*Buteo buteo*), 55cm (22in) from beak to tail. Our most common large bird of prey, found in wooded valleys, and on hillsides of western areas of England and Scotland. Small rabbits and other mammals form an important part of the varied diet of buzzards.

Killer poisons

It is well known that in addition to the legal control of some pests, widespread illegal destruction of protected birds and other animals still occurs. The most worrying aspect of much of this illegal killing is the use of poisons on meat baits or injected into eggs and laid in the open. The most common poisons are strychnine, phosdrin and the narcotic drug alphachloralore. They are used to protect game stocks or reduce predation by crows, foxes or lambing flocks, but as they are non-selective, they account for a tragic catalogue of deaths. Apart from target species, buzzards, ravens, magpies, hedgehogs, badgers, farm dogs and other species are regular victims, and, more serious still, rare birds such as the carrion-eating red kite, golden eagle, goshawk, peregrine falcon, marsh harrier and hen harrier. It is not only the range of species that causes concern, but also the actual numbers of birds and mammals killed in one year are horrifying.

distinguished by a smaller head and slim neck, and bold barring on the tail and under-wings. This is a secretive bird, most at home in a mosaic of mature deciduous woodland and open glades. Honey buzzards winter in wooded country in equatorial Africa, migrating to Europe from early April; some of the crossing points over the Mediterranean are characterised by spectacular concentrations of the birds. A very small breeding population clings to a toe-hold in southern England where they are carefully protected. The best place to see a honey buzzard is the New Forest.

The birds are largely dependent for food on the nests, larvae and adults of various species of wasps and bees, often found by following the flying insects to their nests. These are dug out with the use of strong feet; the stings are nipped off before the insect is swallowed, and the bird's resistance to stings is enhanced by scale-like feathers on the forehead and lores (the area between the eye and upper mandible).

ified their feeding. At present the population is probably stable.

Nesting Most buzzards make substantial nests in trees close to the main trunk. They use sticks, twigs and heather, and line the nest with green foliage before laying. Two or three eggs are a normal clutch, although it is unusual for all to be successful. In areas where buzzards are already numerous, one fledgling young is the normal product of a nesting pair. Eggs are laid every few days, and both parents incubate for 33-35 days. The young are on the wing about seven weeks after hatching, so most have left the nest by early July.

Varied diet A large part of the buzzard's success can be attributed to its resourcefulness and catholic choice of prey. Its most important food items are mammals—small rabbits, voles, mice, shrews and others; it also eats amphibians, insects, soil invertebrates, particularly earthworms, and fledgling birds—their immobility makes them relatively easy prey for the slow and somewhat ponderous buzzard.

Buzzards are not agile like kites, sparrow-hawks or harriers. They patiently sit on a fence or post, carefully scanning a favoured hunting area to find food which they then take by a straight, silent, planing flight from their perch. They also soar over open ground and can hover well or hang in the wind, kestrel-like. They also spend much time walking around fields, picking up beetles and other large insects, and all kinds of other invertebrates such as earthworms.

The rough-legged buzzard is superficially similar to the common buzzard, but it is only a winter visitor appearing in small numbers, most frequently to the east and north. It is a slightly bulkier bird, with deeper wing beats and a larger, markedly patterned tail. A dark belly patch, rare in the common buzzard, is an aid to identification. Its legs are completely covered with feathers. It is a northern breeding bird, nesting in high latitudes, mainly in open tundra areas, well to the north of the range of common buzzards.

The honey buzzard is also superficially similar to the other two, although it is

Above: Buzzard chicks in their nest. The young are cared for by both parents.

Below: The honey buzzard, as its name suggests, is largely dependent on bees, and wasps for food.

Osprey

The osprey has suffered from a history of ruthless
persecution by egg collectors and gamekeepers,
causing it to be absent from Britain for over 40 years.
Since the return of the first breeding pair in 1959,
numbers have been gradually increasing.

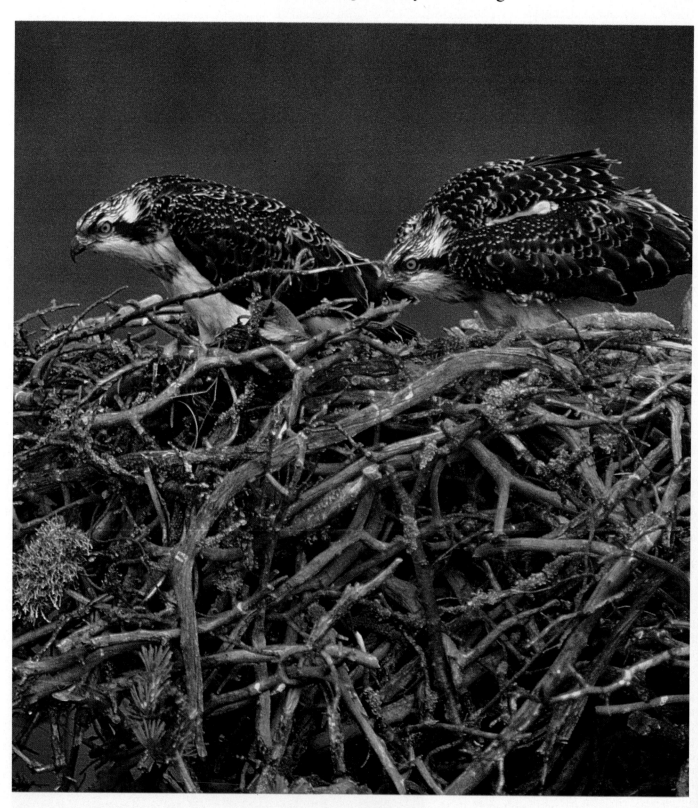

Throughout the long history of their evolution, many different birds of prey have emerged, taking advantage of an immense variety of potential foods, and belying the popular impression that they all live on a diet of small mammals, birds or carrion. From the bat falcons of Central America and the insect-hunting falconets of eastern Asia to the monkey-hunting and even deer-hunting eagles, the range of predatory birds is truly wide, and few potential victims escape the attention of one or another of them. It is hardly surprising, therefore, that among birds of prey some highly expert fishers have evolved. The osprey is supreme among these: it is a large predator that hunts and breeds successfully in many parts of the globe, perfectly equipped to find all its food in water.

Plunging for prey The bird has a striking appearance: the white undersides of its body and wings contrast sharply with its rich brown upper plumage; and its length of 60cm (2ft) is dwarfed by enormous angular wings which, when fully spread, measure 145cm (5ft). It is capable of catching and carrying away fishes of several pounds in weight, but it rarely seizes the larger ones: most frequently it takes fishes between ½lb and 1lb (230-450g).

The osprey's plunge-dive is an awe-inspiring sight. It searches slowly over the water for suitable prey and when it has found a likely victim it banks, circles and hovers. Basking or surface-swimming fishes of many species, such as pike, perch, trout or carp, are all taken by the osprey. Quickly it enters a graceful plunge, at the end of which it takes its selected victim in its talons. Often the dive is fairly gradual, but sometimes it is almost vertical; and often the osprey plunges from heights of 16m (50ft) or more.

As the bird strikes the water, it thrusts its talons forward to take the fish (at the same time they help to absorb the impact of hitting the water). The osprey holds its wings high as it enters the water. It is thought that the bird seldom dives deeper than 1m (3ft), and usually goes a far shorter distance below the surface. Almost immediately it rises from the water again for, provided that the dive has been performed well, the bird has little difficulty in regaining the air.

Terrible talons The feet of the osprey are specially adapted to assist it in seizing and retaining such slippery prey as fishes. The feet and legs are particularly large and powerful; the claws are strongly curved, and the undersides of the feet are equipped with spiny scales that grip the body of the fish. Perhaps most remarkable of all is that one of the four toes is completely reversible–the osprey can turn it either backwards or forwards. With this toe pointing back, alongside the true hind toe, the osprey can hold a fish securely by two claws in front and two behind. Once it has risen from the water, the osprey turns the fish so as to hold it in a fore-and-aft position and carries it away to eat it at leisure. Ospreys

Osprey (*Pandion haliaetus*). Rare summer visitor, 23 pairs recorded in 1981, numbers slowly increasing. Breeding in the Highlands of Scotland. Two or three eggs, richly marked in reddish brown or chocolate colour. Length 60cm (2ft), wingspan 1.4m (5ft).

distinctive white underside of body and wings

fish carried head-first in flight

soaring in search of prey

Opposite: The large nest is made of sticks and a typical site is in the top branches of a Scots pine or other tree. Ospreys have been known to build nests on tall buildings or high cliffs. The two birds seen in this nest are juveniles.

plunge-dive may be nearly vertical

wings raised and talons lowered as bird nears water

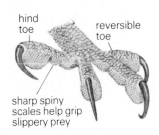

hind toe

reversible toe

sharp spiny scales help grip slippery prey

digest even the bones of fishes without difficulty.

From the edge of extinction In 1981, as many as 23 pairs of ospreys were known to be breeding in Britain, all of them in the Scottish Highlands. For over 40 years in the first half of this century, this splendid bird was extinct as a breeding species–a result of ruthless persecution, mainly by egg collectors. The eggs were considered a great prize by enthusiasts, whose determination to build up their collections led to the disappearance of the species from Britain.

Another major cause of the decline of the osprey in Britain over the past 200 years was the fact that it depends on fishes for its living. Gamekeepers and water bailiffs assumed that this made the osprey a serious competitor with man for the fishes in Britain's rivers and lakes. The latter part of the 19th century was a particularly ruthless period of game preservation and unbridled destruction of any wildlife that seemed to threaten stocks of game fishes such as trout and salmon.

Even today, following its return to the Highlands, the osprey has not been slow to learn the attractions of modern fish farms, and has sometimes caused losses to the owners of these enterprises. However, fish farmers normally have no difficulty in scaring off the ospreys, while many are prepared to tolerate the presence of these beautiful and rare birds, provided their visits are reasonably short.

After its period of extinction, the osprey quite unexpectedly made its appearance in Scotland in 1955, visiting but not breeding during four successive seasons. Then in 1959 a pair of ospreys raised a brood at a site in the RSPB reserve at Loch Garten in Speyside, in Scotland's Highland region. The RSPB set up a visitor centre at Loch Garten, so that while the ospreys regularly breed in the safety of the reserve, thousands of visitors each year have the chance to see these majestic birds without causing them undue disturbance. The centre has become one of the most exciting wildlife facilities provided for the public in Britain.

Summer in Scotland The Highlands of Scotland are the only part of Britain where ospreys breed. Here, a multitude of fresh-water lochs and an unlimited choice of suitable nesting sites are available. Typically the osprey's nest is built on top of a Scots pine, but other species of tree and different sites are sometimes chosen. Some of the legendary Scottish sites in the last century were on ruined island castles. In coastal areas, the nest is sometimes on a cliff or an offshore pinnacle of rock.

In the Highlands, ospreys may travel several miles from one water to another to

Above: A female feeding her young. At first only the male fishes, but later both parents are needed to find food for the growing family.

Below: Mating begins soon after the female has arrived in the nesting area.

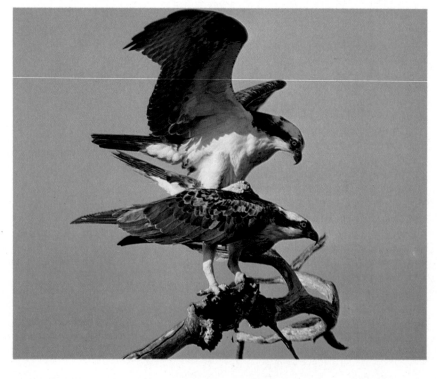

find better fishing if the need arises. Although the British population is essentially a freshwater one, ospreys in some other parts of the world are exclusively coastal birds, and feed at sea and in shallow estuary waters.

The Scottish birds return from wintering in early or mid April – the older, more experienced birds arriving first. Once a pair of ospreys has settled at the nesting site – the male sometimes arriving a few days ahead of the female – they start to breed. The male undertakes all the fishing, while the female remains close to the nest. A spectacular sight at this time is the male's thrilling aerial display of soaring, swooping and undulating flight, which he accompanies with shrill calls. Mating occurs frequently up to the start of incubation, and begins from the first days after the female's arrival. Two or three eggs, which are marked with rich brown or chocolate coloured flecks, are laid; they are incubated for five weeks, and the young hatch at intervals corresponding with the two or three day interludes between laying.

World-wide species The osprey is one of the most widely distributed birds in the world, breeding all across the temperate latitudes of the northern hemisphere. There are some coastal populations of ospreys in the Mediterranean and North African region and in many parts of the Far East as well as Australia. In North America, where there are both coastal and inland populations, a highly successful method of attracting ospreys to nest in a given neighbourhood has been developed. Osprey wheels – usually cartwheels – are set up on top of poles, and the birds soon begin to settle on them.

The northern breeding birds are strongly migratory and, as the fishes move deeper below the water surface with the arrival of autumn, the ospreys set off on the long flight to West Africa. Recoveries of ringed birds – several of these proving to be the victims of hunters – indicate their route through Iberia and north-west Africa to Mauritania and the Gambia. Ospreys en route for the south are frequently seen in many parts of England and Wales (presumably some of these are Scandinavian birds), and they are also seen flying north on the return journey in April and May. In between these times, the birds while away the winter months in the easy fishing of warm tropical waters.

Over 50% of ospreys, as in the case of most other birds of prey, die in their first year, due to various factors including the poor ability of the young birds to feed and defend themselves. Those lucky enough to be still alive remain in their tropical habitat until the third year, by which time they are in breeding condition. At this stage, they are also ready to undertake the long flight to the north. Pairing takes place while the birds are still in Africa. By the time the female reaches Scotland, the male will have found a good site and perhaps begun to build the nest.

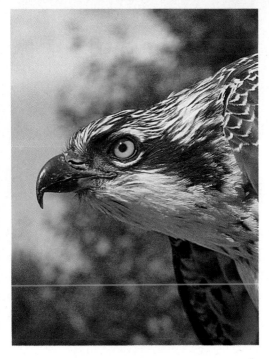

Above: Supervised from overhead by the mother, a young osprey makes its first flight. The father is often away from the nest, either finding fishes or, if he has already brought enough for the day, sitting quietly on a favourite perch near the nesting tree.

Left: A young osprey, in the typically hunched attitude of the bird at rest. The sharply hooked beak is useful for tearing and eating fishes, the only food of ospreys.

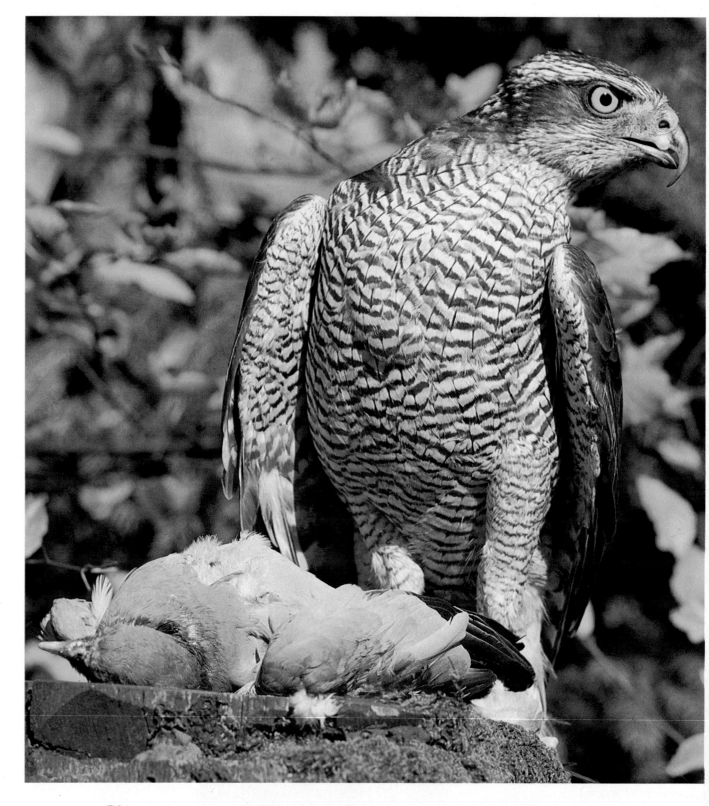

Sparrowhawk and goshawk

The sparrowhawk and goshawk are the supreme
predators of our woodlands. Swift, silent and deadly
in the hunt, they are ideally adapted to the low-level
pursuit of small birds, and specialise in the techniques
of close encounter and surprise attack.

The sparrowhawk is well distributed throughout our more heavily wooded counties and is reasonably familiar to many people. But the goshawk is still a rare bird in the British Isles and its present status is poorly recorded and subject to much local secrecy.

The sparrowhawk and goshawk are extremely difficult to tell apart, although relative size can help. The female goshawk (as large as a buzzard at 50cm [20cm] in length) is about twice the size of a male sparrowhawk, while a large female sparrowhawk approaches the size of a male goshawk. (Like most hawks, the females are much larger than the males.) Both hawks are powerful fliers and, although difficult to tame, can be trained by falconers to take a wide variety of prey.

A hawk or kestrel? Because these two hawks are so similar in appearance, identifying and separating them in the field depends on spotting them at close quarters. What is surprising, and makes for further complications, is the considerable public confusion between the sparrowhawk and the more familiar and conspicuous kestrel (see page 90).

People say they have seen a sparrowhawk hovering over a roadside verge, when this is the kestrel's main hunting method, and something which sparrowhawks never do. Unlike the kestrel (which is a member of the falcon family), the sparrowhawk or broad winged hawk (an accipiter), is a shy, inconspicuous bird and the goshawk even more so. This is because both are predominantly woodland birds, and spend most of their time in the cover of trees.

Apart from a period in late winter and early spring when their high circling displays make them more visible, you are most likely to encounter a sparrowhawk as it sweeps low over gardens, along a country lane or hedgerow, or as it crosses at grass-top level from one wood to another. It sometimes makes a series of 'kek-kek-kek' calls, and also has a short cry 'pew'.

Territory and display The annual cycle of establishing a territory, advertising it to likely mates and courtship, begins much earlier than the usual breeding season of other birds. Sparrowhawks begin to soar and spiral above the nesting woods from late February onwards, especially on clear and breezy days. Females are usually more active than males, and the intensity of their high circling displays reaches its peak as nest building begins in the second half of March.

At this time of year the display also frequently includes a series of exciting, bounding undulations above the nesting wood. These are often so vigorous that the bird seems to 'bounce' upwards from the base of each steep descent. This is the one time of year when the birds are regularly in evidence, and you can expect to look for them with some degree of success.

Goshawks stake out their territories even

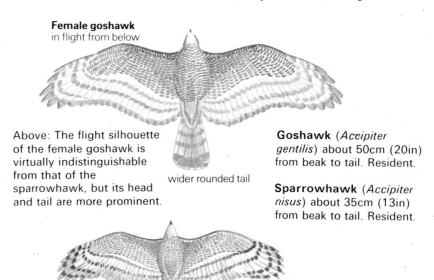

Female goshawk in flight from below

Above: The flight silhouette of the female goshawk is virtually indistinguishable from that of the sparrowhawk, but its head and tail are more prominent.

wider rounded tail

Female sparrowhawk in flight from below

Goshawk (*Accipiter gentilis*) about 50cm (20in) from beak to tail. Resident.

Sparrowhawk (*Accipiter nisus*) about 35cm (13in) from beak to tail. Resident.

Below: The juvenile goshawk has bolder streaks on its underparts and is more amber in colour than the adult.

Juvenile goshawk

bold streaks on underparts

earlier in the year than sparrowhawks. The female can become vocal soon after the new year. She is notably noisy early in the morning –when you may hear a harsh chattering cry ringing through the breeding woodlands even before dawn.

Females call the tune Part of the reason for the louder, more noticeable female display is due to the dominant role that the much larger, more robust females play in each season's pairing. The females also tend to stay in or near their nesting territories throughout the year; this makes them sitting tenants when the new year comes. The females make the first moves in attracting a mate into the territory that they have kept exclusively as their own for the past three or four months.

The hawks probably seek new mates each year, since they go their separate ways at the end of the breeding season. Both the male and female usually remain solitary throughout the autumn and winter, each with its own hunting territory. The female stays in her nest and the male drifts away, or even sometimes migrates south.

The goshawk lays her eggs from early April onwards, and the sparrowhawk some three weeks later. Clutch sizes are surprisingly large; five to six is normal for the sparrowhawk, and three to four for the goshawk. The female is almost exclusively responsible for incubating the eggs while the male does all the hunting–calling the female off the nest tó feed her once or twice each day.

Woodland cover Before the sixteenth century, when the British Isles were still heavily wooded, sparrowhawks and goshawks were abundant. Nowadays their presence and distribution are strongly influenced by the number of suitable woodlands still remaining.

The sparrowhawk survives just as well in a pattern of small woods and open fields as it does in extensive woods. The goshawk, how-

Below and opposite: The adult goshawk has a narrow white tail covert with a darker coloured crown and ear coverts. With its flame-coloured iris the bird looks fierce and alert.

Adult goshawk

pronounced white supercilium

ever, requires a considerably larger territory, often in excess of 8000 acres. About a quarter of this area must be relatively undisturbed woodland. Although both birds once prospered in the former extensive deciduous cover, they are now equally at home in conifers or mixed woodland, provided the cover is not too close. The goshawk favours spruce or pine, while the sparrowhaw prefers larch plantations for nesting, as well as mixed deciduous woodland for hunting.

Falling numbers By the 16th century 90% of the former woodland cover in the British Isles had disappeared. The clearance of this native woodland was a major factor in reducing goshawk and sparrowhawk numbers.

By 1900 the ravages of game preservation had removed the last breeding goshawk from this country, and had taken a heavy toll of sparrowhawks throughout the game-rearing areas. In the 1960s goshawks began to re-establish themselves, helped by the release of falconers' birds. By this time, however, sparrowhawks were suffering from the serious effects of DDT and other organochlorine pesticides. They were virtually exterminated from south and east England, and their numbers were much reduced elsewhere in the country.

The sparrowhawk accumulates DDT through what it eats. Insects and earthworms are the first to take in DDT sprayed on crops, lawns or flowers; they are eaten by birds like thrushes which then fall prey to such predators as the sparrowhawk. DDT interferes with the breeding biology of the sparrowhawk, for example causing the female to lay thin-shelled eggs which break easily, and it also affects their general behaviour. Most of the DDT is laid down in the bird's fat. When

The predator – prey relationship

The phrase 'balance of nature' is well known, and the real meaning of the words is best examined in a predator-prey relationship. It is easy to become angry at the thought or sight of bird predators, such as sparrowhawks, goshawks, magpies or jays, taking garden birds or their nest contents. Such predatory birds are often accused of reducing the number of robins, blue tits and blackbirds. They do, of course, kill these small birds and reduce their numbers, but this is an essential part of the seasonal pattern and cycle of numbers.

The predators do not influence the basic numbers of breeding pairs; indeed the populations of many small birds are increasing. It is rather the numbers of prey that determine the population levels of the predators. So short-eared owls breed additionally well in a year of vole plague, while high numbers of magpies indicate healthy populations of small bird species and other prey.

Sparrowhawks feed almost exclusively on small birds, eating 700-800 in the course of a year. This may seem a great many. However, in 12 acres of woodland there may be, say, 12 pairs of blue tits. If each pair produces an average of 10 young per year, one pair and its successive progeny would multiply to a total of 7500 pairs in five years, if all survived. Together with other woodland species there is a huge surplus and hawks and other birds of prey help to keep the balance right.

it starts to use up the energy stored in the fat – for example, to keep warm on a cold day, or to power itself for a long flight – the DDT is liberated and poisons the bird.

The use of DDT has been restricted or even banned for several years, and the sparrowhawk has recovered some of its former numbers, but the poison is persistent and it is still having a marked effect on the sparrowhawk's nesting success.

Given protection from pesticides and gamekeepers, the prospects for both the sparrowhawk and the goshawk are good. The maturing of many forestry plantations will eventually help to provide the ideal habitat for returning goshawks.

Right: The male sparrowhawk is blue-grey on the upper parts and neatly barred underneath, while the female is much browner.

Left: After the goshawk's 5-6 eggs hatch, the male brings 5-6 kills daily for the mother and young. After two or three weeks even the female joins in the hunting as the youngs' demands increase. The male does not feed the chicks, but brings plucked prey to the nest platform for the female to tear up and give to her hungry young.

Hunting techniques

The hunting methods of the sparrowhawk and goshawk rely mainly on silent observation, stealth and final explosive acceleration. Both hawks exploit rich food sites within a territory, and return to them repeatedly as long as they remain productive.

The hawk sits silently on a perch, hidden in the cover of woodland, waiting for likely prey. It glides low to the ground, only as far as the next perch if necessary, until it singles out its victim. Then it approaches fast and low, using the cover of hedgerow or trees, flicks over the final hedge or bush at full speed and takes the unsuspecting prey with outstretched talons, either while the victim is still perched, or after a short and frantic pursuit.

The hawk's tenacity sometimes leads it to pursue its prey into buildings (even occasionally to fly through glass windows). Sometimes too it chases its victim on foot into bushes. Individuals have been known to take

Male sparrowhawk
catching prey

blue-grey above

orange underparts

Above: The sparrowhawk at close hand has a yellow eye of penetrating alertness, long legs, feet of almost disproportionately huge size and needle-sharp talons.

house martins from under eaves, and young moorhens off the surface of a pond, and sometimes a hawk prospects for prey by soaring high into the air, occasionally stooping (falcon-like) on prey on the wing.

After catching prey (with both feet if it is as large as a jay or wood pigeon), the hawk usually takes its victim into cover and perches on a tree stump, ant-hill or old nest platform to pluck the feathers off with its beak. You can easily identify such plucking posts by the scatter of feathers around them. The bird's sharp talons then make short work of tearing the meat to pieces.

The hawks' food includes game birds, wood pigeons and other woodland species. The goshawk, unlike the sparrowhawk, readily takes prey on the ground – attacking medium-sized mammals such as hares and rabbits.

Neither bird appears to be the specialised villain it is made out to be by gamekeepers, and game birds seldom form a substantial part of their diet. Some farmers and foresters today reckon that the increase in goshawk numbers will provide them with an ally against the destructive wood pigeon.

Marsh, hen and Montagu's harriers

Harriers are large, broad-winged birds of prey. In
Britain only three species occur–the hen, marsh and
Montagu's harriers–out of a world total of about
nine or ten; and all three are now rare and very
restricted in their distribution here.

The shape, size and silhouette of harriers are all distinctive and unlikely to cause confusion with other birds of prey. They are broad-winged, slender-bodied birds with long narrow tails. When seen in flight they are very distinctive, flying buoyantly and gracefully, usually low over the ground, with dexterous turns and changes of direction as they quarter for food or make a half-pass at likely prey.

As with most other birds of prey, female harriers are noticeably larger than the males, in this case by some 5cm (2in) or so. They are also less brightly coloured.

When three apparently similar species occur in the same area, there is usually a clear ecological separation between them, often in their use of different types of habitat. This is amply demonstrated by the three British harriers. The hen harrier is a moorland specialist, and the marsh harrier a reed bed and marshland bird, while Montagu's harrier –a rare summer migrant–has a strong preference for lowland heaths and arable fields. This latter species is a little more catholic in its choice of habitat than the other two although, being confined in Britain to land below 76m (250ft) or so, it no longer overlaps with the hen harrier.

Distinguishing our harriers There are few more exciting sights for bird-watchers in Britain than a dove-grey male hen harrier sweeping buoyantly over the dark, rolling expanses of a heather moor. The males are uniformly pale grey above, relieved only by broad black wing tips and a white band at the base of the tail. At a distance the males can appear so pale that they often resemble a large gull. The females are much darker, being brown birds with a white rump patch that stands out clearly. Hen harriers are confined to heather moors.

Above: A female hen harrier drops down to her nest with prey for the young.

Right: A fluffy young hen harrier; both females and immature birds have banded tails and are often referred to collectively–and evasively–as 'ringtails'.

Opposite page: The head of a harrier is distinctive in shape, appearing strikingly owl-like from the front, with marked facial discs and a very small decurved bill. All species show a distinct neck ruff, in particular the hen harrier, as can be seen here.

Below: A female hen harrier at the nest. On their own territory some birds can be very aggressive, making spectacular diving attacks on intruders.

It was only in 1802 that a Colonel Montagu, studying harriers in Devon, realised that the smaller birds he saw were an entirely separate species from the hen harrier. Montagu's harrier, named after the Colonel, is a summer visitor which formerly bred, albeit sparingly, across the southern half of England and Wales but is now extremely rare.

In appearance and hunting methods it closely resembles the slightly larger hen harrier, but males can be distinguished by the narrow black centre lines on the wing and by the absence of a white rump patch. Balanced and delicate on the wing, Montagu's harrier flies even more lightly than the hen harrier, and its wings are distinctly longer and narrower. The female Montagu's harrier is very similar to the female hen harrier, the two being considerably more difficult to tell apart than the males of the species.

In former times, when great areas of reed bed covered the fenlands of East Anglia and other parts of the country, the marsh harrier was a familiar and widespread bird. Marsh

Identifying harriers

Marsh harrier

black wing bar

3-fingered wingtip

pale crown

smaller and more slender in build than female hen harrier

♂

brown streaks on belly

chestnut-streaked belly

grey tail

Montagu's harrier

chocolate-brown plumage

Marsh harrier (*Circus aeruginosus*). Very rare summer visitor to parts of East Anglia. Largest harrier at 48-56cm (19-22in).

Montagu's harrier (*Circus pygargus*). Very rare summer visitor to Devon, Cornwall and Norfolk. Smallest harrier at 41-46cm (16-18in).

♀

barred tail

The 'food pass'

dark wingtips

♀

brown plumage

pale grey plumage

Hen harrier

4-finger wingtip

white rump

Hen harriers use a special 'food pass' in mid-flight, the female snatching the food from the male in a turning roll as he drops it.

♀

barred tail

Hen harrier (*Circus cyaneus*). Resident in northern heather moors or lower ground in winter. Length 43-51cm (17-20in).

Distribution

☐ hen harrier
⬤ Montagu's harrier
◯ marsh harrier

Above: The distribution of our three harrier species. After a disastrous decline in the 19th and early 20th centuries these birds have shown a small rise in numbers since World War II.

harriers are the largest of the family, distinctly heavier-looking and broader-winged than the others and consequently less buoyant and manoeuvrable in flight. Both sexes are predominantly brown, the male showing grey only on the tail and parts of the wings; the female is a dark-plumaged bird with a prominent creamy head and creamy shoulder patches.

Changing fortunes Our large birds of prey have been persecuted over the last hundred years or so in a systematic and comprehensive way. Harriers were no exception, and all three of our species fell victim to the ruthless control of predators in the name of game preservation in the 19th and early 20th centuries. The gun and the trap have thus been responsible for the wholesale removal of some of our finest birds of prey. Following this, the reclamation of heathland, fen and moorland for intensive farming has drastically reduced the available breeding areas suitable for these species.

In the early years of the 19th century the

hen harrier was a widespread breeding bird in tracts of wild heathland from the Orkneys to the south coast counties of England. In some areas it was extremely plentiful, and accounts of local carnage testify both to the number of birds and the ruthlessness of the killing; on two Ayrshire estates, for instance, 351 hen harriers are claimed to have been killed between June 1850 and November 1854. By the onset of the First World War the hen harrier was extinct as a breeding bird everywhere except the Orkney Islands.

Only after the end of World War II, when keepers had been away for several years, was it evident that a slight resurgence was taking place. The steady spread has continued, and there are now perhaps 600 pairs on moorland in Scotland, Ireland, northern England and north Wales. The bird is still illegally persecuted, however, especially by people with grouse interests, because the hen harrier definitely takes young grouse, but more so because of the effect a hunting harrier has on grouse–forcing them into concealment and thus conflicting with an expensive sport on shooting days.

The marsh harrier has fared little better. It was extinct in Ireland by 1917, by which time it had also temporarily disappeared from England and Wales. The end of World War II again marked a period of modest revival, centred on East Anglia, and by 1958 twelve to fourteen pairs were nesting. Although numbers have fluctuated since, they have remained of this order, with the best-known pairs being those breeding at the RSPB's Minsmere reserve in Suffolk.

There is little doubt that Montagu's harrier was always a scarce bird in Britain, being at the northern edge of its range here, although it, too, fell victim to gamekeepers and egg collectors in the 19th century, and has since suffered from destruction of its habitat. Nowadays it has the most tenuous of toe-holds here each summer, the beautiful dove-grey form of the male being a rare and sporadic sight over the rough commons and heathlands of Devon, Cornwall and Norfolk.

'Dancing' in the sky As the harriers start to re-occupy their breeding territories in spring they also begin to display. The courtship flights of all three harrier species are dramatic and exciting. The male marsh harrier performs high soaring flights above the chosen nesting place, followed by remarkable aerial evolutions, plunging with half-closed wings, steepling high again, tilting, tumbling and

Above: A male Montagu's harrier and (below) a male marsh harrier. Throughout most of their European ranges these two species, and the hen harrier, have been in almost constant decline. Montagu's harrier is, without a doubt, one of the rarest and most threatened birds of prey in Europe, and the hen harrier and marsh harrier have patchy distributions with centres of population interspersed with areas that are now intensively developed and unsuitable for breeding.

looping in an ecstatic flight reminiscent of the wild gyrations of the lapwing. Montagu's and hen harriers, closely related and similar in many ways, also have spectacular diving displays. The males rise to 30m (100ft) or more and then, twisting sideways or somersaulting, plunge headlong earthwards, checking abruptly just above the ground and swinging up again to repeat the process.

At about this time, when the nest site is chosen, the male begins to feed the female, continuing to do so as she incubates the eggs for the four and a half week period. The male now carries out all the hunting, making use of a spectacular technique to pass food to his mate. As he approaches with prey in his lowered talons, the female rises from the nest to meet him. When she reaches him, flying slightly below, she rolls to her side or right over on her back, extending one long slender leg to snatch the food as he drops it, then rights herself so swiftly that the movement is often difficult to follow.

Growing up and feeding After hatching, the young birds stay close to the vicinity of the nest for five weeks, up to the time they fledge, being tended by the female first with food provided by the male but later on with items provided by both parents.

Harriers hunt in a low coursing flight, quartering the ground slowly and methodically, striking at their prey with dexterous turns and making full use of the long reach of their slender legs. Hen harriers prey mostly on voles and other small mammals, together with the chicks of such wading birds as lapwings and golden plovers, and on young grouse and other moorland birds. Montagu's harriers take a higher proportion of lizards, large insects and small birds, while marsh harriers prey on small amphibians and reptiles and a wide range of marshland bird nestlings, as well as on water voles and other small mammals.

By winter Montagu's harrier has moved far south to tropical Africa; many of the marsh harriers, too, move to southern France or the Iberian peninsula. Only the hen harrier – the most northerly of all the harrier species – winters here.

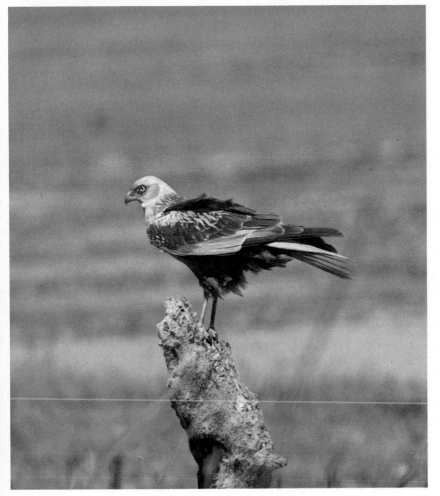

Peregrine

Among all the birds there is none to rival the
peregrine falcon in its powers of flight and its
devastating speed. Even when perched in upright
stance on cliff top or mountain ledge, it seems to
embody the essence of nobility and freedom.

Stooping to conquer

the quarry has been sighted

view from above

view from beneath

going into the stoop—wings held in sickle shape and tail open

the tight stoop—tail and wings closed and flight starting to level off

Everything about the peregrine falcon conveys strength and power. It has powerful shoulders, a short neck, broad chest, large eyes, immensely strong legs and disproportionately large feet armed with formidable talons. The dark eyes, framed in a bright yellow orbital ring, are of enormous size, occupying a large part of the skull, and give the peregrine visual acuity at least four times as sharp as that of humans. The slate grey upperparts of the adults, and the bold black moustachial stripe, contrast with the pale, finely barred underparts.

It is on the wing, however, that the full majesty and speed of the peregrine has to be seen to be fully appreciated. In silhouette from below, as you would normally see it, it is sickle-shaped and heavily built, with a short tail and neck. In level flight it has the rapid wing-beat shared by other falcons such as kestrels and merlins, but it also soars and glides high above the hillsides and sea cliffs where it lives.

In its famous 'stooping' dive, in which the peregrine attacks its quarry (principally other birds), it has been estimated that the bird may reach speeds of between 150 and 200mph, depending on the angle of descent. In level flight the peregrine can attain 60mph or more, with short bursts of speed up to 80mph. But whatever the hunting method it employs—whether it is the stoop or a strike upwards from below—the passing silhouette of the predatory peregrine casts a feared shadow on the ground. It can induce panic in flocks of wildfowl or waders, occasionally putting them into the air to fly at great heights, sometimes for hours on end, and on the ground, nesting grouse, plover and lapwing crouch motionless as the lethal sickle shadow passes over.

Decline and rise The story of the peregrine falcon has not been one of unrestricted success, especially in recent decades for, in the 1960s, it became clear that there was something seriously amiss with the British population.

Ironically, the first signs of this were picked up when a national survey of peregrines was carried out in 1961, following a petition to the

Above: The peregrine feeds almost exclusively on other birds up to the size of a grouse or pigeon, catching them on the wing by sheer force and speed. The most dramatic technique is the stoop, in which the peregrine, having gained height above the quarry, closes its wings and accelerates at breathtaking speed in a stooping dive of several hundred feet or more to hit the unfortunate prey with its talons in a bone-shaking flurry of feathers.

Peregrine falcon (*Falco peregrinus*); resident bird of prey haunting cliffs and mountains. Male 38cm (15in), female 46cm (18in).

Below: An immature female peregrine; it lacks the adults' black 'moustache' and slate grey underparts.

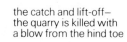

the catch and lift-off—the quarry is killed with a blow from the hind toe

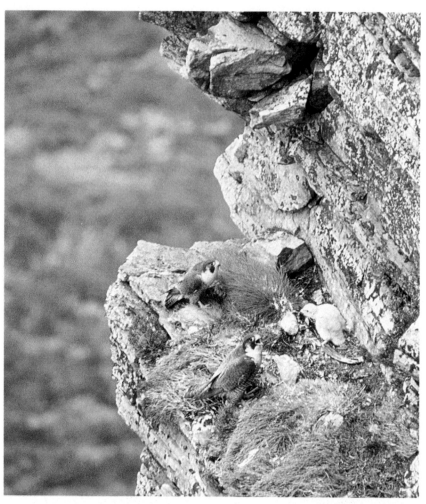

Home Office by pigeon fanciers who claimed that increasing peregrine numbers were making serious inroads into their homing pigeon stocks. The evidence from the 1961 survey showed clearly that there was in fact a serious reduction in pairs and that, in southern Britain, but less so in the north, peregrines were in headlong decline. By 1962 the number of breeding territories occupied was a mere 56% of the total at the beginning of World War II.

As investigations continued, attention focussed on the presence of several synthetic agricultural chemicals being used in seed dressings, principally DDT and the related dieldrin group of pesticides. Not only were these chemicals responsible for killing many song birds, their persistent nature was also affecting predatory birds higher up the food chain. Other birds of prey – sparrowhawks, barn owls, kestrels – were also affected, but it was the peregrine decline that warned of the grave consequences of the extensive use of these chemicals. Government action led to a reduction in the use of the most damaging poisons and slowly the population, by now reduced to a shadow of its former levels, levelled off and then began a slow upturn.

Through the 1970s this increase speeded up and the remarkable resilience of the peregrine has been demonstrated by its recent recovery in Britain to near pre-war numbers. Over wide areas of its northern range, however,

Above: A peregrine family at their cliff-ledge nest. The female is on the left, the male on the right, while the chick, which has not yet lost its grey downy covering, is furthest from the edge. Occasionally peregrines choose to nest in strange places. Some have recently prospected the Post Office Tower in Swansea, but failed to find a suitable ledge.
Below: A peregrine is not such a lordly sight when it is moulting. Notice the extremely powerful talons.

both in Europe and North America, the peregrine has virtually disappeared. It is listed as an endangered species and the British population assumes an ever greater international importance. At present there are some 650 pairs breeding in Britain.

Relationship with man The peregrine has had a chequered relationship with man. Greatly coveted and admired by falconers over the centuries, it has simultaneously suffered attrition at the hands of game-keepers, pigeon fanciers and others. During World War II it was legally controlled to reduce predation on carrier pigeons.

Sadly, since its recovery in the 1970s, the peregrine, despite being strictly protected under the law by special penalties, has been subject to gross predation by both egg collectors and falconers. The RSPB and the police have made strenuous efforts to combat the robberies with protection schemes and a string of prosecutions, but the robberies continue.

Cliff and mountain dweller Essentially the peregrine is a bird of open country. By the nature of its hunting methods it is ill-equipped to deal with birds that can take refuge in the cover of woodland or elsewhere, and it needs to fly down its prey where there is the least chance of losing it once the hunt is under way. Much of Britain is therefore suitable country for the peregrine, but the bird's distribution is restricted for much of the year by the need to find nesting ledges on steep rock faces – it is almost exclusively a cliff-nesting species in Britain. Its breeding strongholds are the mountains and cliff-bound coasts of Scotland, Wales, Ireland and the south-west peninsula of England. Here there are nest sites in abundance and an endless supply of smaller birds as prey.

Nowhere is the peregrine more at home than in the mountains and cliffs of the west and north of our islands. Both inland and on the coasts, pigeons, especially stray homing birds, are the favoured prey, but the range of species taken is very much wider, including birds as large as the shelduck and mallard and as small as house martins and finches.

Many individuals stay in the vicinity of

their breeding cliffs throughout the winter, certainly for as long as the flow of food remains, but others, perhaps predominantly young birds, wander further afield and turn up in river valleys and coastal marshes well away from the breeding area. Here they take a daily toll of the flocks of wildfowl and waders and can often be found using regular perches on flood-drifted logs or fence posts.

Pairs and breeding As in most birds of prey, the female peregrine is markedly larger than the male – as much as 15% in some cases. This sexual size difference means that the female, measurably the more powerful of the pair, is better adapted for taking the largest food items, although the male (called the tiercel) is quicker and more agile.

Peregrines normally pair for life and they and their descendants use the same nest ledge (or a series of alternative sites) with great fidelity generation after generation. Some sites have been used for many hundreds of years and a remarkable fact was that, after birds began to return to the areas from which they had been wholly eliminated in the 1960s,

Above: A peregrine in flight – the essence of aerial power and majesty, and awe-inspiring to watch.

Below: A female peregrine feeding her chick. A brood of three or four chicks is usual for peregrines.

the re-establishing pairs began to occupy the same ledges that their forebears had always used.

Once winter is on the retreat, by late February, occupation of the breeding cliff becomes more regular and the pairs increasingly hunt together in the early morning to satisfy their daily food needs. Successful hunting is often followed by spectacular display flights by the tiercel, careering, speeding, twisting and plummeting over and in front of the breeding cliffs. Mutual chasing often takes place and can be breath-taking in its speed and agility. As in many other bird species, the male feeds the female at this period as part of the process of strengthening the bond between the pair.

Mating takes place three weeks before the laying of eggs, and the first eggs appear in the south of Britain before the end of March. Incubation, predominantly carried out by the female, especially in the early stages, begins around the time when the third egg is laid. A full clutch is usually three or four eggs, occasionally five. They are normally laid at intervals of two days, and are mottled and spotted in different shades of reddish brown.

Incubation takes about 30 days and the newly hatched young are tended with great attention by the female peregrine. During the 40-day fledging period the young birds grow rapidly, passing through a grey downy stage when they appear ungainly and immobile. Over the last two weeks of fledging they develop the brown juvenile plumage. The young males leave the nest first.

The contribution of the female to hunting is small at this time and it is the male who provides for the female and the growing brood on the cliff ledge, although from the third week onwards the increasing demands of the young require the female to hunt.

Prospects The future of the peregrine in Britain at present is bright, and this is one of the few areas of the world where the peregrine population has actually increased over recent years. Nevertheless both here and in the rest of the world, the potential problems of human robbery, persecution and toxic contamination remain.

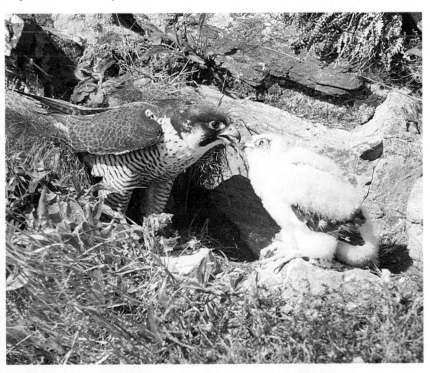

The sport of Kings

Falconry has been practised for over 4000 years and it is reasonable to guess that trained peregrines would have featured from early times. In Britain the Middle Ages were the golden age of falconry, and in the hierarchy of the sport the peregrine was at the very pinnacle, valued above all other birds for its lordly powers of flight and for the size of prey to which it could be directed. Game birds were its principal quarry. The birds were taken to the field hooded and tethered (right). Falconry still has a minority following today and many falconers have a deep knowledge of peregrines in the wild.

Kestrel

The kestrel's old folk name – the windhover – catches the essence of this bird whose most characteristic posture is its skilful, seemingly effortless hovering. If you see a bird with wings winnowing, tail fanned out and head down it's probably a kestrel after prey.

A pair of kestrels at their woodland nest; as with many birds of prey, the male (left) is smaller than the female (right). The nest was not built by this pair; it is an old one made by another bird (possibly a carrion crow) and taken over by the kestrels. When the eggs – up to five in number – are laid, the female does most of the incubating while the male hunts, periodically bringing his mate food – such as the vole she is holding in her beak.

The kestrel is our most common and widespread bird of prey; it is also unique in the way it has come to terms with man and become an independent and resourceful city dweller. Its urban takeover bid has been very successful; in a special survey carried out in 1977 no fewer than 337 breeding pairs were reported in London, at least seven of them right in the heart of the city. The kestrel has also learned to exploit the thousands of miles of infrequently mown grassy motorway verges which harbour the small rodents that make up its principal food. In fact, a stretch of country motorway is one of the best places to see these slim, long-tailed members of the falcon family. Male and female do not look alike. The striking blue-grey head and tail and light chestnu back spotted with black identify the male kestrel, while the female's plumage is barred and streaked in brown and reddish-brown colours. Both sexes have a conspicuous black band on the end of the tail which is clearly visible when the birds are hovering, and both have creamy underparts streaked with black or dark brown.

Varied feeder Towns and motorways are not, of course, the only haunts of the kestrel. It frequents downs, heaths, moors, mountains, parkland, farmland and cliffs – almost every land habitat barring the middle of thick woods where there is not enough room for its particular style of hunting. (In these woods

The kestrel's hunting technique

Left: The hunting kestrel holds its position in the air with continuous small corrective movements of outstretched wings and tail while at the same time keeping its down-pointed head (and eyes) perfectly steady.

the kestrel's place is taken by the sparrow-hawk).

One secret of the kestrel's success is its ability to adapt to a very varied diet. In country areas small rodents such as mice and voles form nearly two thirds of the kestrel's food—making the bird a distinct benefit to the farmer. The next most important items of diet are insects, particularly grasshoppers and beetles, and some small birds such as finches. Some enterprising individuals have been known to take turtle doves and lapwings—birds almost as large as themselves.

In towns where small outdoor mammals are in short supply, the kestrel preys principally on small birds such as house sparrows and starlings. Distance is no serious obstacle if the kestrel knows that a good supply of food awaits it at the end of a journey; for instance, one pair of outer London kestrels flew five miles regularly to hunt at a sewage works frequented by starlings.

Skilled hunter The kestrel is an exceptionally keen sighted bird—as it has to be since it often hunts from heights of up to 60m (200ft). As it hovers, the kestrel keeps its head absolutely still—eyes fixed on the prey far below—while maintaining its position in the air with constant small adjustments of wings

Right: To catch its prey the kestrel must be fast and accurate. When its keen eyes have picked out the movements of a mouse or vole on the ground below, the kestrel swoops down on it in a series of stepped descents. The kill is made with the strong, fearsomely sharp talons which clutch the victim in a deadly grip. Open ground is essential for this type of hunting—in dense woodland with tangled undergrowth the kestrel could severely damage its long, pointed wings.

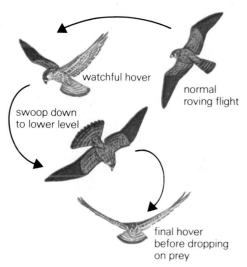

watchful hover

normal roving flight

swoop down to lower level

final hover before dropping on prey

Below: After the kill, the kestrel sometimes 'mantles' its prey, with its wings outspread and its tail forming an almost circular cover. It is thought this is done to screen the prey while the bird recovers from the flurry of the hunt.

Left: Although the kestrel will sometimes eat its prey on the ground, it prefers to carry it to a secluded perch. The feet grip the prey firmly while the strong hooked beak tears off flesh.

and tail. Even when facing into a high wind, the head remains quite steady though the body may be wobbling frantically from side to side and the wings and tail lashing furiously.

Once the victim is spotted, the kestrel swoops towards it at great speed, sometimes catching up short halfway to adjust position, and seizes the unfortunate animal with its powerful outstretched talons. The prey either dies instantly from the impact, or when a talon pierces a vital organ during a tussle on the ground. If the kill is made on a roadside verge or other exposed place, the kestrel flies off at once to a private perch, clutching its prey firmly in its talons. Alternatively, the kestrel will crouch over its kill on the ground, 'mantling' it with outspread wings and tail – like an open umbrella. It is thought that this is done to screen the prey from other birds while giving the kestrel time to regain its breath after the exertion of the hunt; it is an aspect of behaviour typical of all falcons. Small birds are sometimes caught on the wing in a swift 'swoop, clutch and away' movement. The prey is usually carried off to a suitable perch or post, where the kestrel can eat it in peace and quiet. Fence posts, telephone wires and tall trees are often used as convenient perches from which the kestrel can watch for prey; its alert, straight-backed posture on these perches is almost as characteristic a pose as the hovering. The swoop down on a victim is made just as effectively from this position.

Choosing a nesting site Like other falcons, the kestrel does not build a nest. In the country it often lays its eggs on cliff ledges, in hollow trees or, in wooded areas, in the old nest of another bird – particularly that of the carrion crow. On the Orkney Islands which have a good supply of food to offer but neither cliffs nor trees, the kestrel has learned to nest in long heather on the ground.

In towns, however, the kestrel's adaptability is especially evident in its catholic choice of nesting site. Ruined and deserted buildings have long been used as substitutes for cliffs and from these it seems to have been a simple stage to nesting on occupied buildings. Most early town-breeding records refer to public buildings like churches. One famous pair of kestrels managed to raise their family on the tower of the Imperial Institute in South Kensington! More recently, kestrels have been discovered breeding in window boxes on high-rise buildings – perhaps the ultimate in city acclimatisation.

Kestrels are great opportunists; in the Netherlands, for example, they were quick to benefit from the invasion of rodents on the newly reclaimed Zuider Zee polders, and readily occupied the large open-fronted nest boxes put up for them by the thoughtful Dutch.

Courtship display Kestrels are rather solitary birds, so it is only during courtship that you are likely to see male and female together.

The pair soar up into the sky with extended wings, the male usually higher than his mate. Soaring is followed by much wilder movements – the male repeatedly 'stoops' upon the female like a fighter plane in aerial combat, sometimes even brushing her with his wings. This dramatic display is often accompanied by loud, rather shrill 'kee-kee-kee' calls.

The soaring display flight is perhaps the only time when you might confuse the kestrel with our other small bird of prey, the sparrowhawk. Both birds are similar enough in size to cause confusion, both have a long tail and both soar in the breeding season. However, if you watch for the sparrowhawk's distinctive low-level interception method of killing (as opposed to the kestrel's characteristic hover), and broad, blunt wings (unlike the kestrel's long pointed ones) identification should not be too difficult. Sometimes, however, the kestrel's wings can look broad and blunt-ended when they are stiffly extended during soaring.

Raising young The female kestrel lays her eggs between mid-April and mid-May, at intervals of two to four days. The eggs, from one to five in number, are a rich, mottled red brown in colour.

The female incubates the eggs for about a month, sometimes assisted by the male. Occasionally, she will start incubating as soon as the first egg is laid (instead of when all are laid, as is more usual), so the young may hatch

out at two- to four-day intervals. This is an adaptation for species survival, for in years when food is scarce the smallest and weakest (and probably the youngest) quickly starve to death; in this case it is better to raise just one healthy, strong chick rather than four or more weaklings.

Both male and female take part in feeding the chicks; these develop not one but two successive coats of greyish fluffy down before fledging at about 28-30 days old. The young are meat eaters from the start of their lives and greedily swallow the chunks of flesh and insects offered them by their parents until they are old enough to leave the nest and hunt for themselves.

Above: Female kestrel and her brood on a rocky cliff ledge nesting site. Both male and female feed the chicks, bringing voles, mice and insects.

Left: The kestrel chick has two successive coats of down, the first shorter and thinner and the second longer, coarser and usually darker. Feathers start to appear when the chick is between 12 and 20 days old, and the chick is able to fly at anything from 27 to 39 days.

Kestrel (*Falco tinnunculus*), also called the windhover; 34cm (13½in) long from beak to tail; distribution very general, including open woods, moors, cliffs, farmland, motorway verges and city centres.

How birds see

Vision is the dominant sense of nearly all birds. In most, the eyes are placed so far to the side of the head that they have mainly monocular vision—each eye scanning a separate area—a feature shared by all hunted creatures who depend on vision to warn them of possible danger. The thrush turns its head sideways to look (not to listen), and some birds, such as the woodcock, even have all round vision. Birds of prey and owls have eyes set more to the front of the head, offering a wider angle of binocular vision—vitally important for judging distance. The kestrel, for example, has a 150° field of vision, over the middle 50° of which both eyes work in binocular vision, scanning an overlapping area.

We see only the cornea of a bird's eye, but the eyeball within the skull is proportionately huge. For example, if our eyes were like the starling's, they would be as big as tennis balls! A bird focuses by means of powerful muscles which alter the shape of the lens. Light passing through the lens falls on the retina—a complex surface of minute cells. Part of the retina—the fovea—is more densely packed with cells: in the buzzard there are one million per square millimetre, while in man there are only 200,000. The more cells there are, the greater the detail transmitted to the brain. (Some of the cells are responsive to light, while others respond to colour.) Elsewhere within the bird's eye is a small, fleshy projection called the pecten, which supplies oxygen and nutrients to the cells and also enhances the ability of the eye to detect movement. Many birds have oil droplets within their eyes which serve to sharpen contrast (as a photographic filter does), making it easier for the bird to distinguish its prey. Also birds have a third 'eyelid'—a transparent nictitating (winking) membrane—which moves sideways across the cornea and keeps it moist without interrupting vision. This makes birds look as though they blink.

Accuracy is crucial for a hunting bird like the kestrel which relies on its keen eyesight, first to spot prey and then to catch it; the kestrel's eyes are therefore positioned sufficiently far forwards to give it binocular (three-dimensional) vision over a third of its visual arc.

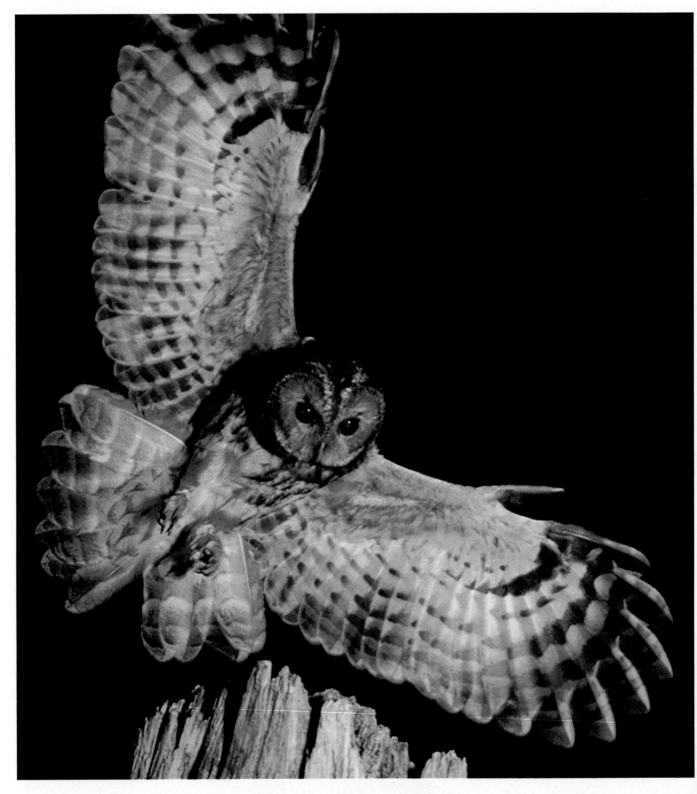

Tawny owl

The tawny owl is most in evidence during the hours of
darkness when its exceptional hearing and sensitive
vision–through 360°–make it a particularly
effective hunter. You are more likely to hear its call
or pick up its outline as it flies past the lights of your
car than to see it perched in a tree.

Tawny owls are highly specialised nocturnal hunters. Although the head may seem disproportionately big, inside the skull are two large, asymmetrical ears so sensitive that they can pick up the rustling and high-pitched squeaks of nearby prey after dark. They can pinpoint a moving target like a mouse with such accuracy that a miss is rare. In addition owls have unusually large eyes. These are forward-facing—like human eyes and binoculars—for three dimensional vision, which enables owls to judge distance accurately. (Most birds have eyes on the sides of their heads.) The retina of each eye is extremely sensitive to light and so designed to enable the owl to see in very poor light.

The owl can turn its head both left and right (like a radar scanner) to inspect a full 360°, so the bird can search for and locate its prey while keeping its body still. The 'facial disc' of rather stiff, bristly feathers serves as a reflector, collecting sounds and focusing them on the ears.

Silent hunter The essence of effective nocturnal hunting is the silent approach—and again, in the tawny owl, evolution has come up with the necessary adaptations. The outer surfaces of the feathers have a velvety finish to deaden noise, and the feathers of the leading edge of the wing have a special comblike fringe to silence the wing as it cuts the air.

Tawny owls will usually sit motionless on a branch, waiting for some unwitting meal to pass below. The owl then drops silently on to its victim, seizing it in the fierce grip of large, sharp talons. If this does not kill the prey instantly, the death blow may be administered by a sharp bite at the base of the skull.

In flight, tawny owls seem dumpy and top-heavy with broad, rounded wings and rather moth-like, fluttering wingbeats. They often appear misleadingly pale in car headlight beams but, when seen in daylight, the blacks, browns, buffs and chestnuts of their streaky plumage provide excellent camouflage against a tree trunk. This so-called 'cryptic' plumage has its values: if the tawny owl were not well concealed, its daytime resting period would be rudely shattered by tormenting groups of mobbing birds, trying to drive it away.

Food supply Although the tawny owl is primarily a rodent killer (voles, mice and rats are all acceptable), shrews and small birds have good reason to be concerned by its presence, as their remains regularly feature in pellets. Owls often swallow their prey whole and the regurgitated pellets are made up of the indigestible remains of its prey such as bones, fur and feathers. These left-overs can provide valuable clues to its diet. In the case of the tawny owl, rodents and birds occur prominently, but the wide variety of its diet (and thus the adaptability of the species) can be gauged by the regular presence of fish, amphibian and reptile remains. Nocturnal observations show that invertebrates, particularly worms which do not leave easily

Opposite: A tawny owl lands whilst hunting.

Right: A dark triangle on the crown is a distinctive marking of the tawny owl.

Above: Primary and secondary feathers are soft to deaden the noise of the owl's descent—giving it the element of surprise and enabling its sensitive ears to do their job without disturbance.

Holes in trees provide a safe nest for the round white eggs which fit compactly in a small area.

Tawny owl (*Strix aluco*) Also called brown or wood owl; 38cm (15in) from beak to tip of tail; 40-45cm (16-18in) high; distribution widespread but absent from Ireland and some Scottish islands.

upper left ear

lower right ear

Below: The tawny owl uses its disproportionately large feet to good purpose when hunting. The formidable talons often penetrate a vital spot to administer an immediate death blow and, because they are widely spread and can grip effectively, they enable the owl to carry even small rabbits.

Top: Asymmetric ears enable the owl to locate its prey.
Above: Ear holes are so large that a human finger can fit inside.

The owlets fledge (leave the nest) after five weeks, but for the next three months they continue to demand parental attention with hungry 'ku-wek' calls at their regular feeding stations, scattered through the woodland. After August, the parent owls begin to re-establish their territorial boundaries and the familiar calls, 'hoo-hoo-hoo' and 'tu-whit', are often heard. The youngsters finally move off or are driven away by the parent owls. This territorial activity increases in January and is probably at its height in February and March. Autumn and winter are the times when mortality is at its highest, particularly for the young birds, when cold weather and food shortages take their toll. Sadly, some also die in collisions with cars after dark on country roads, when the owls are dazzled by headlights.

Favourite nest sites are hollow trees, or cavities found in deserted buildings. One give-away sign of an owl's nest—or roosting site—is pellets around the base of the tree. Occasionally, eggs are laid in old nests of other birds such as magpies and carrion and hooded crows. If there is a scarcity of trees, tawny owls will even nest on the ground, perhaps choosing an old rabbit hole. Tawnies also take readily to nestboxes, and a barrel with good drainage holes, if slung at an angle beneath a high branch sheltered from direct wind and rain, will often tempt a pair of owls. The best time to go out and see tawny owls is on a clear night and at dawn, when they are returning to roost for the day.

The tawny is Britain's most numerous and widespread owl, though absent from Ireland; it's place there is filled by a different species, the long-eared owl (Asio otus). We think of it very much as a woodland bird, and to a degree this is true. However, there are plenty of mice, rats and house sparrows in towns, plenty of parks and large gardens with trees large and old enough to have holes for nesting—and of course there are plenty of suitable buildings like churches in which to nest. Add to this the very catholic diet of tawny owls, and it becomes less surprising that these adaptable birds have taken to urban and suburban life so well.

recognisable remains in the pellets, also feature largely when more substantial prey is in short supply.

Family planning In some uncanny way tawny owls seem able to assess the likely food supply at the start of the breeding season. In years when small mammals are low in number, clutches of eggs tend to be small; the number of eggs increases when mice, moles and small rabbits are more plentiful. Tawny owls usually have a single brood of young each year—and this occurs from mid-March onwards.

Unlike small birds, which wait until their clutch of eggs is complete, the female tawny owl starts incubating as soon as she has laid her first egg, which is like a ping-pong ball in size, shape and colour. The chicks hatch at about two-day intervals, each egg taking 28-30 days to hatch. The chick waits fretfully in the nest for food—usually mice, shrews and sometimes even small birds. The first born tends to get more than its fair share of the food, the result being a considerable difference in size between youngest and oldest. If food is plentiful, then all is well. Should food fail, then the biggest chick eats the smallest one. It may sound unduly brutal, but for the survival of the species it is better that two chicks die to provide food for a third, than for all three to die of starvation. In exceptionally hard years when the shortage of food is acute, the tawny owl may not breed at all.

Above: Wedged into the tree hollow so they can't fall out, these chicks rely on their parents for food. The larger one is about two days older than the other.

Owl pellets

Pellets are found under a roost or nest site, usually at the base of a large tree. They contain the indigestible parts of a meal—mostly fur and bones—which have been compacted in the gizzard before being coughed up. The average length is 42mm (1¾in). The average width is 19mm (¾in).

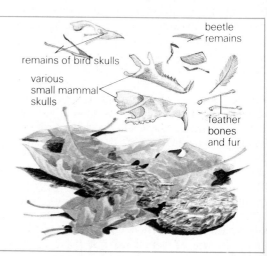

beetle remains

remains of bird skulls

various small mammal skulls

feather bones and fur

Birds and their feathers

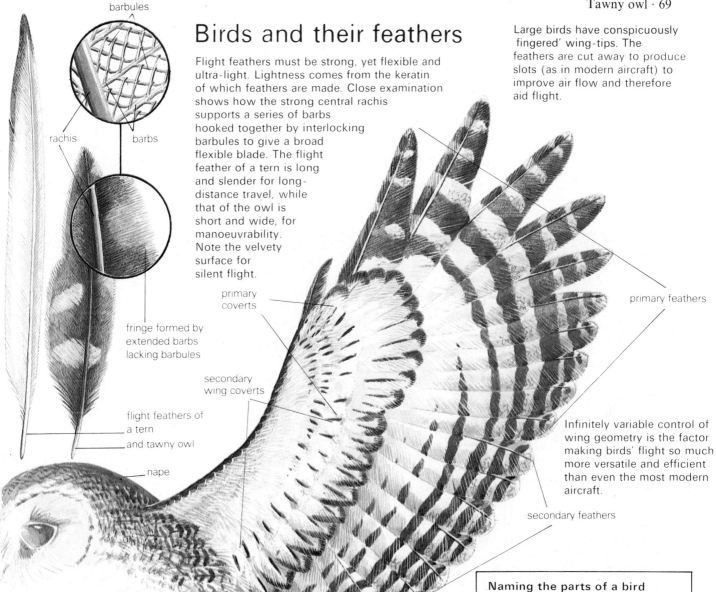

barbules

rachis   barbs

Flight feathers must be strong, yet flexible and ultra-light. Lightness comes from the keratin of which feathers are made. Close examination shows how the strong central rachis supports a series of barbs hooked together by interlocking barbules to give a broad flexible blade. The flight feather of a tern is long and slender for long-distance travel, while that of the owl is short and wide, for manoeuvrability. Note the velvety surface for silent flight.

Large birds have conspicuously 'fingered' wing-tips. The feathers are cut away to produce slots (as in modern aircraft) to improve air flow and therefore aid flight.

fringe formed by extended barbs lacking barbules

flight feathers of a tern
and tawny owl

nape

primary coverts

secondary wing coverts

primary feathers

Infinitely variable control of wing geometry is the factor making birds' flight so much more versatile and efficient than even the most modern aircraft.

secondary feathers

The streamlined outline of the owl is formed by stiff, specially shaped contour feathers. Between this surface layer and the body is a layer of down feathers—the bird's 'thermal underwear' —very necessary for survival through cold winter nights. This insulation may be provided by an aftershaft attached to the contour feather or by special down feathers.

Feathers are vital to a bird's survival. They power flight and supply warmth, and the colours and patterns used in courtship, aggression or camouflage are all in the feathers. Thus their maintenance is of utmost importance. Disarranged barbs must quickly be put straight to maintain flight efficiency, and this is the purpose of preening, which seems to occupy so much of a bird's time. Preen oil is applied by wiping the beak across a gland above the tail and then passing each feather through the beak, when rapid nibblings re-adjust any displaced barbules.

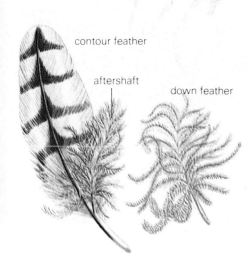

contour feather

aftershaft

down feather

Naming the parts of a bird

primary feathers

primary coverts

secondary coverts

nape

crown

chin

secondary feathers

mantle

rump

breast

ankle

cheek

bill

belly

flank

feet   tarsus

tail

Whether you want to describe a bulky bird like an owl or a slim tern, the same words apply to both. The parts vary in colour and shape, providing a means of identifying each species. To help identify an unfamiliar species, it is worth keeping a note book and making a rough sketch, labelling the colour of each part.

Barn owl

The barn owl, sometimes called the white owl,
is–apart from the rare snowy owl–the palest of the
six species of owl nesting in the British Isles.
Although lacking the camouflage of its relatives, it is
well adapted to a nocturnal predatory life.

The barn owl, probably the best known and most widely distributed owl in the world, is primarily a tropical species. Most live between the latitudes of 40°S and 40°N of the equator, and in Scotland barn owls are at the northernmost part of their range. They seem to benefit from Britain's relatively mild maritime climate, the winters in other countries further from the sea being, by comparison, too harsh. However, even in the British Isles, barn owl numbers are severely reduced in cold winters, and they tend to avoid mountainous areas.

Most owl species are well camouflaged so they can rest in trees during the day without being constantly mobbed by other birds. The barn owl, with its white face and underparts, has no such camouflage, so it hides away in holes and old buildings by day to avoid being noticed. Females are larger than males and tend to be greyer above and slightly spotted below. On the continent, and occasionally in south-east England, you may see very grey-looking barn owls with buff-coloured breasts.

Barn or tawny? Barn owls are smaller than tawny owls (see page 67) and have even been killed by them. However, they usually avoid competition for food and nesting sites by staying outside the tawny owl's woodland habitat. Also, the barn owls' wings are relatively longer than the tawny owls' and therefore more suitable for flight over open ground than among trees. Barn owls prefer to hunt over rough grassy areas, farmland, marshes and bogs, scrub and young forestry plantations.

Unlike tawny owls, barn owls do not call. They mark out their territory with a wild shriek, often made while flying. If you approach a nest you may hear the parents or

Above: A clutch of seven young chicks peer out from their hay-loft nest.

Below: The female owl, in a crouching, defensive posture, shelters her young behind her spread wings.

Opposite: The male barn owl has a white face and underparts. The upper parts are orange-buff, delicately spotted with grey, brown and white, while the tail has four greyish bars.

Right: The female barn owl, larger than the male, is greyer above and slightly spotted below.

young birds hissing ferociously or perhaps making a snoring noise. Alarmed barn owls also make an audible snap with their beaks.

Man-made homes Holes in old, fairly isolated trees, rock crevices and old nests of birds like the jackdaw are often used to rear the barn owl family. However, many barn owls depend on man-made nest sites such as barn lofts, unoccupied buildings, ruins and church towers, even in the middle of towns. Many old barns were made with a special hole high on an end wall to encourage barn owls to nest inside and hence control the local population of mice.

Even modern barns can be adapted by cutting an access hole about 20cm (8in) square. Some barn owls have been trapped inside buildings when the doors were closed and there was no other way out. Recently, in buildings where suitable nesting ledges are not available, they have readily taken to large nest boxes placed in a high, dark corner. We should be careful to make sure they have somewhere to nest, especially as their more natural nest sites are becoming scarce.

Incubating the eggs Barn owls do not add any nesting material to the chosen site, although an untidy scattering of pellets might provide some sort of bed for the eggs. The female usually lays three to seven eggs (though sometimes up to 11) at two to four day intervals, generally in April or May. Their eggs, like other owls', are white; but unlike the normal spherical shape of owl eggs, the barn owl's are oval.

Survival of the fittest Successful nesting is dependent on the availability of food; in good years barn owls may breed in almost any month. Like other owls, the female starts incubating as soon as the first egg is laid, each egg hatching after about a month. During this time the male brings food to his mate at the nest; later on, both parents have to work hard to satisfy the growing family. If, when the chicks are young, food becomes short, the last to hatch – and therefore the smallest – may not survive. The larger chicks are given what food there is to make sure that when they leave the nest in late summer they are healthy enough to survive in the wild. More food means more chicks survive, and also gives the adults a chance to rear a second brood.

Owlets Newly hatched owlets are covered in short, white down, but they replace this after a week or two with thicker creamy-buff coloured down. It is 9 to 12 weeks before the owlets leave the nest and even longer before they can hunt for themselves. By this time they have grown their third coat of feathers, like that of their parents, though you may see some fluffy remains of down. Despite the young owls' natural instinct to hunt and kill their prey, they must learn, often by trial and error, how to do it efficiently. If they manage to survive the first winter they

can raise their own family the following year.

Visions of the night The barn owl sees on the darkest night and can spot prey clearly while remaining unseen itself. Most birds avoid flying at night because they cannot see clearly. Long migrations are often made at night, but usually at great heights – away from dangerous obstacles. However, barn owls' eyes are specially designed for night vision, and are forward-facing to give them a wide degree of binocular vision. They can therefore fly in safety and hunt with astonishing efficiency.

Stealthy hunter Most diurnal birds of prey rely on speed of flight to catch their prey, but the barn owl is master of the silent approach and surprise attack. The unfortunate prey gets no warning because marvellously soft plumage and several hundred sound-deadening hair-like projections on the owl's wing feathers enable it to fly in complete silence.

The barn owl's head looks enormous, but it is exaggerated by feathers that form a characteristically heart-shaped facial disc.

Barn owl (*Tyto alba*), 34cm (13½in) from beak to tail. Distribution widespread.

Opposite: The bulk of the barn owl's diet consists of field vole, common shrew, wood mouse and brown rat. Once captured, the prey is swallowed whole or taken back to the nest site (in this case an old brick loft) where it is torn to pieces for the hungry chicks. Indigestible parts are later coughed up in shiny, blackish pellets about 5cm (2in) long by 2·5cm (1in) wide.

male in flight

male hovering

The barn owl has a very light body compared with the area of its wing (technically known as a low wing bearing). This makes it buoyant in flight, and eliminates the need to flap quickly; the barn owl often glides (above left). As it searches methodically for prey it hovers (above) over ditches and by hedges. The barn owl also dangles its long, feathered legs ready to make a quick kill and can move the outer toe to maximise the deadly grip of its sharp, curved 2cm ($\frac{3}{4}$in) long claws (left).

In the same way that a dog raises and twists its external ear flaps, the barn owl moves these feathers to focus tiny sounds onto its large, sensitive ears–especially receptive to high-pitched sounds like the squeak of a mouse. On very dark nights the owl can range in on its prey by sound alone.

On the other hand, barn owls see perfectly well in bright sunshine, as the pupils in their eyes contract to cut out excess light. You are most likely to see them hunting at dawn, in the afternoon in winter when food is short, or when they have a family to support. Sometimes you may see barn owls perched on fence posts or other vantage points waiting for unwary quarry to pass beneath. You are, however, more likely to see them in flight.

Carnivorous diet Barn owls live on animals that man regards as pests and are certainly more efficient at controlling the rat population than cats or poison. In England, Scotland and Wales, voles and shrews are the most often caught–but only if they are available close to the nest site. However, in Ireland and the Isle of Man, neither short-tailed voles nor common shrews are found.

Sometimes barn owls catch small roosting birds like starlings and sparrows, and they have been seen plunging feet first into water like an osprey to catch fish. They are also known to eat frogs, beetles, moths and bats, but only rarely do they take larger prey such as rabbits.

Of all owls, the barn owl is the most closely associated with man. But for centuries it was regarded with extreme suspicion and attributed all sorts of evil powers. This is, perhaps, not surprising since it seems to thrive in many of the situations we would find unfamiliar and uninviting. Since it depends on the silence of the night to hear and locate the squeaks and rustlings of its prey, it favours such places as lonely ruins and churchyards for hunting and nesting.

In flight, or perched upright on a post, the barn owl has a ghostly man-like appearance with long legs and a distinct face in which the forward-facing eyes and hooked beak are situated just where we would expect our own eyes and nose to be.

Mortality Many barn owls are hit by fast-moving cars and trains, and some collide with wires in strong winds. In this country information from ringed birds has shown that very few live for more than eight years. In the past there was a time when barn owls were frequently shot because, along with all other predatory birds, they were thought to kill game birds.

More recently, population declines have been attributed to the use of toxic chemicals in agriculture. Add to this a steady reduction in good habitat and it is not surprising, though sad to say, that barn owls are not as common as they once were.

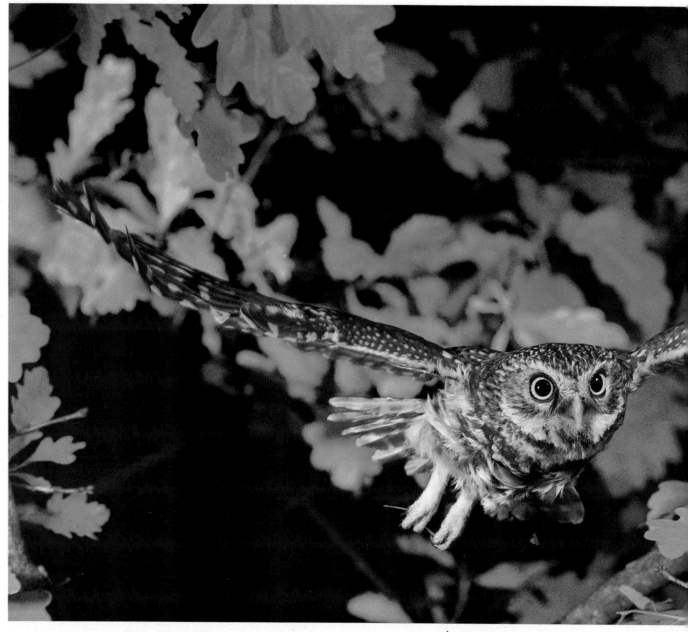

Little owl

Owls are usually regarded as birds of the
night, but not all of them fit into this stereotype.
The little owl (above) is active during the day and can
often be seen perching in some prominent place,
although it does most of its hunting at dawn and dusk.

Little owl (*Athene noctua*).
Resident bird of prey; at
23cm (9in) long, the
smallest British owl. Its
habitat ranges from open
farmland and wasteland
to urban areas, but it
avoids woodland.

Owls are well known for their extraordinarily
keen eyesight that enables them to hunt at
night. Yet they can see just as well during
the day, though few owls take advantage of
this to hunt while the light is still good.
The reason for this is that their victims – mice,
voles, worms and insects – are mostly nocturnal creatures.

A few species of owl, however, prefer to be
active throughout the day. One of these is the
little owl, which does most of its hunting at
dawn and dusk. In this way, it can hunt both
daytime and nocturnal creatures.

Where to see little owls The ideal habitat for
little owls is open farmland with old trees and
buildings to provide nesting sites. Other
favourite haunts include old orchards,
quarries and wasteground, and it is not unusual to find them near the coast among sand
dunes or around cliffs and islands. Some have
even adapted to an urban environment and
nest in city centres. The only habitat they seem
to avoid is woodland, probably because this
is the domain of the much larger tawny owl,
which is known to eat little owls.

The best way to see a little owl is to scan
its favourite perching places: telegraph poles,
fence posts, stone walls, the roofs of buildings
and prominent rocks and branches of trees.
Seen from a distance the little owl is easily
overlooked because its greyish colour and

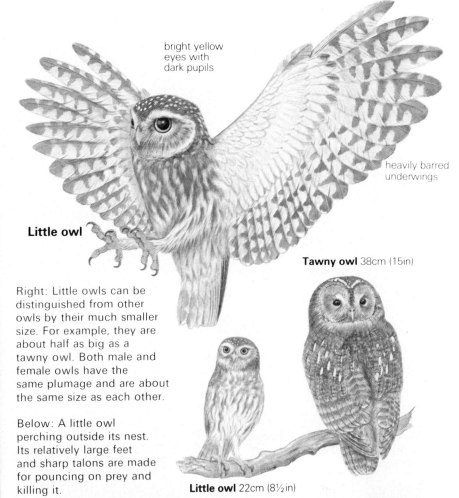

bright yellow
eyes with
dark pupils

Little owl

heavily barred
underwings

Tawny owl 38cm (15in)

Right: Little owls can be
distinguished from other
owls by their much smaller
size. For example, they are
about half as big as a
tawny owl. Both male and
female owls have the
same plumage and are about
the same size as each other.

Below: A little owl
perching outside its nest.
Its relatively large feet
and sharp talons are made
for pouncing on prey and
killing it.

Little owl 22cm (8½in)

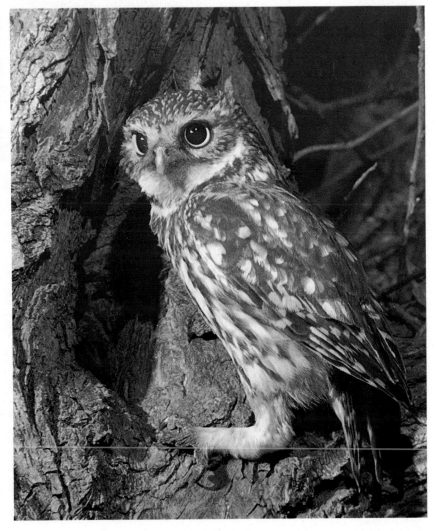

squat rounded shape blend well into the
background.

The little owl's flight and call are useful aids
to identification. Its flight is deeply undulating and resembles that of a woodpecker. The
two most distinctive calls are a shrill barking
'werro' and a more plaintive mewing 'kiew',
noises that can often be heard when two little
owls call to each other. Little owls also make
a high-pitched penetrating 'ooo', repeated
every few seconds, and they have an alarm
call–a loud 'kip-kip-kip'–used by adults to
warn their brood of danger.

Distinctive markings At close quarters the
little owl is easily identified by its beautiful
and distinctive markings. Both the male and
the female have grey-brown upperparts with
white bars and spots. The underparts are
whitish with dark brown streaks. Their eyes
are a distinctive bright yellow with large
black pupils.

As its name suggests, the little owl is small
in comparison with other owls. At 23cm (9in)
from head to tail it is by far the smallest

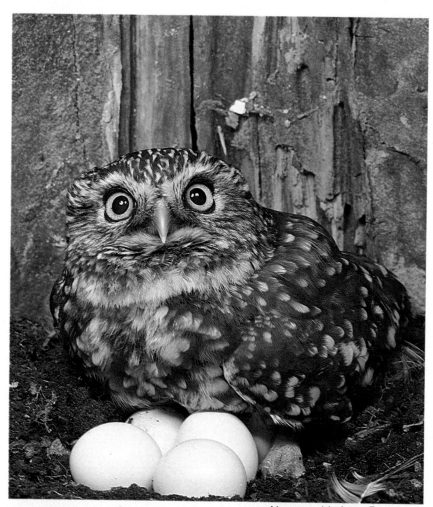

done in the stomach. Each day the owl coughs up a pellet consisting of the indigestible parts such as bones, fur, teeth and feathers. These pellets are about 2.5-4cm (1-1½in) long and can be seen accumulating around the owl's daytime roosting sites.

In times when food is plentiful little owls establish secret hiding places where they build up larders of food. As well as providing a store of food for the future they seem to prefer their food a little 'high'. And there is an additional advantage: the rotting food attracts flies and beetles, which the owls eat as well.

Nesting in holes Little owls nest in holes, usually in old trees, in which case they are likely to choose a hole that has two exits. They may also nest in a cavity in a stone wall or an old building, or in a disused rabbit warren. Like other owls they do not add material to their nest, though they may nest in a hole that has already been lined, for example an old jackdaw's nest.

In April or May the female lays her eggs. The typical clutch is three to five eggs, which are white and elliptical rather than the more usual egg shape. The female often waits until the clutch is complete before she begins to incubate it. Incubation is performed by the female alone and takes between three and four weeks. During this time she is fed by the male. Once the eggs hatch both parents help to feed the young. At first the young owlets are covered with short white down that makes them look rather like fluffy tennis balls with feet. They grow their adult plumage still in the nest and are ready to leave when they are about five weeks old. Sometimes the parents will then raise a second brood, but

British owl and is about as long as a song thrush. But its large rounded head and broad wings make it look much bigger.

Feet for killing For such a small body the little owl's feet seem abnormally large, but they need to be since the little owl sometimes kills quite large prey. A little owl can pounce on unsuspecting prey with astonishing speed, and the strength of its talons usually kills the prey outright. If it does not then one swift slash from its razor-sharp beak is enough to finish off the victim.

As with all other owls, the little owl has keen eyesight and acute hearing with which to detect its prey—the slightest movement or noise attracts its attention.

Little owls often hunt for food standing still, waiting until they see a potential prey moving and then running to catch it. They also watch for prey from perching sites.

The little owl's diet depends largely on what is available in its vicinity. It includes slugs, snails, centipedes, minnows, frogs and even jackdaws and mistle thrushes, which are both larger than itself. But the usual diet of the little owl consists of small rodents, insects, earthworms and a few small birds.

Prey up to the size of a mouse is swallowed whole but the larger catches are usually taken away to a roosting site such as a hole to be dismembered. As with other owls, the little owl makes no attempt to sort out the digestible parts from the rest of the carcass. This is

Above and below: From three to five white eggs are laid in April or May. The young are white and downy at first, but soon darken as their adult plumage develops.

only when food is plentiful.

Young little owls are not abandoned by their parents straight away. They have a month or two to learn where and when to look for food, what to eat and how to catch it. But after that the young are on their own. Many inexperienced young owls die in hard winters when food is scarce. For example, the British population fell dramatically during the harsh winter of 1962-3. However, their numbers always recover quickly.

Imported from Holland Fossil records show that little owls existed in prehistoric Britain but then became extinct. Our present population is descended from birds brought over from Holland during the last century. In 1888, a flock of little owls released in Northamptonshire bred successfully. Once they were established their population grew rapidly since, in open habitats, they have no competitors. By 1930 little owls were breeding in every county south of the River Humber.

Since then they have continued to spread, but at a slower rate. Some little owls now breed in Scotland, but in general the climate there is too harsh for them, and it seems that the Irish Sea is too wide for them to fly over and invade Ireland. There has even been a decrease in their numbers in southern England, possibly because of the presence of pesticides in their prey.

Friend or foe? Little owls were popular when they were first introduced to Britain, but public opinion turned against them in the early part of this century as people began to claim that they killed chickens and game-bird chicks. Many little owls were shot, but in 1935 the British Trust for Ornithology, worried at the number of little owls that were dying, carried out an enquiry. It examined the stomach contents of dead owls, the remains of prey found at nest sites, and thousands of pellets. It soon became clear that, although little owls do occasionally eat game-bird chicks, most of their diet consists of animals that are themselves pests. So, instead of being the pests that people thought them to be, little owls are actually beneficial to man by helping him to control his natural enemies.

Right: Three young little owls at their nest hole. When nervous both young and adult little owls bob their heads up and down in a characteristically comical manner.

Below: The young are fed largely on a diet of insects and earthworms. Both parents help to catch the food and feed the young. At about five weeks old, the young owls leave the nest, but they remain dependent on the parents until they learn to hunt.

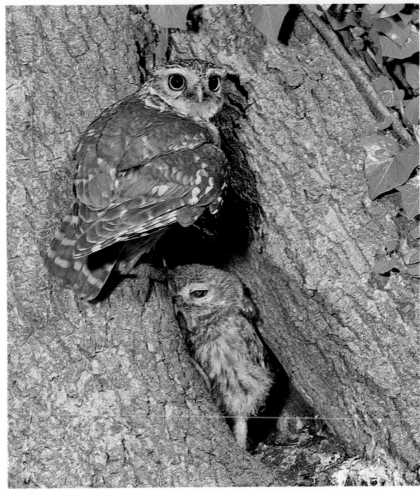

Snowy owl

Owls are an almost universally successful group of birds. Few of the world's terrestrial habitats have not been exploited by this adaptable family, and one owl species, the snowy owl, even lives in the Arctic wastes. This species has also bred in Shetland.

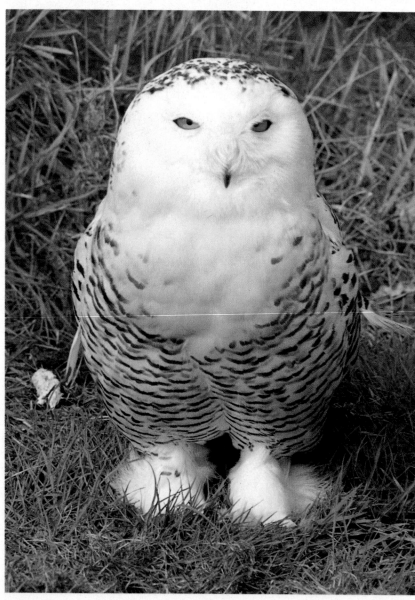

Below: A captive female snowy owl poses for the camera. High quality insulation is provided by the dense plumage, the heavily feathered legs and feet, and the long feathers of the facial disc, which partly conceal the strong black bill.

Snowy owls are very rare birds in Britain, although they have long occurred in small numbers during winter, usually as part of the post-breeding season dispersal of some of the population in northern Scandinavia and other Arctic regions. The Shetland Islands, far to the north of mainland Scotland, are the nearest part of Britain to the snowy owl's regular breeding grounds, and it is here that individual vagrant birds, normally males, have been seen with comparative regularity since the early 1960s.

Large, white owl The male is much the whiter of the two adult birds, often with no markings other than a few dark flecks on the wings and back. The female, noticeably larger, with a wingspan of up to 1.5m (5ft), is more heavily barred on the upperparts and slightly less so on the underparts. This barring, which acts as camouflage for the female when incubating on the nest, tends to become less marked as summer advances because of wear and tear. The chicks, thickly insulated with grey down, resemble the adults by the end of their first summer. It barely needs saying that body insulation needs to be of the highest order for a bird which spends so much of its life in a devastatingly cold and hostile climate. This requirement is amply met by the bird's thick and fluffy plumage at all ages.

The Arctic habitat The true home of the snowy owl is on the inhospitable tundra, frozen solid and buried in a blanket of snow for more than half the year. The tundra is a flat, empty expanse of land, but in the brief Arctic summer it is far from being a barren desert, for once the days lengthen and the strengthening sun thaws the snow and ice, this landscape pulses with life. Migrant birds and mammals return to breed in the bounty of plant, insect and aquatic life, and with them come the inevitable predators, which sustain themselves at the expense of others—arctic fox, gyr falcon, skuas, glaucous gull and snowy owl.

Breeding on the tundra Snowy owls have a circumpolar breeding distribution, nesting on the tundras around the coasts of the Arctic Ocean, as well as on most of the archipelagoes. In a few areas, they breed further south, for example in Iceland and the mountainous snow-covered spine of Scandinavia. Wherever they are, however, the breeding grounds of the snowy owl are among the most inaccessible and desolate places in which any birds choose to nest. Observations suggest that these remarkable birds stay in the same range through the icy cold of the Arctic winter as well.

A diet of lemmings In its Arctic and sub-Arctic home in summer, the snowy owl feeds mainly on lemmings, and to a considerable degree the cycles of both brown and collared lemming populations determine the abundance or scarcity of the owls themselves. The number of lemmings normally rises to a peak every four years; at peak times the owls thrive, rearing large broods. After the peak summers, as the supply of lemmings wanes, numbers of snowy owls tend to move south, and in winter these 'emigrants' are seen in areas where the species is not normally encountered. This is the background of all the sightings in Shetland.

If lemmings form the bulk of the diet, howver, they are by no means the only prey of the snowy owl. Willow grouse and arctic hares are taken, and in summer a variety of smaller birds—waders (especially their chicks), snow buntings and occasionally young wild-fowl. In winter the main birds taken are ptarmigan and seabirds.

Shetland discovery In the spring of 1967 the RSPB's Shetlands Officer, Bobby Tulloch, observed a female snowy owl several times on the island of Fetlar, and on 7th June he

Snowy owl (*Nyctea scandiaca*). Arctic species of owl visiting Scotland as a vagrant, mainly in Shetlands. Length: males 53cm (21in), females 60cm (24in). Wingspan of female 1.5m (5ft).

Below left: A snowy owl chick on the typical low vegetation of its habitat.

gliding, buzzard-like flight

numerous streaks on wings and back

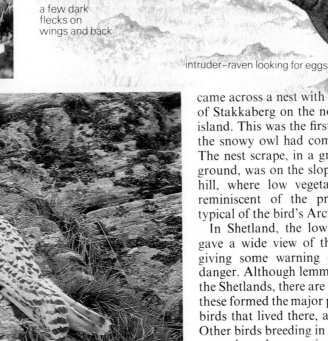
defence posture

a few dark flecks on wings and back

intruder—raven looking for eggs

came across a nest with three eggs on the hill of Stakkaberg on the northern slopes of the island. This was the first time on record that the snowy owl had come to nest in Britain. The nest scrape, in a grassy patch on rocky ground, was on the slopes of this windswept hill, where low vegetation all round was reminiscent of the prostrate plant cover typical of the bird's Arctic breeding grounds.

In Shetland, the low hill on Stakkaberg gave a wide view of the surrounding area, giving some warning of any approaching danger. Although lemmings do not occur on the Shetlands, there are rabbits in plenty, and these formed the major part of the food of the birds that lived there, and later their young. Other birds breeding in this part of the island were also taken—arctic skuas, oystercatchers and other waders. In 1967 the Shetland pair produced seven eggs, and eventually in August five young successfully flew.

Fetlar is much visited by birdwatchers, and from the outset in 1967 it was clear that the secret could not be kept.

In 1968, to the delight of the many bird-watchers among whom word had gone round about this exciting phenomenon, the original pair of snowy owls were still on Fetlar and reappeared on the breeding site. During the seven years from 1968-75, these two parents raised a further 11 young. In some years a second female was seen to have laid eggs, but these did not result in new families. Eventually, the old male snowy owl disappeared and, having previously driven off all the young males, left the females without a partner. The short, exciting phase of snowy owl breeding in Britain had ended, for since then only a few individual birds have lingered on, and none has paired or bred.

Above: A female snowy owl roosting on a limestone outcrop. Her plumage is richly barred with brown, especially on the back and wings. This is good camouflage at breeding time in the Arctic, when the background often consists of broken patches of snow.

Right: The long feathers of the facial disc of a male snowy owl. He lacks the mottled crown of the female. The eyes of both sexes are a liquid golden yellow.

Short-eared owl

Food is first in the short-eared owl's life—a life totally governed by the availability of field voles, its main prey. Not only is the size of its brood influenced but also its territory, lack of voles often forcing the owl into a nomadic existence.

The short-eared owl is one of the most widespread of the world's 133 owl species. Found throughout most of Europe and North America, the northern half of Asia and the southern half of South America, it has even made its way to a dozen remote oceanic islands, such as the Galapagos Islands, 965km (700 miles) west of Ecuador, and Hawaii in the very centre of the Pacific.

Despite this enormous range, the short-eared owl is not a common bird in Britain—barn, little, tawny and long-eared owls all have much larger populations. Although it has been breeding in Scotland, Wales and northern England for many years, it has only recently colonized the coastal marshes of East Anglia and Kent. Nevertheless, since it is primarily a day-time hunter, and since the population is augmented by migrants from the Continent in winter, it is not difficult to find. You may come across several of them together, roosting on the ground, or floating like giant moths over the wild and treeless terrain they tend to favour.

Bouncy flight Extensive tracts of moor, bog, heath, rough grass, dunes and coastal marsh are ideal habitats for the short-eared owl, quite unlike those of its relative, the long-eared owl which is a rarely seen, highly nocturnal forest dweller. Gliding just a couple of feet above the grass, with slightly raised, extraordinarily long, outstretched wings, you might well mistake one for a harrier, were it not for the large, round head which could only belong to an owl. Compared to the weight of the body, the wing area is very large and the resultant buoyant, rather bouncy, flight is characteristic.

When seen flying close-to, the striking appearance of this owl becomes obvious. The black-centred, pale yellow eyes are each highlighted by a ring of smoky black feathers which merge into the pale buffs and greys of the facial discs. Almost hidden among these feathers, like a secret weapon, is the cruelly hooked, razor-sharp beak.

The back is mottled and streaked with buff and brown, while the wings are a similar colour but with white spots. In contrast the underparts are pale, boldly streaked with brown on the breast but fading to fine, rather delicate streaks on the belly. Like other owls, the thick and muscular legs and feet are covered with tiny white feathers right down to the long, curved, needle-sharp claws. In flight the wings and tail are noticeably barred and there is a dark patch at the angle of the wing—the carpal patch.

Cunning hunters Short-eared owls use a 'glide, surprise and grab' hunting technique which makes them proficient hunters, each one able to catch several thousand voles a year. Using eddies and upcurrents in the wind, they often glide for considerable distances without a single flap, their soft, well-padded plumage ensuring totally noiseless flight, so

Above: In flight the short-eared owl is identified by its long wings which have a dark 'carpal patch' at the angle of the wing.

Opposite: This species is not often seen in trees, preferring to perch on posts or even on the ground.

Below: The owl's short 'ears', which can be raised or lowered at will, have nothing to do with hearing, but are thought to convey its mood—fear, excitement and so on—to other owls.

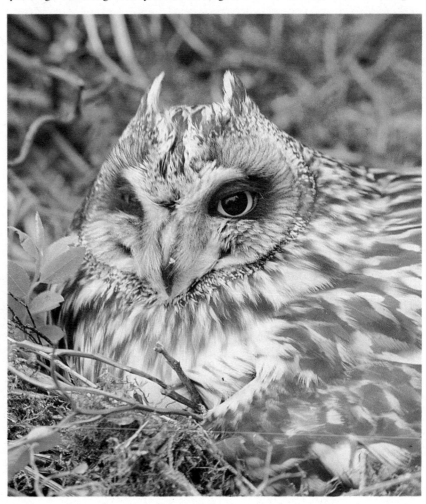

Round-up of British owls

The tawny owl is found among trees and the long-eared in fir woods; the short-eared owl favours open country, and the barn owl old buildings and farms. The little owl has a more general habitat, unlike the snowy owl which is limited to the Shetland Isles.

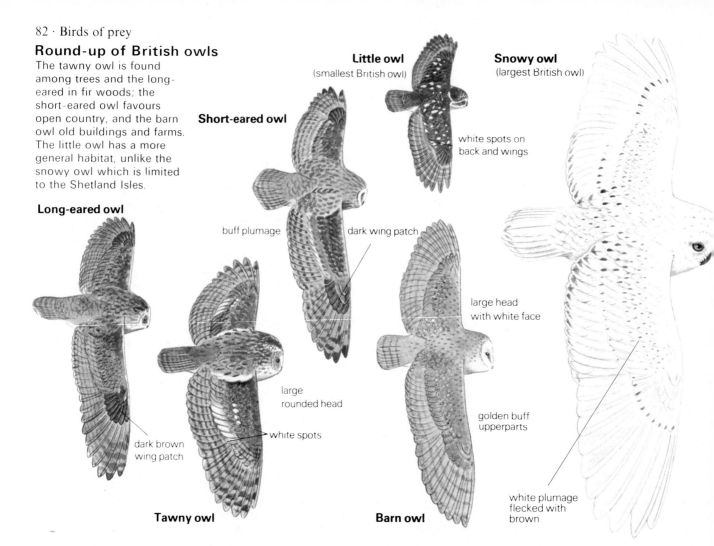

Short-eared owl

Little owl
(smallest British owl)

Snowy owl
(largest British owl)

white spots on back and wings

Long-eared owl

buff plumage

dark wing patch

large head with white face

golden buff upperparts

large rounded head

dark brown wing patch

white spots

Tawny owl

Barn owl

white plumage flecked with brown

Below: Young short-eared owls are a comical sight, covered in white and later grey down, quite unlike their parents. Fledging takes 20 to 30 days but they do not stay in the nest all this time. After only a fortnight they venture out and hide in the surrounding vegetation, even though they cannot yet fly. This behaviour makes it more difficult for predators to find them.

that the unsuspecting vole gets no warning.

Their prey-detection equipment is no less ingenious. The forward-facing eyes give superb binocular vision for accurate judgement of distances, while the discs of feathers surrounding each eye focus the slightest rustle on to enormous, highly sensitive ears, so that even in the gloom of dusk, when owls (and voles) are most active, they can pinpoint the position of their prey with ease.

Nomadic existence It is often thought that predators control the numbers of their prey. This is not true—the opposite usually applies, as is the case with the short-eared owl, whose own life is dominated by the field vole which forms most of its diet. Since vole populations

are far from stable, the fortunes of the owl and the strategies it adopts vary dramatically from month to month and from year to year.

Apart from hiding among long grass, the voles' only defence against short-eared owls is prolific breeding. During the summer they produce litters at the rate of five young every seven weeks. As the youngsters can themselves breed when about six weeks old, vole populations often reach plague proportions (on average about once every four or five years).

Evidently short-eared owls thrive during these vole plagues, especially since the voles become noisy and may eat much of the grass that would otherwise conceal them. This has two main effects: first, owls from many miles around flock, as if by magic, to the bountiful food supply, and secondly, the owls capitalise on the easy pickings by 'breeding like voles'—laying 10 or more eggs (14 is on record) and sometimes having two broods in a season. The glut is usually short-lived. In such crowded conditions voles stop breeding and this, combined with the heavy predation, results in a population crash. Consequently, in the year following a vole plague, any owls that have not moved on find the larder seriously diminished and may not breed.

The most dramatic demonstration of the nomadic nature of the short-eared owl comes from Vancouver airport in Canada. Here, the neatly mown grass bordering the runways

Above: This female is adopting an almost horizontal stance – a characteristic peculiar to short-eared owls. Breeding starts from April onwards when the female lays her rather conspicuous white eggs in a hollow among tall grass, heather, gorse or brambles, where there is some shelter. She is a good mother, incubating for hours at a time and leaving the nest only when absolutely essential. Throughout the 24 to 28 days of incubation, and while the chicks are young and still need brooding, her mate brings food for the whole family. Their diet consists mainly of field voles although other rodents, insects and even small birds may be brought to the nest by the male.

Short-eared owl (*Asio flammeus*); resident bird joined by migrants from Continent in winter. Found mainly in Scotland, Wales and north of England where it favours open country. Length 38cm (15in).

attracted flocks of roosting gulls and waders which became a serious bird-strike hazard to aircraft. In an effort to remedy the situation the authorities let the grass grow longer, hoping it would force the birds to roost elsewhere – it worked. However what the authorities didn't bargain for was the vast influx of owls which came to hunt the newly thriving vole population breeding in the long grass. Over 500 owls were trapped and taken elsewhere in only three years.

Family life In spring the male is seen displaying high over his territory, booming out his song at the same time. From a lofty position he twists his wings down and back to meet behind his tail and rapidly claps them together several times, meanwhile plummetting several feet towards the ground.

Following the courtship and mating procedure, the female lays her eggs in a sheltered hollow on the ground, at any time from April onwards. During incubation she rarely leaves the nest – her mate brings all the food needed for her and the young family.

While the owls can, to a certain extent, judge the amount of food available and vary the size of their clutch accordingly, they also have an additional safety mechanism which ensures that the maximum number of healthy young will fledge. The female lays eggs at two-day intervals and incubates right from the start, ensuring that the chicks also hatch at two-day intervals. Then, if the adults have

judged the food supply correctly there will be sufficient for all the family – from the oldest (and strongest) to the youngest – but if they overestimated the number of voles, only the youngest chick dies. The logic for this strategy is very simple: it is better to raise a few healthy nestlings than many weaklings.

Fledging takes 20 to 30 days depending both on the number of voles and the number of owlets – the more food there is to go round, the faster the owlets grow and the sooner they fledge. Initially the mother tears up food for the young, but before long one vole is just one mouthful. They cough up the indigestible bones, teeth and fur in a pellet about 5cm (2in) long and 2cm (¾in) in diameter. Analysis of these pellets shows that several small rodent species supplement the field vole diet, on the Isle of Man brown rats being particularly important. On the coast, particularly in winter, short-eared owls also catch birds such as finches and waders – even in flight – showing a surprising turn of speed and agility when necessary.

Today, when so many of our native birds are declining, it is good to report that short-eared owls are probably more common now than at any other time this century. One reason for this is that young forestry plantations, now a common sight in many upland areas, have proved to be an excellent habitat for them. While the trees are small and the grass is long, voles and owls thrive.

Birds of fresh water

Freshwater birds are, perhaps not unnaturally, as wide-ranging as their habitat, which embraces waterways and their immediate surrounds from their source in the hills down to the sea. Included are streams and rivers, as well as the ponds, pools and lakes into which they run: these are long-established components of the countryside, and many of them are natural features, like the moorland lochs that provide breeding sites for the diver family. But man has influenced the course of streams and created, usually many years ago, many of the lowland ponds and lakes that today have a natural, rather than an artificial, appearance. There are also more recent man-made additions to the landscape, and bird populations have been quick to adopt them as habitats. Some are now of considerable ecological importance, particularly to grebes and to the various species of diving ducks which congregate on them in winter. These 'newcomers' to the scenery include reservoirs and sewage works (the latter being particularly popular with snipe) and, most recent and most important, flooded mineral workings. These may be sand pits or clay and ballast workings, are usually to be found on the flood plains of river valleys, and are all valuable replacements for wetland lost to drainage schemes.

The wetland system begins with streams. Upland streams often flow over stony beds, and they are fast-running and clear, particularly so on higher ground. This is the typical habitat of the dipper. In contrast, on lower ground with deep soils streams are few and far between, and the rivers that they feed are often cloudy and meander sluggishly through a flat countryside. These slow-moving waters are the haunts of the kingfisher, heron and moorhen, and are often adjoined by extensive swamps, reedbeds, or marshland.

If one could design the ideal marshland habitat for birds it would be an extensive low-lying area, fringed with an almost impenetrable stunted woodland of alder and willow, intersected with ditches. At the heart would be an open expanse of water, deep in the centre but shallowing rapidly to give a band of exposed damp mud, out in the open, on which snipe would feed, before a thick belt of that most typical of marshland plants, the common reed (*Phragmites*), home of reed and sedge warblers during the summer.

Any birdwatcher who has visited freshwater wetlands during the warm days of summer will be able to testify to the potential richness of the food supply: some midges are content to perform their mating dances in smoke-like clouds, but other insects such as mosquitoes seek warm-blooded mammals for a meal! Thus, in summer, there is abundant food for the warblers, and for visiting swifts, swallows and martins. The larvae of these insect hordes are aquatic, and ensure that fish are in plentiful supply–hence the popularity of such sites with fish-catching birds ranging from kingfishers and grebes to herons and ospreys. But these are habitats for all seasons, except when all the water freezes over. Once the summer migrants have gone, it is the wintering ducks, grebes and coot that predominate. Never is this a dull habitat.

Opposite: Bewick swans flight into the Wildfowl Trust reserve at Slimbridge, Gloucestershire.

Great crested and red-necked grebes

The great crested grebe, the largest member of its family in Britain, is a resident but the species often mistaken for it–the red-necked grebe–is a winter visitor here.

Above: A family party of great crested grebes. The adult male and female are very much alike in plumage, although the male is larger, with a heavier bill and larger crest and tippets. In the 19th century these handsome birds were ruthlessly hunted and shot in Britain for their exceptionally soft, silky feathers.

The great crested grebe has a slender body that sits rather low on the water, and a long thin neck that is generally held upright. In the breeding season this handsome water bird is readily identified by its black crest and prominent chestnut and black frills, usually called 'tippets', on either side of its head. The bill is dagger-like and brown, strongly tinged with red, in colour. The upperparts are grey-brown, while the face, neck and underparts are gleaming white. The tippets are shed in the autumn and the great crested grebe in winter is then an altogether duller bird, with a white face, dark crown and a thin white stripe over the eye. In this winter plumage it can sometimes be mistaken for our other large grebe species, the winter-visiting red-necked grebe.

Sad story with a happy ending The great crested grebe is a common breeding bird throughout the lowland areas of Britain and much of Ireland, being found on shallow lakes, reservoirs and gravel pits. It also breeds on some stretches of river. At the time of the last countrywide census in 1975, there were some 6500 pairs nesting in Britain.

This is very different from the bird's breeding status about 100 years ago, when the species was brought to the brink of extinction in this country. Up until about the middle of the last century, great crested grebes bred freely, though in comparatively small numbers, in some 13 counties of southern and central England. At about that time, however, the skins of grebes, with their thick layers of down feathers, became highly fashionable as articles of decorative wear. It is thought that as a result of being hunted for their skins there may have been as few as 32 pairs of great crested grebes left in the whole country.

Many efforts were made to protect the species, and gradually matters improved, with laws passed in the 1870s and 1880s to stop the exploitation. The number of pairs slowly increased, probably helped by immigration from the Continent. In 1931 a census taken throughout Britain revealed a total of just over 1200 pairs, nearly all of them in England

Grebe distribution

☐ great crested (breeding)
▦ red-necked (winter)

extensive
black crown

yellow bill

grey face
and neck

Red-necked grebe
(*Podiceps griseigena*).
Winter visitor found in ones
and twos on estuaries and
sheltered waters of England/
Wales; larger numbers found
on Scottish firths. Length
43cm (17in).

predators. Once the attractive, striped young have hatched, the parents take them straight on to the water. The brood often rides on the back of one parent while the other dives for food to bring them.

The young are fed on small insects at first, graduating to smaller and then larger fishes as they grow. After about four weeks, the brood may be split between the two parents, each adult taking some of the chicks to different areas of the nesting lake. After about two and a half months, the young fledge and become independent of their parents.

Elaborate courtship The displays of the great crested grebe, as in other birds, are a form of communication between the male and female. They are used first to establish a strong bond between them, forming a pair that can breed successfully and then be maintained through to copulation and egg-laying. Most of the courtship takes place on the water.

There are four different displays in the great crested grebe's courtship ritual: the 'head-shaking' ceremony, the 'discovery' ceremony, the 'retreat' ceremony and the 'weed' ceremony.

The commonest of the four displays is the head-shaking one. It is performed by both male and female birds, one starting off and the other soon joining in. The crest is raised into two shaggy ear-tufts rising from the back of the head, while the tippets are fanned out to the sides. Each bird slowly swings its head

and Wales. In the next few decades the number increased, the grebes at the same time spreading north into Scotland and westwards into Ireland.

Nesting and breeding The nests made by great crested grebes are huge floating platforms of waterweed, anchored to stands of reeds or rushes, or even an overhanging willow branch trailing in the water. The nest often projects only a couple of inches above the surface, although there is usually a much more substantial pile of waterweed lying underneath.

Great crested grebes usually lay three or four whitish eggs. When the incubating bird leaves the nest it flicks a few pieces of weed over the eggs to conceal them from passing

Above: In winter plumage the red-necked grebe, a winter visitor to Britain, lacks the white eye stripe of the great crested grebe, and has grey areas (not white) on the face and neck, a more extensive black crown, and a yellow (not red) tinged bill. In summer plumage the red-necked grebe's rich chestnut colour on the neck contrasts strongly with a white face and black crown. Very small ear tufts also develop, but are not nearly as obvious as the great crested grebe's crest.

Left: A great crested grebe on its egg-filled nest. The grebe suffers somewhat in very severe winters—a factor which may slow down its rate of increase in this country. In the past it also suffered from organo-chlorine residues in its fish diet. However, it is probably man's leisure activities—such as wind-surfing and water-skiing—that are the main causes of a grebe's failure to breed today. Strong wave action from motor boats can swamp the grebe's nest, and noise and disturbance can drive the bird away altogether.

Great crested grebe
(*Podiceps cristatus*). A resident bird on shallow lakes, reservoirs and gravel pits throughout lowland Britain and much of Ireland. Lays 3-4 blotchy white eggs any time from April-July. Length 48cm (19in)—our largest member of the grebe family. Winters on estuaries and on the sea, like the red-necked grebe.

Ceremonies of courtship

head-shaking

discovery

one bird fluffs out its feathers and crest

one bird dashes away then turns to face its mate

retreat

weed

each bird shakes its head, slowly or rapidly, from side to side

the other bird dives, then re-emerges, rising on its tail but with bill pointing down

the birds dive, emerge with waterweed in their bills, then rise up in the water breast to breast, shaking their heads

The great crested grebe has one of the most elaborate and distinctive courtship displays of any British breeding bird. When displaying, the pair are extremely intent on each other. At first the displays may appear to have little pattern, but close watching reveals that they occur in four parts or phases: the 'head-shaking' ceremony (**1**); the 'discovery' ceremony (**2**); the 'retreat' ceremony (**3**); and the 'weed' ceremony (**4**). In the picture (right) a display has been interrupted by an aggressive intruding male.

from side to side, sometimes with the bill pointing down, sometimes up, or even vertically to the sky. The pace of these movements varies from slow to fast, giving great variation to the character of each performance. Every so often one or other bird suddenly stops and bends its head down to preen among its scapulars (long feathers at the base of the wings). One bout of head-shaking may last for up to three minutes at a time.

In the head-shaking ceremony, both birds perform the same movements, but in the discovery ceremony they perform different movements, although either male or female can do both. If, while you are watching a pair of grebes which are some distance apart, one

Below: A male great crested grebe feeding its striped chick with fish. The grebe catches prey under water, submerging gracefully with little more than a ripple. Having located the prey by sight, the grebe pursues and captures it, swimming entirely with its feet and keeping its wings tightly folded to its sides. All but the smallest items of food are brought to the surface and eaten there. Fishes are turned in the bill until they can be swallowed head first.

of them dives, then watch its mate closely. If the birds are indulging in the discovery ceremony, this bird will fluff out all its feathers and raise its wings, crest and tippets. The diving bird will be swimming straight for its mate, often leaving a tell-tale ripple on the surface. Then it abruptly emerges right beside its partner, rearing up on its tail but pointing its head and bill sharply downwards.

The head-shaking ceremony is often ended with the retreat ceremony. One of the pair suddenly ceases head-shaking, lowers itself in the water, and dashes away. At some distance away, it turns and faces its mate again, perhaps to come back and start the whole procedure once more.

The weed ceremony – the climax The climax to the displays is undoubtedly the weed ceremony, which has often been called the penguin-dance ceremony. The birds start by moving together with their necks held bolt upright, crests raised, then first one, followed by the other, dives. They emerge clutching large pieces of soft waterweed in their bills.

At this stage the birds come together to perform the spectacular culmination, the weed-dance. The birds rise up out of the water, breast to breast, paddling vigorously with their feet, at the same time swinging their heads, and loads of weed, from side to side. After as many as 40 such head swings, the water churning under their feet and tails, they subside, drop the weed, and finish quietly with a few shakes of the head. Either the male or the female can initiate any display, but you can tell which is which because in the weed dance his head swings higher than hers.

Red-throated, black-throated and great northern divers

A rare and thrilling sight on remote lochs and islands, divers–hardy, Arctic birds–are experts at diving and underwater swimming. At breeding time their wild, shrieking calls ring out by day and night.

Below: A black-throated diver walks ashore to its nest. Divers sometimes build a substantial heap of waterweed and grass, but the simple type shown here –a grass-lined hollow–is more usual for all species.

All four of the world's species of divers are to be seen in Britain and Ireland, although one, the white-billed diver (which breeds in Arctic North America), occurs very infrequently, usually only one or two individuals being seen during a year. The two smaller species, the red-throated and black-throated divers, breed in the north and west, but travel south to spend the winter at sea around all our coasts, so that they can be found somewhere in Britain and Ireland at any time of the year.

The great northern The huge and spectacular great northern diver was made famous for many in Arthur Ransome's book for children, *Great Northern*. In most years, some adults spend the summer on remote lochs in northern Scotland, and once every few years a pair attempts to breed. Only once in recent decades, in 1970, has breeding proved successful and resulted in a couple of youngsters.

Most great northern divers breed in northern North America, Greenland and Iceland. On the other side of the Atlantic they are called 'loons', a name which is often thought to derive from their song. Of all bird calls, that of the great northern diver must count as one of the most thrilling. Its weird cry, like a whooping, lunatic laugh, echoes wildly across the lochs between the mountains and forests of their breeding grounds.

Breeding areas of Britain's divers

The great northern and white-billed divers are too rare to be shown on our map. Black-throated divers are slightly more numerous, with 150 breeding pairs in Scotland; while only the red-throated divers are outside the class of rare birds, for there are about 1000 pairs of these in Scotland and Ireland. They are also the only ones that breed in Orkney and Shetland, for the lochans (small lochs) there are too small for the other divers, which need plenty of room for taking off and landing.

black-throated diver

red-throated diver

In full summer plumage, the bird is as spectacular as its song. Great northern divers are goose-sized, but with a short, thick neck and a powerful, dagger-like beak. The head is black with a greenish metallic sheen, and the back is black, but chequered with many brilliant white squares. On the side of the neck is a small black and white striped patch. In winter the plumage is much drabber: dark grey-brown above, shading to greyish white below.

Black-throated diver In summer, this bird could be mistaken for the great northern, as its plumage colours are an equally crisp combination of black and white. However, the black-throated diver is considerably smaller and slimmer, and has a less powerful looking neck and beak. The underparts are white and the back is black, with a chequer-board pattern of white blocks similar to that of its larger relative, but the head and nape of the neck are a plain dove-grey, while the throat, as the name suggests, carries a large, pure black 'bib'.

In winter, although the basic colours are

The calls of the black-throated (above) and red-throated diver (below) are similar—gruff, barking noises, and wailing calls interspersed with cackling or yodelling phrases—but less exciting to hear than the great northern diver.

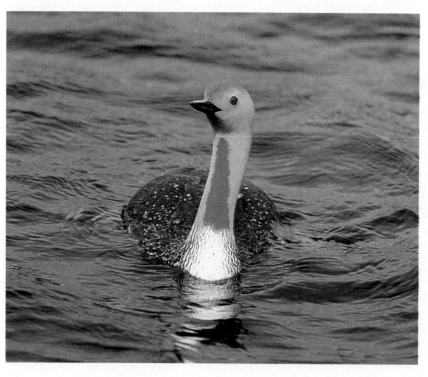

similar, the dividing lines between dark upper parts and pale underparts are far more precisely defined than the smudged margins of the great northern, and head and beak sizes remain a good identification feature.

Red-throated diver This is the smallest of the family, though only slightly smaller than the black-throated. In summer it is easily recognisable because the upperparts are clearly brown, not black, and quite uniform rather than spotted. The head and neck are a finely streaked grey, and the 'bib' is a rich deep chestnut red, though at long range this may look black. An excellent identification feature at all times is the beak, which is slender and always seems to be tilted upwards.

In winter, the beak remains the best distinguishing feature separating red-throated from black-throated divers, but in addition the red-throated diver's back is brownish-grey and densely speckled with small white spots—a useful guide at close range.

Divers in flight The divers have a very characteristic flight silhouette, which helps (particularly in winter) to separate them from cormorants, shags, ducks, geese and grebes. The body is pencil slim, the wings slender and set well back, and the flight is straight and fast with powerful wingbeats. In the case of the black-throated, the wingbeats are conspicuously (and surprisingly) shallow. There are no interruptions for spells of gliding, as in the gannet or cormorant, for example. The tail and feet often seem to be held slightly depressed, and in the two smaller species the head and neck also droop a little, giving a hump-backed appearance.

The quiet of the loch All divers choose remote lochs for their British breeding grounds, the great northern and black-throated divers needing relatively large areas of water. The red-throated seems happy on the smallest of moorland pools, which explains why it is so widespread in the Orkney and Shetland Islands, where the lochans (small lochs) are tiny, and why the black-throated diver is absent there. Also, red-throated divers often fish far from their home pool, flying off to a larger loch or out to a sea-

Divers in summer plumage

Great northern diver

chequered back
and forewing

thick powerful
neck

**Black-throated
diver**

head and
nape grey

striped neck with
black throat

striped neck patches

Great northern diver
(*Gavia immer*); mainly
winter visitor, rarely
breeding. Length 69-90cm
(27-36in).

White-billed diver (*Gavia
adamsii*); largest diver;
vagrant. 76-90cm (30-36in).

Red-throated diver (*Gavia
stellata*); smallest diver;
resident (breeds April-Sept).
Length 53-69cm (21-27in).

Black-throated diver
(*Gavia arctica*); resident
(breeds April-Sept). Length
58-73cm (23-29in).

bill frequently
held upright

red throat

Red-throated diver

bill yellow
in summer

White-billed diver

loch perhaps some miles away, and so can be content with a small pool for nesting.

Winter on sea or reservoir Divers can be seen in coastal waters during their spring and autumn migrations. Many, probably including Scandinavian birds, spend all winter around our coasts, often well out at sea but coming closer inshore in bad weather. Many large reservoirs, often well inland, have also become regular places for seeing divers in winter.

These reservoir birds offer by far the best chance to watch the fishing technique (and time the diving durations) of the various species. The hunting diver patrols the surface, often putting its head underwater to scan for fish or other prey, including molluscs and crustaceans, and even large insect larvae and worms. If a likely food item is sighted, the diver slips beneath the water surface, sinking easily from view and hardly causing even a ripple.

Once under the water, they are mobile and speedy. The great northern and red-throated divers regularly reach a depth of 10m (30ft), and there are records of divers caught in fishing nets 70m (230ft) under water – surely a world record for diving birds.

Ancient species The earliest diver-like fossils date from 100 million years ago, placing the divers among the first recognisable fossil bird groups. The continued presence of such a seemingly 'primitive' line must surely testify

to the success of divers as underwater fishers. The body is well streamlined for underwater movement, being torpedo-shaped, and the wings are relatively small in proportion to the body, offering little resistance in the water. The feet, set back near the tail, are highly efficient in propelling the bird under water, though rather ungainly on land.

Above: A great northern diver incubating eggs on its nest, a task that takes about 33-35 days. Fledging is slow in this large species, taking 10-11 weeks. Both processes are quicker in the smaller species.

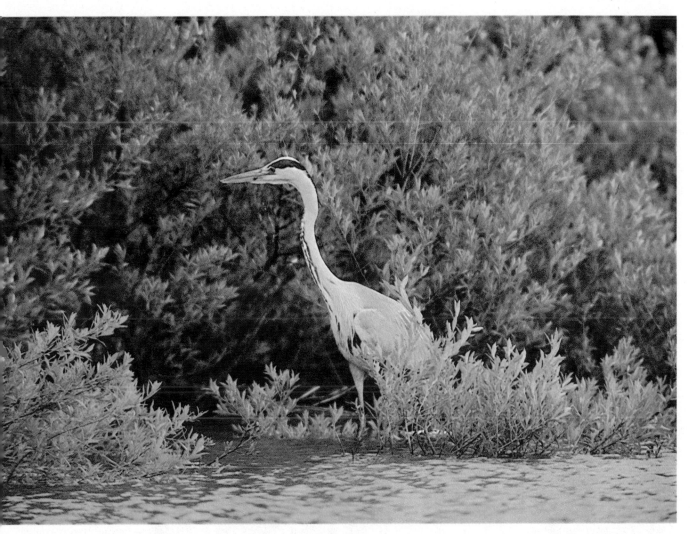

Grey heron

The grey heron is the top bird predator of the freshwater food pyramid – a status which affords it a wide range of diet, but also makes it most vulnerable to the build-up of toxic chemicals in the water. Despite this and other threats, the number of British heron pairs remains at a stable 4000–5000.

Above: A magnificent bird with a wide wingspan of 175-195cm (68-76in), the grey heron has a white head with a dagger-like beak, and a broad black streak running from the eye to the tip of the crest.

Opposite: A grey heron catches a fish on the shoreline. Although mainly seen near fresh water, herons sometimes venture on to estuaries in search of food.

The large, stately and distinctive-looking grey heron is generally found beside or in fresh water. You may also spot it flying with its long neck tucked in against its body and its legs stretching far beyond the tip of its tail. The harsh, honking 'fraank' call of the heron is a familiar sound on the marshes, instantly recognisable to birdwatchers and the many anglers who come across herons while they themselves are fishing.

Colonies Herons breed in colonies, preferring huge nests in trees; but sometimes they nest on cliffs, or at ground level on islands in lakes and lochs, especially in Scotland. A very few colonies, including the one at Tring in Hertfordshire, have nests in reed-beds –

sites more commonly favoured by the purple heron on the continent. Most colonies contain 10-30 nests, but a few colonies in England exceed 100 pairs.

Herons at a colony refurbish their old nests in January, or even December, ready for the early breeding season. Most colonies have traditional 'club' areas close by, where the 'off-duty' herons stand around. These gatherings are called 'sieges' and provide the sites where the birds begin their courtship display.

The male choses a site and then advertises himself and his site to the females. When one of the latter shows interest, both sexes display together; this leads to mutual preening and the start of nest-building. The male generally

Grey heron (*Ardea cinerea*), total length about 95cm (36in), body length about 43cm (16in). Distribution beside almost any freshwater margin, especially marshes. Resident.

collects sticks, twigs, leaves, grass and other nest material and the female arranges them—in most cases using the base of the original nest. The birds mate on the nest or in the immediate vicinity.

From February right through to May, and even June, the female lays her eggs, which both parents incubate; two broods are rare.

Migration Herons often fly long distances to find new sources of food during cold spells, and are good at locating springs, sewage farms and other open water. In severe weather they also forage on the shore, as the salt in the sea prevents the water from freezing.

Herons from Scandinavia arrive in Britain for the winter as they are not able to survive this season in the colder parts of Europe. A few British herons leave for France, Spain or Portugal, but the majority remain within 100 miles of their native heronry.

Predator and pest Herons forage for a mixed diet of fish, eels, frogs, small mammals (quite often voles) and sometimes large

drin, accumulate in animals from the bottom of the heron's food pyramid upwards, and concentrations of these poisons increase until they reach the heron, which is the top bird predator of this pyramid. Analysis shows that the build-up of chemicals in the heron's body causes its egg shells to thin—to the point where in some cases they collapse or are broken by the weight of the brooding parents.

Population The effects of toxic chemicals and the gun put severe pressure on the heron population. In 1954 protection was granted against shooting, though it was sometimes difficult to enforce, and numbers returned to previous levels (as they also do after a fall in heron numbers caused by a hard winter). The most recent census figure for Britain stands at just over 4000 pairs—rising to 5400 in a really good year. This makes a maximum population at the start of the breeding season of 12,000 birds. These census figures, which have been kept for over 50 years, are only possible because herons breed in colonies.

Right: A heron lays 3-5 chalky, blue-green eggs (surprisingly no bigger than hen's eggs), which hatch 3½-4 weeks later. The nestlings fledge after a further 7-8 weeks.

Below: The heron flies to a nearby field to beat its prey to death or swallow it.

Below: The heron spots its prey and stands motionless, with neck outstretched and head near the water ready to strike.

Left: The heron stabs its victim (in this case an eel) with a very fast, accurate blow. Just before the strike the heron often re-adjusts the position of its head, to make sure the final stab tells.

Below: All herons, including the purple heron (*Ardea purpurea*), can keep the head still, while swivelling the eyes downwards.

insects such as grasshoppers and emerging dragonflies. In the past, water bailiffs persecuted herons for their fish-eating habits, and trout farm owners today find individual herons persistent and expensive pests. Herons also welcome the source of food provided by suburban fish-ponds—goldfish are particularly easy to see.

With such a varied and abundant source of food, it is perhaps not surprising that herons have long lifespans. The record is held by a German bird that survived for 24 years; the two oldest British herons lived for 18 years.

Mortality Life can be hard for herons. All sorts of hazards may cause death—choking on large fish, being shot, becoming entangled in barbed wire, being killed by foxes, and (8% of all ringed recoveries) flying into overhead wires. The British Trust for Ornithology's sample census of heronries, which is the longest running survey of bird numbers in Britain, also shows how devastating the effects of severe winters can be.

Toxic chemicals, such as DDT and diel-

Relatives The grey heron is the only one of its group that occurs regularly in Britain, although its close relative, the purple heron, visits occasionally during the summer. Our native heron has a soft grey plumage, while the purple heron has darker, richer colours which are easy to distinguish. At a distance the young grey heron with its darker plumage is sometimes confused with the purple. The latter, however, is still very rare in Britain.

Apart from the bittern, which is a distant relative, the only other regular herons in Britain are the dazzling-white little egret and cattle egret – and both are even rarer than the purple heron.

Historical birds Heron colonies are generally in traditional sites – the oldest one, recorded in 1293, is at Chilham in Kent. The long history of this heronry is no accident. In the Middle Ages, falconry was an aristocratic sport, and herons were the most prestigious quarry. Herons also featured regularly as a *piece de resistance* at medieval banquets where they were often called cranes. It was therefore well worth noting the presence of a heronry in the land deeds. Heronries are commemorated in the names of houses, farms and villages – Herne Hill in London implies the hill with a heronry on it, and there are records to confirm this.

The bird's name has only recently been established as 'grey heron' and it is still known by local names such as herne and heronsew.

Preening

Preening is feather maintenance; as birds rely on their feathers for flying, for keeping dry and for insulation, they must keep their plumage in top condition. Close examination of a bird preening, scratching and shuffling, shows that these are very exacting activities. Individual feathers are teased through the bird's bill to ensure the barbs are aligned properly. The uropygial gland, situated above the base of the tail, provides natural oils for grooming, but not for waterproofing as one might expect. Herons (and bitterns) are particularly likely to get slime on their feathers from the food they catch. So they have a special tract on the breast (right), and two more on their flanks, providing a crumbly, powdery material ('powder down') which they use in preening. It is as if they are able to carry a natural, constantly renewed powder puff around with them.

Some birds, including nightjars that prey at dusk on moths whose wing scales then soil the birds, use their central claws to preen such scale material from their feathers. During the breeding season especially, you may see two birds preening each other. This could be helpful for feather maintenance, but it has a much deeper significance. It reinforces the pair bond between male and female (very like petting in humans) and is an important part of heron courtship.

claw comb

Above: The heron uses its comb-like claws and the powder down located in its breast (below) to preen.

Mute swan

The mute swan that once graced the tables of medieval banquets is now protected from this fate. It is, however, vulnerable to the modern hazards of overhead power cables and lead weights in fishing tackle. Despite its name, the mute swan will snort and hiss noisily if it feels threatened.

Mute swan (*Cygnus olor*) length (bill-tip to tail-tip) 152cm (5ft); weight—cob (male) 12-20kg (26-44lb), pen (female) slightly less; distribution: on most slow-flowing waters.

Opposite: A stately cob mute swan swims across the water of his riverside home.

Below: Downy cygnets take to the water early and are guarded carefully by their parents, who pull up underwater vegetation for them. It has been suggested that the adults also paddle vigorously to bring food to the surface for the young.

You will find mute swans wherever there are sizeable expanses of relatively still water. These majestic birds are at home on slow-flowing rivers, lakes, gravel pits, large ponds —even in heavily built up areas such as London, where they add a touch of serenity to stretches of the Thames. Their haunts are not, however, restricted to freshwater, since they also frequent harbours and estuaries and have been sighted as far offshore as the Solent on the south coast of England.

Striking appearance The mute swan is one of the most easily identifiable of British birds. The adult's plumage is pure white and the thickly feathered neck is long and curves in a graceful 'S' shape. The head is small with a down-pointed, orange-red beak tipped with a black nail, and there is a black knob over the nostrils at the base of the bill; this knob is more pronounced on the male than the female —and most obvious in spring. The webbed feet are black. The young swan has a greyish plumage which begins to turn white during the first winter and becomes pure white by the third spring, while the beak takes two years to assume its bright orange-red colour.

The swan uses its long neck to feed on underwater plants; pondweed and semi-aquatic plants make up the bulk of its diet. It also eats algae and shore plants and occasionally will take worms, insects and fish; it swallows grit and fine gravel for

Taking to the air

An adult swan is too heavy to take off from a standing position. To gain momentum it runs along (on land or on the surface of the water) with its neck outstretched and its wings thrashing violently. In a strong wind, may have to run as far as 100m (300ft) before taking off. In flight the wing beats make a loud rhythmic noise. In order to land, the swan slows itself down by spreading out its wings and using its feet as brakes.

roughage. In deep water, where its neck is not long enough to reach certain food, it upends like a duck.

Its calls are quite out of character with its name and appearance, since it will snort, grunt and hiss threateningly when provoked; it also gives a shrill, trumpet-like call—particularly to the young who reply to the adult in a high-pitched tone.

Mating breeding and nesting Mute swans pair up, often in the autumn, when they are between two and four years old. Paired swans are not gregarious, preferring to nest isolated in their own aggressively defended territory. Non-breeding individuals and those of pre-breeding age may congregate together in areas where there is plenty of food and space. In spring, when their courtship and mating rituals reach a peak, you can see a pair of swans facing each other, swaying their heads sideways or dipping their heads in the water, extending their necks and bills vertically and even upending. Once the pair has been established, the cob (male) and pen (female) return annually to the same territory to breed again. Swans seldom change their mate, unless they fail to breed.

The cob selects a nest site close to the water's edge and well away from other nests. Building the nest is mainly the pen's task, although the cob helps by gathering vegetation, often from previous nests, and passing it to her. The pair makes little attempt to camouflage the nest, which is a huge pile of reeds and sticks lined with a thin layer of down.

The pen lays her chalky, round-ended eggs every other day for up to 12 days; this occurs any time from April to July. The pen does most of the incubating, although the cob will take his turn and keep guard over the nest.

The eggs hatch after 36 days and the pen carries the broken shells to the water's edge. The young, which are born with their eyes open, are covered with soft, fur-like grey down; this is replaced by woolly feathers which change slowly to a drab brown colour. At five days they are independent enough to leave the nest during the daytime, although for up to a month they may continue to gather

in the nest at night. Cygnets will walk long distances to water, marching along in single file behind their parents. If you are lucky, you may see one riding on its parent's back between the arched wings. They fly at four months and are usually driven away from the nest area in the following spring, when their plumage has changed from grey and when territories are redefined and their parents begin to prepare for the next brood. After leaving the nest the young join the summer flocks of non-breeders until they are ready to mate.

Less than half the swans in the British Isles are breeding stock. You can easily identify the non-breeders, which are immature birds or those which have yet to form a nesting pairs, since they have pale pink bills and small nostril-lobes.

Moulting and migration If you come across a scattering of white feathers in July or

This mute swan is in aggressive mood as it protects its eggs (which lie in the large platform nest of reeds and sticks) from intruders. The wingspan can reach 2m (7ft).

August, do not assume this is the result of a fight; swans moult their flight feathers in the summer after nesting. When moulting they are vulnerable because they cannot fly.

Some breeding adults, whose young cannot yet take to the air, moult at the nest site, but most make long journeys to find a safe place where they will not be threatened during the flightless period. Up to 1000 swans arrive annually on the River Stour in Essex to moult while others use Fairburn Ings in Yorkshire, the Tweed estuary and Loch Leven in Kinross. They moult 15 to 30 days after arrival, losing first their primary feathers and then the secondaries. They are able to fly again after a month, four weeks before the feathers have reached full length again. The return journey is made in September or October.

Swan ownership The mute swan is frequently described as a royal bird, and in fact all swans were once proclaimed to belong to the Crown, just as forests were reserved for royal deer hunting. Noblemen and city guilds were also given a right to own swans; a marking system of cuts and nicks on the swans bill was used to identify the ownership of each bird.

Today the Dyers and the Vintners City of London livery companies are the last lawful owners (apart from the Queen). The Dyers use a single nick on the side of the bill, while the Vintners use two. The Queen's birds are not marked at all. This ownership of swans is taken as applying only to the Thames; elsewhere swan populations are unmarked and are treated as wild birds.

Swan upping Each July the colourful ceremony of swan upping—when the cygnets are rounded up and marked—takes place on the Thames. Three groups of swan uppers— one from each livery company and one led by the Queen's swanherd—row for four or five days up the Thames, from Maidenhead to Pangbourne, herding each brood of cygnets and marking them according to the marks found on their parents.

Threats to the swan The swan has no serious natural predators, although foxes and pike will sometimes take unguarded cygnets; and pike have been known to drown adult swans by holding their heads under water. The only real threat to the swan comes from man's increasing encroachment on its natural habitats. Overhead power cables are a major hazard to swans in flight and a number also die every year from oil pollution and mercury poisoning.

An increasingly common cause of death, which is currently under investigation, appears to be lead poisoning. Swans often become entangled with fishing tackle and swallow the angler's lead weights. They also swallow lead shot and fishing hooks which have been discarded in the water at the end of the fishing season—a worrying result of modern disposable fishing hooks, lines and weights.

An adult swan that is fortunate enough to escape all those threats to its life, however, can live up to 15 years and sometimes even longer; but on average a swan that succeeds in fledging will only survive for two to three years.

The mute swan establishes a territory at the start of the breeding season and defends it aggressively, driving away intruders with a threatening display or, as here, by chasing the other bird off its patch.

mature

immature

The mute swan's head is small compared to the rest of its body. The down-pointed, orange-red beak is tipped with a black nail. The characteristic black knob over the nostrils does not develop until the bird becomes fully mature.

Brent, barnacle and Canada geese

Brent and barnacle geese visit various coastal sites of the British Isles in winter, after breeding in separate areas in the Arctic Circle. Canada geese (below) are mainly resident here, though they were originally introduced from America 200 years ago.

The Brent Goose, the smallest goose species, is not much bigger than a large duck. It has a circumpolar distribution and breeds on coastal tundra and small islands in the high Arctic. Over thousands of years, separate populations have evolved plumage differences – with underparts ranging from dark grey to silvery white – sufficient for them to be described as sub-species.

Breeding and migration The dark-bellied Brent Geese have dark grey underparts and breed in northern Siberia. These birds migrate to north-west Europe for the winter, living in estuaries in eastern and southern England, the Netherlands and France.

There are also three separate populations

of light-bellied Brent Geese, which have silvery-grey underparts. The largest, numbering about 100,000, breeds in eastern Arctic Canada and winters on the east coast of the United States. A second population of about 9000 birds, breeds in the very north-east of Arctic Canada and northern Greenland, and winters in Ireland. The smallest population, of under 3000 birds, breeds in Spitsbergen and winters in Denmark.

Arctic breeders Brent Geese breed in the far north, almost all of them well north of the Arctic Circle. Here the brief summer is only just long enough for them to complete the breeding cycle. Indeed, in order that the young are on the wing before the cold of winter returns in September, the eggs are often laid while the snow still lies on the ground, in late May. The nest sites, on low ridges and hummocks, are free of snow, but the flat, marshy tundra around them is still covered. Until the snow melts there is no food for the geese, which graze on marsh plants in the summer, and they have to live on their fat reserves built up before the spring migration.

With timing so critical, any delay in the start of the breeding can be disastrous. If the spring is late and the snow is deeper than usual, or takes longer to thaw from the marshy ground, then either the birds are unable to lay their eggs at all, or if they do, then continued bad weather may force them to abandon their nests. Heavy rain or snow in the period when the eggs are hatching, or the young are still very small, can cause severe mortality.

The effects of weather Bad summers occur quite regularly, but clearly, since the birds do breed in the far north, there are also sufficient good summers. When the geese arrive in the autumn on their wintering

Geese migration routes

☐ Brent

☐ Barnacle

☐ Canada

Below: The male and female Brent goose are similar: the upperparts, head, neck and chest are completely black, the only relief being a small white patch on either side of the neck. Underparts vary from dark grey to silvery white.

grounds in north-west Europe, it is possible to ascertain how well they have bred that summer. The young birds show pale barring on the wings, but lack the white neck marks, and by scanning through the flocks with a telescope the number of young can be assessed. A flock can consist of as many as 50% young birds in a very good breeding year, to none at all in a bad one.

These enormous variations in breeding success naturally have a considerable effect on the overall size of the population and the way it changes. For example the dark-bellied Brent goose experienced rather more good years than bad through the late 1960s and early 1970s, and this coincided with increased protection as first France, and then Denmark, banned the shooting of them. Britain and the Netherlands, the other two main wintering countries, had protected the Brent in the 1950s. The population rose sharply from about 25,000 in 1964 to 120,000 in 1975, and has gone on rising, though more slowly, to its present level of 150,000.

Finding food While such a massive increase in numbers might seem an excellent thing, causing the bird to be quite common instead of rather scarce and vulnerable, the whole process could be reversed by a sequence of bad years at any time. There has also been an unexpected problem as a result of the increased numbers. Brent geese normally feed on tidal mudflats, grazing on eel grass

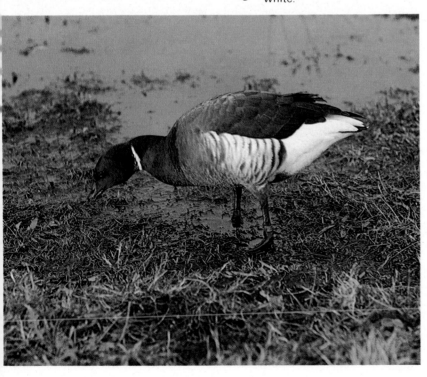

(*Zostera*), and on various green algae. The population explosion meant that this food was no longer sufficient for them in some areas so the geese have taken to flying inland to graze on winter wheat fields and on pastures. This has brought them into conflict with farmers who claim that the geese are damaging their crops. Various scaring techniques have been tried, with mixed success, and currently conservation groups are trying to have some feeding reserves set aside for the geese, which will relieve the pressure on the farmers.

Barnacle geese If some of the Brent goose populations have been separated from each other sufficiently long for plumage differences to evolve, the same has yet to happen with the barnacle goose. There are three distinct populations of this species, but the birds in them cannot be told apart.

The three populations breed in East Greenland, in Spitsbergen, and in north-west Arctic Russia. They winter respectively on islands off the west coasts of Scotland and Ireland, on the Solway Firth between England and Scotland, and in the Netherlands. The Russian breeding population is the largest, numbering about 50,000 birds, while the east Greenland stock is rather smaller at about 30,000. Easily the smallest is the Spitsbergen-Solway population, which now numbers about 9000, though it has been much less than this.

Before the war there were a few thousand barnacle geese in the Solway, but disturbance during the war from the several airfields set up in the area to guard the Western Approaches, coupled with shooting for food, was so great that by 1946 only some 500 birds could be found wintering there. There was a very slow increase for the next few years, until in 1954 shooting of barnacle geese was prohibited, and two years later a National Nature Reserve was set up covering the main wintering site at Caerlaverock near Dumfries. There followed a steady increase to 4000 by 1969. Further areas of feeding ground were protected, by the Wildfowl Trust, in 1970, and two years later several of the breeding islands in Spitsbergen were declared sanctuaries. The population responded immediately to this extra protection and rose to 6000 in 1975 and 9000 in 1980.

The barnacle geese arrive on the Solway in late September, and spend the next four months mainly on and around the reserve area. Here they feed on grasses on the salt-marsh and pastures, and glean the barley stubbles. Their distribution is governed to a considerable extent by the amount of wild-fowling which goes on around the Solway. There are other areas of good feeding for them away from the reserve, but they can make little use of them until after the end of the shooting season in February. The barnacles themselves are protected but shooting of other geese, pinkfeet and greylags, and of the wide variety of ducks on the Solway, is very heavy and the geese prefer to remain where there is no shooting, on the reserve.

Canada geese In contrast to the highly migratory Brent and barnacle geese, the Canada goose is largely resident in Britain. It is a large bird, with a black head and neck, a white face patch, dark brown upperparts and whitish underparts. This species was originally introduced into Britain from North America in the 17th century. Charles II kept Canada geese with other ornamental water-fowl on his lake in St James' Park in London, and large landowners with lakes in their beautifully landscaped parks followed suit. It was not until the 1950s that birdwatchers or biologists began to take an interest in the Canada goose, by which time the birds were beginning to colonize the many gravel pits being dug along the lowland river valleys of Britain. They also started to move on to reservoirs. A first census of Canada geese in Britain, in 1953, found about 3500 birds. By the time of the next census, in 1968, there were 10,500 and this had risen to 19,500 by 1976.

The great majority of Canada geese in Britain are sedentary, rarely moving more than 20 or 30 miles. However, there is one notable exception to this. Canada geese from North Yorkshire make a summer migration to the Beauly Firth near Inverness, 300 miles away. This is not for breeding, which takes

Brent goose (*Branta bernicla*), about 60cm (23in) from beak to tail. Winter visitor.

Barnacle goose (*Branta leucopsis*), about 65cm (25in) from beak to tail. Winter visitor.

Canada goose (*Branta canadensis*), about 100cm (40in) from beak to tail. Mainly resident.

Below: Barnacle geese are medium-sized, black, grey and white. They have a black head and chest, rather like the Brent goose, but with a creamy white face. The back is black, lightly barred with white, while the underparts are white with pale grey flanks.

place on the many lakes and reservoirs in North Yorkshire, and on some of the high moors. Instead the migration is made by one and two-year-old birds, not yet old enough to breed. They leave Yorkshire in early June and move to the Beauly Firth. Here they spend the period of the annual moult, when like all wildfowl they shed their wing feathers simultaneously and become flightless for a period of about four weeks while their new feathers grow. The Beauly Firth provides them with ample food on the high saltings around its shores, and safety out on the wide expanses of mudflats and water.

Such moult migrations, as these movements by immatures are called, are undertaken by many wild populations of geese, including Canada geese in North America. The main purpose behind them seems to be to take the non-breeders of the population away from the breeding grounds at a time when all the resources of the area are needed by the breeding pairs and their young. They need as much food as possible in order to grow rapidly, before it is their turn to migrate. Most of these movements are to the north, often to areas that are not fully suitable for breeding by geese, but which nevertheless can provide the food and sanctuary required by moulting birds, though for a shorter period than needed for a full breeding cycle. The extraordinary thing about the moult migration of the

Canada geese from Yorkshire is that neither of these reasons is applicable. There seems to be plenty of room in North Yorkshire for all the Canada Geese to spend the summer, and there is no reason to think that they could not live all the year round on the Beauly Firth if necessary. The moult migration is thought to have started in the early 1950s, or nearly 300 years after the original Canada geese had been brought over from North America. We shall probably never know what started the migration–initially by 40 or 50 birds and now undertaken by up to 800–but it appears to be some remarkable throwback to the behaviour of their wild forbears in North America.

Above: In spring, barnacle geese feed intensively, putting on weight to last them through the migration and also, in the case of the females, to provide the energy necessary for the formation of eggs. The birds generally leave the Solway Firth in late April and fly direct to north Norway where they pause for two or three weeks, feeding on some of the myriad small islands lying off the coast.

The pecking order – social status in birds

In communities of birds of the same species, such as geese, living together, it is quite common for an order of dominance, a 'pecking order', to become established. You can see this phenomenon frequently in farm yards, where the principal cockerel lords it over the other cocks and hens. Under him there will be a second, subordinate, bird able to defeat all the others (in a dispute over food for instance), and so on all down the line. If a particular hen becomes the favourite mate of the cockerel, she will adopt his dominant status, however lowly her previous position.

Pecking orders also occur in the wild. The Bewick's swan, for instance, wintering at Slimbridge in Gloucestershire, has such an order. Larger families with four or five young are dominant over smaller families with only one or two young. These in turn can successfully drive off a pair without any young, or unpaired birds, from a favourite part of the lake.

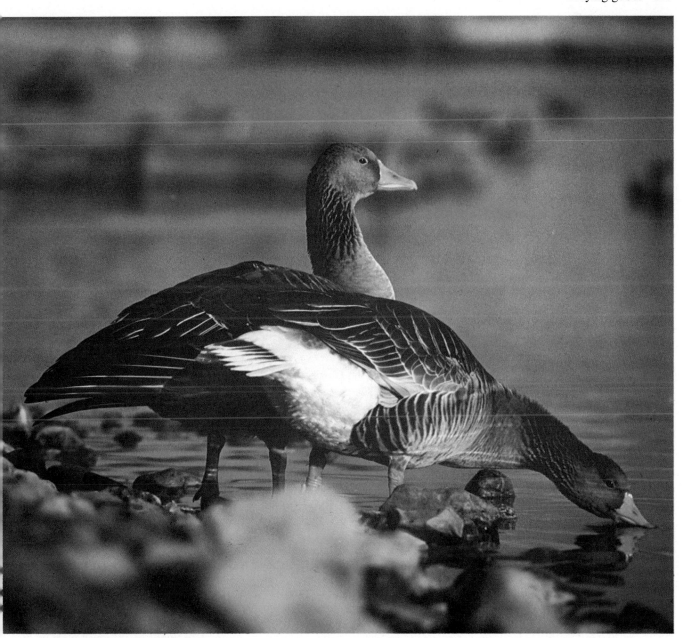

Greylag goose

The greylag goose is the ancestor of the familiar white goose of farmyards and fairy tales. Semi-domestic greylags are widespread, but wild birds are confined to the north.

The greylag goose is one of several species of so-called 'grey' geese found in Britain. The others are the pink-footed, bean and white-fronted geese; all have predominantly grey plumage which distinguishes them from the Canada, Brent and barnacle geese, which are brown or black.

The greylag goose is the heaviest of the grey geese–an adult weighs about 2-3kg ($4\frac{1}{2}$-$6\frac{1}{2}$lb)–and differs from the others in its combination of large round head, stout orange-pink bill and pink legs. No other grey goose has all these features. In flight the bold pale grey forewings of the greylag show up clearly and also help to distinguish it from other geese.

Visitors from Iceland Although Britain supports a small but growing population of breeding greylags, the great majority found in this country are winter visitors from their breeding grounds in Iceland. Most of these birds can be seen in lowland areas of Scotland, particularly Aberdeen, Perth, Kinross, the Lothians and the Solway Firth.

These winter visitors arrive during the second half of October and head immediately for the stubbled fields of harvested barley and wheat, where they feed off spilt grain. Soon afterwards, the potato harvest is gathered and the greylags perform a useful service to the farmers by eating all the broken and small

Above: Many greylags are semi-domestic.

Opposite: Greylags and other wildfowl at Slimbridge, Gloucestershire.

Below: Greylag distribution.

flocks fly
in V-formation

orange bill

pink legs

pale grey
forewings

white rump

Greylag goose (*Anser anser*). At 75-90cm (30-35in) long, the largest of the grey geese found in Britain. Apart from size, it is distinguished from other species of grey goose by its paler plumage, pink legs and orange bill – though some birds in eastern Britain have pink bills.

eastern race
has pink bill

Below: A typical brood consists of between four and six chicks. Both parents help to look after the chicks, and the family stays together into the winter.

tubers left behind. Without this 'mopping up', these tubers would sprout again the following year as 'rogue' potatoes.

These food sources are soon exhausted, however, and from late November through to the spring the geese turn to feeding on grass, so becoming the farmer's enemy rather than his friend. At first the problem is not serious since, in winter, sheep and cattle are usually brought in and fed with hay and other foodstuffs. But as soon as the animals are turned out to graze on the spring grass they and the geese come into direct competition.

Numbers increasing The conflict between the migrant greylag geese and Scottish farmers has intensified in recent years because of the steadily increasing population of winter visiting greylags. Since 1960 their numbers have more than doubled to their present total of about 90,000.

This increase is due partly to better protection, with reserves being set up to prevent the birds being shot. The other major factor is the change in Scottish agriculture in recent years. Much more barley and potatoes are being planted now, and more pastures are being improved and fertilised. So, as the farmers grow more and improved crops, they provide better feeding for greylag geese. Farmers now use scaring devices to keep the geese away from certain fields, but only with partial success.

Return to Iceland In late April the winter migrant greylags return to their breeding grounds in Iceland. Their favourite sites for breeding are lowland river valleys, and marshy areas beside rivers and shallow lakes. The nest is usually a simple scrape, hidden among thick vegetation. The eggs, usually between four and six, are incubated by the female alone while the male stands guard: the process takes 28 days.

The family stays together throughout the autumn migration and following winter, so that the young learn directly from their parents the best migration routes and where to feed and roost over winter.

Resident greylags Not all our winter population of greylags depart for Iceland in the spring. A few wild greylags are resident in Britain, mainly in the north-west of Scotland and the Outer Hebrides. These are the remnants, no more than 2000-3000 individuals, of a population that once bred widely in England and Scotland. As recently as the 17th century greylag geese bred commonly in the fenlands of East Anglia. But gradually man's activities have reduced their numbers to their present level, both by direct persecution and by draining the bird's marshland habitat.

Fortunately, the tiny Scottish population is now increasing. Greylag geese have begun breeding on uninhabited offshore islands and on islands in large lochs. One of our largest breeding colonies is on Loch Druidibeg in South Uist, where there are many small islands covered with bracken and scrub – ideal habitat for greylags. The Loch is now a part of the National Nature Reserve.

Semi-domestic greylags All the greylags described so far can be seen only in Scotland and the far north of England. Yet greylags appear in many different parts of the British Isles. These birds are neither the winter migrants from Iceland nor the indigenous wild greylags of Scotland. They are semi-domestic and have been introduced to their present breeding grounds. Over the years, landowners, people with private collections of wildfowl and wildfowlers themselves have all established free-flying flocks of greylags. Some people have done this to produce birds or shooting, others simply for the pleasure of seeing a flock of geese.

There are now at least 3000 semi-domestic greylags scattered around the country, mostly in small flocks, though in south-west Scotland round Stranraer there is a resident population of about 1000 birds. These are all descended from eggs and young brought down from the Outer Hebrides in the 1930s, and most of the semi-domestic flocks in the rest of the country are, in turn, descended from the Stranraer birds.

A few greylags found in eastern England have pink bills but otherwise resemble ones with more orange bills. These greylags are the descendants of birds found in eastern and north-east Europe; they were introduced to Kent in 1973.

Domestic geese Almost all the domestic farmyard geese we see today are descended from the greylag goose. Greylags have been domesticated for a very long time. Egyptian frescoes dating back to 2000BC contain recognisable drawings of domestic geese. The birds represented are patterned like greylags but the drawings are clear enough to show details of shape that are typical of domestic birds. For example, the birds depicted are bulkier, with longer necks and a more erect stance than wild greylags; all these are typical features of domesticated rather than wild geese.

The ancient Greeks and Romans also kept

Above: When an intruder comes too close, a greylag goose adopts a threat posture in which it juts its neck out.

Right: The large round head, stout orange-pink bill and pink legs make the greylag unmistakable.

Below: A winter flock of greylags with some domestic geese in the background. At night greylags fly off in their familiar V-formation to their roosting places on lakes and reservoirs. Come the morning they return to the fields.

geese descended from greylags. The Romans kept geese as guards, relying on their vociferous calls to alert them to the presence of intruders. On one famous occasion, the calling of geese is supposed to have saved Rome from a surprise attack.

Of all the species of geese in the world, the greylag was the obvious one for man to domesticate. The reason is that greylags breed freely in temperate and sub-tropical regions, whereas nearly all other species migrate to the uninhabited Arctic to breed. So the eggs and young were readily available for stealing. Gradually the birds began to be bred selectively for size – to increase the yields of meat and eggs – and over thousands of years this process of continual inbreeding led to all-white geese being born. Today all-white domestic geese are a familiar sight around our farmyards.

Triumph ceremony

Greylag geese have a highly ritualised form of courtship display known as the triumph ceremony. In this, both birds extend their necks forward with their heads held low and close together – but side by side so that neither bird is face-on to the other. Established pairs also perform this ceremony when they meet.

Mallard

The mallard is a popular bird because it takes to many man-made surroundings, and tamely accepts food from the hand. In summer it moults its feathers and cannot fly.

The mallard is the most common, widespread and best-known duck in the British Isles. Although it is a water bird, the mallard has followed the example of other successful species—for instance starlings, pigeons and house sparrows—by adapting to man-made habitats.

Many water-birds have declined because pollution and the drainage of marshes have destroyed their natural environment. But the mallard has managed to outweigh such losses by colonizing the artificial lakes and ponds in many town and city centres, as well as taking to the smallest farm ponds. Even in the centre of London, you'll find mallard on the ponds in all the major parks. It is also invariably a mallard which features in press photographs of a policeman holding up the traffic to allow mother and brood to cross the road safely.

Courting You can see the courtship behaviour of the mallard on any mild winter's day, as the birds begin to form pairs ready for the summer breeding season. Ducks form a new pair in winter or spring, and then break up again after the breeding season. The female is actively courted by the males (drakes), often several at a time. From a group of displaying males the female eventually chooses her mate. She presumably selects the one which is displaying with greatest vigour, showing him-

Above: The dappled brown female mallard leads her downy nestlings to the water, almost as soon as they are hatched. They feed themselves without any parental help.

Right: The traditional mallard nest site in the wild is in thick vegetation—nettles, brambles, bracken and heather. Unusual sites, more associated with Man, include water tanks, flower boxes and bridge supports. The female builds her nest using plant debris, grasses, and down feathers plucked from her own chest. She usually lays 7-11 pale bluish-green eggs, which she alone incubates. The young become independent at the same time they fledge—about six weeks after hatching.

Duck displays

There are a number of behavioural gestures, mostly associated with courting, which the male performs.

Grunt whistle is the most common display. The male tucks his head down to his chest, and lifts the front half of his body right out of the water. He then just flicks the surface with the tip of his bill, sending a little spray of water droplets up into the air. At the same time he lets out a low grunt, followed immediately by a clear whistle.

Head-up, tail-up involves both chest and tail coming up off the water. This emphasises the colouring on the male's neck and breast, as well as the black and white pattern on the tail.

Raised wing is another action where the male tucks his head behind the raised wing, as if to preen. This really serves to expose a blue-green bar (speculum) edged with white, along the rear of the wing.

Though not actually involved in the courtship rituals, this male (4) is alerted to the proceedings and quacks in response. When there is a surplus of males, they continue to court females already paired.

self off to be the brightest and largest bird present, and therefore the most suitable to fertilise her eggs.

Choice of nest site Mallards tend to choose nest sites on the ground, where they will be concealed in marshy vegetation; but they also adapt to all kinds of artificial situations – including nest boxes and holes in, and even under, buildings. They may nest a trifle precariously in the crowns of pollarded willows, and even on broad branches many metres off the ground. One much-publicised site was in a window box of the house next-door to the Iranian Embassy in London, facing on to Hyde Park. The duck sat through the trauma of the 1980 siege and rescue, apparently without budging from her nest.

Nest construction When nesting off the ground, the female mallard uses little or no nest material because she cannot carry things in her bill. On the ground, however, the duck constructs a shallow cup of such vegetation as it can reach from the nest, pulling and pushing stems and leaves into a circular rim.

2 head-up tail-up

female

1 grunt whistle

The female (above) remains passive prior to pairing but once she has a mate she sometimes 'incites' him to drive off contending suitors. She dabs her head and bill in the direction of the interloper, while quacking noisily.

3 raised wing

4 alert, quacking

As the mother begins to lay the clutch of seven to eleven eggs, she also begins to pluck down from her breast. This process starts slowly with a few bits at a time, but by the end of the egg-laying–she usually manages one egg per day–there is a thick layer of pale greyish down under and around the eggs. The down serves two functions: first it insulates the eggs from the cold, and often damp, ground; secondly, when the female leaves the eggs for her twice daily feed and bathe, she pulls the down and some of the nest material over the eggs, concealing them completely from any passing predator.

Incubating the eggs The drake takes no part in the incubation, and rarely has any contact with the female once she finishes laying and begins to sit on the eggs all day. Sometimes he waits nearby to meet her when she comes off the nest. He also keeps watch while she has a hasty feed, but only does this for a week or so. In fact this is just as well: the female's mottled brown plumage is perfect camouflage, and fits in with the nest surroundings, but the contrasting green, purple and white plumage of the male could catch the eye of a fox or crow, and lead such predators to the nest with its precious clutch of eggs.

Brooding the chicks The female incubates the eggs for 26-28 days. The young hatch out over a short period–all within 24 hours. Depending on the time of day and the weather, the female will brood them in the nest for

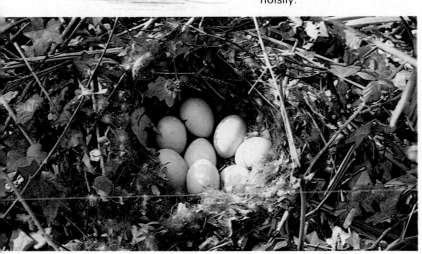

several hours, during which their down dries, and they become fluffy and active. Then she leads them off the nest, and takes them to the nearest stretch of suitable water where they can find food. Most nests are within a hundred metres of water, but some ducks may have to trek double that distance, and even cross roads to get there.

The young can run and swim as soon as they leave the nest, and also feed themselves, pecking instinctively at any small object. They quicly learn to distinguish between small seeds and insects which are good to eat, and surface debris, which is of no value to them. The town park mallard eats crusts and scraps, but the true diet of those living in more natural surroundings includes seeds of rushes and grasses, a wide variety of insects and the tips of leaves and stems of growing plants.

The mother broods her young at night or during rainy periods, defending them against predators. However, many of the ducklings fall prey to pike and rats and, during a cold wet spell, they may even starve. From a brood of ten young, perhaps four or five survive to the flying stage. They reach this all important stage in about six weeks, and may incur further losses while they learn to fly properly. Nevertheless the number of young mallard reared each year is ample to compensate for losses of adult birds, and the overall population is buoyant.

Population In December and January there are probably between 300,000-400,000 mallard in the country. Many of these are migrants coming from northern Europe to overwinter, but when they depart in the spring, about 50,000 pairs of mallard remain behind to breed.

Although most of the town park lakes in Britain only hold small numbers of mallard, a few hundred at most, there are some notable concentrations – over 8000 have been seen together on the estuary of the Humber near Hull, and nearly 6000 on the floods of the River Derwent. Counts of 4000 to 5000 have been made on Abberton reservoir in Essex, and on the Ouse Washes in Norfolk.

Distribution Mallard occur throughout the northern hemisphere, in Europe, Asia and North America. They have also been introduced into Australia and New Zealand. Those that breed in the British Isles are completely sedentary, rarely moving more than

30 miles throughout their lives. Those that migrate from Scandinavia on the other hand, move considerable distances.

The breeding range for birds wintering in Britain extends north from southern Sweden and Finland to the arctic circle, and deep into the Soviet Union to the east. The majority of these birds leave Britain in March and move north-east in a series of short hops, to reach their breeding quarters by the end of April. Once the female is sitting safely on her eggs, the male may start to move back south-west as early as July.

Many males pause for some weeks on large lakes and reservoirs while they undergo their annual moult, changing all their feathers, and actually becoming flightless for a couple of weeks. They then continue their migration, arriving back in Britain in September. The females and the young stay on the breeding grounds until well into August.

Mallard (*Anas platyrhynchos*), 50-65cm (20-25in), one of the most widely distributed of our breeding birds. The male (above) is a handsome bird, with a bottle-green head and neck. A neat white collar separates the purple-brown chest and pale grey back. Small black feathers above the white tail curl upwards in a small but decorative feature. By contrast, (shown on the nest below) the female is a subdued mottled brown all over. This makes her well camouflaged for sitting on the eggs and nest.

Tufted duck and pochard

Two of our most attractive diving ducks, the pochard and its close relative the tufted duck, are becoming increasingly common on Britain's lakes and reservoirs. Many are now breeding here, but most are winter visitors from northern Europe.

Above: A male tufted duck. The female has a much less pronounced tuft.

Tufted duck (*Aythya fuligula*). Resident duck, breeding next to lakes, gravel pits and reservoirs throughout much of lowland Britain. Length 43cm (17in).

Pochard (*Aythya ferina*). Resident duck, but far less common in the breeding season than the tufted duck and confined mostly to natural lakes. Length 46cm (18in).

As with so many species of duck, male pochard and tufted duck are strikingly coloured birds. The females, on the other hand, are dull by comparison since they need to be well camouflaged when they incubate their eggs and raise the young.

The male tufted duck has black upperparts set off by brilliant white sides and belly. It gets its name from the tuft on the back of its head, although this feature is not always conspicuous. The female tufted duck has only a rudimentary tuft and is brown with slightly paler sides. Sometimes, she has a pale patch at the base of her bill. In flight, both sexes show a long white bar on the upper side of each wing.

The pochard is larger and more heavily built than the tufted duck. The male is unmistakable, his pale grey body contrasting sharply with a black chest and dark chestnut neck and head. From a distance, the male seems to have a uniformly dark head, neck and breast, and a pale body. The female resembles a larger version of the female tufted duck, but she has a paler back and buff markings around the bill and eye. In flight, the pochard shows pale grey wing-bars, the only species of duck with this feature.

Winter visitors The numbers of tufted ducks and pochards breeding in Britain has increased considerably during the last hundred years – in the case of the tufted duck the increase has been spectacular – yet most of the birds seen in Britain are still winter visitors from other parts of Europe. It is estimated that there are between 40,000 and 50,000 of each species wintering in Britain, compared to the summer breeding figures of about 5000 pairs of tufted duck and only 300 pairs of pochard. It is, therefore, not surprising that they are our commonest diving ducks to be seen on lakes, reservoirs and gravel pits during winter.

Many tufted duck wintering in Britain arrive here from Iceland, the rest coming from northern Scandinavia and northern and arctic Russia. The former population winters mostly in Scotland, western England and Ireland; the latter usually settles in southern and eastern England. Flocks of several thousand may gather, particularly on large areas of water such as the reservoirs around London.

Our wintering pochard come to us from Russia, though further south than the tufted duck's breeding grounds. Like the tufted duck, pochard form huge flocks numbering several thousand. A notable gathering point is a tiny pool, called Duddington Loch, lying within the city limits of Edinburgh, which used to hold a staggering 8000 pochard crowded together, though their numbers are now declining. The London reservoirs and gravel pits in the Thames Valley also support large winter populations of pochard.

Favourite foods During winter, large numbers of both pochard and tufted duck happily coexist on the same lake or reservoir–happily, because they are not in direct competition with each other since they have different food preferences. Generally, the tufted duck is carnivorous and the pochard is herbivorous. However, both species feed on the other's food if it is abundant. The main food source for the pochard is the stoneworts and pondweeds; the tufted duck feeds mainly on insects and shellfish.

Both species feed by diving, usually beginning with a slight upward jump to give them impetus to dive deeper. Once under water they swim with their feet alone, keeping their wings tightly closed. The dives last for about

With its striking black and white plumage and tuft, the male tufted duck is far more distinguished than its dull brown and white female. After mating, the male adopts a characteristic 'bill-down' posture.

Tufted duck

white wing-bars

tuft

♂

'bill-down' posture

♀

pale patch at base of bill

Right: The head of a male tufted duck is black but, in certain lights, its glossiness can give it a purplish tinge. Notice the bright yellow iris, a characteristic shared by the female.

Below: Pochards and tufted ducks share the same habitat but rarely compete with each other for food since they have different preferences. Tufted ducks generally feed on animals, whereas pochards concentrate more on plants.

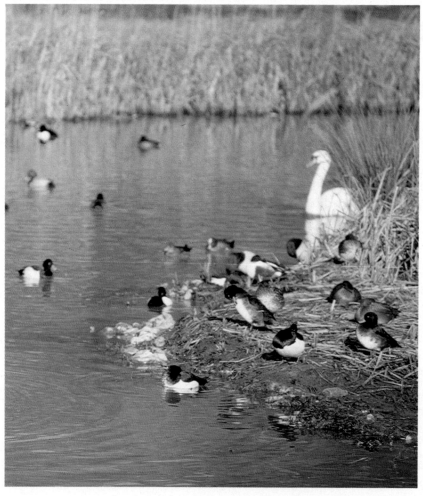

15-20 seconds and the birds emerge close to where they submerged.

Segregated flocks In both species, the winter flocks consist predominantly of one sex or the other, rather than being evenly mixed. The reason for this is that the males leave the breeding grounds well before the females and so arrive at their wintering grounds much earlier. By the time the females arrive the more northerly wintering sites (the ones nearest to the breeding grounds) may already be full of males, so the females have to move on further south.

Even if a flock comprises males and females it is noticeable how often the sexes remain separated. The males tend to feed in deeper water further from the shore. Being larger, they can dive deeper and stay submerged for longer, up to 20 seconds compared to the females' 15 seconds. By feeding in deeper water the males reduce the competition for food by exploiting a different source.

Resident tufted ducks Most pochards and tufted ducks migrate in spring back to their summer breeding grounds, but increasing numbers are now breeding in Britain. The earliest recorded instance of tufted ducks breeding in Britain was as recent as 1849, when a pair bred in Yorkshire. Other records uickly followed; the speed of their increase an be gauged from the breeding record at och Leven, where the first pair bred in 875 but only five years later there were more an a hundred breeding pairs.

The excavation of numerous gravel pits in wland parts of southern England has rovided the tufted duck with large areas of ew habitat, and there are now few pits with-ut nesting pairs. The presence of an island the gravel pits is a great advantage since e birds are then safe from foxes.

The tufted duck's nest is a hollow on dry round near water, hidden in grass or rushes nd lined with grass, down and feathers. The sual clutch of eggs is between seven and welve. Only the female incubates the eggs; e male leaves to congregate with other ales, its part in the breeding cycle having ow been completed. The eggs hatch after bout 24 days, and the female leads the young hicks down to a shallow sheltered area of ater close to the shore, where she rears them.

The young take about six weeks to fledge, ut they are often abandoned by the mother vo or three weeks beforehand. The reason or this is that the female moults immediately fter the breeding season; by leaving the rood early she gives herself more time to arry out the moult.

head-throw display
crouch display
neck-stretch display

grey back
distinctive chestnut-red head
black breast
Pochard
♂
♀
ale face

Above: Male pochards have several unusual courtship displays. The commonest is the neck-stretch display, where the male's neck is held upright and appears thickened, possibly due to its feathers ruffling out. It may also perform the head-throw display, in which it whips its head far back and then forwards again while calling, and the crouch display, in which its neck is pulled in.

Left: A male pochard. During winter, male and female pochards often form separate flocks. If they stay within the same flock they are likely to feed in different parts of the lake.

Left: The characteristic chestnut brown head of a male pochard contrasts sharply with its black chest and pale grey wings and back. The female pochard is dull brown.

Below: A female tufted duck with chicks. The chicks fledge after six weeks, but the mother often abandons them before that.

Resident pochards Pochards have bred in Britain in small numbers for centuries. How-ever, as with the tufted duck, their population began to grow during the latter half of the 19th century. Pochards now breed in most parts of Britain, except upland areas, though they are still much less common than tufted ducks. This is probably due to their breeding habits, which are much more restricting than those of the tufted duck. Instead of nesting on dry land, the pochard builds its nest close to, or actually in the water, and so it needs dense stands of vegetation growing in shallow water. Its natural habitat used to be marshlands but, as these have been drained and reclaimed, the pochard has had to find alternative sites. Unlike the tufted duck, the pochard has not yet been able to colonize recently established gravel pits and reservoirs since the margins still lack the necessary vegetation.

The breeding habits of the pochard are broadly the same as those of the tufted duck. The female alone incubates the clutch of six to eleven eggs and rears the brood. But she does not abandon the chicks before they can fly (at about seven weeks old). Possibly, this is because pochards nest earlier than tufted ducks and so have more time for moulting.

Pintail and shoveler

The pintail is easy to recognise with its long, fine tail, as is the squat shoveler with its remarkably large bill. Both breed in Britain and Ireland, although breeding pintail are rare; and both populations are outnumbered in winter by visitors from northern USSR, coming in their thousands.

Above: A male shoveler in breeding plumage. When swimming, shovelers have a distinctive appearance, lying noticeably low in the water. The stoutness of the neck is emphasized by the large head, ending in the great spatulate bill, held pointing slightly downwards as if a little too heavy for the bird.

Below: Both species breed in lowland areas with marshes and flood meadows

Of the 20 species of wild duck seen regularly at some time of the year in Britain and Ireland, seven belong to the genus *Anas*. These are mallard, teal, garganey, wigeon, gadwall, pintail and shoveler. Here we look at two of these, the pintail and the shoveler.

Measured from bill to tail tip, the pintail is the second longest of the group (after the mallard) at 56cm (22in), while the shoveler shares third place with the gadwall at 51cm (20in). As a breeding species the pintail is the rarest of the group, while the shoveler has the third largest population after the mallard and teal. Apart from the garganey, which is a summer visitor, the breeding populations of these ducks are reinforced by large numbers of

birds migrating to Britain and Ireland from more northerly breeding grounds.

Pintail The slender body of the pintail is enhanced by its long thin neck and greatly elongated central tail feathers. The latter make up one fifth of its total length. The dark chocolate-brown colouring of the male's head continues down the back of the neck to the mantle (lower back). The front and sides of the neck are a bright and contrasting white which continues as a narrow streak up each side of the head. The underparts are also white, while the back and flanks are finely vermiculated (marked with tiny wavy stripes) in grey.

The squat, heavy-headed silhouette of the

Distribution

■ pintail
□ shoveler

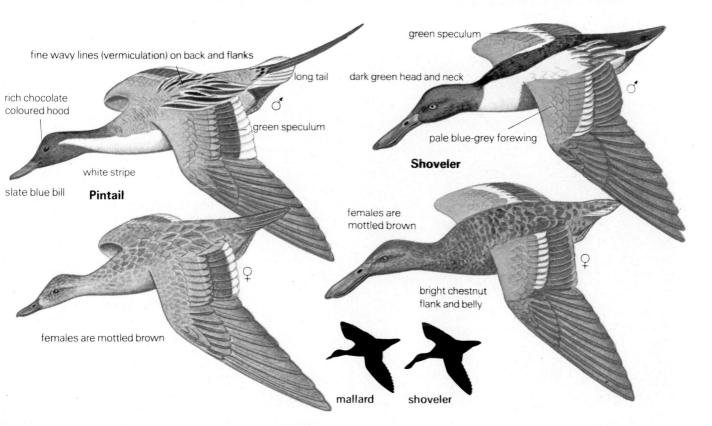

fine wavy lines (vermiculation) on back and flanks

long tail

rich chocolate coloured hood

green speculum

white stripe

slate blue bill

Pintail

females are mottled brown

green speculum

dark green head and neck

pale blue-grey forewing

Shoveler

females are mottled brown

bright chestnut flank and belly

mallard   shoveler

hoveler is in direct contrast to the graceful pintail, though the male is not unattractive, having colourful plumage. The male is visible from a great distance thanks to its gleaming white chest. The head and neck are dark green, appearing almost black, while the flanks are a bright chestnut, further set off by a white patch between them and the black undertail coverts. The back is black but has two white stripes running from front to rear, one on each side. Female shoveler are a mottled brown all over, their bill and squat shape serving to identify them.

Breeding grounds The pintail and shoveler both breed in Britain, but the pintail is comparatively scarce, with probably no more than 0 pairs, while the shoveler, following a period of increase in recent years, is now estimated to total about 1000 pairs. The pintail has been found breeding in scattered small groups of one or two pairs, quite widely over northern England and Scotland; but many of the sites are only used once or twice in several years. Some of the more regular breeding places are to be found in East Anglia and north Kent. Here they nest in wet pastures, concealing their eggs under overhanging tussocks of grass, and never very far from shallow areas of fresh water.

Similar habitats are chosen by the shoveler, one of the major breeding sites for the species in Britain being on the Ouse Washes on the Norfolk/Cambridgeshire border. Here there has been a considerable increase in pairs, also reflected elsewhere in the country. In the 1950s there were probably no more than 50 pairs, but this had increased to about 100 by the 1960s, reaching a peak of over 300 in 1975, or perhaps a third of the total for Britain. Elsewhere there are few concentrations, but the species is widespread in all but the more

upland areas of the country.

Winter numbers In winter the relative status of the two species is reversed. The pintail is much more common, with a regular peak of about 25,000 and perhaps occasionally as many as 30,000. The shoveler, on the other hand, rarely numbers much above 5000-7000, with an absolute peak of perhaps 10,000. A few years ago a peak of 5000 would have been unusual, but the increase noted in breeding birds has been reflected by an increase in wintering numbers, at least during the early part of the winter.

Pintail migration The great majority of the pintail wintering in north-west Europe breed in the northern part of the USSR. But this is only a small part of the total number of pintail migrating out of this area each autumn. Perhaps 75,000 winter in north-west Europe, compared to some 300,000 in the Mediterranean and Black Sea areas. Some of these even cross the Sahara to winter in Senegal and Niger, West Africa.

The pintail start to arrive in Britain and

Above: Recognition features of the birds in flight. The silhouettes show how different a shoveler looks from a mallard—chiefly because of the bill. Also, the shoveler looks as if its wings are set further back because the bill extends so far forward. The pintail has a slim body with a long tail. It also has a green, shiny area (a speculum) behind the forewing. The shoveler, on opening its wings, reveals a pale blue-grey forewing and behind it a green, white-edged speculum.

Below: A male pintail preens his back feathers, of which the remarkably long scapulars are clearly seen pointing outwards across the front of the wing.

Above: A group of wintering pintail stand in the safety of the ice on a pond. As in most duck species, the winter plumage is identical to the summer plumage. During late summer most duck species, including shoveler and pintail, enter an 'eclipse' phase of several weeks during which males take on the mottled brown colouring of the females. The pintail eclipse is from mid July to late September, after which the males resume their colourful appearance, as seen here.

Right: A female shoveler sits on her nest. The breeding habitat is uncut waterside meadowland, and this picture shows how suitable it is as cover for the shoveler.

Ireland in late September, and continue through October and November, reaching their peak in December. This is followed by a steady decline until the middle of March when most of the migrants have left. Although pintail are quite widespread in small groups in Britain in winter, the great majority of them are concentrated on only a few sites. Indeed as many as three-quarters of the total British wintering population have been counted at just one place—the Mersey estuary near Liverpool.

Shoveler migration The movements of the shoveler are more complex than those of the pintail because of the existence of a substantial British breeding stock. While these birds move away south for the winter, other birds come from Russian breeding grounds to replace them. The British stock seem to move away during late autumn, probably not until November. The monthly wildfowl count organised by the Wildfowl Trust show that peak numbers are often present in Britain in November, suggesting that some Continental immigrants have already arrived, while many British birds have not yet left. The British shovelers generally go south into Spain and southern France, with a few crossing the Mediterranean to winter in North Africa. Many more birds come from further east to winter in the Mediterranean area, probably totalling some 150,000. The November peak in Britain has reached 9000, but 5000-7000 is more usual. During December, January and February, probably only the Russian immigrants are present in the country, and numbers fall to perhaps 4000-5000.

On one occasion in the 1960s there was a further peak in shoveler numbers in March and early April, and it was assumed that this represented both the Russian birds, not yet on their way back east, together with the British breeders already returned to their nesting areas. In recent years, however, this peak has failed to materialise, and it may be that the Russian birds are now leaving earlier, though the reasons why this might be so are not clear.

Changing sides These varying movements by different stocks of shoveler have been re

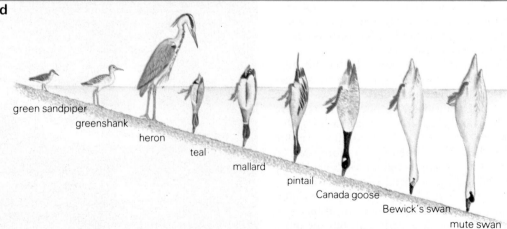

Reaching for the mud
Feeding in winter on estuaries and floods, and in summer on ponds, lakes and rivers, 'upending' species of water birds can each exploit waters of different depths. The duck with the longest reach is the pintail, followed by the mallard. Differences in upending depth allow many species to feed in the bottom mud without competing for the same sites.

green sandpiper
greenshank
heron
teal
mallard
pintail
Canada goose
Bewick's swan
mute swan

The filter feeding method

Shovelers swimming in this close 'raft' formation are exploiting two sources of food that are suitable for straining through a filter: the plankton just below the surface, and any food items stirred up from below by the paddling feet of many shovelers as they swim round and round.

water is sucked in at the front and strained out at the sides   lamellae

The shoveler is a highly adapted filter feeder. The sides of its enormous bill are thickly fringed with fine tooth-like lamellae, like the teeth of a comb. The bird sucks the water in through the tip of the bill, which is broadened out, so permitting a greater throughput, and then squirts it out through the sides, trapping food items in the lamellae.

vealed by marking the birds with leg rings. What has also been shown is that occasionally a bird joins the 'wrong' population. For example, there have been a few cases of shoveler ringed as young birds in Britain, being recovered in subsequent years in Russia. This has mostly occurred with males. What seems to happen is that the British-reared male meets an attractive Russian female shoveler, arriving in Britain for the winter; and instead of ignoring her and setting off on his own southerly migration, the male pairs up and then flies back to Russia with her during the following spring. A special term has been coined to describe this behaviour—abmigration.

How pintail feed The largest flocks of wintering pintail in Britain are found on estuaries, and on flooded marshes and pastures. Easily the biggest concentration is on the Mersey estuary near Liverpool, where a maximum of over 18,000 have been counted together. There are other important sites for pintail in the same part of Britain, particularly the Dee and Ribble estuaries, and on the freshwater pools of Martin Mere north of Southport. The natural foods of pintail are quite varied. They take small snails and other invertebrates from tidal mudflats. They also 'upend' in shallow fresh water and eat a great variety of seeds. In many areas, however, they 'flight' out (fly in formation) in the early morning to feed on nearby areas of farmland.

Here they glean spilt grain from harvested wheat and barley fields, and even pick up pieces of potatoes and sugar beet after the harvesting machines have been through.

The plankton specialist Shoveler rarely occur in Britain in flocks greater than 500. Most of the larger flocks are on reservoirs, for example those around London, and on flooded pastureland, such as the Ouse Washes, where many pairs breed. Shoveler pick up quite large seeds and insects in their bills, and frequently feed by picking and nibbling round the edges of pools and reservoirs.

However, while classed as 'dabbling' ducks, they have a unique feeding method. Their large bills are specially adapted for filter feeding, enabling them to exploit plankton, which other water birds are not able to use. Even so it takes a lot of feeding to gather enough to live on, and it is probably for this reason that, while small numbers of shoveler are often seen on lakes, reservoirs and gravel pits throughout Britain, large flocks of these birds are rare.

Above: A pair of shoveler, demonstrating the use of their specialised bills.

Shoveler (*Anas clypeata*). Breeding population of c. 1000 pairs; most of our wintering birds breed in northern USSR. 51cm (20in).

Pintail (*Anas acuta*). Small breeding population below 50 pairs; most of our wintering birds breed in northern USSR. 56cm (22in).

Below: A pintail upending. Not only do the different species of bottom-feeding waterbirds share the feeding grounds by each specialising in a particular depth; the male pintail can feed in deeper water than the female, thus reducing competition between the sexes within a flock.

Coot and moorhen

Coots and moorhens are freshwater birds but, unlike the ducks, they spend much of their time feeding on land, running about on their disproportionately long feet. In the breeding season both species become very aggressive in defence of their territories.

Below: A moorhen among the grasses at the edge of a pond. The bright red beak 'shield' and the white area under the tail distinguish it from the coot. Another characteristic is its habit of jerking its head back and forth as it swims.

The coot and the moorhen, close relatives belonging to the rail family, are common and widely distributed throughout the British Isles. The coot is all black, with a white 'shield' above its white bill, and a faint whitish wing bar (as it does not fly very much, however, this last feature is rarely seen). Its legs are greenish in colour. The moorhen is brown-black in colour, tending to grey on the sides and underparts. Its shield, smaller than that of the coot, is bright red, as is its bill. There is a whitish bar down the flanks, and the area under the tail is also pure white. Its legs are green.

Both coots and moorhens can become totally accustomed to man. Moorhens, especially, breed beside the smallest farm or village pond, and also appear throughout the year on lakes in city and town centre parks. At a distance, both species can be confused with ducks. The moorhen, however, is smaller than most ducks, raises its tail well out of the water, and jerks its head backwards and forwards as it swims. The coot has a rounded dumpy outline–very different from the straight-backed appearance of most ducks. Once you see the short, pointed bill you can easily distinguish both birds from the broad-billed ducks.

Territory, nests and chicks During the breeding season coots and moorhens defend territories against others of their own species. The area of the territories varies greatly, but

lobe

ike ducks, coots swim well
nd dive for food. Instead of
aving duck-like webbed
eet, however, the coot has
road lobes on each toe (see
elow) which help to propel
he bird through the water.
The moorhen is less aquatic
n habits than the coot and
as no lobes on its long
oes.)

he coot usually defends a much larger one up to an acre or more) than the moorhen. Some moorhen territories may be less than 100 square metres (123 sq yards) in size. The erritories provide all that the pair needs in he way of food and nest sites.

The nests of coots and moorhens are built of dead leaves and the stems of rushes and other water plants. They are often placed n shallow water among concealing vegetation, sometimes anchored to the bottom, out often just floating on the water. Moorhens, more than coots, also build on dry land, occasionally a little way off the ground in thick bushes. A shallow cup at the top of the nest is lined with green leaves and finer material. Both species lay between six and nine pale buff eggs that are liberally spotted with brown.

Young coots and moorhens are able to walk and swim within a few hours of hatch-ing; moorhen chicks tend to stay close to the nest for the first few days at least, returning to it to be brooded by the parents at night or in cold, wet weather. Around the time of hatching the adult male coot builds one or two 'platforms' within the breeding territory. These are similar to the nest but flatter on top and are provided with one or more ramps leading up from the water. The young coots are brought to these platforms and brooded there rather than in the nest.

The young of both species are blackish in colour, with reddish heads. In the case of the coot this colouring comes from the tips of the down plumules, but the moorhen's head is bare–it is the skin that is red. This colour also extends to the bills and tiny shields of the young of both species. The bright colour in the middle of the reddish head shows as a central 'target' area for the parents who are feeding the chick. It is noticeable that as the young grow and begin to feed themselves, the reddish colour fades.

Above: Coots just taking off for flight from a lake. The lobed toes on the feet assist the bird in its laborious take-off from the water surface. To gain the necessary speed and impetus the coot has to patter over the water for several metres. It always looks rather laboured in flight.

Coot (*Fulica atra*); 38cm (15in) from beak to tail; distribution widespread, on lakes and meres. Resident.

Moorhen (*Gallinula chloropus*); 33cm (13in) from beak to tail; distribution widespread, on ponds, marshes, lakes and rivers. Resident.

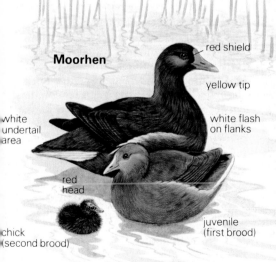

Moorhen · red shield · yellow tip · white undertail area · white flash on flanks · red head · chick (second brood) · juvenile (first brood)

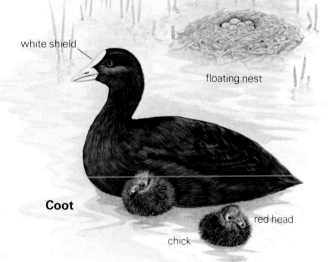

white shield · floating nest · **Coot** · chick · red head

Threat and aggression

prominent white
undertail feathers

fluffed plumage

threat display

outstretched neck

rearing
posture

outspread
wings

fighting

Above: The outstretched neck, raised wings, fluffed plumage and conspicuous presentation of the red shield (left) are typical moorhen display postures. If neither bird gives way after display, fighting begins. The birds come together breast to breast, rearing up on their tails to strike at each other with their feet (right).

Below: The threat display of the coot.

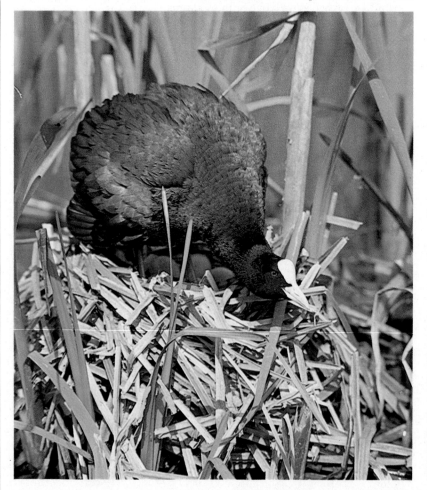

In defending their territories, both species become aggressive, displaying vigorously at intruding birds and often fighting with them. The white frontal shield of the coot, and the red one of the moorhen, are the principal 'signals' used to indicate aggression. The bird holds its head low over the water, with neck outstretched, then fluffs up its plumage and slightly raises its wings. As well as making the bird look larger, and therefore more threatening, the shield is effectively presented to the opponent against a background of black feathers.

Two moorhens in a dispute, perhaps at the boundary of their territories, not only fluff themselves up to show off their shields, but also cock up their tails and swim round so that their brilliant white undertail feathers show to maximum advantage. If neither bird gives way after this, they rear up on their tails, coming together breast to breast and striking at each other with their feet. Sometimes the long claws interlock and the two birds tumble over and over, even rolling into the water (if the encounter was started on land), and generally making a considerable commotion. It is not uncommon for the mates of the fighting birds to join in so that all four moorhens form a flapping, grappling mêlée. The fights can end in one of two ways. Either one bird, or pair, gives way and is chased off by the victors, or the combatants mutually decide that enough is enough, and they break off and retreat slowly from each other, hunched and ready to resume battle at the slightest sign of further aggression.

The coot indulges in similar fighting, preceded by showing off its white frontal shield. It also raises its tail and swings round like the moorhen but, as the underside of its tail is black, the significance of this is not so obvious. Fights between four birds—two pairs—occur as with the moorhen. All four may be involved in one scrap, but not uncommonly the two male birds and the two females have separate fights alongside each other.

Aggression and fighting is very important as each pair of birds tries to establish a territory large enough for its breeding and feeding needs. Actual damage during the fights is rare: as in most close encounters between birds, the winner, if there is one, is the stronger or older bird, and the loser gives up before it gets injured. Researchers have found some evidence to suggest that the same pair of birds return in spring to hold and defend the territory they had the previous year. This certainly happens with some moorhens, but it has not yet been conclusively proved that the same thing happens with coots.

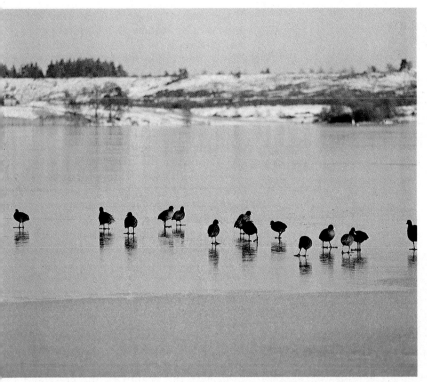

Adaptation to life in the water

Water is an attractive habitat for birds: it is fairly safe from land predators such as cats and foxes, and can provide a great diversity of food. To help them swim, the feet of water birds are often lobed (coots and grebes), or webbed (ducks and gulls). Penguins and puffins actually 'fly' under water, using their stiff, flipper-like wings. Birds that spend most of their time on water need warm, waterproof plumage. A thick layer of down keeps out the cold and traps air which helps the birds float. The down is covered by long overlapping body feathers that prevent any water from penetrating. To keep the feather waterproof, the birds must oil them regularly from a special oil gland situated at the base of the tail. The birds rub the oil into their feathers with the bill while preening. Grebes do this after each feeding session, rolling over in the water to oil the feathers on the belly. Well-kept feathers are unwettable; water forms droplets on the oily surface and quickly runs away. Land birds also have oil glands, but their feathers are rainproof only, not completely waterproof.

Above: Coots walking on ice. They rarely breed on waters of less than an acre in extent, but in winter appear in flocks on many town park lakes, becoming completely tame and joining the swans and ducks in taking food from people. The rounded, dumpy silhouette of the coot, clearly visible here, distinguishes it from most ducks, which have straight backs.

Below: Coot chicks hatching. The red colouring on the head seems to reinforce the strident calls of the chicks as they beg for food from their parents. When the chicks beg they raise their heads towards the parents and sway them slightly from side to side.

Family affairs The coot normally rears just one brood of young in the year, but the moorhen often manages to raise two, and sometimes even three. In nearly all other species of birds that raise a second brood, the first brood youngsters move, or are driven, away from the nesting area. In the case of the moorhen, however, the young of the first brood help to rear the next lot of chicks. Occasionally they may help to incubate the eggs, but more usually they assist in the feeding of the chicks after hatching.

It is obviously advantageous for the parents to have help in finding food and giving it to their chicks, but it does also mean that the territory has to be large enough for all the birds—parents, first brood young and second brood young—to be able to live and feed within it.

Seasonal movements Moorhens in the British Isles and north-west Europe are almost entirely sedentary. Movements of ringed individuals have rarely been recorded over more than about 10 to 15 miles. Further east, however, where the winters become very icy, moorhens are forced to move away south and west to warmer areas, but few if any come as far as Britain. Many moorhens stay on their breeding territories throughout the year.

British coots, too, are with us all the year round, but are joined by fairly large numbers coming from the Continent to spend winter here. Ringing has shown that these birds come from as far afield as western Russia, as well as from the countries round the Baltic and nearer Britain. For a bird that always looks very laboured when in flight, coots travel surprisingly long distances on migration. Unlike the moorhen, coots spend the winter in large flocks, with few birds staying on their territories. On some of our reservoirs and gravel pits, flocks of up to 5000 may build up.

Diving for food Moorhens are omnivorous birds, eating a wide variety of plant leaves, stems and seeds, as well as molluscs, worms, the larvae of many different freshwater invertebrates, and whatever the generous public feeds to them. They feed on land as much as on the water. When swimming they often dip their heads under water, and even upend, but only very occasionally dive.

Coots, on the other hand, dive quite competently, first pressing the air out of their plumage, and making a little upward and forward leap to give themselves the necessary impulsion to submerge. Normally they go down only about 90 or 120cm (3-4ft), but greater depths, of 4.5m (15ft) or more, have been recorded. Coots are omnivorous, like moorhens, but tend to eat mostly plants. They graze short vegetation on land, and pluck aquatic plants growing in and under the water.

Lapwing

The lapwing is one of the easier birds to spot in our countryside, with its distinctive crest and dark green plumage with white wing patches. It can be seen at all times of year, breeding on hillsides, marshes and farmland, or wintering near ploughed fields.

Peewit, green plover and lapwing are just three of a multitude of colloquial names for this particular bird, an indication of how diverse and confusing local names can be. Nevertheless, each name has a meaning: 'peewit' clearly comes from the plaintive rasping cry so familiar over meadows and marshes. 'Green plover', too, is a more appropriate name than would, at first, seem. Take a close look at this apparently black-and-white bird on a sunny day: the 'black' back is really deep bottle-green, shot with iridescent purple. Often you see lapwings in the air, when their floppy, clumsy looking wingbeats give a clear indication of how this, their most widely accepted name, was derived.

Lapwings are medium-sized waders, about as large as a pigeon but with the horizontal body posture and long legs of a wader. Besides their pied plumage, they have other useful identification features, such as the short beak and the slender, upturned crest, which is rather longer in the male than in the female lapwing. It is well worth seeking a closer look (using a car as a hide is an excellent idea) to appreciate the beauty of the crest and the sheen of the back feathers.

When they hatch, the young chicks are superbly camouflaged: the basic coloration of the down is a sandy fawn, with copious black or dark brown markings. There is a conspicuous white patch on the back of the head, easily seen when the chick is upright and running about, and doubtless an aid to its parents in keeping track of its whereabouts. When the chick squats, this prominent mark vanishes. As they grow, the chicks begin to resemble their parents, but with much reduced crests and with fawn fringes to the greenish-black back feathers, giving them a markedly scaly appearance.

Many habitats Lapwings are classed among the wading birds, but unlike the majority of these their prime habitat is not the shore. Their short, typically plover-like beaks are ideal for catching small ground insects and other invertebrates. They often feed well away from the water, and in Africa many of their close relatives are birds of arid grassland.

In winter, most lapwings are found on

Above: A male lapwing incubating the eggs. Even a small tuft of rushes is sufficient cover for the lapwing's nest.

Left: The lapwing's nest is relatively elaborate for a wader, but the eggs are typical: irregularly blotched, and laid with their pointed ends inwards.

Right: When the parent bird gives an alarm call, the chicks squat down to hide in the grass.

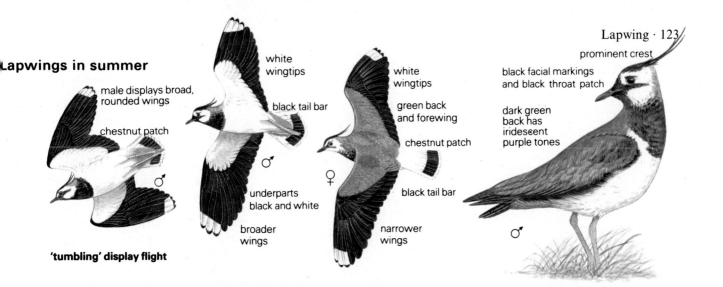

damp grassland or ploughed fields, with relatively few on the moors. They occasionally visit the shore, but usually only when snow or hard frost has made feeding difficult inland. On farmland, it is amazing to see how a flock of such conspicuously black and white birds can apparently vanish into the ground when they land. Their food at this time includes a great many worms and insect larvae driven out of the soil by the shallow flooding associated with winter rainfall. Often, lapwings congregate in flocks, sometimes hundreds of birds strong, but towards the end of winter these flocks begin to fragment as migrants return to their breeding areas overseas and as local birds begin to take up their territories.

Lapwings breed in a considerable range of habitats, but these do have a common feature: the territories always have patches of short vegetation or bare ground nearby, suitable for feeding. In some areas, most breeding birds are found on waste or marginal land, such as that surrounding gravel pits, chalk quarries, refuse tips or sewage farms. Elsewhere, they are farmland birds, breeding on permanent pasture or on freshly ploughed land sown with winter or spring corn. In upland areas, lapwings tend to congregate in the more sheltered situations, rather than on the moors. They usually set up their territories in the valleys, where any arable farming also tends to be concentrated, so improving the range of feeding habitats available.

Defending the home Territories are easily recognised as the air overhead in spring is full of tumbling, calling birds performing their aerobatic displays. Besides the calls, the wingbeats themselves are audible: the rounded, 'fingered' wings of the lapwing produce a unique 'whooshing' noise. Interestingly, male and female can be told apart at this time by the width of the wings: with the major role to play in display, it is natural that the male's wing is noticeably broader and thus noisier. Wing noise is not just used for display, but also as a terror weapon to repel invaders of the pair's territory.

Ground-nesting birds are vulnerable to attacks from predators – magpies, crows and

Above: The breeding plumage of the lapwing. The pied plumage proves, on closer inspection, to be a combination of black on the outer part of the wings, white mainly on the undersides and bottle-green with iridescent purple tones on the back. The winter plumage is similar to the summer plumage, but looks mottled, for many of the feathers have buff edges.

Lapwing (*Vanellus vanellus*). Wader adapted to inland habitats including farmland and upland meadows. Resident, with additional wintering population from Europe. Length 30cm (12in).

Below: A small flock of lapwings over a ploughed field in winter.

foxes – and any marauders, even humans, are instantly attacked by both birds as they cross the territorial boundary. The swooping, screeching lapwings, with these thumping wingbeats, are usually enough to put off any intending predators and thus increase the chances of the eggs being unharmed and the young surviving. It need not be the threat of losing in combat that deters the predator, for if there are other good hunting grounds nearby that are free from the distracting noise and behaviour of lapwings, the predator simply takes the easier option and hunts elsewhere. It is the aggressive appearance of the lapwing, rather than its fighting capability, that keeps danger away.

Often quite innocent parties become involved, and the sight of a pair of partridges straying accidentally into a lapwing territory while feeding, and then attempting to withdraw and maintain some dignity under such an onslaught, can be extremely amusing to watch.

The breeding season The lapwing's breeding

behaviour is, in many ways, typical of all the wading birds. The nest, at first, is a mere scrape in the ground. The male makes several of these, using his feet to do a little excavating and then his breast to round off the hollow. The female chooses one of these nests, which both birds then line with fine, dry grasses. Almost always it contains four eggs, though on rare occasions clutches of three or five are found. The eggs are stone-coloured, with copious black blotches giving excellent camouflage, and are arranged points facing inward in a neat square.

The sharply pointed shape of the eggs is characteristic of most waders, and has a logical explanation. Young lapwings hatch down-covered and with their eyes open, and as soon as they are dry they scamper around, feeding themselves under the watchful eyes of their parents. To do this, they must have well-developed and relatively long legs, and it is these that are housed, compactly folded, in the pointed part of the egg.

Both sexes share the work of incubation, which lasts about a month. Although the sitting bird may seem conspicuous in the middle of a field, it is likely to leave the nest and go into hiding if danger appears: once the bird has gone, the eggs are so well camouflaged that they are difficult to find. During the five weeks that it takes the chicks to fledge, each parent may take responsibility for part of the brood. Alternatively, the female may shepherd them about while the male stands guard.

A nomadic bird The movements of the lapwing lack the routine patterns that are characteristic of migration, and might, therefore, better be called nomadism. After the breeding season, the birds disperse widely. A lapwing may not necessarily breed in the same area in successive years, nor does it always migrate to the same wintering areas. Young birds bred

Above: A flock of several hundred lapwings lifting off from a winter field. Lapwings on the wing usually form ragged and shapeless flocks. Towards the end of winter these flocks begin to fragment: some birds are migrants from further north, and these return early in the year. Non-migrants depart to take up their breeding territories for the new season.

Below: A male lapwing broods the chicks: his dark throat is clearly visible.

in Britain or Ireland are as likely to be found nesting the following spring in central Europe as in the country of their origin.

This nomadism may be a factor that has prevented the species from subdividing into distinct regional groups (subspecies). This effect is seen in several widespread bird species: one example is the yellow wagtail, subspecies of which occur in different parts of Europe and Asia. The lapwing's distribution also extends into Asia, but it is thought that the bird's nomadism helps to mix the stock together, thus preventing a separation into distinct groups.

In winter, lapwings in Britain and western Europe react very quickly to changes in the weather. Any really cold spell is usually heralded by flocks of lapwings, flickering black and white across a stormy sky, heading westwards in the hope of finding warmer weather. If the cold is short-lived, a return movement may be seen as soon as the thaw sets in.

Lapwings are our most widespread species of wader, and are among the most numerous members of this group, in both summer and winter. Winter numbers depend greatly on their nomadic wanderings, and on the weather, but are always greater than those in the breeding season. Various estimates have put the breeding population in the region of 200,000 pairs, a figure that drops sharply after a very cold winter.

In the north of Britain, breeding numbers are on the increase, while in the south (probably as a result of land drainage and other changes in cereal production), some areas show signs of a decrease. Thus there are indications of a geographical shift in the population, though the total numbers are not changing.

Snipe and jack snipe

Snipe, noticeable for their long, straight bills, are small wading birds most often seen in inland marshy areas, damp meadows and river valleys.

The two species of snipe regularly seen in the British Isles are both birds of rank vegetation in damp, fresh-water areas. Both birds have richly mottled and striped brown body plumage, with characteristic creamy stripes along each side of the back. The jack snipe is known only as a winter visitor and is the smaller of the two species, with a shorter beak. The common snipe is a widespread breeding species, and its numbers are augmented during winter by an influx of larger birds from the rest of Europe; it has a very long bill.

Common snipe breed in damp meadows, river valleys, coastal fresh-water marshes, bogs, and over damp moorland throughout the British Isles. They are thinly scattered in the more populated areas of south-eastern England but become increasingly common in western and northern Britain. There are particularly large breeding populations in the boglands of central Ireland, over much of the Highlands of Scotland and on many Scottish islands, especially the remote St Kilda group. The birds are quite small–roughly the size of a starling, but look much longer as they have 6cm (2½in) long bills.

'Drumming' flight It is easy to discover that common snipe are holding territory, as the birds have a conspicuous aerial display called 'drumming'. The displaying bird flies above its territory, periodically swooping down with its outer tail feathers pushed out into the passing airstream. The feathers are strengthened and stiff so that they whirr as the air passes them, causing the 'drumming' sound. In fact, to most people the sound is not so much a drumming noise as a bleat, sounding rather like a goat. Such displaying birds also utter a 'chippering' note.

These noisy displays may take place at any time of day but are most usual early in the morning or during the evening; some birds display at night as well if there is a bright moon. There is another territorial call, generally given from an elevated perch such as a fence post or tree stump, and this is a sharp, loud 'tock'.

Territorial displays may take place as early as February in southern England–at

The jack snipe is a winter visitor that breeds in the north-eastern parts of Europe and western Siberia. It is smaller than the common snipe but less shy; if approached it does not fly away until the last possible moment.

Jack snipe
(*Lymnocryptes minimus*), 19cm (7½in) from beak to tail. Shorter bill and rounder wings than common snipe and no white on tail. Sept-April visitor.

Common snipe
(*Gallinago gallinago*), 27cm (10½in) from beak to tail. Very long bill. Resident.

Above: Common snipe feeding in marshland—their typical habitat. You usually see them in groups, probing with their exceptionally long bills for worms and other food. They also take insects from the surface.

least two months earlier than the displays of birds in northern Scotland.

The snipe makes its well-concealed nest on the ground (see photo captions, page 127). The chicks are most attractive, with striking markings. They are able to fly after 18-20 days but, like all waders, they leave their nest within a few hours of hatching. In some areas two broods may be reared, but most pairs are thought to be single brooded.

Long sensitive bills The common snipe's long bill is used to obtain food from deep in the ground. It is a precise and sensitive tool and a bird can insert the whole length of the bill into soft ground and still open the tip to take worms or other food. Snipe take food

items from the surface as well.

When the marshy areas where snipe normally feed freeze rock hard, they are adept at finding areas which have not frozen, such as where a spring has kept the ground open. Here they may congregate in large numbers. Flocks of snipe, known as wisps, flushed out from the marshes by shooting parties, usually number fewer than 10 birds, but in freezing weather favoured areas might provide flocks of 50-100 birds. If frosts persist native birds may be forced to move to Ireland, where it is generally warmer in winter, or southward to France or Iberia.

Worldwide distribution The common snipe is a widespread species away from the British Isles. The main population breeds right across northern Europe and northern Asia, and another group occupies most of South America; there are even common snipe breeding over much of East Africa. Some of the island populations, such as those on St Kilda and other outlying Scottish islands, are slightly bigger and darker than the general run of British and European birds. The birds in the Faeroes and Iceland are certainly big and dark, and it is probably the influence of the island's isolation which causes these differences in colour and size.

The jack snipe is much rarer than the common snipe and is a native breeding species of the north-easternmost parts of Europe and western Siberia. The wintering birds reach the British Isles in October and leave again in March or early April. The birds are superficially similar to common snipe, but their bills are shorter and they are, overall, about two-thirds the size of the common snipe. Their choice of habitat is much the same, but they allow a closer approach, and when they fly off they do not

Common snipe

twisting flight

Jack snipe

short hopping flight

Left: When flushed out of the vegetation in which it hides, the common snipe twists as it rises steeply away, but the jack snipe flies slowly in a broad loop and usually for a shorter distance.

very long bill with sensitive tip

Common snipe

Jack snipe

usually call or 'jink' in flight. Indeed, they often pitch again within a few dozen yards. They are quite often found along the edges of paths or ditches in marshy areas, and may sometimes be in small flocks—especially shortly after they have just arrived in autumn on the east coast.

The great snipe is the only other snipe found regularly in the British Isles. A handful is recorded each winter as visitors from the breeding areas of north-east Europe. They are difficult to distinguish from the common snipe, although they are actually plumper and show more white on their tails in flight. The great snipe is the long-distance migrant record holder for the group. Many are recorded in Africa in winter.

Fair game All snipe are liable to be shot during autumn and winter, both in the British Isles and in other European countries. Game species such as pheasants and grouse are shot in a highly organised fashion, but most snipe are shot by people walking through marsh-land, accompanied by dogs. The birds are disturbed as they rise and jink away. They

outer tail feathers produce drumming sound

Common snipe

cambered outer tail feather

The superbly marked fluffy chicks (above), the eggs (right), and a newly hatched egg being guarded by a parent (below), of the common snipe. The nest is usually made within a grassy tussock in freshwater marshy surroundings, and four eggs are laid. Like those of most waders, the eggs are pointed with dark blotches on an olive background. They are incubated for 20 days by the female alone. When the chicks hatch, their basic ground colour is dark, rich chestnut, spangled with gold and silver markings.

are always difficult to kill, and at present there is no evidence that the population is suffering through shooting. Indeed, there are records of much more intense shooting pressures in the past than now. Drumming birds are, of course, safe from being shot as they display only during the close season, which starts at the beginning of February and lasts until 11 August.

However, it is not possible to be complacent about these birds and their chances in the future as their habitats are under increasing pressure. In southern Britain areas of marsh-land are being drained and taken into arable agriculture, and many of the smaller field ponds that in the past provided shelter and food for one or two birds during winter have been filled in. Old-fashioned sewage farms, with their large settling ponds with muddy margins, have been replaced by systems with little, if any, chance for snipe to feed. As fresh-water wetlands are drained, what are now commonplace birds could become rare over the span of just a few decades.

Dipper

Dippers (above) nest beside fast-flowing streams and flit low over the water, alighting on favoured stones and boulders. They stand bobbing and bowing for a while, and then plunge into the rushing water to hunt aquatic creatures–they even walk beneath the surface, gripping the stream bed with their powerful claws.

Dipper (*Cinclus cinclus*) seen mainly beside fast, stony streams in upland areas; solitary dweller. Resident. Sexes look alike. Length 18cm (7in).

Below: The dipper is found in areas between 320 and 640m (1000-2000ft) above sea level; but in the north, in places where hills descend steeply to the sea, dippers nest close to the shore as well.

With its bold plumage and strong association with rivers and streams, the dipper is normally an easy bird to identify. Perhaps best likened to a 'thrush-sized wren', it has a jaunty, tail-cocked posture, and as it stands on some stone or boulder it frequently bobs up and down. Its legs are strong and look similar to those of a starling, while its beak is like that of a thrush in both colour and size. The upperparts are a rich, plain-chocolate brown, and the wings and tail look short in proportion to the distinctly plump body. By far the most conspicuous feature is the large, strikingly white 'bib' extending across the throat and breast, and down on to the belly.

In the case of English and most Scottish-breeding birds, this white bib has a broad chestnut margin which merges gradually into the near-black of the flanks and belly. Irish-breeding dippers (and also those in the Hebrides) have considerably less chestnut, and birds of the Continental race (which sometime stray to east and south-east England in spring and autumn) have almost no chestnut at all. The Continental race of dipper is in fact known as the black-bellied dipper.

Stony stream dwellers Just as characteristic as the plumage is the habitat of the dipper. Apart from stray migrants, which are sometimes seen on the coast or on slow-moving

Dipper distribution

The British and Irish dippers

British race

tail cocked

stout body

sturdy legs with strong feet

white bib

chestnut margin

Irish race

chestnut margin almost invisible

often in mid-stream, and the dipper stands on them, bobbing up and down continuously. Against the background of broken white water, the clear white bib offers surprisingly good camouflage. As the dipper bobs and dips its tail, it also blinks, using its so-called 'third eye lid' or nictitating membrane, which travels fore-and-aft, rather than up and down, to wipe the eye surface clean. In the dipper, the nictitating membrane is conspicuously white. Under water, this membrane is thought to protect the dipper's eye from gritty particles; when submerged it becomes transparent and does not hamper the bird's underwater vision.

Underwater hunter From the boulders in

streams in the lowlands, dippers are typically birds of fast-flowing streams and the shallow rocky shores of lochs and tarns in hilly or mountainous country. In Britain, only those dippers that inhabit the south-eastern edge of the breeding range (roughly along a line from Swanage in Dorset to Flamborough Head in Humberside) frequent slower-moving lowland rivers or streams. These birds usually favour stretches near weirs or sluices, where the water flow is broken.

Most dippers are sedentary birds, establishing a territory on a suitable stream or river and rarely straying far from it. Those in the far north, or at higher altitudes, do descend to lower waters during the winter, but in general, severe winters (especially those with a sudden, rapid-freezing onset) are fatal for many dippers.

Dippers are usually to be seen singly or in pairs (except when they have newly fledged young), and most pairs maintain their territories through the winter months. They are reluctant to cross the 'border' with adjacent territories, and double back when reaching this invisible line. Usually their flight is low and fast, with frequent, penetrating 'zit . . . zit . . . zit' calls, generally over their home reach of water; occasionally, if alarmed, they fly overland.

Not only do they have a 'home reach' of water, but also a number of favoured boulders within this, from which they hunt. These are

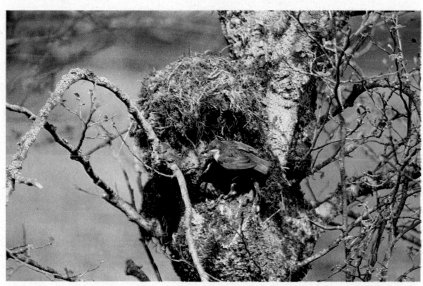

Above: The dipper's nest is dome-shaped and built of grasses and mosses. Many dippers nest behind waterfalls, and nowadays in man-made sites such as mills, weirs or under bridges.

Below: In lowland territories, two broods a year are usual, the first eggs being laid in early March. In the Scottish Highlands, laying is up to a fortnight later, and often only one brood is raised.

its stream, the dipper hunts, often beneath the surface but occasionally just 'up to its waist' in the shallows. To submerge, the dipper may jump straight into deep water, or gradually walk into the stream until lost from sight. Once beneath the surface, it hunts on foot, and this is where the disproportionately stout legs and powerful, sharp-clawed feet serve a vital purpose in holding the bird's buoyant body down on the stream bed. Under water, the wings are used like the fins of a fish, both for propulsion and to maintain balance in strong currents—sometimes dippers swim for considerable distances.

Most small underwater animals form part of the dipper's diet at some stage, but favourite items include caddisfly larvae (in their 'portable homes' of tiny fragments of shell, stone and vegetation) and water-beetle larvae; worms and small shellfish; freshwater shrimps; the occasional small fish; and, in season, tadpoles.

The breeding season This begins early in the year. The tunefully sweet, if slightly disjointed, warbling song can be heard in the territories from October onwards through the winter, until towards the end of the nesting period in the subsequent June. Both sexes indulge in song with equal enthusiasm: yet another colourful feature of this attractive waterside bird.

Reed, marsh and sedge warblers

Three small songbirds that live in our waterside habitats
in summer are the reed, marsh and sedge warblers, welcome
visitors which come to breed here each year.

Warblers are a large, world-wide family of insect-eating birds, most of which migrate south to Africa in autumn, returning in spring to breed. During their few months in this country, most British warblers are inconspicuous, tending to stay hidden within trees and bushes—one reason why many people are not familiar with them. There are three main groups in this country—'leaf', 'bush' and 'reed-bed' warblers; the reed, marsh and sedge warblers belong to the last of these groups.

The 'reed-bed' warblers have a characteristic shape and appear to be pointed at both ends. At one end the fine, relatively long bill merges smoothly with the head. At the other, the graduated tail with shorter outer feathers is supported by unusually long tail coverts (the small feathers that lie above and below the tail). In colour the birds are generally sandy brown above and creamy white below.

Broadly speaking, the group contains streaked and unstreaked species. Sedge warblers, with contrasting colours on the head, back and wings, are streaked. Reed and marsh warblers are typical of the unstreaked category, although both have a pale, indistinct stripe above the eye. These two species are so similar that they can only be safely distinguished by the colour of their plumage if a very good view is obtained.

Adult marsh warblers have more olive upper parts, while reed warblers tend to be more rusty in colour. Ornithologists have to catch the young birds before they can positively identify them, and even then some are indistinguishable.

Habitat Reed-bed warblers tend to stay within thick cover. When they fly they rarely cover much distance, although their wings flap rapidly, before diving back into the vegetation. Consequently even sedge warblers may not be easy to identify. Often the habitat is of little help since there is considerable overlap and all three species may nest together.

Perhaps reed warblers are the most aptly named, since they are frequently found among stands of common reeds, close to water. Their ability to cling to vertical reed stems is obvious as they slide up and down, one foot always higher than the other. Sedge warblers are less dependent on water and inhabit overgrown hedges and marshy ground with bushes and ditches, as well as reed-beds. Marsh warblers require vigorous undergrowth of plants such as nettle, willowherb and meadowsweet, although they will also inhabit reedy places with bushes. All three are found in colonies in a suitable habitat; the edges of lakes and flooded gravel pits are favoured.

Opposite: The sedge warbler can be identified by the creamy stripe with a dark outline above the eye; its wing feathers have pale edges. The nest is cup-shaped and rather bulky, and is attached to supporting reed stems.

Reed warbler (*Acrocephalus scirpaceus*) 12.5cm (5in) long from beak to tail; distribution reed-beds and marshes in England, rare in Wales and north, none in Ireland; summer visitor, arriving April and leaving August-September.

Marsh warbler (*Acrocephalus palustris*) 12.5cm (5in) long from beak to tail; distribution bushes, trees near water, also hedgerows and wood margins, rare in central and southern England; summer visitor, arriving late May.

Sedge warbler (*Acrocephalus schoenobaenus*) 13cm (5¼in) long from beak to tail; distribution widespread in waterside habitats, bushes, hedgerows and crop fields throughout British Isles; summer visitor, arriving early April.

Migration All three species leave Britain in August or September to winter in Africa, choosing the risks of long-distance migration rather than the high probability of acute food shortage in Britain. While there, they moult all their feathers, even though the body feathers were replaced before the autumn migration. When they return, the earliest arrivals–in April–are always sedge warblers, followed by reed warblers about a fortnight later, although some individuals of both species do not arrive at their breeding sites until late May or even June. Marsh warblers, one of our latest migrants, are rarely recorded before late May, although most arrive before mid-June.

Compared with other small birds, reed warblers are known to live for a long time. There are records of individuals over 11 years old, about twice as old as most other British warblers. Such a bird, travelling 3000 miles to tropical Africa every year, might fly over 60,000 miles during its lifespan.

Song is most intense when territories are established in spring. The start of the song period for each species therefore depends on when the birds arrive. Of the three, marsh warblers sing for the shortest period–only three weeks at the end of May and early June, although little song is heard from any of them after July. The song is probably the best identification feature available to birdwatchers.

Above: A marsh warbler feeds his mate on the nest they have woven together; the nest is attached to the reeds with a kind of basket weave. Unlike reed warblers, these birds rarely build over water.

In general, reed-bed warblers sing in rather unpunctuated manner with repetitive 'chirruping' and 'chirring' for several seconds at a time. These phrases are interspersed to variable extent with more musical notes. At one extreme, the reed warbler often chatters slowly and methodically, repeating each phrase two or three times in succession with little more than regular changes of pitch for variety. Sedge warblers are less repetitive and frequently utter high-pitched trills and clear musical phrases in their rather hurried delivery.

Both birds will imitate the songs and calls of other species, which can give rise to confusion with the marsh warbler that has, without doubt, the most musical and varied song. Its rich and diverse warblings often give the impression that a variety of birds are all singing within the same bush, for its ability to mimic others is quite remarkable. Over 5 species may be imitated, although any single bird will have a much smaller repertoire. Other calls, often scolding 'chirrs' and 'rattles', are uttered when danger threatens, for example when someone approaches the nest.

Breeding The nests of reed warblers are often supported by two or three vertical reed stems, and the female does the bulk of the building. The nest is particularly deep cupped, and cylindrical to ensure that eggs and nestlings do not fall out when strong winds cause the reeds to sway. Many build nests low down over the water where wind is not a problem. Marsh warbler nests are similar in construction but sited in dense vegetation such as nettles, while sedge warblers build nests low down in deep cover.

Sedge warblers lay six or seven eggs, while broods of five or six are quite common among their unstreaked relatives. The eggs of the

Song-flight
Of the three species only the sedge warbler (left) has a true song-flight. Singing boldly, the bird flutters up for a metre or so before parachuting down again. More usually the song is delivered from the cover of vegetation or in the sedge from an exposed perch, particularly by marsh warblers. Reed and sedge warblers often also sing at night.

edge warbler are generally mottled brown, uite different from the off-white, brown-otched eggs of the reed and marsh warblers. lso, incubation is chiefly by the female edge warbler, while both parents of the other pecies share this duty. When parents are eding young, both sexes can be seen flying and fro over the reeds, each carrying eakfuls of food. It takes a full month to lay nd incubate the eggs and then rear the estlings.

After leaving the nest, the young birds rely n their parents for food for a while. Marsh arblers, many of which leave the country y mid-August, have insufficient time to rear wo broods. Early arriving sedge warblers, nd reed warblers in southern England, do roduce a second brood.

Diet The breeding birds collect much of heir food outside the defended territory, but arsh-haunting and aquatic insects and their rvae form the bulk of the diet. The birds o take other animal foods, such as spiders, orms and slugs, and in autumn some berries re eaten. Reed-dwelling aphids are known to e important before migration. At this time ome sedge warblers double their weight in outhern England; the extra fat provides the nergy needed for the long flight south.

Distribution One striking difference be-ween the three species is their distribution vithin the British Isles. Sedge warblers occur a every county and are common even in

Above: The reed warbler, similar in appearance to the marsh warbler, does not have the conspicuous marking of the sedge warbler. It is pale brown above and buff white below. Male and female reed warblers have the same colouring so are difficult to tell apart. The female builds a deep, cylindrical-walled cup-shaped nest among common reeds; the sides are woven round the reed stems (left). Here it is feeding time for the chicks.

northern Scotland and western Ireland, where most other warblers are scarce. Only in upland areas and in Shetland are they thin on the ground. In contrast, the reed warbler is confined largely to the south and east of England and Wales, with perhaps a tenth as many breeding pairs. Sadly the best songster, the marsh warbler, is rare.

While shortage of habitat may be partly responsible for these differences, a study of the European distributions is revealing. Sedge warblers, for example, occur farther north than all European warblers except the willow and arctic, and therefore might be expected to be common throughout the British Isles. Reed warblers have a more southerly range and seem to need warm, dry summers which prevent colonisation of the north and west, even where suitable habitats appear to exist.

British-breeding marsh warblers are on the extreme western fringe of their range and, unless the European population extends westwards, our population is unlikely to increase significantly.

Kingfisher

The kingfisher is one of our most brilliantly coloured birds but its small size and rapid flight can make it difficult to spot. However, once seen it is seldom forgotten.

In flight the kingfisher looks like a flash of bright blue light as it skims fast and low over the water. It is one of Britain's most beautiful birds, with upper parts of an iridescent cobalt blue – or emerald green depending on the angle at which the light catches them – and a very noticeable paler blue streak stretching from nape to tail. The underparts and cheeks are a warm chestnut colour, which is most obvious when the bird is perching, and there's a patch of white on the throat and sides of the neck. And as if all this colour were not enough for one bird, the legs are a bright sealing-wax red. Juveniles generally have a duller plumage, shorter bills with a white tip and dark legs.

Opposite: Chalk streams such as the River Itchen in Hampshire are favoured haunts of the kingfisher. Inset: A stickleback meal helps to show the size of a kingfisher.

Below: Apart from its distinctive colouring, the kingfisher can be easily identified by its stumpy body, large head, short tail and long, dagger-shaped beak.

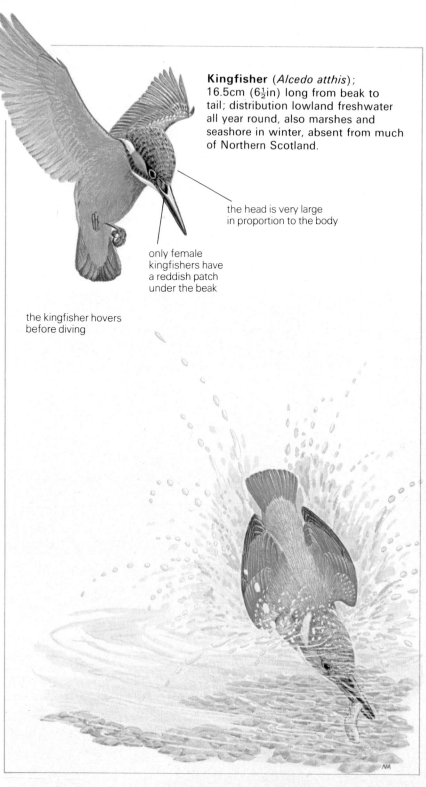

Kingfisher (*Alcedo atthis*);
16.5cm (6½in) long from beak to
tail; distribution lowland freshwater
all year round, also marshes and
seashore in winter, absent from much
of Northern Scotland.

the head is very large
in proportion to the body

only female
kingfishers have
a reddish patch
under the beak

the kingfisher hovers
before diving

the kingfisher's diet; but it will eat insects such as caddis fly larvae and dragonflies, as well as tadpoles, small molluscs and crustaceans such as crayfish.

As its name implies, the kingfisher is an expert fisher. It normally perches on a post or branch over the water, watching intently for fish; if a suitable perch is not available, it hovers over the water. The instant a fish is spotted the kingfisher dives headlong straight into the water and grabs its prey with its open, dagger-like beak; the complete action, from leaving the perch to returning to it, is over in a matter of seconds. Minnows may be immediately swallowed head first, but spiny fish such as sticklebacks are beaten against the kingfisher's perch until they are dead and their spines flat enough for the bird to swallow them comfortably. You might see the kingfisher juggling the fish in its beak to get it the right way up to swallow. On average, adults catch a fish once every two or three dives, while juveniles only catch one every eight or ten dives until they gain expertise. In learning the art, some young birds drown because they dive too often and their feathers become waterlogged.

Pairing and nest-building Throughout autumn and much of the winter individual kingfishers keep to their own territory, male and female using separate areas of water; but in January or February the pair bond is established or renewed. The birds chase each other, often at considerable heights, in a swooping, diving aerobatic display, or they perch on a branch bobbing and bowing to each other. The attentive male will even fetch fish to feed to his partner.

From mid-February to mid-April you may hear the infrequent song of the kingfisher—a rapid, high-pitched succession of varied whistles. The bird's normal and very distinctive call is a loud, shrill 'chee' or 'chikee'.

As the weather warms up the pair look for a nesting site, usually in an exposed bank of a stream or lake. Once a suitable location is found they excavate a tunnel, which they start by flying at the bank and driving in their strong bills; they then build a chamber at the end of it. The tunnel, anything from 15-100cm (6-40in) long depending on how hard the soil is, slopes gently upwards. If a suitable waterside bank is not to be had, the kingfisher will nest among the roots of a fallen tree or in a sandpit, sometimes as much as 300m (330yd) from the nearest water. If you spot a kingfisher flying through woodland, the chances are it will be fetching food to take to an inland nest.

You can recognize the nest by the circular entrance hole to the tunnel, positioned near the top of the bank. Later in the season, disgorged fish offal round the opening will provide evidence of a nest, as will the dark slime trickling from the hole—the excrement of the young which is directed into the tunnel from the nest chamber.

It would be surprising if such a colourful bird had escaped mention in myth and legend; the most attractive story comes from the ancient Greeks who said the bird—which they called 'halcyon'—bred in a floating nest at sea at the time of the winter solstice, calming high winds and stormy waves. Today 'halcyon' has come to mean any calm, peaceful and happy time.

Expert angler The place to spot the elusive kingfisher is near fresh, rather slow-flowing rivers, canals, lakes, ponds, streams, flooded gravel pits and even tiny streams in towns—almost wherever a ready supply of small fish such as minnows, bullheads and sticklebacks is to be had. These fish make up the bulk of

Raising a family Kingfishers lay eggs at any time between the end of March and early July. Pairs can rear two broods a season and sometimes even three. Male and female share in incubation, when the clutch – usually seven eggs – is complete. At first the eggs are a translucent pink but they turn a shiny white colour during the 19-21 day incubation period. Both adults diligently feed the young which are blind and naked when they hatch. The young are fed a diet of tiny fish at first. After about 10 days their eyes open and the first signs of feathers appear; after two weeks they can manage much larger fish. To encourage their parents to keep them well supplied with food, the young keep up a continuous trilling or purring sound; the hungriest stand at the front of the chamber calling for food while the more contented sleep at the rear. The accumulation of fish bones and regurgitated pellets, as well as the youngsters' excrement, make such a mess of the tunnel and chamber that the adults have to take a quick bath every time they leave the nest.

At the end of the breeding season the juveniles are chased out of the territory by their parents, who threaten them unmercifully and drive them out in noisy chases. Most go no more than six miles away, although some have been recorded as travelling up to 160 miles, mostly in the autumn, in search of fresh sources of food.

Hazards to survival Winter is an occupational hazard for all our resident birds and kingfishers are particularly vulnerable if the weather turns cold enough to freeze lakes and ponds and cut off the supply of fish. Many die of cold and starvation. Those lucky enough to find enough food to survive face an additional hazard – the alterations made by man to the watersides. Removal of trees used for perches, water pollution, the regrading of banks which destroys nesting sites and the levelling of streambeds which reduces the numbers of fish – all drastically affect the kingfisher's chances of survival. Fortunately, the kingfisher is still widespread over most of England, Wales and Ireland.

Above: Both male and female birds feed the young, who clamour incessantly for food; soon the nest chamber becomes littered with discarded fish bones.

Below: As part of the courtship ritual the male kingfisher offers his partner a fish. The female is the one with the reddish patch on the lower bill.

Birds of coast and estuary

Western Europe has a tremendously varied coastline, and nowhere is this more so than Britain. Much of it is low-lying, giving rise to wide, sandy and shallow bays so attractive to holidaymakers, and to sheltered and equally shallow estuaries. Here rivers bring some of the richness of the land to mingle with the richness of the sea in a warm environment, the mixture producing areas of mud and water, aesthetically pleasing to some people and unsightly to others, but undeniably extremely rich in a wide variety of food items for birds. The ooze teems with minute animal and plant life, as well as with worms, crustaceans and shellfish. Its surface carries plentiful seaweeds, and these harbour still more animals— especially snails. On the waters that ebb and flow above, fishes flourish in wide variety.

Such a richness in food is of great value to birds like gulls which are to be found all year round as well as to the few species of ducks and waders that breed on estuaries. Outside the breeding season, many other ducks and waders benefit from this food source. Many of these breed in the far north on the Arctic tundra, but move south to overwinter in unfrozen habitats. In consequence, they often have extensive migratory journeys to undertake, and so the estuaries of western Europe are vital 'staging posts'. Here the migrants may pause to rest, recuperate, perhaps moult, and 'refuel' by building up fat reserves, either to keep out the winter cold or to provide the energy necessary for those species migrating even further south into Africa.

Sadly, this estuarine habitat is under threat. Little known, poorly understood and often considered unsightly, it is a prime target for reclamation and subsequent industrial development with ready access by sea. From a conservation viewpoint, it is important that the vital role which this habitat plays in our ecosystem is more widely understood.

In the north and west, much of the European coast becomes spectacularly rocky, with towering cliffs, and here in the summer months huge seabird colonies develop. The safety of cliffs and offshore islands encourages the development of colonies of seabirds often tens or hundreds of thousands strong. The various species, though densely packed, each choose a slightly different nest site, and thus make full use of the terrain.

Just as important, although the seas nearby must be rich in fish, how do the various seabirds share out this resource? As in the case of the structural adaptations of duck or wader beaks, comparing cliff-nesting seabird foods and feeding techniques makes fascinating reading, and includes the spectacular dive and plunge of the gannet, emerging triumphantly with its wriggling prey, to the seemingly impossible food gathering feat of the puffin, which somehow manages to carry as many as sixty sandeels, held cross-wise in its beak, at one time.

Opposite: Herring gulls on a quay awaiting the arrival of the fishermen and the inevitable free meal.

Fulmar, Leach's and storm petrels

Petrels are ocean-going birds that include the gull-like fulmar and its smaller, sooty relatives, the storm petrel and the Leach's petrel. They spend their lives gliding over the waves in search of food, only visiting land to breed.

Gliders and flutterers

The fulmar, together with the storm petrel and the Leach's petrel, are all related to that giant among oceanic birds, the albatross, as well as to the shearwaters, aptly named after their habit of skimming low over the waves.

The fulmar looks completely different compared to the other two petrels. It is about double the size of its relatives, mainly white and much like a gull. It nests on open cliffs and in summer can be seen all day long near the coast. The storm petrel and the Leach's petrel, on the other hand, are quite small for seabirds (lighter in weight than a song thrush) and are sooty black all over save for a white patch on the rump. They come ashore to their nests, in deep burrows or natural crevices in the rocks, only after dark.

Tubular beaks All petrels are distinguished from other seabirds by their complex beak structure. Viewed close up, the beak is made up of a series of plates of horny material, with clearly visible joints or sutures in between. In addition, the ridge of the beak is topped with a horny tube that gives the group another colloquial name—the 'tube-noses'.

The precise function of this narrow tube is not properly understood. One theory is that it serves these seabirds—most of them extremely efficient high-speed gliders—as an air-speed indicator, in much the same way as does a 'Pitot tube' on a modern aircraft. Another theory suggests that it functions as a genuine nostril. The sense of smell is poorly developed in most birds, but many petrels emit a powerful, musty odour, and returning birds may possibly 'scent out' their mates not only after dark but also deep in nesting burrows.

Success story The fulmar is at the centre of one of the most amazing bird success stories of the last 100 years. For over 900 years, the only known British breeding station was on the remote island of St Kilda, 50 miles west of the Outer Hebrides. Then, in the middle of the 19th century, the Icelandic fulmar population began to expand, and in 1878 other colonies began to be reported on Scottish islands, the first on Foula.

Since then, there has been no stopping the birds extraordinary spread. First the northern islands were colonised, followed by the cliffs of both the east and west coasts of Britain and Ireland, until by 1970 fulmars were nesting on all suitable stretches of rocky coast. Even in some apparently quite unsuitable areas they find a way to succeed. In the Hebrides, there are now nests on the ground in remote and undisturbed sand dunes, and on the cliff-less coasts of southern and eastern England. The birds have even commandeered nuclear power station window sills as the nearest alternative to a cliff ledge.

Fulmars have also moved inland. Nesting was first reported on ruined buildings in the Shetlands, but now quarries several miles from the sea in northern England have breeding pairs.

There is no certain reason for this success. It may be that there was a sudden genetic change in the birds themselves, or that the North Atlantic warmed slightly and produced more fish. A more likely explanation is related to the fulmars' diet, which consists mainly of offal. The rise in numbers coincided with the time when whaling reached a peak in the Atlantic—with abundant supplies of offal both at sea and near the shore. Although whaling has now been curtailed, modern fishing (with a great deal of the catch gutted at sea) has taken over this food-providing role.

Fulmar (*Fulmarus glacialis*), 47cm (18½in) from beak to tail. Long stiff wings, grey upper parts, white underparts.

Storm petrel (*Hydrobates pelagicus*), 15cm (6in) from beak to tail. Pale wing bar, white rump, squarish tail.

Leach's petrel (*Oceanodroma leucorrhoa*), 20cm (8in) from beak to tail. Diagonal paler wing band, white rump with dark stripe, forked tail.

Above: The fulmar slices through the air like a guided missile, while the much smaller storm petrel, resembling a large black moth, flutters feebly on an erratic flight path. The Leach's petrel is more positive in flight, but retains the erratic flight of its smaller cousin.

Opposite: At their nesting site on an open cliff, fulmars will 'spit' a foul smelling fluid (regurgitated from the stomach) to deter any intruders.

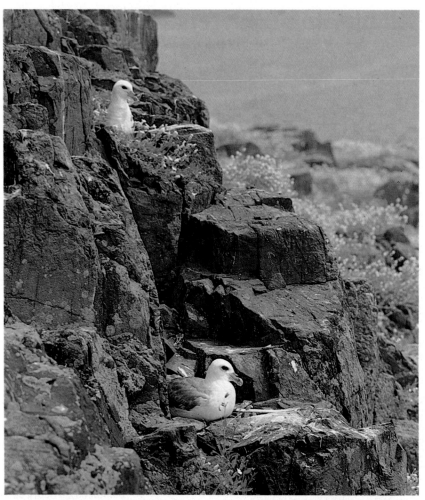

Slow breeders The fulmars' success is particularly surprising in the light of their low reproductive capacity. Once they have fledged from their simple cliff ledge nests fulmars remain 'adolescent', roaming around the North Atlantic, for at least five years. After this period they visit the cliffs in spring and summer – prospecting for a nest site and seeking a mate – for another two or three years before they breed for the first time at about eight years old.

Only a single large chalky-white egg is laid and this often cannot be replaced if it, or the chick, is lost to a predator. And these losses do occur, despite the fulmar's vigorous defence of its nest (see the box on aggression).

Long life The dangers inherent in such a lengthy breeding cycle seem to be offset by the lifespan of this bird. (Research workers have found it difficult to make a ring strong enough to resist the abrasion caused by the fulmar shuffling about awkwardly on the rocks.) But those results obtained from detailed studies by Aberdeen University suggest that many fulmars live for as long as 30 years, and a proportion may be a good deal older. At that rate, even laying only one egg a year, the fulmar pair have ample time to produce offspring several times over and ensure the population explosion that we have witnessed.

Fulmars in flight Out at sea or twisting and turning in the eddies and updraughts near

Aggression in birds

Birds normally resort to aggression only to protect their breeding territory from competitors, or defend their feeding areas from predators. Competition between birds is almost always confined to birds of the same species, other birds being tolerated or ignored. The response to predators varies. Starlings, for instance, just gather and swoop around – or 'mob' – a hunting kestrel, while the meadow pipit may press home an attack against a marauding cuckoo to the point of causing feathers to fly.

The fulmar is unusually well equipped to repel intruders. Once in its digestive system, the fulmar's plankton food is converted into an oily and smelly fluid. The fulmar can 'spit' this with great accuracy at predators venturing near its nest – even at several metres range. Sometimes it will pursue an intruder and 'shoot it down' in mid-air, the predator landing immediately and preening vigorously to remove the foul-smelling oil that is clogging its plumage.

Most birds, however, rely on plumage and posture to convey their aggression. The fluffed-up cock blackbirds patrolling each side of the invisible boundary between their territories are a good example. Robins use their red breasts to warn rivals off their territory (see page 272), even going to the extent of attacking with great ferocity stuffed 'model' robins placed in their territory by researchers.

Above: These fulmars are nesting among the rocks and flowering sea campion on the island of Inner Farne, off Northumberland.

Right: The fulmar lays only one large, dull-white egg in its clutch, usually in some sort of surface hollow. Incubation – at around 50 days – is long and potentially hazardous.

Below: This young Leach's petrel, a ball of sooty down, is hidden in a burrow excavated by the parents.

heir nesting cliffs, fulmars provide the birdwatcher with a flying spectacular. They are expert gliders, rarely flapping their wings except on a still day. Gull-sized and grey and white in colour, they may look rather dumpy with short, slender and stiff wings held slightly down-curved. But they are very well streamlined. Their large eyes are set deep in grooves in the feathers and, except when the birds are on the nest, the feet are normally concealed, tucked up out of the way in the body feathers.

Near the cliffs, fulmars use their webbed feet to assist in steering or to make fine adjustments to their flying techniques. They seem able to take advantage of any wind, cutting at speed diagonally across the wind and also downwind in a shallow dive before turning sharply into the wind to gain height again. They then repeat the process. Even the slight up-currents raised by the face of oncoming waves are exploited to give that extra bit of 'free' aerodynamic lift.

Storm petrels are sooty black, save for a white patch along the rump which divides off the square, black tail. They nest on many islands to the west and north of Britain – and often apparently enormous numbers can be heard purring in their burrows. However, any census of these small black birds, which nest in holes and come ashore only after dark, is difficult to carry out with much accuracy.

The Leach's petrel is slightly larger than the storm petrel, with a grey patch on the wing, a forked tail and a dark line down the centre of its rump. One of our scarcest birds, it nests only on a handful of remote islands like St Kilda, where its wild whooping and whistling song can sound quite chilling to the birdwatcher.

Nocturnal activities Towards dusk petrels journey back home to land, either loaded with plankton food for their single dark, fluffy offspring, or anxious to relieve their mate incubating the small, almost spherical white egg. Before they enter their nest these birds gather offshore to await the dark and the safety that darkness brings from predators such as the great black-backed gull.

In winter, these small petrels truly become birds of the open sea (pelagic). They cover the oceans in their search for minute food items from the surface plankton, which they gather while swimming or by dipping down to the waves in flight. Often storm petrels follow in the wake of ships, sometimes pattering their feet on the surface, for mile after mile in the hope of collecting a meal from the scraps tossed overboard. In the days of the sailing ships this habit endeared them to sailors on long voyages and earned them the name 'Mother Carey's chickens' – the reason for which remains obscure, but probably refers to *Mater Cara*, the sailors' name for the Virgin Mary.

Above: The storm, or stormy, petrel is among the smallest and most fragile of seabirds. It touches land only during the breeding season, and then only from dusk to dawn. At other times it is a truly oceanic bird, often following ships in pursuit of scraps, and skimming low over the water.

Below: From humble beginnings nearly 1000 years ago on the island of St Kilda (circled in red), the fulmar population has now spread dramatically round the British coast.

○ distribution in 1800
■ current distribution

Manx shearwater

Manx shearwaters nest in burrows, and the sound of their wailing calls, coming from underground at dead of night, has inspired legends of trolls.

Manx shearwaters are slender-winged sea-birds about the size of a small gull. As their name suggests, shearwaters at sea skim low over the water, occasionally touching and 'shearing' through a wave-top as they bank and turn. The wings are relatively long and narrow, in comparison with those of a gull, and in flight they are usually held at right angles to the body, with the leading edge held very straight. For much of the time the wings are stiff, and the tips are bowed slightly downwards.

The plumages of adults and young are similar; dark, oily black above, and white below. The boundary between dark and light comes roughly at water level when the birds are swimming on the sea; although apparently very conspicuous, this distribution of colour hides the somewhat vulnerable shearwaters well from predators such as gulls that approach from above, or large fishes approaching from below.

In flight, however, their plumage is conspicuous; together with the characteristic flight pattern, it makes them easy to recognise at all but the longest ranges. They fly fast and low, often vanishing from view in the wave troughs, which may cause some difficulty in spotting them; but then they bank and turn, first presenting a white undersurface, then black upperparts, to the birdwatcher.

Long-distance gliders At sea, shearwaters cover prodigious distances, and are masters of the art of energy-conserving flight. Most often, they fly in a long, shallow glide down and along the ocean wind, then suddenly turn into the wind, using it to gain a violent uplift at the expense of flight speed, before heading off downwind again in another long glide. Shearwaters are seen performing this spectacular type of flight as they pass along the coast, either on migration or, in the breeding season, on fishing excursions. They often fly in groups, usually in a straggling line.

They are most frequently seen off our south and west coasts. In summer they can be watched in the vicinity of any shearwater

Above: A Manx shearwater: the name 'Manx' refers to a historic colony on the Calf o Man. After centuries of breeding there, shearwaters were absent for 150 years, returning in the 1960s.

Manx shearwater
(*Puffinus puffinus*). Summer visitor. Sexes alike. 36cm (14in).

Manx shearwater distribution

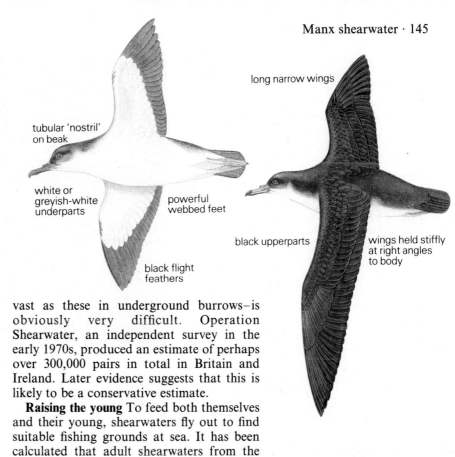

tubular 'nostril' on beak

white or greyish-white underparts

powerful webbed feet

black flight feathers

long narrow wings

black upperparts

wings held stiffly at right angles to body

colony. These are located on the Isles of Scilly, Lundy, Skokholm, Skomer, Anglesey, some of the islands off the eastern Irish coasts, and many of the islands off the rocky western Scottish and Irish coasts.

Island colonies Most shearwater breeding areas are on remote islands, often uninhabited or at most with just a few human occupants. Shearwaters are clumsy on land; they have powerful webbed feet, and their legs are situated close to the rear of their bodies–which makes them effective swimmers. However, this makes walking on land rather difficult for them. They can only drag themselves along at a painfully slow rate. As a result, they easily fall victim to marauding gulls.

Greater black-backed gulls, in particular, specialise in catching shearwaters. It takes these large gulls only a couple of powerful bites to open the carcase and snip the wings off the shoulders. Then, with a few flicks of the gull's strong neck muscles, the shearwater is skinned and ready for eating. Around the nests of these predatory gulls, the discarded shearwater skins accumulate in a gruesome midden. Despite this vulnerability, shearwaters seem to be maintaining steady populations in most of the areas they inhabit.

As dusk falls, shearwaters gather offshore, floating on the sea in huge 'rafts'. They remain there for some hours, deriving a measure of safety in numbers, and venture ashore only when it is completely dark. Most colonies are on the cliff top, or close to the shore of low-lying islands. One striking exception to this norm is more than a mile from the sea and about 600m (2000ft) up on the rocky screes in the heart of the island of Rhum in the Inner Hebrides.

By day, anyone walking along the cliff top could be excused for not suspecting that there was a shearwater colony nearby. There is little outward sign of their presence in daylight except for the occasional carcase of a shearwater that fell victim to a gull the previous night.

At night, especially on a dark and stormy night, the scene changes dramatically. Homecoming birds fly past overhead with a rush of air, and call to their partners in the nesting burrows with extraordinary cackling, cooing and caterwauling calls. Those in the burrows make similar calls, and the sound of these, coming from the ground and after dark, has inspired legends. The troll legends of Norway, in particular, are said to have originated from these weird sounds.

Shearwater numbers Shearwaters are always colonial, but while some new colonies may only hold a few dozen pairs, others are huge. The one on Rhum was estimated to contain over 100,000 pairs in 1976, while the one on Skomer was estimated at 95,000 pairs in 1973. Counting birds such as shearwaters–which have black upperparts, come ashore only after dark, and nest in numbers as

vast as these in underground burrows–is obviously very difficult. Operation Shearwater, an independent survey in the early 1970s, produced an estimate of perhaps over 300,000 pairs in total in Britain and Ireland. Later evidence suggests that this is likely to be a conservative estimate.

Raising the young To feed both themselves and their young, shearwaters fly out to find suitable fishing grounds at sea. It has been calculated that adult shearwaters from the

The shearwater's underground nest

Often nests are made in rabbit burrows. The shearwaters evict the hapless rabbits, using their sharp claws and hooked beaks to secure vacant possession of a suitable-sized burrow.

entrance   nest chamber

Above: Shearwater pairs that do not take over rabbit burrows dig new ones for themselves in the soft, peaty soil of the cliff top. A typical burrow consists of an entrance tunnel and a slightly larger nest chamber, which is lined with fronds of bracken and pieces of grass.

Right: A shearwater nesting site, as it appears after many years of burrowing.

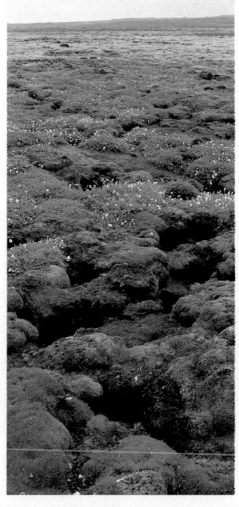

Welsh colonies travel as far afield as the Bay of Biscay to find food, returning within one to two days. Most of their food is small in size and taken from the zooplankton, and includes many species of fishes and the young stages of crustaceans and molluscs. The shearwaters fish by diving from the surface and swimming powerfully under water.

The young shearwater, on emerging from the egg, soon develops large quantities of fluffy grey down, and resembles a ball of fluff from which eyes, beak and feet appear incongruously. The parents feed it with a smelly, oily mixture of fish and plankton which is regurgitated from the crop, where it is stored on the long fishing journeys. This mixture is highly nutritious, and the chick grows quickly, becoming very fat. The layer of fat it acquires provides a useful reserve food store for the chick. This is vitally needed, for the parental feeding visits are made after dark, and may not occur every night.

Expert navigators A shearwater has remarkable powers of navigation. Around its 70th or 80th night, the chick fledges: it spends a short time performing vigorous wing-flapping exercises before taking off on its maiden flight. On this journey, without the guidance of an accompanying parent, the young shearwater heads for wintering grounds out at sea off the coast of Brazil. Some birds, however, certainly do go astray. They are liable to be diverted by the violent winds of the south Atlantic. There is one record of a ringed shearwater washed up dead on the coast of southern Australia.

Manx shearwaters have good homing powers, too. Some years ago, an adult female was removed from the egg she was incubating in a burrow on Skokholm, Pembrokeshire, and flown (by aircraft) to Boston in the United States. There, she was released from a tall building. She had returned to her burrow before the letter announcing her release had reached the island!

Above: A Manx shearwater chick in the burrow. Its parents feed it on fishes and marine plankton.

Right: The single egg is usually laid in late May or June. It is oval in shape and a non-reflective white, although its colour soon changes, for it becomes stained by the peaty soil. The parents share the task of incubating, sitting in spells of three to five days and changing over at night. Change-overs may be delayed if bright moonlight illuminates the area and makes the returning bird easily visible to predators such as gulls. Bad weather may also delay the return of the partner bird. Incubation lasts just over 50 days.

Left: A young shearwater, about to reach the age when it will depart on its migratory flight. Fledging usually takes between 70 and 80 days; for about the last 10 days the chick is not visited or fed by its parents. By the time they cease feeding the chick, it has grown far too heavy to fly, and its excess weight is used to complete feather and muscle development as well as for day-to-day sustenance. Eventually, it will struggle out of its burrow and indulge in vigorous wing-flapping exercises to bring its muscles into tone for its maiden flight.

Goosander and red-breasted merganser

The goosander and the red-breasted merganser—two quite similar fish-eating ducks—are often called sawbills. They get this name from the tooth-like serrations along the sides of their long, narrow bills. These savage-looking features enable them to take a firm grip on their fishy prey.

Below: The male goosander has a greenish-black head and back, with white underparts.

Bottom left: A female goosander, followed by ten young: she is probably fostering several broods.

Bottom right: Both the goosander and the red-breasted merganser breed in northern Britain, but only the latter breeds in Ireland.

The goosander is a large bird, about 65cm (26in) long, with a wingspan of up to 95cm (38in). The male has a black head, neck and back, with a glossy green sheen. His head bears a distinctive crest of feathers, and his long bill and his legs are reddish orange. His underparts are pure white, contrasting strongly with the head and back. The rump, belly and tail are grey. In flight, even more white shows, as virtually the whole of the inner half of the wing is white, with just a few black streaks; the outer half is black. The female is grey above and white below, with a chestnut head and neck, and a slight shaggy crest. In flight the rear half of her inner wing is white, and the forewing grey.

Arrival of a species Goosanders breed in northern latitudes throughout the Northern

Goosander distribution

Red-breasted merganser distribution

Hemisphere. Rather confusingly, they are known in North America as common mergansers. It has been estimated that there are about 75,000 goosanders in north-west Europe, with between 900 and 1250 pairs breeding in the British Isles, mainly in Scotland. Yet the first definite breeding record of a goosander in Britain was as recent as 1871, when single pairs bred in Perthshire and in Argyll.

There had been rumours of breeding attempts earlier than that, in 1858 and again in 1862, but certainly the goosander was a rare winter visitor to Scotland before the 1870s. However, from about that time it became increasingly common, with winter influxes presumably leading to birds staying for the summer and breeding. By the turn of the century it had spread to most western Scottish counties, from Sutherland to Argyll, and was moving eastwards across the country.

During the first part of this century, breeding spread to the east coast counties of Aberdeen and Angus, and southwards to Renfrew, Selkirk and Dumfries. In 1975 it was estimated that there were up to 950 pairs in Scotland.

Summering birds were present in Northumberland from the late 1920s onwards, but it was not until 1941 that the first breeding record for England occurred in that county. The first nesting in Cumberland was in 1950, and during the next 10-15 years the birds spread south into County Durham, Westmorland and Lancashire, and bred in North Wales from about 1968. Today there are about 150 pairs breeding in Northumberland, with at least another 100 pairs in other English counties, and about 10 in Wales.

This increase and spread, welcome as it might be to birdwatchers, has been met with considerable opposition from fishermen, river bailiffs and others involved with trout and salmon fishing. It is claimed that goosanders cause great damage by taking young fish, and the birds are widely shot, although there is no direct evidence that they are harming the fish populations.

Two fish-eating ducks

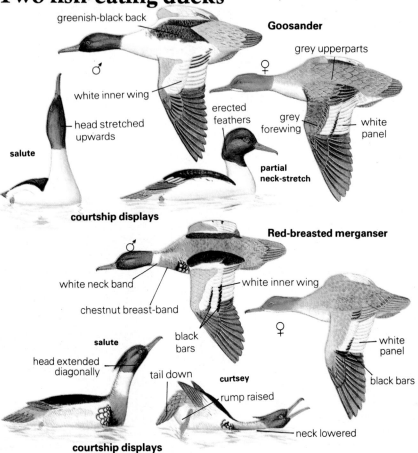

Goosander

greenish-black back
grey upperparts
white inner wing
erected feathers
grey forewing
white panel
head stretched upwards
salute
partial neck-stretch
courtship displays

Red-breasted merganser

white neck band
white inner wing
chestnut breast-band
black bars
white panel
black bars
salute
head extended diagonally
tail down
curtsey
rump raised
neck lowered
courtship displays

Goosander (*Mergus merganser*). Resident duck, nesting beside upland rivers and lakes. 65cm (26in).

Red-breasted merganser (*Mergus serrator*). Resident duck, mainly coastal. Up to 58cm (23in).

Below left: The red breast of the merganser is really bright chestnut, while the female goosander (below) has a chestnut head.

Both goosanders and red-breasted mergansers have serrated bills, with which they grip their catch. They feed on many fish species, mainly those between 10 and 20cm (4-8in) long.

sharp teeth

Lakes and upland rivers Goosanders generally nest in holes in trees or banks, or among rocks, though they readily breed in nest-boxes and have used holes in buildings, from the cellar to the roof-space. The nest is usually within a few metres of water, though it can be up to a kilometre away. The female excavates a slight hollow within the selected hole, and lines it with whatever pieces of material or debris are within reach. She lays 8-11 eggs, and incubates them for about 30 days, the male taking no part in this, nor in rearing the young. The latter takes about two months.

Goosanders nest beside freshwater lakes, and along the upper reaches of fast-flowing rivers and streams. In winter they descend to the broader lower reaches, including estuaries, and also appear on reservoirs and gravel pits in small numbers. The principal food is fish, which they catch by diving, though they may first locate their prey by swimming on the surface with just the head and neck submerged. Underwater, they use only their feet to propel themselves, keeping their wings closed tightly. Dives can last for as much as two minutes, but half a minute is more usual, and they probably do not dive deeper than about 4m (2 fathoms).

The red-breasted merganser This duck is between 50 and 58cm (20-23in) in length, with a wingspan of up to 85cm (34in). The male has a black head, shot with green, ending in a ragged crest. His neck is white, contrasting with a broad chestnut breast-band. His upperparts are mainly black (with a green gloss) and grey, with grey flanks, though a broad white band shows on the closed wings. The underparts are white. The bill and legs are red. The inner half of the wing is white, but crossed by two black bars, and with a dark leading edge. The outer wing is dark.

The female is very similar to the female goosander, but has a larger shaggy crest and a duller chestnut head, and no sharp dividing line between the colour of her neck and breast. In flight, her wing pattern is more obviously barred black and white.

Expanding population The red-breasted merganser has a very similar distribution to that of the goosander, occurring all round the

Above: A male red-breasted merganser with his shaggy crest. Unfortunately, both goosanders and red-breasted mergansers are persecuted on Scottish rivers because they are believed to eat too many young trout and salmon. There is, however, little direct evidence of just how much damage the birds may be doing to fisheries. Despite extensive shooting, and destruction of nests, the birds continue to flourish.

Below: Red-breasted mergansers on the sea. They are almost purely fish-eaters, obtaining their prey by diving. Unlike the goosander, they use their wings to propel themselves, being one of the few species of birds that 'fly' under water.

Northern Hemisphere, but extending further north, well into the Arctic. There are thought to be about 40,000 birds in north-west Europe, of which up to 2000 pairs breed in Britain.

The red-breasted merganser has probably always been a British breeding species, but at the same time that the goosander was colonizing the country, it underwent a marked expansion, in both range and numbers, which is probably still continuing. It now breeds throughout the northern and western parts of Scotland, extending south through south-west Scotland into north-west England, where it first bred in 1950. It is now quite widespread in Cumbria, particularly in the Lake District, and has bred in North Wales since about 1953.

A coast dweller The red-breasted merganser is mainly a marine species, breeding around the coasts of Scotland, in sheltered bays and inlets as well as in estuaries. The birds also enter the lower parts of rivers, remaining separate from the goosanders, which breed in the upper reaches. During the winter they are found mainly on the sea, though sometimes occurring on inland freshwater lakes. Some large flocks are seen in certain estuaries, for example the Beauly Firth near Inverness, where up to 1000 have been counted.

The nest is nearly always on the ground, concealed in thick vegetation, or among tree roots or in hollows and crevices on banks and low cliffs. Small islands are favoured for nesting, presumably for added safety from predators. The nest is rarely more than a few metres from the water. The female scrapes a shallow depression and lines it with any available grass or leaves. In it she lays 8-10 eggs and incubates them for about a month. Neighbouring broods may amalgamate, some being cared for by a single foster mother.

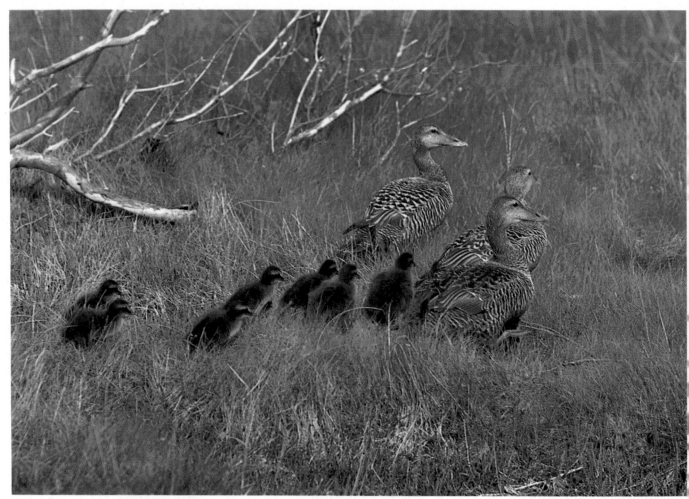

Eider, common and velvet scoters

Eiders and scoters are seafaring ducks that dive in shallow coastal waters to wrench mussels and other shellfishes from the rocks of the sea-bed. They have in common a broad, strong bill to crunch the shells of their victims, and in almost all species a proportion of the male's plumage is black.

Seen at a distance, the male eider is a handsome black and white bird, with black sides and tail and a black cap on its head, set off by a white chest, neck, face and back. Closer to, one can see more subtle colouring: pastel green on the back of the head, and soft pink on the breast. The bill is dull green and has a lobe on either side running back towards the eye. In complete contrast, the female is brown all over, much mottled and barred in shades of brown to produce perfect camouflage. This is vitally important when she is sitting on the nest, for she must conceal herself from predators.

The male eider also appears in other plumages, for example during the annual moult in late summer: at this time, he loses the majority of his white plumage and for a time looks much more like a dark female. Then, during the time when the males are developing their full plumage, there is a period when the black and white patterning is rather variable between individual males.

Another variation is seen in the immature males. Male eiders do not attain their full adult plumage until they are in their second year, and in their first year they have a distinctive immature plumage; this consists of a white breast, with light and dark brown on all other parts of the bird.

Life on our northern coasts The eider breeds commonly all round the coasts of Scotland, except in the extreme south-west; it penetrates into northern England in Northumberland and, on the west coast, at a few locations in Cumbria. It has been estimated that there

Above: When the young eiders have hatched, they are soon able to walk. The parents immediately lead them to the sea, where they learn to swim. Here, three adult females lead seven chicks—doubtless a 'crèche' in which three broods are combined—to the water. Once on the sea, the chicks have survived their time of greatest danger, for they are out of range of foxes and other predators. These chicks may be all that remain of an original total of about 16.

Distribution

☐ eider
■ common scoter

are about 20,000 to 25,000 pairs of eider breeding in Britain, making it our second commonest breeding duck after the mallard.

In most of the breeding locations, the pairs nest several metres apart; each nest is placed in a slight hollow, or in the shelter of a boulder or tuft of vegetation. In certain locations, however, especially where there is a degree of protection, for example on a small islet, or where man actively discourages predators such as foxes, large colonies form, hundreds or even thousands strong.

Eiders are not long-distance migrants: after the breeding season, the parents take the young ducks down to the sea and the families leave the breeding grounds. They gather together in flocks in sheltered estuaries and bays. In some locations on the sea, for example the Moray Firth and the mouth of the Firth of Tay, several thousand eiders congregate.

A crusty meal Eiders eat various kinds of shellfish, including mussels, as well as crabs. They crush these in their powerful beaks,

Above: Down falls out of the female eider's plumage, particularly from her breast, and she uses this to good purpose. If she has to leave the nest, she covers the eggs with down (as shown) to conceal them from predators. To keep the eggs warm, she also lines the nest with down. In Iceland and Norway, eiders are 'farmed' or encouraged to breed in special reserves; when they have completed breeding, the down is collected for sale. The down from over 100 nests is needed to fill one sleeping bag.

Above left: A female eider incubates her eggs. Clutches usually contain 4-6 eggs.

Eider (*Somateria mollissima*). Diving duck, resident. 58cm (23in).

Common scoter (*Melanitta nigra*). Diving duck; small breeding population; large wintering population. Length 48cm (19in).

Velvet scoter *(Melanitta fusca)*. Mainly a winter coastal visitor. 55cm (22in).

discard the hard shells and eat the soft meat inside. Because they live most of their lives in tidal waters, eiders have adapted to feeding in a variety of water depths. Thus they can dive as deep as 15m (45ft) in order to reach mussels growing on the sea-bed. They wrench them off the rocks on which they are attached, and bring them to the surface to eat them.

In shallower water, eiders merely upend to reach their food, while in shallower water still they need only dip their heads under the surface to reach the bottom. Another feeding technique is adopted to catch crabs in soft mud. When the mud is covered with a few centimetres of water, the eiders sit over a likely patch and then paddle vigorously with their feet, stirring up the mud and forming a shallow crater. They then probe into the crater with their bills, hoping to feel and then grasp an unwary crab.

Vagrant species Three other species of eider occur in Britain, all as vagrants. All three breed in the Arctic (the king eider most widely) with some colonies in Iceland and many more in Greenland and Spitsbergen. The spectacled eider breeds in north-east Siberia, and Alaska, while the small Steller's eider also breeds in Siberia, with just a handful of pairs in Norway. One or two king eiders and Steller's eiders are seen in most years in the waters around the Hebrides, Orkneys and Shetlands, and some individuals stay there for months or even years.

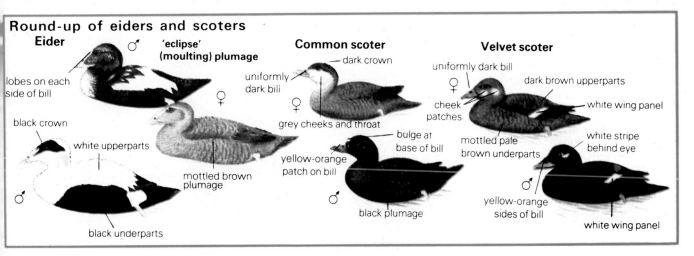

Round-up of eiders and scoters

Eider
'eclipse' (moulting) plumage
lobes on each side of bill
black crown
white upperparts
mottled brown plumage
black underparts

Common scoter
dark crown
uniformly dark bill
grey cheeks and throat
bulge at base of bill
yellow-orange patch on bill
black plumage

Velvet scoter
uniformly dark bill
dark brown upperparts
cheek patches
white wing panel
mottled pale brown underparts
white stripe behind eye
yellow-orange sides of bill
white wing panel

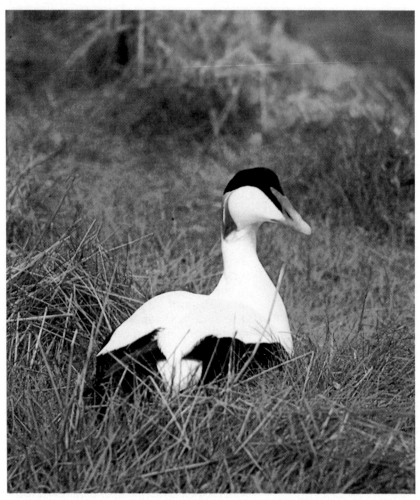

Two main scoter species Scoters are shell-fish divers like the eider, but can be recognised easily because a greater proportion of their plumage is black. Indeed, the male common scoter is black all over, with a glossy sheen of either purple or green. The only relief to the dark colouring is on his bill, the upper mandible of which has a large yellow-orange patch, outlined in black. Another interesting feature is the black knob at the base of the bill.

The female common scoter is a dull dark brown, with a paler brown face and under-parts. Her bill is dark. The pale cheeks and dark crown to her head give a distinctive 'capped' appearance.

The velvet scoter is very similar to the common scoter, and is best distinguished, both male and female, by the white markings on the wings. These show clearly in flight, but when resting on the water they are often concealed. The male velvet scoter has a tiny white patch behind the eye, and the sides of the bill, rather than the top, are orange-yellow. The female has two pale brown patches on her cheeks either side of the eye, and lacks the 'capped' appearance of the female common scoter.

Scoter populations The common scoter breeds in very small numbers in Britain and Ireland; there are a little over a hundred pairs in Ireland, mostly in the north and west, and perhaps 50 pairs in Scotland, again confined to the north and west. In winter,

Above: The strikingly coloured—and thus very conspicuous—male eider takes no part in the incubation or rearing of the young. This one is therefore merely resting.

Below: A male velvet scoter. In general, the scoter's dives last for as long as 20 or 30 seconds, compared with the eider's longer dives of 30-35 seconds. Both eiders and scoters do, however, sometimes make exceptionally long dives, lasting for over a minute.

however, many thousands of scoters visit our shores from Scandinavian and Russian breeding grounds, and some also come from Iceland. These flocks are found in various sections of our coastal waters, always where the sea is shallow and usually in a location that is sheltered from the worst weather. Thus flocks of thousands can be seen in the Moray Firth, the Firth of Forth, the Wash, the Thames Estuary and Carmarthen Bay in South Wales. It is thought that between 35,000 and 45,000 winter in Britain.

The velvet scoter does not breed in Britain, but winter visitors from Scandinavia and Russia can be found in eastern Scotland, particularly in the Moray Firth and the Firth of Forth; numbers are usually between 2000 and 3000.

Lakeside breeding grounds The common scoters breeding in the British Isles do so on the banks of freshwater lakes, usually quite large ones. The nests are concealed in clumps of vegetation, often heather, and may be placed on the shore, or on a small island. If there is a suitable island, then several pairs may nest in close proximity. The female carries out all the tasks of incubating the eggs and rearing the young, without any help from the male.

When on the freshwater breeding lakes, scoters live mainly on the larvae of dragon-flies and caddisflies, as well as eating fresh-water mussels.

Wintering on the sea Both the common and the velvet scoter live on the sea in winter. Here they feed mainly on shellfish—mussels, cockles, clams and whelks. These they obtain by diving, usually in water depths between 2m and 6m (6-20ft). Common scoters and velvet scoters often occur together in flocks in winter, and it seems probable that their diet is similiar, though velvet scoters are more frequently seen close to the shore, and probably find a slightly different range of food here.

The surf scoter This is the only other species of scoter to occur in the British Isles. It occurs as a rare vagrant, chiefly in the north and west of Scotland and Ireland. Its breeding grounds are in North America.

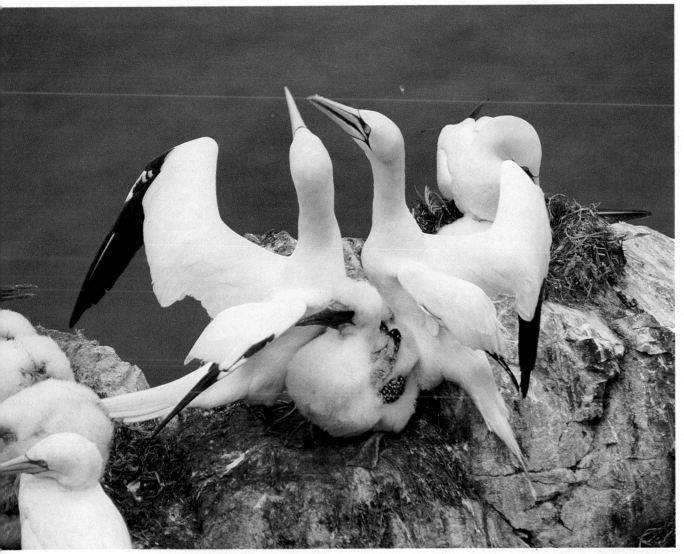

Gannet

Above: Gannets greet each other with raised bills.

A gannetry in spring or summer is a breathtaking spectacle:
the cliffs and rocks are white with many thousands of
these large seabirds. The air, too, is filled with gannets in
soaring flight, each ready to plunge into the sea for fish,
perhaps from a height of 30m (100ft) or more.

Gannetry sites

1 Herma Ness; **2** Noss; **3**
Foula; **4** Fair Isle; **5** Sula Sgeir;
6 Sule Stack; **7** Flannans; **8** St
Kilda; **9** Bass Rock; **10** Ailsa
Craig; **11** Scar Rocks; **12**
Bempton; **13** Gt Saltee; **14**
Little Skellig; **15** Bull Rock; **16**
Grassholm; **17, 18** Alderney.

The gannet is our biggest and most spectacular seabird, with a body length of about 1m
(3ft) and a wingspan approaching 2m (over
5ft). It is essentially a maritime bird, breeding
in cliff colonies called gannetries, although
very occasionally storm-driven gannets are
seen on lakes and reservoirs inland.

Goose-like bird The adult gannet is a large,
almost goose-like white bird with a yellow
ochre tinge to the head and nape and conspicuous black wingtips. The yellow colour is
mostly lost in winter. In flight, its appearance
is less goose-like, mainly because the stout
neck and beak in front are counterbalanced
by a long, pointed white tail, whereas geese
have very short tails and a characteristically
unbalanced appearance in flight. The wings,
long and noticeably slender, are white for
much of their length but with mostly black
primaries, or flight feathers. Gannets are often
seen flying along the shore, maintaining a
height of about 10m (30ft) above the water.
The steady flight pattern consists of a series of
slow wingbeats, followed by a glide. In small
flocks, often all or most birds will pause to
glide with precisely timed synchrony.

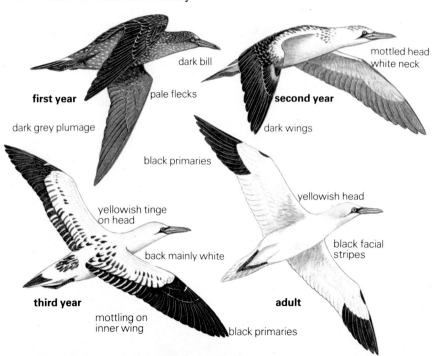

first year
dark bill
pale flecks
dark grey plumage
black primaries

second year
mottled head
white neck
dark wings

third year
yellowish tinge on head
back mainly white
mottling on inner wing
black primaries

adult
yellowish head
black facial stripes
black primaries

In close-up view when perched, the gannet's webbed feet can be seen to be lead grey, with a neat blue-grey line running along each toe and down the front of the 'shin' or tarsus. The beak, stout and dagger-like, is almost 15cm (6in) long, and is silver coloured, with black lines. On the face a patch of grey or bluish naked skin surrounds a glaring eye with a strikingly pale iris.

Remote gannetries Gannets are colonial breeders, and their expansion in numbers over the last hundred years is one of the more striking bird success stories. There are now 18 gannetries off our coasts, no less than 11 of them founded this century.

The current increase in gannet numbers may partly be a restoration to an earlier situation following an intervening decline. Certainly during the 18th and 19th centuries gannets were persecuted by man, the fat and nutritious nestlings being slaughtered for food in tens of thousands by the inhabitants of some of our remote islands. This pressure has ended with the modernisation of our food industry, and with bird protection laws.

At the same time, it seems most unlikely that the current rate of increase, some 3% per annum, can be solely due to the relaxation of hunting pressure. Probably a major additional factor is climatic change, influencing the numbers and location of such surface-shoaling fish as mackerel, on which the gannets feed. Certainly the rate of increase is high for such a large bird which lays only one egg per season.

During the present century, the world population of the gannet has trebled, and with some 140,000 breeding pairs, Britain and Ireland hold 70% of the world total. Perhaps as many as one third of the world total now

Gannet (*Sula bassana*). Resident seabird; 70% of world population found in British Isles. Sexes are alike. Length 90cm (36in), wingspan 1.8m (6ft).

Left: A juvenile gannet. In its first autumn and winter it is dark chocolate brown, flecked with pale grey or white. The plumage develops to the adult stage over four or five years.

Below: Herma Ness gannetry, at the extreme northern tip of Shetland.

Diving for a fish

sighting the fish

dive may be over 30m (100ft)

wings are swept back on entering water

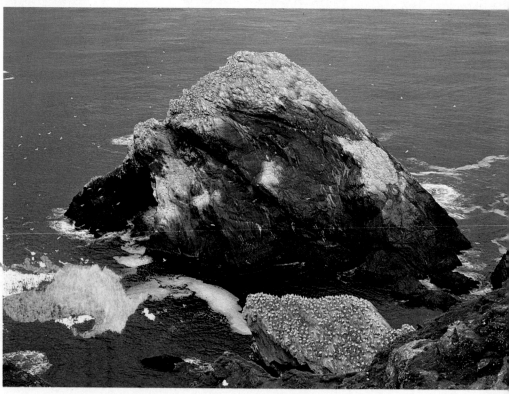

ests on Boreray and its associated giant rock pinnacles, Stac Lee and Stac-an-Armin, which form part of the St Kilda group of islands. This gannetry may hold over 60,000 pairs. Calculations of the daily catch of fish when the Boreray colony is fully occupied in spring and summer indicate that a prodigious 00 tons or more of fish a day are needed to supply it.

Adapted to fishing In the vicinity of a gannetry, the birds are seen performing their fishing plunge, often from a height of 30m 00ft) or more. When fish are present in huge numbers close to the surface, or when the weather is particularly rough, making visibility poor, the gannets sometimes dive at a slant into the water from a height of only a few feet.

Anatomically, the gannet is admirably well adapted to this way of life. Its eyes, for example, can swivel freely in the sockets, enabling the gannet to look vertically down into the water while maintaining its head in a horizontal position for good aerodynamic 'trim'. Feathers and tough skin assist a robust skeleton in resisting the impact of high dives, and the eyes are set in sockets lined with special 'padding' tissue which acts as a shock absorber.

Gannets differ from sea eagles, ospreys and other dive-plunging birds in the position of their wings during the dive. Instead of entering the water with their wings bent, the 'elbow' pointing forward, gannets allow their wings to trail, stretched out alongside and behind the tail as they penetrate the surface.

The food of the gannet consists almost entirely of fish, the choice depending more on easy availability than on any particular preference. Mackerel, herring, cod, capelin, saithe and pollack all feature regularly in the diet. Most food items are swallowed with a convulsive gulp just as the gannet surfaces from its dive, and can often be seen as a large bulge, steadily descending the gullet.

Colonial breeding Adult gannets begin to return to their nesting ledges in late winter, and by the spring noisy honking displays are commonplace; pairs alternately raise and lower their bills to one another in a complex and ritualised pattern. Gannets are monogamous, and usually pair for life (which is on average about 16 years), although the two sexes go their separate ways during the winter.

Over the years, most nests have become substantial mounds of seaweed and flotsam, held together with guano. As part of the courtship ritual, the male brings frequent 'gifts' of seaweed to the female on the nest, which helps to become even bigger. The single egg is relatively small for the size of the adult bird, being 7.5cm (3in) long and 5cm (2in) broad. is chalky blue when laid, but rapidly becomes stained brown. Some eggs are lost to predators such as gulls, or by rolling off the nest (usually during a squabble with the neighbours), but in a study of the gannets on

Bass Rock it was found that over 80% hatched. Eggs lost in the first three weeks of incubation are usually replaced.

Gannets in winter Once they leave the breeding colonies at the end of summer, adult and young gannets separate to go their own way during the winter. The adults, with their superior skills at fishing in poor conditions gained over several seasons, disperse from the colonies but tend to remain in coastal waters round Britain and Ireland or slightly to the south, rarely travelling further than Portugal or Spain. The young birds of the year, on the other hand, migrate purposefully south, first to the Bay of Biscay and later to the waters off North and West Africa.

Above: Over 10,000 pairs of gannets breed each year on the Bass Rock, off the coast of Lothian.

Below: A gannet incubating its egg. The bird has no brood patch of bare skin on the belly to warm the eggs, but instead laps the webs of its feet over the egg to warm it. Incubation takes about 45 days—the longest time for any bird of Britain and Ireland. Fledging takes about 90 days, so there is time for only a single brood each summer.

Cormorant and shag

Cormorants and shags (below), two of our largest
sea birds, are common around our coasts at all times
of the year, often bobbing about in the water in
their continual search for fish, or standing motionless
with their wings spread out wide to dry.

roups of large, black, long-necked birds pparently just standing idly around, are a miliar sight on British coasts. They are rmorants and shags. Although totally pendent on diving in water to catch food, ese birds have wing feathers that are less ater repellent than those of most other ater birds. After each feeding session they ve to seek an open, breezy place and hang eir saturated wings out to dry. At favourite afing spots, such as low rocky ledges, lets, piers, breakwaters, moored boats and uoys, you can often see several birds stand-g in a row. Sandbanks exposed at low tide estuaries are also often used.

Ancient birds The cormorant and shag mily has one of the longest fossil records f all birds. Remains of one cormorant-like ird found in Hungary are thought to be 100 illion years old. Today there are 31 species f cormorants and shags in the world, cluding a flightless species found only in the alapagos Islands.

In the British Isles we have only two ecies, and shags outnumber cormorants out four to one. Our species of cormorant as an extensive world distribution and ves in every continent except South America. contrast, our shag is restricted to Europe nd North Africa.

Near-black look-alikes Even experienced rnithologists sometimes have difficulty dis-nguishing between shags and cormorants.

Of the two species, the shag is smaller and slighter, with a narrower beak. Neither species is really black; shags are glossy green-black with a brownish tinge to their wings and back. Cormorants have white cheeks and chins.

In summer, identification of adults is easier, since both species develop temporary breeding plumage. Shags grow a character-istic recurved crest about 5cm (2in) long. Cormorants grow whitish wispy feathers on their heads, and a white patch on each thigh which is often conspicuous in flight.

Immature shags and cormorants have brown upperparts. Young shags may only be a little paler beneath, whereas young cormor-ants can be almost white. The plumage of both species becomes darker with each successive moult until they reach full adult plumage in the second or third year.

In common with their close relatives, the pelicans, gannets and frigate birds, shags and cormorants have patches of bare skin around the beak and eyes. These are analogous to the pelican's enormous fish-carrying pouch. *Phalacrocorax*, the Latin name for shags and cormorants, refers to these patches, and means 'bald raven'. The name cormorant is apparently an English corruption of the Latin *Corvus marinus*, or sea crow.

In general shape and habits both species resemble divers. However, in the water you can easily spot cormorants and shags by their

Shag
(Phalacrocorax aristotelis); 76cm (30in) from beak to tail. Found all round the coast of the British Isles and occasionally inland. Population currently on the increase. Resident.

Cormorant
(Phalacrocorax carbo); 90cm (36in) from beak to tail. Less common than the shag, but more widespread, being found inland as well as around our coast. Resident.

Below: Cormorants breed in colonies, often in very exposed sites where storms can be disastrous. Eggs or young are easily chilled by sea spray and whole nests can be washed away by the waves.

Cormorant display postures

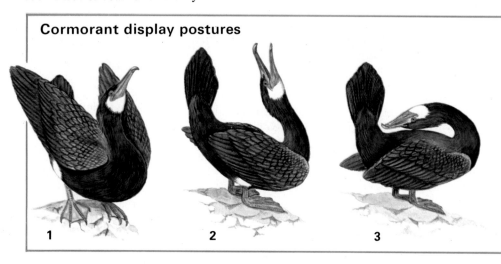

Cormorants and shags perform elaborate displays at their nest sites. The male cormorant, having claimed a suitable site, advertises to prospective mates by a series of dramatic gestures such as spreading his head feathers and raising his long wedge-shaped tail (**1**), calling with head and bill thrown back (**2**), and by rotating his head noisily from side to side whilst touching the base of the tail with his closed beak (**3**).

Below: A shag parent with its chicks in a typically defensive posture, its long neck outstretched as it utters a loud call, and its wings held slightly away from its body.

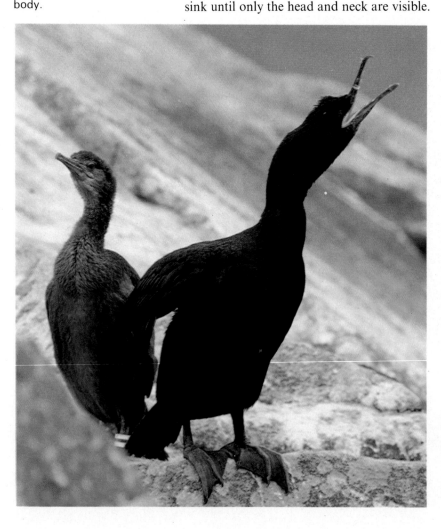

long, thin, upstretched necks and narrow, hooked beaks which they hold up at an angle. In flight they hold their necks horizontally or slightly raised, while divers allow their necks to droop below body level.

Low-lying swimmers As you would expect, most water birds are waterproof. However, cormorants and shags probably find their lack of waterproofing advantageous. On entering the water they expel air from their feathers and so increase their overall density, becoming heavier and therefore diving more easily. Both species tend to swim low in the water with their backs just awash, and when they are afraid of attack by predators they sink until only the head and neck are visible.

Nevertheless, they cannot stay in the water indefinitely, and always remain within reach of land where they sleep, preen and dry out. Unlike many other sea birds, cormorants and shags are never oceanic.

Cormorants and shags are powerful swimmers, both above and below water. For maximum efficiency in the water their legs are placed well back along the body, but this means they are poor walkers on land. Most water birds have a small hind toe that is useless for swimming. However, the hind toe of cormorants and shags is long, turned inwards and webbed to the inside front toe, giving them three webs instead of the usual two on each foot. Their close relatives also have this pattern of webbing.

These species are two of our largest sea birds and in calm weather without the help of the wind they have difficulty in rising from the surface of the water. However, once they are airborne, their flight is powerful with steady wing-beats and neck outstretched. They usually fly in a straight line low over the water. In silhouette they resemble geese, and if flying far, perhaps to good feeding areas or back to communal roosting sites, they often travel in lines or a goose-like formation. Cormorants also fly inland, sometimes soaring to a great height. They follow river valleys where they find lakes and slow-moving rivers.

Vicious fishers If you watch cormorants and shags fishing you will probably be able to spot their catch. They actively pursue fish beneath the water; once grabbed by the strong, hooked beak the fish has little chance of escape. The birds usually return to the surface to swallow their prey, and often juggle the fish in their beaks to be sure it goes down head, not spines, first.

In the past these birds were accused of depleting fish stocks—a cormorant eats up to 700g (1½lb) a day—and thousands were shot. However, studies show their feeding habits are rarely detrimental, although in fresh water they may take the occasional trout as well as eels, perch and young salmon. In some places the birds may be beneficial, helping to control the predatory fish which ould otherwise eat species more favoured by man.

On the coast cormorants prefer shallow bays and estuaries where they dive to catch flatfish such as flounders. They also eat cod and whiting, and shore fish such as blennies.

Typically the nest is a heap of seaweed, bracken and heather. Both sexes build, although the male often concentrates on collecting the material and the female on arranging it. The species may nest singly, in scattered groups or in large colonies (rookeries) and you may find all three types together. In a colony, nests may be almost touching, though usually they are just out of pecking distance. There are fights for the best sites when two opponents grab each other by the beak and try to pull or push the other.

The females lay three or four eggs in April or May, usually at two or three day intervals. The eggs are pale blue and covered with a chalky deposit. Storms can destroy many eggs and chicks and pairs may have to build a new nest and lay a second clutch. The timing of the breeding season partly depends on the food supply; in Wales shags have been found breeding in winter.

Both parents incubate the eggs in 12-hourly shifts, each fearlessly defending the clutch against marauding gulls. Many species develop a brood patch (an area of skin on the belly without feathers but well supplied with blood vessels to keep the eggs warm). Shags and cormorants, however, have warm feet that they shuffle beneath the eggs during incubation.

Shags fish only in the sea. They swim in deeper water than cormorants catching mid-water fish such as sand-eels, sprats, whiting and saithe. They rarely eat flatfish.

Coastal nests In the British Isles cormorants and shags nest on rocky coasts. There are a few in southern and eastern England but most are found in Scotland. Cormorants favour small rocky islands and broad cliff ledges, their nests up to a metre (3ft) wide and over 80cm (2½ft) high. Some nest inland, and in Ireland they nest in trees, a habit widespread elsewhere in Europe that was more common in this country before persecution took its toll. Shags prefer more sheltered coastal sites such as crevices in rocky gullies, ledges in the roofs of caves or among boulders on steep slopes. They can nest on a ledge only 30cm (1ft) square. Both nests and surrounding rocks become plastered with odorous white droppings (guano). However, it makes excellent fertilizer and is collected for this purpose in many parts of the world.

The first egg hatches after a month, and for almost a week the nestlings are blind. Each parent feeds them once a day on a diet of regurgitated fish. The young birds leave the nest after about seven weeks and become independent about two months later.

Both species disperse a few hundred miles during their first winter. They breed when

Above: A juvenile shag in a rock pool. Young birds are dark brown, and they do not have paler underparts like young cormorants.

they are two or three years old, often in their natal colony. After this they are relatively sedentary.

Compared with many birds, shags and cormorants are long-lived. Of those that survive the first few years, only 10-20% die in each subsequent year. Their average life expectancy has been estimated at about seven years, but some live to be 20 years old.

Both species were heavily persecuted in the last century, and even now many are shot each year. Some become entangled in fishing nets and others suffer from oil from ships washed ashore. Nevertheless, the shag, and probably also the cormorant, are currently on the increase.

Cormorant
adult

Shag
adult

white cheeks

adult in breeding plumage
drying wings

Cormorant

white thigh patch

Oystercatcher

With its pied plumage, pink legs and red bill the oystercatcher is one of our most distinctive shore birds. It has several strange patterns of behaviour, including an unusual 'piping display' performed in the breeding season to defend its territory.

Oystercatcher *(Hematopus ostralegus)*. Resident wader, found on rocky shores (exposed headlands as well as sheltered bays), mud flats and sometimes inland, particularly in Scotland. Length about 40cm (17in).

Most of our coastal waders are dull brown and difficult to distinguish from each other, but the oystercatcher is an exception. Its orange-red bill, red eyes and pink legs stand out strongly from its stark black and white plumage. Yet if you come across an oyster-catcher while it is quitely feeding it can seem an inconspicuous bird, particularly if its

back is turned towards you. Only when it i disturbed and looks up does it reveal it remarkable colouring.

Sexes alike Male and female oystercatcher are similar in appearance. The upperparts ar predominantly black, with white wing-bar rump and base of the tail. During the breedin season in spring and summer the black part c their plumage becomes glossy. In winter is duller and the birds develop a white colla round the front of their necks. Young oyste catchers retain the white collar and dull plumage all the year round.

The adult bill is orange-red, tending t become yellower towards the tip. In younge birds the tip is duller yellow-brown. The bi is about 7cm (3in) long, the female's bein slightly longer than the male's. The legs of th adult are pink but in young birds are greyis The colour of the eyes also develops as th birds mature. In their first year, oyste catchers have brown eyes. As they grow olde these become yellow, then orange and final red by the time the birds reach adulthoo The red of the eye is accentuated, aga primarily in the adult, by a ring of red feathers surrounding it.

Coastal and inland habitats Oystercatchers occur in a variety of habitats, primarily coastal. On rocky shores they feed on both exposed headlands and sheltered bays, though the number of oystercatchers found there is never·great. Larger numbers are found on mud flats, where the birds can probe for worms and shells. On extensive mud flats, such as those of the Wash, Morcambe Bay, Solway Firth and the Burry Inlet, huge winter flocks numbering 10,000 or more can be seen. As high tide approaches the birds fly off noisily in flocks to roost together in dense packs above the high-water mark.

During the last hundred years oyster-catchers have been moving away from the coast to take advantage of inland feeding sites–after all, probing for worms in soil is much the same as probing for worms in mud. In northern Britain and particularly in Scot-land they are now common farmland birds often seen feeding in association with lap-wings, rooks, starlings and those other inland invaders of recent years: gulls. The reason for this movement is not known, but increasing human disturbance of the coast, and even a genetic change in the birds themselves, have been suggested.

Oyster catchers no more The name 'oyster-catcher' is a misnomer, for the bird rarely eats oysters these days. Inland feeders live off earthworms and other soil invertebrates; coastal dwellers eat mostly crabs and shellfish such as limpets, cockles and mussels, though worms are commonly eaten.

The oystercatcher shows great skill in the way it extracts the meat from a shellfish. It takes the shell to a rocky or sandy surface that will give good support, placing the

broad white wing-bars and white rump

pink legs

white underside

chick

short black bill

legs dark at birth

bove: A pair of ystercatchers during the reeding season. In winter heir coats are much less lossy and the birds evelop an irregular white ollar round the front of heir necks.
ystercatchers usually mate or life and, during the reeding season, are trongly territorial.

ight: In winter ystercatchers form hemselves into large ocks.
o identify an ystercatcher in flight, ook for the white nderparts with black head nd wing tips. Of the nore colourful parts of an ystercatcher, only its ink legs are distinct in ight.

Left: An oystercatcher's nest is usually a simple hollow, sometimes lined with stones, shells or dead vegetation. The number of eggs laid is normally three, but may be two or four. The eggs are large, about 6cm (2½in) long, and often pointed.

Below: If the chicks are threatened, one of the parents sometimes feigns injury or pretends to be brooding to draw the predator towards it and away from the young.

weakest part of the shell uppermost. Then it either stabs through the gap between the shells or hammers the shell repeatedly until it can get its bill inside. Once inside the shell the oystercatcher uses its bill to sever the muscle attaching the flesh to the shell and eats the flesh.

This method of feeding illustrates some interesting adaptations. The bill is sensitive enough to detect food when probing in sand or mud, yet it is also tough enough to break through hard shell.

Close examination of shells attacked by oystercatchers show another strange feature equivalent to our own right-handedness or left-handedness. The birds have a preferred side from which to attack the shell. For example, if you investigate damage to limpet shells made by oystercatchers you'll see that most blows are delivered with the head and bill turned to the right.

Strange displays Throughout the winter oystercatchers flock together but in March, with the start of the breeding season, they separate into pairs–oystercatchers mate for life–and establish a territory.

The courtship and territorial behaviour both include some unusual displays. During courtship the 'butterfly-flight' display is performed; in this the male flies over his territory with slow exaggerated wing-beats. Sometimes he pursues a female but equally often the male is alone.

More bizarre is the territorial display with its associated 'piping' call. This begins with a series of clearly spaced, loud notes. These gradually quicken until they become a prolonged trill. At the same time the bird adopts a peculiar posture with the neck partly extended, the shoulders raised in a 'hunchback' attitude and the bill open and pointing downwards. A bird performing this display to

Bill shape and feeding

An oystercatcher attacks shells in one of two ways, depending on how it was taught by its parents. Which method it uses is reflected by its bill. If the bird stabs its bill between the shell valves the bill remains sharp, but if it hammers the side of the shell the bill becomes blunt.

Below: During the breeding season an oystercatcher announces and defends its territory with a piping call and a strange posture: the neck is extended with the bill open and pointing down. Both partners may perform the display.

worn bill due to hammer-style feeding

stabbing bill remains sharp

defend its territory may be joined by its mate and by birds from adjoining territories to form a party of piping birds. The piping call may also be given in flight, again to defend territory.

The more usual call of an oystercatcher is a tuty 'kileep'. When alarmed or excited this may be varied to a repeated 'kleepa, kleepa, kleepa'.

Nest, eggs and young The typical oystercatcher nest is a simple hollow or scrape, sometimes lined with stones, shells, or dead vegetation. Favourite sites include coastal shingle, rocks and dunes, and river banks and loch-sides. As inland feeding becomes commoner, so does inland breeding, with nests being established in open cultivated fields.

Egg-laying usually takes place in May. The normal clutch is three. The eggs are incubated for about 25 days, mostly by the female. A few hours after hatching the chicks begin to wander, closely guarded by their parents. If danger threatens the parents sometimes try to distract the intruder by feigning injury or by settling into a brooding posture some distance from the chicks. More often they fly around calling: the warning cry causes the chicks to 'freeze' in a secluded spot where their camouflage makes them hard to find.

Oystercatcher chicks are unusual among waders in being dependent upon their parents for food; not surprisingly, since their bills are too small to break open shells. This depend-

ence lasts until the chicks fledge at about 35 days old.

Numbers increasing Without doubt, the oystercatcher is our most successful wader, though why this should be so is not clear. The numbers of our own breeding birds – now well over 30,000 pairs – and of wintering migrants from Iceland, the Faroes and Scandinavia have increased dramatically in recent years, and a significant part of this increase stems from the oystercatcher's movement inland. This process is continuing, in both Britain and Europe. There seems little doubt that the population of our pied pipers will continue to increase for some years to come.

Above: A flock of oystercatchers waiting for the tide to recede. Notice how several of the oystercatchers are standing with their heads turned round and their beaks tucked into their backs. This is called the 'false sleeping posture'. The birds are pretending to be asleep but, in fact, they are carefully watching an intruder in case it approaches too closely.

Oystercatchers and the cockle industry

The oystercatcher's fondness for cockles has brought it into conflict with cockle fishermen, who harvest this shellfish and depend on it for their livelihoods. The problem is particularly acute in South Wales, where our largest cockle beds are to be found, and is made worse by the fact that oystercatchers prefer two-year old cockles, which is also the main age-group taken by the fishermen. The abundance of cockles fluctuates considerably from year to year, making the life of a cockle fisherman precarious enough without oystercatchers adding to his problems, and limited shooting of these birds is now allowed in certain areas.

However, the impact of oystercatchers on the cockle population is still disputed, some people arguing that oystercatchers consume large quantities of cockles only in years when they are plentiful. Either way, short of extreme measures there is little that can be done to control the activities of such a successful species.

Turnstone and purple sandpiper

Our wintering waders are generally seen on mudflats and estuaries, except for two: the turnstone, which visits rocky shores as well as beaches and nearby fields; and the purple sandpiper, which is a true specialist of the rocky shore. The two species can be seen together in mixed flocks.

Those of us who brave winter weather to walk around muddy shores are probably familiar with the most noticeable features of a typical wader – a long bill for probing into the mud for hidden food, and long legs to permit the bird to walk in the shallow water among breaking waves without getting its belly feathers too wet. It is somewhat surprising, therefore, to discover that these features are little used for these purposes on the breeding grounds, for most waders breed during the short summer of the high Arctic, where their staple diet consists of the myriads of midges and their larvae abounding on the tundra.

Two of the waders that visit our coasts in winter have tended to forsake the mud and

manage, instead, to eke out a living from our rocky shores. These are the purple sandpiper and the turnstone. Like other waders, they breed in the Arctic, except that in some recent years perhaps one single pair of purple sandpipers has bred in an unpublicised locality in Scotland. For all practical purposes, therefore, the two species are migrants visiting Britain and Ireland for the winter months only.

The purple sandpiper This species is almost entirely restricted to rocky shores during its stay in Britain and Ireland. It is a stocky bird, about 20cm (8in) long, and is usually found feeding in small flocks. The head and breast are sooty brown, while the back is a little

Above: A mixed flock flies along the strandline between feeding grounds. About a third of them are purple sandpipers and two thirds are turnstones. The purple sandpipers are slightly smaller, dark birds with long, down-curved bills. The turnstones can be identified by a white stripe along the back and an extra wing stripe, which shows as a clear white area, often L-shaped, almost on the shoulder.

Purple sandpiper (*Calidris maritima*). Winter visitor to rocky shores all round Britain and Ireland. Though classed as a wader it is very much a rocky shore specialist. Sexes are alike. Length 20cm (8in).

Turnstone (*Arenaria interpres*). Winter visitor to rocky, sandy and muddy shores round Britain and Ireland. Frequently lifts stones to find prey. Sexes are alike. Length 23cm (9in).

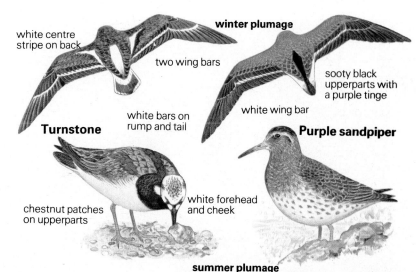

white centre stripe on back

winter plumage

two wing bars

sooty black upperparts with a purple tinge

white bars on rump and tail

white wing bar

Turnstone

Purple sandpiper

chestnut patches on upperparts

white forehead and cheek

summer plumage

Right: A turnstone in full summer plumage. You can see varying degrees of summer plumage on turnstones in Britain and Ireland, for in spring some of them begin their seasonal moult before departing for the breeding grounds; and in autumn some arrive with their breeding plumage still showing. However, such birds are in the minority and it is commoner for turnstones in Britain and Ireland to be seen in complete winter plumage. Purple sandpipers, too, are sometimes seen in summer plumage, but this is normally only in spring, for in autumn they almost all arrive in winter plumage.

Below: A purple sandpiper resting on a shingle beach. This bird is clearly in winter plumage, looking dark with a slight purple tinge. The shingle is a good place for roosting after tirelessly hunting for food amid the harassment of the waves.

darker, at close range showing a purplish tinge. The eye is surrounded by a fine white ring. The throat, belly and under-tail are white, and in flight the upper wing shows a white wing bar.

In addition to being stocky, the purple sandpiper also appears somewhat squat, for its legs are a little shorter than many of its mud-dwelling relatives. A useful identification feature is that the legs are yellow, as is the base of the slightly down-curved bill.

As the birds develop their breeding plumage, brownish feather edgings on the back give them a more mottled appearance. Some-

times this occurs before they migrate northwards in spring, so that you can see purple sandpipers that look lighter than usual while they are still on our shores.

The turnstone Squatness and stockiness are features the purple sandpiper shares with the turnstone, but the latter is a little larger, being around 23cm (9in) long, and with much more boldly marked plumage. In winter the back and breast are dark grey-brown, and while the head is the same general colour it has suggestions of white markings behind the eye and on the cheeks. The throat and belly are white, the latter being separated from the dark breast by a clearly defined line. The contrast between the dark breast and the white throat and belly gives the appearance of a distinct, dark breast band.

In flight, even a winter plumage turnstone is readily distinguished from the purple sandpiper, for it is much more strongly patterned, with a double white wing bar and broad black and white bars on the rump and tail. The turnstone's legs are generally orange and its pointed bill is black.

In summer, the turnstone takes on a completely new appearance, to become one of our most striking shorebirds. The head and breast become strongly patterned in black and white, and the back develops rich chestnut patches, giving a 'tortoiseshell' look. While you are most likely to see winter plumage birds in Britain or Ireland, in the spring and autumn you can find turnstones in all stages between winter and summer.

Arctic migrants To breed in the Arctic imposes considerable restrictions on the breeding season of shorebirds, for they cannot begin their reproductive activities until the snow and ice have thawed, and they must depart before freezing conditions return. The breeding season is thus necessarily short, and most of their life is spent in warmer climes.

The purple sandpiper has a comparatively short migration for a shorebird, going little

Above: A purple sandpiper attempts to feed at the shore of a lake. The commonest cause for these birds to leave the rocky seashore is when high tides cover it for too much of the day. This happens in the Scottish winter, with its short daylight period. The birds then feed either on the rocks and strandline at night, or in grassland and fresh water habitats during daylight hours.

further south than the British Isles. Ringing has shown that the birds wintering on our coasts, mainly on the flatter rocky coasts of the north and east, breed mainly in Norway, although a few come from Iceland. It has been estimated that somewhere around 20,000 purple sandpipers winter on British and Irish shores.

Although many turnstones winter around the coasts of the British Isles, the proportion spending the winter at such northern latitudes may well be small compared with that which passes on beyond Britain to winter on the shores of tropical Africa and even further south. Our own shores provide homes for the winter visitors and also for birds simply picking up food in preparation for an onward journey south. Those that winter on British coasts have bred or were born in Greenland or north-eastern Canada, but in autumn our North Sea coasts provide temporary lodging for turnstones that breed in northern Europe; these birds then continue their journey southwards to winter in Africa.

Feeding on the rocks Although the purple sandpiper does not use its wader features – long bill and long legs – to enable it to probe in mud like its relatives, these features nevertheless serve it well on the rocky platforms where it is usually to be found. It is an agile bird, well able to run out of the way of advancing waves, but if it cannot run from a particular wave it hovers above the water until the

Birds of the rocky shore

Herring gulls
open shellfish such as mussels by dropping them on to rocks

Purple sandpipers
forage at the water's edge, moving with the tide, in search of food

Eider ducks
can be seen diving to take food, principally mussels, from the rocky bottom

Oystercatchers
use their long bills to prise apart or hammer open mussel shells

Turnstones
stoop to turn stones or expose seaweed on the strand-line in search of food items, mainly crustaceans

Rock pipits
breed in sheltered coves and gullies and feed on periwinkles and insect larvae, picked from stranded seaweed

wave has receded.

It is on gently shelving reefs, at the water's edge, that the purple sandpiper finds its food most easily. Here, the crustaceans and shellfish that it eats are active, whereas higher up the shore, where it is drier, the same animals tend to retreat into crevices, cling firmly to the rock or close their shells tightly in order to avoid the danger of desiccation.

The purple sandpiper's diet is varied and consists of many of the common animals found on rocky shores. Small winkles and dogwhelks are taken in large numbers, while barnacles, mussels, tiny shore crabs, shrimps and even worms are eaten from time to time. Some of this variability in the diet is due to the birds' habit of feeding at the edge of the water, for as the tide moves in or out, so the different kinds of animal living at different levels on the shore become available for the birds to eat.

One problem for purple sandpipers in northern Britain is that high spring tides—submerging the reefs—can last all through the daylight hours; so they are forced to feed at night, or go inland during the day.

Varied feeding grounds Turnstones are altogether more versatile, both in the habitats in which they live and in the kinds of food they eat. Although they are commonly found on rocky shores, often feeding in mixed flocks with purple sandpipers, they are by no means restricted to these places. Estuaries, muddy and sandy beaches and even rubbish tips near the shore all support flocks of turnstones, while a visitor to the tropics is often surprised to find them in coastal coconut plantations.

Turning over stones The turnstone has, in fact, a unique style of behaviour which enables it to move away from the water's edge and feed elsewhere. Even when the tide is out, some animals—the ones protected from drying out by being hidden under stones or seaweed—remain active on the shore. The turnstone does exactly as its name suggests and uses its short bill, squat body and strong neck to take advantage of these hidden resources. In all of this bird's feeding areas, one can see individuals running to stones or pieces of seaweed

Above: Turnstones feed in a variety of places. On rocky shores they take crustaceans and shellfish; on mud or sand (as seen here) their bills are too short for probing, and so they feed on shrimps, worms and shellfish exposed by the receding waves; they eat insects when found, and scavenge—picking at dead fish, birds and any other carcases washed ashore.

Below: A small party of turnstones investigating a stony beach.

and flicking them over to expose whatever might be revealed beneath.

This is the winter behaviour of these squat-looking waders: both seem to be perpetually on the move, running energetically in search of small items on the rocks. But this is only a part of their life, for in spring they move north again to await the melting of the ice in remote Arctic regions. There they change their ways and become inland birds, dwelling away from the sea on the expansive, empty landscape of the tundra. They raise another brood in the short time available to them, and with their young they reinvade our shores after a brief season far to the north, in the land of the midnight sun.

Left: The rocky seashore provides nourishment for a special 'clientele' of birds. The herring gull cracks shellfish open by taking them overhead and then dropping them on the rocks; the eider duck dives for mussels on submerged rocks; the oystercatcher is often seen visiting rock pools; the rock pipit is found at low tide in almost any part of the rocky shore except in the sea; the purple sandpiper feeds at the water's edge—as does the turnstone.

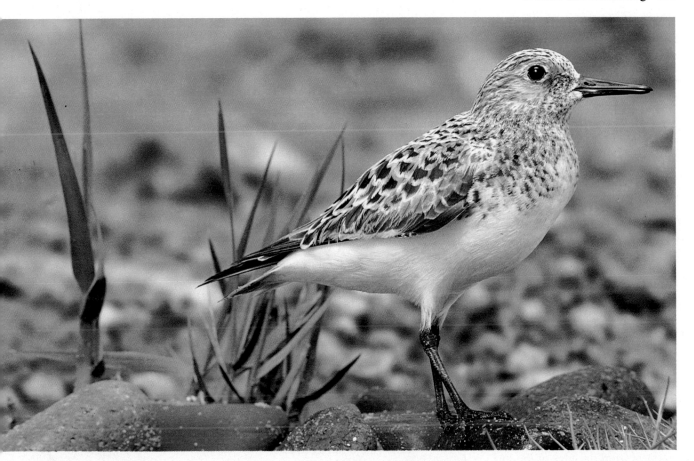

Dunlin and sanderling

In spring, large numbers of these dainty waders gather on our shores before setting off for their summer grounds far to the north. Just a small population of breeding dunlins is left behind.

Above: A sanderling in its summer breeding plumage. Although the sanderling does not breed in this country it can be seen here in full breeding plumage in the spring when it migrates north along our coasts.

The dunlin and the sanderling are both small gregarious waders often seen on our larger expanses of mudflats and long sandy beaches, especially in the winter and during the spring and autumn migrations. Indeed, the dunlin is our most common wading bird in mid-winter; some 700,000 individuals are found around the coasts of Britain and Ireland at that time of year–more than twice as many as any other wader. Dunlins also breed here, though in far smaller numbers, but the sanderling is a winter visitor or a migrant; it never breeds in the British Isles.

Delicate dunlins At about 18cm (7in) long, the dunlin is one of our smallest waders. Throughout the year, it can be seen at almost any estuary, muddy beach or harbour. Inland, it is surprisingly common; sewage farms, flooded fields and the shores of reservoirs are good places to see dunlin in winter, and in summer it can be found in the moorland areas where it breeds.

The dunlin is easy to recognise in the summer because it has a characteristic black patch on its belly. The upperparts are a rich

rufous brown streaked and spotted with black. The breast is heavily streaked with brown. In the autumn, the dunlin moults to its winter plumage, losing both its body and wing feathers (in spring, when it regains its breeding plumage, only the body feathers are moulted and replaced). The dunlin's winter plumage is quite drab and inconspicuous, the upperparts being grey-brown and the underparts a dull white.

Dark-shouldered sanderlings The sanderling is slightly larger than the dunlin and usually inhabits sandy estuaries and long sandy beaches. In Britain, it is most often seen in its winter plumage, which is much more striking than that of the dunlin. Its underparts and much of its head are pure white and its back and wings are pale grey. Often, there is a dark patch on the 'shoulder' of the wing (technically called the wrist).

Like the dunlin, the sanderling moults its body and wing feathers in the autumn and just its body feathers in the spring. Its summer plumage resembles that of the dunlin, except that it has a white belly. The best chance of

Opposite: Dunlin and knot in flight (top) and sanderlings (below).

Dunlin (*Calidris alpina*). Resident wader; numbers augmented in winter by migrants from the Continent and Greenland, when it becomes our commonest coastal wader. It is also found inland, and breeds in moorland areas. Length 18cm (7in).

Sanderling (*Calidris alba*). Winter-visiting wader, confined mostly to sandy beaches and estuaries. Length 20cm (8in).

seeing a sanderling in full breeding plumage is in spring, when many birds migrate north along our coasts, having just grown a new set of body feathers.

Beak differences A good way to tell the difference between the dunlin and the sanderling is to look at the beak. British dunlins have downward-curving beaks about 3cm (1¼in) long, whereas the sanderling has a shorter (2.5cm/1in), straight beak. There is considerable variation in beak lengths among dunlins, the British birds in general having shorter beaks than those breeding further north. For example, Canadian dunlins have beaks averaging about 4.5cm (1¾in).

The beaks of these two species are different because they have different methods of feeding. The dunlin, when feeding, walks with a purposeful air, head held low, constantly pecking at the surface of the mud and probing for tiny molluscs. The tip of its beak is particularly sensitive and allows the bird to detect, by touch, food lying below the surface of the mud.

The sanderling, on the other hand, feeds at the water's edge, hurrying back and forth like a clockwork toy following each wave as it breaks and recedes. It can be seen skilfully snatching small creatures such as sandhoppers from the edge of the surf.

Both dunlins and sanderlings feed until high tide and then fly off to special roosting

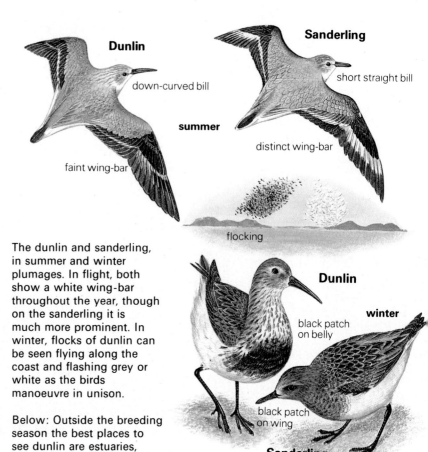

Dunlin
down-curved bill
summer
faint wing-bar

Sanderling
short straight bill
distinct wing-bar

flocking

Dunlin
winter
black patch on belly

black patch on wing

Sanderling

The dunlin and sanderling, in summer and winter plumages. In flight, both show a white wing-bar throughout the year, though on the sanderling it is much more prominent. In winter, flocks of dunlin can be seen flying along the coast and flashing grey or white as the birds manoeuvre in unison.

Below: Outside the breeding season the best places to see dunlin are estuaries, beaches and harbours, where food is always plentiful.

sites on shingle banks and marshes or sometimes, on grassy fields. There the birds gather in their thousands for two or three hours until the tide has retreated and they can return to feed. Both on the ground and in flight the two species form their own groups. In the winter, a large flock of dunlins flying to or from the feeding and roosting areas can be a marvellous spectacle. Each bird in the flock flies in precise formation only a few inches from its neighbour, and with each change of direction the colour of the flock changes. First, you see the birds' dark upperparts then, as they swerve to one side, the dark changes to the white of their underparts.

Migration routes Most dunlins seen in Britain, and all sanderlings, are winter visitors or passing migrants. Migrating sanderlings arrive in the British Isles each July and August from their breeding grounds in Greenland and Siberia. Some spend the winter here and the remainder fly on south to France, the Iberian Peninsula and Africa. In May, our wintering sanderlings return to their summer grounds, joined by migrants passing through Britain from further south.

Britain is one of the few countries in the world with both breeding and wintering dunlins, so their passage through Britain is not as distinct as sanderling migrations. Nevertheless, dunlins breeding in Greenland, Iceland, the Netherlands and around the

Above: A flock of dunlins in spring. Some of the birds still have their winter plumage but most have moulted ready for the breeding season. Soon they will be migrating to their breeding grounds far to the north.

Below: A sanderling feeding in winter. With their short straight beaks, sanderlings pick up small creatures from the surface of the sand, whereas dunlins have longer, curved beaks for probing beneath the surface.

Baltic Sea all migrate through Britain on their way to or from their wintering areas in southern Europe and North Africa. Dunlins breeding here also fly south for the winter, but this loss is more than compensated for by the arrival in Britain for the winter of large numbers of dunlin from Scandinavia and Russia. As hard weather sets in further north, so more and more dunlin arrive on our coasts; their numbers usually reach a maximum in January. In spring, our wintering dunlins return to their breeding grounds, to be replaced by our own breeding population. Most of our breeding dunlins settle in Scotland and northern England, but a few nest in Wales and Ireland and there are even some on Dartmoor – the most southerly breeding dunlins in the world.

Upland breeders The breeding season for dunlins usually starts in April or May. A typical site is a damp, peaty, upland moor, though some nest beside lakes and others in salt marshes.

The nest is a tiny hollow, hidden among heather or a grassy tussock to provide shelter. The female lays four eggs – the typical number for a wader – at the rate of one every day or two. Both parents help to incubate the eggs until they hatch after about three weeks.

Dunlin chicks are superbly well camouflaged with yellow, buff, black and white down. When danger threatens they lie down and become almost invisible. They feed mainly on midges and cranefly larvae, which are plentiful at that time of year. The chicks grow quickly and can fly after about 25 days, when they leave for the coastal feeding sites.

Occasionally, dunlins manage to raise two broods in a season, but this is rare. The sanderling, on the other hand, usually succeeds with two broods by laying one clutch of eggs in a first nest, followed immediately by another clutch in a second nest. Both clutches contain four eggs; one is incubated by the female and the other by the male.

Sanderling chicks have the same camouflaged down as dunlin chicks and they fledge in much the same length of time. Soon after, they begin their long migration south.

Curlew and whimbrel

The curlew (above) is a common British wading bird, while its relative the whimbrel is scarce, being chiefly a bird of the Arctic. But you may see whimbrels flying past on their migratory flights to Africa in autumn, and on the way back in spring.

Curlew (*Numenius arquata*).
Largest European wader. Resident, breeding in moorland, grassland, marshes and dunes. Winters on estuaries and coasts. About 50,000 breeding pairs. Length 53-58cm (21-23in).

Whimbrel (*Numenius phaeopus*).
Summer visitor, smaller than curlew. Breeds in dry moorland and grassland in north Scotland and Shetlands. Under 200 breeding pairs. 41cm (16in).

The curlew is a truly unmistakable bird: a large, robust wader, common on estuaries in autumn and winter, and familiar in the west and north as a breeding bird of inland pastures and hayfields in spring and summer. Its silhouette, with long legs, slightly hunched attitude and long, curved bill is unlike that of any other bird except for the whimbrel which, although it looks similar to the curlew, is rarely seen in Britain. Look closely at the curlew and you will see that its strong legs are a delicate pale grey, while the plumage is a warm ashy brown, paler below, and streaked with darker brown on the neck and upperparts. Like other large waders it has a long neck, but the most remarkable feature is the surprisingly long, downward curving bill.

On the wing, curlews are bulky birds with strong, steady flight, less rapid than most other waders and looking a little like gulls at a distance – even in their habit of dropping down to their feeding grounds on estuaries in a long, planing glide. They are shy and wary birds, whose measured, dignified movements set them apart from the scuttling activity of the mass of other waders on the shore.

Introducing the whimbrel The much scarcer, but less timid, whimbrel is superficially similar to the curlew, but the main differences are a shorter and less curved bill, shorter legs and a distinctive pattern of two dark bands of feathers on the crown. In general, it is a slightly darker and smaller bird than the curlew, although if it were not for the simple and distinctive call of the whimbrel it is probably fair to say that a great number of individuals passing through on migration would go undetected.

Whimbrels are essentially birds of passage in Britain, and so if you hear the sound of a whimbrel at all, it is likely to be flying overhead, giving its presence away by a call of about seven rapid, whinnying notes. Whimbrels stay to breed only in small numbers, chiefly in the north of Scotland and the Shetland Islands. In their northerly habitat they replace the curlew, which is a bird of the temperate zone. They breed chiefly in the Arctic zone all round the northern hemi-

How shore birds share their prey

The many birds that feed on estuaries and mudflats do not all compete for the same food. The curlew and the whimbrel can locate deep-burrowing creatures with their long, sensitive bills. For shorter-billed species of birds, such as shelduck and oystercatcher, there are shallow-burrowing shellfish, while turnstones and gulls feed on surface-dwelling crabs and mussels.

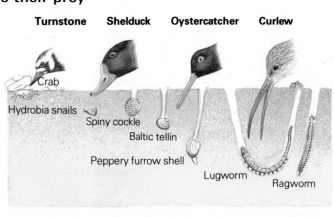

Turnstone · Shelduck · Oystercatcher · Curlew

Crab
Hydrobia snails
Spiny cockle
Baltic tellin
Peppery furrow shell
Lugworm
Ragworm

plain crown
long bill
Curlew
both species show white rump in flight
striped crown
shorter bill
Whimbrel

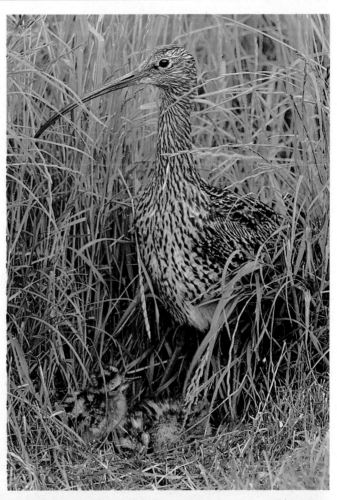

Far right: Adult curlews incubate their eggs for just over four weeks and the young hatch at about the end of May. The curlew and whimbrel, in common with other large birds, have only one brood per year, but lay a replacement clutch if the first one is lost.

Below right: Curlews lay four green-brown eggs, which are large and strongly pointed. The chicks have short beaks, which grow rapidly during fledging.

...phere. They nest on dry moors and old peat hags (mounds), and although much of this habitat exists in northern Scotland, the whimbrel remains a very scarce breeding bird in Britain, which lies at the southern limit of its breeding range. Fewer than 200 pairs of whimbrels breed in Britain each year.

The curlew in spring The return of the curlew to its nesting fields is one of the unfailing signs of spring. There are few sounds that are more welcome at the end of a long winter than the strident, bubbling song of the curlew. The song begins with a series of slow, graceful notes and then gains momentum, strengthening and rising in pitch to a rapid trill before descending again in a series of

Above: A whimbrel nesting on Fetlar, one of the Shetland Islands, makes contact calls to its 12-hour old chicks.

Left: A curlew balances in a typical one-legged posture while it rests and preens its plumage.

Below: Whimbrels prefer dry upper moorland as a nesting area. They also choose sites on the dry mounds left by the erosion of numerous small streams on peat moors.

low, single notes. This song is performed during a beautiful song flight in which the bird rises high with trembling wings and then descends in a shallow, gliding plane.

Curlew migration In the south of England, curlews begin to arrive in their nesting areas as early as the last days of February, but it is usually well into March before those that breed in Wales, northern England and Scotland reach their strongholds in the hills and valleys. Often at this season the birds can be heard calling at night, as they follow the river valleys up to the foothills. At one time curlews were thought of exclusively as birds of upland moors, but in the last 50 years or so there has been a sharp increase in Britain's curlew population, together with a marked spread into the lowlands. Now the curlew is as familiar in some lowland areas as in the uplands. There are probably about 50,000 pairs in Britain and Ireland.

Curlews are comparatively short-distance migrants: the main British population leaves the breeding areas in July, but travels no further than our own coasts. Many of the curlews of Europe's mainland, too, escape the Continental winter by flying across to Britain's coasts. However, a particularly severe British winter is also a threat to the curlew, so that even here they may not be out of danger.

Whimbrel migration Whimbrels on the other hand, like many of the species which migrate to the Arctic to breed, are among the great long distance travellers. At the end of the short breeding season they journey south, stopping to find nourishment on the estuaries in western Europe. Most travel in August, and by October the movement has finished except for a few stragglers. They have far to go—the majority seek the fertile tropical shores of West Africa, and some even go as far as South Africa. In spring the same movement occurs in reverse, most birds travelling up the coasts of western Europe in late April and May. Relatively few touch down in Britain, but the bulk of those that do use the low wet meadows of the Somerset levels as their main staging post.

Following the tide Outside the breeding

season, both whimbrel and curlew share the mudflats and estuaries with hordes of other wading birds. Their activity is linked with the ebb and flow of the tides, both by day and by night. As the rising tide covers the feeding grounds they fly to the quiet of a safe roosting site; as the tide ebbs again, they rise and follow it down, feasting on the harvest left behind by the tide. The curlew searches deeper than any of the other waders, and the whimbrel searches deeper than most. The tips of their bills are highly sensitive and enable them to feel the lugworms and ragworms in the sand. Both species also eat crabs and the smaller crustaceans, and small shellfish.

Life in the breeding grounds After flying inland to their breeding grounds, both whimbrel and curlew change to terrestrial habits of feeding. In this habitat of fields and moorland, they continue to use their bills to probe into the ground, where they find earthworms–although there are less of these to find on the moors than in grassland. Most of their food is taken from the surface of the ground, in the form of insects and their larvae, spiders, woodlice and other invertebrates. They also feed on the vegetation, including berries.

While the conspicuous song flight makes the curlew's breeding territory easy enough to locate, the nest itself is much more elusive. The birds become very secretive once they have laid their eggs, slipping off the nest and moving away through the grass long before an intruder comes near. The eggs are laid in a scant nest of grasses, well concealed in a deep tussock or in other rough vegetation, such as standing hay.

In those areas where the breeding areas of the curlew and the whimbrel overlap, for example in the Shetland Islands, the separation between the two is clear: the curlews inhabit the hay meadows and water valley bottoms, and the whimbrels resort to the upper areas of dry moorland. The picture becomes confused as the season advances, for then the whimbrels lead their young down to feed in the lower valleys. Once the eggs hatch, or towards the end of incubation, the adults become much more conspicuous and noisy if approached. They defend their brood boldly against crows, birds of prey, foxes, dogs or other ground predators. Parents often divide a brood between them, and go separate ways–increasing the chance that at least one group will come safely through the vulnerable weeks of fledging. Once on the wing, the families reunite before leaving the breeding grounds.

Hopes of protection Until the recent passing of the Wildlife and Countryside Act (1981), curlews and whimbrels were both legitimate quarry for shooting. The new Act gives total protection to both at all times of year, and the whimbrel, one of our scarcest breeding birds, is additionally protected by special penalties.

Above: A flock of curlews in the sea, with several oystercatchers and a shelduck. Both curlews and whimbrels are gregarious in winter, and flocks on large coastal flats can run to thousands.

Below: The curlew breeds in most parts of Britain and Ireland. The extreme north of its range overlaps with that of the whimbrel, while in the Arctic zone the whimbrel replaces the curlew altogether.

Curlew

Whimbrel

Common, wood and green sandpipers

Sandpipers are among the most dainty of our wading birds. Three species are found in Britain, of which only one is common here. The other two are migrants on their way to or from their breeding grounds.

Above: The common sandpiper, seen here at the edge of a loch in Scotland, is the only sandpiper to breed in large numbers in th British Isles.

Common sandpiper (*Actitis hypoleucos*). At 19cm (7½in) long, the smallest of the three species It is a summer visitor, arriving in April.

Green sandpiper (*Tringa ochropus*). Length 23cm (9in); the largest of the sandpipers. Passing migrant sometimes seen in spring or autumn. A few pairs have bred in Britain.

Wood sandpiper (*Tringa glareola*). Length 21cm (8in). Like the green sandpiper, usually seen as a passing migrant, though a few pairs now breed here.

Several species of small and medium-sized waders are known as sandpipers. They all have pointed beaks with which they probe mud for food, in typical wader fashion. But, because their beaks are not as long as those of many waders, they can also feed by pecking at morsels on the ground.

Of the three species of sandpiper found in the British Isles one, the common sandpiper, is a summer visitor and breeds here in large numbers. The other two species, the green sandpiper and the wood sandpiper, are sometimes seen in the spring and autumn on their way to or from their breeding grounds in north-east Europe. They are known as passing migrants. Both, however, occasion-ally breed in this country in very small numbers.

Which is which? The common sandpiper is the smallest of the three species and it has the shortest legs and neck. It has dark olive-brown upperparts, with a dark rump and tail. The underparts are white except for some brown streaks on the neck and breast.

On the ground, the most distinctive feature of this species is the way it constantly bobs its head and tail up and down. In flight, it can be distinguished from other sandpipers by a conspicuous white wing bar.

The other two sandpipers are similar to each other, especially when seen on the ground. Both have dark upperparts speckled

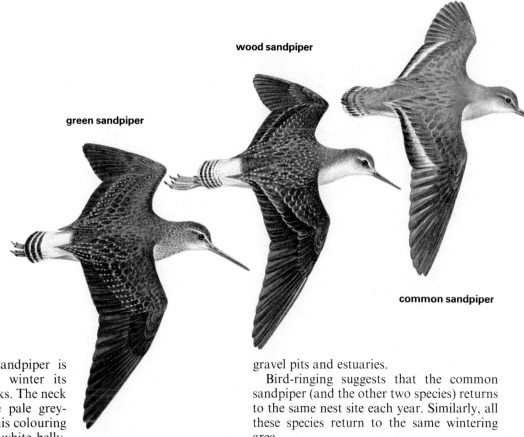

green sandpiper

wood sandpiper

common sandpiper

Above: The common sandpiper is widespread in upland Britain and Ireland, whereas the wood sandpiper is confined to a few sites in the Scottish highlands.

...ith buff, though the green sandpiper is ...arker (almost black) and in winter its ...peckling is reduced to a few flecks. The neck ...nd breast in both species are pale grey-...rown; in the green sandpiper this colouring ... sharply demarcated from the white belly, ...hereas on the wood sandpiper the two areas ...erge. Both species have a white rump, and ... paler face than that of the common sand-...iper.

The best way to tell the wood and the green ...andpipers apart when they are flying is to ...ook at their legs. On the green sandpiper ...ey are greenish and reach only as far as the ...p of the tail, or a little further. On the wood ...andpiper they are yellowish and reach well ...eyond the tail. Another difference is in the ...ndersides of their wings. These are dark on ...e green sandpiper, contrasting with its ...hite belly, but on the wood sandpiper the ...ndersides are buff-white. Neither species has ...e white wing-bar of the common sandpiper.

One final way to distinguish between the ...ree species is by their calls. The green ...andpiper gives a ringing three-note call: ...luit-weet-weet'; the common sandpiper ...tters a shrill piping 'pee-wee-wee', while the ...ood sandpiper has a shrill repeated 'chiff-...f-iff'.

The common sandpiper In April, after win-...ering in Africa, the common sandpiper ...igrates to Europe for the breeding season. ...uring migration it can be seen in many ...arts of Britain on its way to its breeding ...rounds, and it becomes widespread again ...a the autumn as it heads back to Africa for ...e winter. But during the breeding season ...t is confined to upland areas of Wales, ...cotland and the north of England. It is also ...ommon in the west of Ireland.

Common sandpipers breed beside clear ...reams, rivers and lakes. In the spring and ...utumn, during migration, good lowland ...tes to see them include reservoirs, flooded

Below: The nest of a common sandpiper is a simple hollow scraped out of the ground, sometimes lined with vegetation and usually sited beneath overhanging plants at the side of a stream or lake. The eggs (usually four) are laid in May or June. They are pale cream, speckled with reddish- or blackish-brown. Both parents help to incubate the eggs.

gravel pits and estuaries.

Bird-ringing suggests that the common sandpiper (and the other two species) returns to the same nest site each year. Similarly, all these species return to the same wintering area.

Exhilarating display flight Once the common sandpiper has reached its breeding ground, the male stakes a claim to an area that will be his breeding territory and defends it against rival males.

He also needs to attract a mate. To do this he performs a display flight, flying round and round, often soaring high into the air then descending steeply with stiff or quivering wings. Sometimes a female joins him and the pair fly round and round in fast pursuit flights. During these displays the birds sing a series of rapid trills and liquid notes.

The nest is a simple hollow or scrape, some-times lined with plant material or debris from

Left: Common sandpiper chicks. The young of all sandpiper species can feed themselves from birth.

Below: A green sandpiper. Its upperparts are darker than those of the common sandpiper, and speckled white. It has a white rump (not seen here) and the legs are greenish.

Bottom: The wood sandpiper is similar to the green sandpiper, apart from being smaller and having paler legs and underparts.

Accidentals

We take for granted the skill with which migrating birds return to the same nesting place year after year. But these are the successful ones. For a few birds things go wrong. A gale blows them off course, fog confuses them, or they get caught up in a migrating flock of a completely different species. Many perish, but a few survive, eventually turning up perhaps thousands of miles from their intended destination. These lost birds are called accidentals.

Each year, accidentals are sighted in Britain, causing great interest among birdwatchers since it may be the only chance in their lifetime for them to see a particular rare species.

a river or lake. Usually it is built under overhanging vegetation.

The number of eggs laid is usually four a typical number for a wader. The incubation is carried out by male and female equally, a is the rearing of the young. Among the three sandpiper species, only the common sandpiper shares these tasks equally between the parents.

The young are born downy and develop quickly. As soon as the down dries they leave the nest. At about two weeks old they begin to fly and a week later they are proficient.

The wood sandpiper This species is usually just an occasional visitor to these shores resting here during its migrations in spring and autumn.

A pair of wood sandpipers was recorded breeding in Northumberland in 1853, and again four years later, but there were no further reports until as recently as 1959. In that year two birdwatchers in Sutherland accidentally stumbled across an adult wood sandpiper and two recently fledged young. A pair of birds (presumably the same ones) bred there for the next three years, and since then several new breeding sites have been found, all in the north of Scotland.

The wood sandpiper usually nests among clumps of marsh vegetation. Both parents share in the incubation, but once the eggs have hatched the female leaves the breeding area, either immediately or within a few days. This behaviour is not uncommon among waders breeding in northern latitudes. The most likely reason is that there is more food available for the chicks if one parent goes.

The green sandpiper Like the wood sandpiper, this species is an occasional passing migrant in this country, its main breeding grounds being in north-east Europe. Very rarely a pair breeds here. The last recorded instance was in 1959.

Small numbers of green sandpiper spend the winter in Britain, particularly in the south west. They can be seen beside lakes and reservoirs, and are sometimes found feeding in the bottom of ditches and streams. The first indication of their presence is an explosive take-off and rapid flight up into the sky accompanied by a ringing call.

The green sandpiper is unusual among waders in that it often lays its eggs in trees using old nests of other birds. Very occasionally, the wood sandpiper also does this. The nest can be as high up as 10m (30ft) above the ground. Once the chicks have hatched and dried they have to be got down to the ground. This is done by the female calling to them from below so that the chicks jump from the nest. Being light and covered with soft down they rarely come to any harm.

Once the chicks are a week or two old, the female leaves them in the care of the male and begins the long flight to her wintering grounds. Once the young become independent, they and the male follow on the trek south.

Ringed plover

The ringed plover's plumage pattern serves two contrasting purposes: during nesting it is camouflage, and yet in display it is vivid and eye-catching.

Above: A ringed plover at rest on turf. There are two ways you can tell it is not a little ringed plover, even without seeing both birds together: this bird lacks a yellow eye ring, and there is no white border at the back of the black band on the forehead. The ringed plumage is good camouflage, but also has a vivid visual effect when the bird adopts a demonstrative posture: thus it plays a part in the highly developed display behaviour of the species.

Ringed plovers can be found on virtually every beach in Britain, at least for part of the year. They are selective in summer, choosing shingle, shell and sandy beaches, but some disperse in autumn to join flocks of other waders on mudflats and estuaries.

Confusion of identity In Britain, the only bird likely to be confused with the ringed plover is the little ringed plover. Both are aptly named since, especially in summer plumage, they have conspicuous black and white rings or collars on the head and neck. The difference in their size is only slight, so plumage features provide a much better way of distinguishing them.

The head pattern of both species is com-

Ringed plover distribution

Leap-frog migration

From extensive northern breeding areas, most of the world's ringed plovers migrate long-distance to Africa. In doing so, they 'leap-frog' the ringed plovers of Britain and Ireland, some of which migrate 'short-haul' to the Spanish and French coasts, while others winter on the south coast of England, or even nearer their breeding sites.

short migration
long migration
long migration

breeding area   wintering area

Identification features

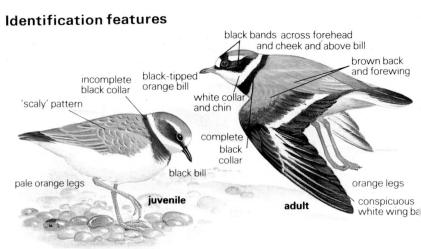

black bands across forehead and cheek and above bill

brown back and forewing

incomplete black collar

black-tipped orange bill

'scaly' pattern

white collar and chin

complete black collar

pale orange legs

black bill

juvenile

adult

orange legs

conspicuous white wing ba[r]

plicated. Each has a pale brown and black cap and a white forehead. Each is also black in front, behind and around the eye, and there is a white collar and chin, and a second black collar below this. However, of the two species, the ringed plover has more black on the crown, and it also lacks the yellow eye ring and a white border at the back of the black forehead band, which are characteristic features of the little ringed plover. The ringed plover's best distinguishing feature is a bold white wing bar, totally absent from its relative.

Such striking patterns prompt one to ask what purpose they serve. Recognition of other individuals of the same species is one obvious answer, but a study of the behaviour of these birds shows that two other factors are important: camouflage and display. It might seem surprising that the same plumage should suffice to enable a bird to be either inconspicuous or conspicuous, but this is certainly true of the ringed plover.

Camouflage for nesting Effective camouflage is essential during the breeding season because ringed plovers nest on the ground on wide, open beaches. Shells and pebbles typically give a very varied pattern of stripes and curves in a wide range of colours and shades, and the ringed plover's plumage blends perfectly into such a background. Even sandy beaches usually have a scattering of seaweed and stones which the plover can mimic.

The nest is a shallow depression, lined with small stones and odd bits of vegetation collected nearby. Predictably, the eggs are stone-coloured, being grey to buffish in ground colour, spotted and blotched with black and grey. They are laid one every day or two, four eggs being the usual clutch. The chosen site always has a good all-round view—rocks and other obstacles are avoided—so the incubating bird is able to watch for danger.

On the approach of a predator, or perhaps someone walking along the beach, two alternative strategies are usually possible. If the intruder is unlikely to approach closely, the incubating bird bird may sit tight and rely on its own camouflage for protection. How-

Above left: The ringed plover is a sand and shingle nester, and the form of its nest is typical of all the wading birds: a simple scrape in the ground. The pointed eggs are laid in May, June and July.

Ringed plover
(*Charadrius hiaticula*).
Wader breeding on beaches. Partial migrant, some birds wintering on mudflats and estuaries in the British Isles. Sexes alike. Length 15cm (6in).

Below: The distraction display is performed in order to lead an intruder from the nest. The bird feigns injury and runs or shuffles along with one wing raised and the other dragging over the ground or (as here) folded.

ever, if the intruder is likely to come within a few yards of the nest, the better alternative i[s] to leave the nest quietly, run some distanc[e] and then fly to safety. The logic behind thi[s] course of action is that the nest and eggs ar[e] even more difficult to see than the incubatin[g] bird, and unless the intruder knows exactl[y] where to look they are almost impossible t[o] find. When the danger is past, incubation ca[n] be resumed. Like other waders, ringed plover[s] have very rapid flight, so it would be possibl[e] for them simply to wait and then fly to safet[y] at the very last moment, but this sudde[n] movement would almost certainly reveal th[e] nest site and so jeopardise the eggs.

High failure rate Incubation is shared mor[e] or less equally between the two sexes, change[-] overs occurring at least once each hou[r] throughout the day and night. Off-duty bird[s] usually fly off to feed or stand sentinel on [a] raised piece of ground nearby, ready to soun[d] the alarm when necessary. Incubation last[s] 23-25 days, typical for waders but about twic[e] as long as the average garden bird. Throug[h]

stony banks.

Displays for many occasions Both male and female ringed plovers frequently perform eye-catching mock-injury displays in defence of their young, drawing the predator away from the nest. The birds also defend their nesting and feeding territories from one another, though in this the male is usually more active. Intruding ringed plovers are greeted with a marvellous threat display, in which the feathers on the breast, back, crown and under-parts are increasingly erected, greatly accentuating the black and white head patterning. To complete the effect, the tail is fanned, and constant calling draws attention to the display.

Yet more displays are adopted during pair formation, mating and nesting. The easiest one of these to see is the male's song flight. Throughout the breeding season, and particularly during the early stages of the nesting cycle, you can see him circling the territory, flapping his wings with deep, demonstrative strokes and constantly uttering melodious, piping notes.

Animal eaters Ringed plovers feed primarily on terrestrial and coastal invertebrates, using a characteristic 'run-stop-peck-run-stop-peck' technique. Even at night they hunt by sight, watching carefully for their prey to move and then pouncing. Marine polychaete worms, crustaceans and molluscs comprise the main diet, though at inland sites insects, spiders and even sticklebacks have been recorded. On mudflats where food is plentiful, they often group together, but they never form such tight flocks as other waders like dunlin and knot. When the tide covers feeding areas, ringed plovers retreat to roosting sites that they choose for their safety from disturbance: saltmarshes, beaches off-shore islets and farmland are all suitable.

out this time the eggs must be kept warm, even f this means enduring Easter snowstorms in heir bleak, windswept habitat.

It has been calculated that 60% of ringed plovers' nests in Britain are unsuccessful, and perhaps as many as 87% of those in eastern England. However, repeat clutches are laid and the majority of pairs probably raise at least one brood; some occasionally manage three. The very first eggs are laid in late March, and the last in July.

Ringed plovers are always careful to position their nests above the high tide mark, but some are still flooded by spring tides. However, the main cause of failure is predation, gulls, crows, foxes, dogs and rats all being to blame. Here, too, we can include ourselves, for many a clutch of eggs has chilled when people have inadvertently stood or sat close to a nest for too long. In cases such as these the camouflage of both birds and eggs is perhaps too effective, for the culprits are usually quite unaware of the problem.

With ever-increasing tourist pressure on our beaches, birds are adapting to alternative sites, so their overall population is probably not declining. Power station and oil refinery compounds have proved ideal, and some birds have nested on farmland by the coast. Further inland, particularly in northern England and Scotland, ringed plovers can be found in a variety of situations near water. Rivers, lakes, gravel pits and reservoirs may all have suitable

Above: Ringed plover chicks 'freeze' when they are alerted to danger.

Below: These eggs are beautifully matched in colour with the soil of the ploughed field.

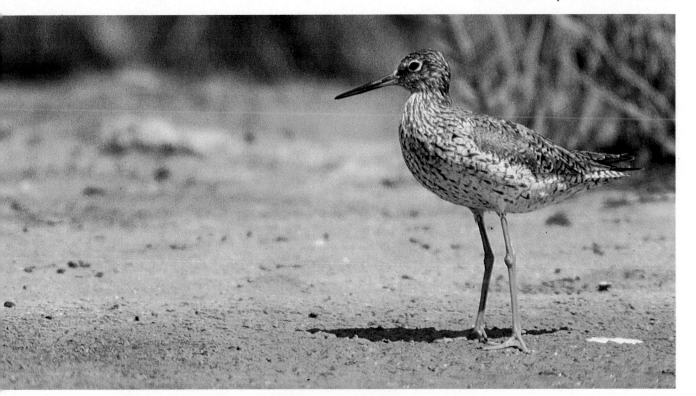

Redshank and spotted redshank

The redshank, famous for its bright red legs, is called the 'sentinel of the marshes' for its habit of calling loudly to warn of approaching intruders.

Above: On mud or a grassy nesting meadow, the redshank is a shy and restless bird. When it is suspicious, it bobs both its head and its tail as it walks along – just like the various sandpipers, which belong to the same genus.

The redshank is a slender, medium-sized, grey-brown wader with striking bright red legs. (In young birds, however, the legs are a dirty yellow.) The beak is long and thin, dark brown at the tip but deep red near the face. In summer, the redshank's back is a warm golden brown, with black patches, and the head and neck have well-defined black streaks. In winter the back is grey-brown with darker flecks, while the head and neck are greyish with sooty streaks. The flanks are speckled and streaked grey-brown, shading to a pure white belly.

Recognising redshanks By far the most conspicuous plumage feature of the redshank – in summer or in winter – is its pattern in flight. The rump is white and a broad white streak extends up the back between the wings. The tail is white, with narrow brown bars, and the wings are brown, but with a very broad white bar along their trailing edges. This striking pattern, coupled with the continuous noisy calls the bird utters, makes the redshank one of the easiest waders to identify.

In flight the redshank is vigorous, fast and rather erratic, somewhat reminiscent of a snipe in its sudden changes of direction. Often, immediately after landing, the redshank lifts both wings vertically over its back, as if stretching to relieve tired muscles after a long flight.

When walking it is normally a slow and graceful bird, something that is particularly apparent as it moves among other waders on the mud. Except at high tide, when all species are forced to pack together on the few remaining spots of dry land, redshanks rarely form large flocks.

Musical calls All of the redshank's many calls have a special musical quality, even the noisiest and most frantic of its alarm notes. The commonest notes, uttered by undisturbed birds, are a single beautiful but slightly mournful 'tuuu', and a trisyllabic 'tu-hu-hu'. The song, a series of yodelling variations on the calls, includes a 'tu-oodle' sound. It may be produced by a male standing on a prominent song perch – an old fence post, for instance – or in a yo-yoing hovering display flight.

Opposite: The bright red legs from which the redshank gets its name are clearly visible in this portrait of an adult bird.

Redshank (*Tringa totanus*). Resident wader, found inland in the north, and on eastern and southern coasts, on damp marshland, flooded fields, estuarine marshes and saltings; joined by migrants in winter. Length 28cm (11in).

Spotted or **dusky redshank** (*Tringa erythropus*). Passage migrant, appearing in Britain in April and May, sometimes overwintering on estuaries in south and south-east England and western Ireland. Length 30cm (12in).

Above: The nest of a redshank, with its usual clutch of four eggs, is always well-concealed. Both male and female takes turns to incubate the eggs. One parent often perches on a conspicuous post or pole (right) to keep watch for the approach of predators.

Below right: Change-over time at the redshank nest. One parent is rising off the eggs so that the other can take its turn with incubation. The incubating bird tends to sit tight until danger is right on top of it. Then it explodes noisily upwards, its flashing white wingbars usually being sufficient to distract more predators. Both parents will pursue an intruding animal with relentless dive-bombing attacks until it leaves the vicinity of the nest.

and feed themselves as soon as they are dry. Normally each parent keeps guard on half the family, both staying in close and alert attention until the young fly at about one month old. The parents may walk, or even swim, their family for considerable distances between feeding grounds. In the water the youngsters bob about buoyantly, propelled by their long-toed feet.

Delicate feeders For food redshanks concentrate mostly on small animals like worms and arthropods, especially midges and their larvae, which they catch on their inland marshy breeding ground. On their estuarine breeding and wintering areas they feed more on small shellfish and shrimps. The redshank's needle-fine beak is ideally adapted for picking up such tiny items of food as small spiders and even occasionally seeds.

Dual distribution Broadly speaking, the redshank is predominantly an inland bird in the north of Britain, but coastal in the east and south. It is relatively scarce in Wales and the Devon/Cornwall peninsula. Most breeding pairs seem to prefer damp marshland, fields with flooded patches and estuarine marshes.

Unlike so many of the waders, redshank are with us all year round. Because of their inland breeding habits, they tend to be more widely distributed in summer, but thinner on the ground. In winter they gather on the coast, usually in sheltered sandy or muddy estuaries. At this time the redshanks are joined by migrants from further north. Our own young birds tend to disperse after fledging; most do not travel far, but some cross to Ireland or France.

The spotted redshank A relative of the redshank, the spotted redshank is a slightly larger bird with longer legs and beak. In flight its white back, visible between the wings, is conspicuous, but the white trailing edge to the wing, so obvious in the redshank, is

Risky breeding Redshanks breed early, sometimes taking up territories in February. Eggs appearing in March are not unusual, while the season continues until late June or early July. It is thought that most pairs are single-brooded. The eggs, however, are so often taken by predators (crows, foxes, rats, weasels and even hedgehogs) or destroyed by the trampling of unwary cattle or flooded by unusually high tides or heavy rains, that replacement clutches must frequently be laid.

The nest is built in the heart of a large tussock of grass or sedge. The leaves of the tussock arch overhead to conceal the nest and eggs from flying predators such as crows. The four (occasionally three or five) olive eggs with darker spots are laid in the deep nest cup, which is lined with dry grasses. Both sexes share the incubation period, which lasts just over three weeks.

The young chicks, which hatch with well-developed legs and a thick covering of camouflaging down, are able to run about

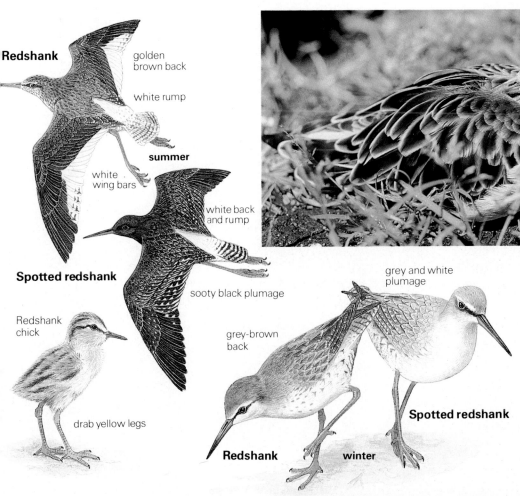

Redshank
golden brown back

white rump

summer

white wing bars

white back and rum

Spotted redshank

sooty black plumage

Redshank chick

drab yellow legs

grey and white plumage

grey-brown back

Spotted redshank

Redshank   **winter**

Above: Redshank in roosting posture. Redshanks are resident here, but harsh winters can take a severe toll. The winter of 1962-3 eliminated the breeding population of redshanks in Devon and it took a decade before they reappeared there.

Below: Spotted redshank in autumn plumage. At this time of year, it can be told from its relative, the redshank, by its larger size and paler colouring. Also, its legs and beak are noticeably longer.

lacking. The wing feathers are delicately barred and spotted with white instead of being uniformly brownish grey.

Towards the end of the spring passage in May, some migrant spotted redshanks start to acquire their spendid full breeding plumage. They become sooty black all over, with a few grey crescent-shaped bars on the breast and belly, and upperparts flecked with white spots, against which the reddish beak and long dark red legs are well set off. This beautiful plumage gives rise to the most commonly used colloquial name: dusky redshank.

This bird's delicate, rapid pecking technique of feeding is much the same as that of the redshank, but the spotted redshank takes advantage of its longer legs and can be seen wading out from the margins of marshland dykes or lagoons and feeding on small surface animals even when the water comes halfway up its flanks. At all times, though, the flight call is characteristic and unmistakable: an emphatic, two syllable 'chewitt', carrying well over the mudflats.

Spotted redshanks breed in the Arctic tundra of northern Europe, across Russia to Siberia, but winter mostly from the Mediterranean south to South Africa. Thus they can appear in Britain on passage in April and May or, in greater numbers, on the more leisurely return migration between late June and October.

Avocet

The avocet is a beautiful bird with long grey-blue legs, startling black and white plumage and a gracefully up-curving bill. It is very rare—your best chance to see this wader is through the viewing slots of a hide on one of two RSPB reserves.

Above: The avocet is an elegant, graceful bird with a strongly up-curving black bill about 9cm (3½in) long. It feeds on small invertebrates on the shoreline.

Although the avocet is still a rare British bird, there is certainly never any problem of identification or recognition. The snow-white plumage is strikingly marked: on the outer third of the wings there are convergent black bands on the back and across the wing coverts, and the nape and top of the head are also black. The most unmistakable recognition feature is the up curved bill. The avocet is a wading bird and frequents seashores where it feeds on invertebrates living in shallow water.

Speedy swimmer Most waders can swim adequately if necessary; but the avocet does so more easily than most because, unlike most waders, its feet are partially webbed. It frequently gets out of its depth when feeding, swimming positively and quickly to the next shallow area, and occasionally upending for food items while swimming. A characteristic feature is its walk—it has a brisk and busy gait and holds its body almost horizontal, carrying its neck in a graceful forward curve.

Pairing and nesting In most waders court-ship display is prominent and often lively, but avocets are remarkable in having virtually no courtship display. Male and female pair in spring and the bond between them appears to be strengthened through mating.

Although courtship is limited, the avocet's mating ceremony is distinctive and attractive. The female adopts an inelegant position of readiness in thigh-deep water. This stimulates the excited male to execute a particular dance in which he runs round the rear of the female several times from one side to another before mounting. After mating he jumps to one side of the female and both run forward together for several yards. Often one of his wings extends over the back of his mate—a touching gesture in human terms. The avocet's call is an unvarying 'kloot' or 'kluit'—the latter being the Dutch word for avocet.

The avocet is a gregarious bird which lives in colonies during the breeding season. This is probably a result of specialised breeding and feeding requirements, and a consequently limited choice of sites.

The parents scrape out a nest hollow on

Opposite: The shallow brackish water pools which form on saltmarshes are favourite feeding areas for the avocet.

Above: Apart from its more obvious attributes, the avocet is distinguished from other waders by its partially webbed feet.

sandy ground close to the water. They sometimes collect and arrange dead grass or other vegetation around the nest scrape, but they do not build a nest as such. Both parents share in the incubation, which begins once the final egg is laid and lasts for 22-24 days. The chicks start to feed themselves almost immediately after they hatch, pecking for insects and shrimps on the surface of the mud.

Feeding habits The avocet's feeding technique is unique among waders. It frequents saline and brackish pools and its food comprises the narrow range of creatures which can tolerate varying levels of salinity and desiccation–these include several species of shrimp, water beetles, midge larvae, aquatic flies and ragworms. The bird feeds by sweeping the upturned bill from side to side as it moves through the water.

The availability of food differs as lagoon water evaporates in summer and salinity increases. This is a critical factor in the survival of avocet young. The size of a family feeding territory is determined by the abundance or scarcity of food. The adults take their brood to areas rich in food and defend them aggressively from neighbouring families in a manner which contrasts with their mutual tolerance in nests positioned close together before the eggs hatch.

Numbers and distribution The avocet's numbers in the British Isles are on the increase today–an astounding fact considering that before World War II they had not bred in Britain for over 50 years. Although the full extent of the avocet's former breeding distribution and numbers in Britain is not known, it was probably never great, and almost certainly restricted to coastal areas in the south eastern part of Britain between the Humber estuary and the Sussex coast. What is known for certain is that the avocet's decline occurred well before the end of the nineteenth century. The drainage of fens and coastal marshes was a root cause of the decline; later, egg collecting and shooting for mounted specimens completed it.

In 1947, when access was again permitted to many of the east coast areas which had been fenced off during the war, it was discovered that avocets were breeding in two sites in Suffolk: Minsmere Marshes and Havergate Island, near Orfordness. Both these sites had

Above: The avocet turns its eggs to ensure they get an equal amount of warmth. The eggs are pale brown with black blotches, and four is an average clutch. The avocet's long legs have a strong blue tint which is particularly evident in the bird shown here. The legs account for about half the bird's total height.

Right: Avocets protect their chicks vigorously. The chicks, which already show some of the familiar marking of the adult bird, have partly webbed feet at birth. Initially the chick's bill is straight, but it develops the sideways feeding motion of the adult before the beak gets its characteristic up-turned shape.

een flooded during the war, and now provided perfect conditions of shallow water and low banks for the birds to return and breed. During the hot summer of 1947, round-the-clock vigils were organised under great secrecy at both sites by pioneers of the RSPB. Four pairs of avocets bred at Minsmere that year and the same number at Havergate.

The RSPB link Within two years of the discovery of breeding avocets the RSPB–then a body of only about 5000 members–negotiated a lease on Minsmere and strained its slender resources to the limit to buy Havergate Island outright. As a result of this act of boldness and foresight on the part of the RSPB, the avocet population built up steadily through the 1950s and 1960s. During this period the number of pairs increased at both sites to a maximum of about 100 on Havergate and 50 at Minsmere. The avocets are now dependent, like so many other breeding species, on the man-made lagoons that have been developed and are managed for the purpose.

The problems have been immense at both sites, both for the avocets and for the RSPB. They have had to combat the 1953 east coast floods, salinity variations leading to poor food supplies, as well as egg collectors and predation by gulls. These reverses have been successfully overcome, and the avocet is now

firmly established. The RSPB have taken the avocet as their own special emblem–an emblem that reflects the parallel successes of both the society and the birds.

Need for protection The avocet is an outstanding example in the British Isles of a bird that needs the security of tightly wardened reserves, as well as the skilful management that permits them to share a crowded lagoon with other species. It is unlikely that the avocet would maintain its toehold here, were it not for the reserves at Minsmere and Havergate.

Whether the avocet can spread much further in the British Isles is doubtful as suitable habitats are so restricted. Nevertheless as the avocet is a partial migrant we may expect visiting birds–usually from Denmark and Holland–on many estuaries in the South of England.

The breeding range of the avocet extends far beyond our coastline to the shores of Africa–though those at Minsmere disperse only to Iberia, or other parts of the British Isles. This shows the enormous thermal range of the world population–from the roasting hot lakes of East Africa, to the chilly, uninviting mud flats of East Anglia.

Avocet (*Recurvirostra avosetta*), 43cm (17in) from beak to tail. Breeding distribution restricted to Minsmere and Havergate. Non-breeding winter visitors around south coast.

Below: The black crescents and black wing-tips across white wings, make a striking pattern when the avocet is in flight.

adult in flight

adult using sweeping motion of bill to feed

Left: In cloudy water, where the avocet cannot see prey clearly, it traps its food by feel. The bird holds its bill slightly open under water, sweeping from side to side to catch small invertebrates. In clear water or from the surface, it pecks at its prey.

up-curving bill

adult in defence posture protecting chick

Below: Both parents incubate the eggs using their brood patches—feather-free areas that give direct contact from the adult's skin to the eggs and so transfer heat. The chicks are a sandy, brownish colour on top, which provides some camouflage.

chick with camouflage coloration

drooping wings

Gulls are generally but not exclusively coastal birds; and at least six species are common around the British Isles. Here we look at four of our larger, familiar gulls: the herring, the lesser black-backed, the great black-backed and the common—which is not quite so commonly seen as its name suggests except in Scotland and Northern Ireland. These four gulls are difficult to tell apart, especially the immature birds.

Herring gulls are the most numerous of our gulls. They breed all round the coasts of Britain and Ireland, except the stretch from Flamborough south to the Thames. In this area only a few isolated pairs have been recorded—in north Norfolk and Orfordness. The further north and west you go, the more abundant herring gulls are. In 1969-70 there were more than 333,000 pairs–157,000 in Scotland, 52,000 in Ireland, 70,000 in England and 54,000 in Wales and the Channel Islands. These numbers are increased in winter by visitors from north-west Europe.

Herring gulls nest along the steep cliff edges, among rocks, on ledges and stacks, and sometimes on shingle banks or in sand dunes. Many nests are isolated, but where there are plenty of suitable sites then something like a colony develops–though this is more because of opportunity than design.

During the 1920s, a few herring gulls began to nest on buildings in south-west Britain; now many more are choosing this

Above left: The herring gull, an opportunist feeder, is a persistent scavenger behind trawlers and also finds food on ploughed fields and refuse tips.

Herring, common and black-blacked gulls

Identifying gulls by sight is not easy, nor can you rely on habitat as a guide. Although we associate these birds with our cliffs and shore-line, not all are coastal.

Below: The herring gull frequents rocky coasts and cliffs while the lesser black-backed gull prefers flatter sand dune areas or grassy cliffs. The great black-backed gull nests on rocky coasts, as does the common gull which also nests inland in northern Scotland.

Herring gull

Lesser black-backed gull

Great black-backed gull

Common gull

type of nesting site. In seaside hotels and boarding houses, landladies complain that visitors' sleep is disturbed by the gulls' early morning chorus.

Both parents build the nest using grass, seaweed and other plant material. The nest, which is located in sparse vegetation among rocks, offers no protection against such predators as the great black-backed gull and the crow. The adult gulls therefore have to guard their eggs and chicks in, or close to the nest.

The male and female herring gull share the work of nest building, gathering grass, bits of seaweed, lichen and heather. In May or June the female lays a clutch of two or three (rarely four) eggs. These are greenish-blue to umber-brown in colour, with darker blotches and spots. The interval between the laying of each egg is usually only one day, but may be as long as five days. Both parents share in the incubation which lasts 25-27 days.

The chicks hatch at two day intervals and are fed by both parents. The red blob on the tip of the adults' lower beak gives their offspring an aiming point when taking food. No matter how wheedling their cries, the young will not get fed unless they peck at the red spot; the adult then regurgitates food from its crop.

When the young are seven weeks old, they are able to fly, feed and fend for themselves. In their first year they are almost indistinguishable from lesser black-backed gulls–both are mottled brown with darker flight feathers, and a dark end to their brown tail. After a spring moult, the young herring gulls' second summer plumage is much like the adults, but with a few brown flecks. However, their wings are still fully mottled. By their fifth year the juveniles have caught up with the adults both in colour and maturity –they are ready to breed.

After the breeding season, herring gulls disperse only as far as the nearest sources of food, usually provided by man–behind his ploughs, on refuse tips and round fishing harbours. They scavenge for carrion and kill anything they can, including other gull nestlings. Herring gulls take potatoes, turnips, grass and fruits in season, as well as crustaceans, insects and worms. In fact the herring gull is omnivorous to a degree rivalled only by Man.

Anyone who has visited the seaside, or seen these gulls following a farmer's plough, will be familiar with their raucous calls. These include a low-pitched 'kyoo-kyoo', an excited 'kee-u-kee' and a brief loud 'oww' or 'e-oo'.

Lesser black-backed gulls often breed close to or in mixed colonies with their close relatives the herring gulls. Their distribution is similar but their numbers are smaller– under 50,000 pairs.

Lesser black-backed gulls always nest in

Great black-backed gull *(Larus marinus)*, 70-75cm (27-30in) long, wingspan 165cm (65in). White except for black mantle and wings. Legs are pale flesh pink.

Lesser black-backed gull *(Larus fuscus)* (left), marginally smaller than herring gull. Dark slate-grey back, yellow legs.

Herring gull *(Larus argentatus)* (right) 55-60cm (22-24in) long. Wingspan 130cm (52in). Pale silvery back, flesh-pink legs.

Common gull *(Larus canus)*, 45cm (18in) long, wingspan 120cm (48in). Back is mid grey, legs greenish-yellow. Unlike others, no red spot on beak. Smallest of this group.

dense colonies well back from the edge of the cliff. They may even take to islands in lakes. Unlike herring gulls, newly hatched lesser black-backed gull chicks leave the bowl of the nest as soon as they have dried out, to find shelter from predators. They hide in vegetation such as bluebells and bracken. Another difference is the lesser black-backed gulls' defensive behaviour: they attack any intruders into a colony with threatening dive-bombing displays that avoid actual physical contact.

The nest and eggs of lesser black-backed gulls closely resemble those of herring gulls, and the parents have similar behavioural characteristics in nest building, incubation and parental care. Their calls also follow a similar pattern, but the notes are generally quieter and lower-pitched. They include a noisy 'quow', a quickly repeated 'kook-kook-kook' and a lively 'eck-eck-eck'.

Lesser black-backed gulls are choosy in their diet, feeding mainly on the shore and arable land. Here they feed on crustaceans, worms, molluscs and insects, as well as occasionally scavenging for carrion. They hardly ever touch plants.

Most lesser black-backed gulls migrate southwards in winter to north-west Africa and the Iberian Peninsula. An increasing number, however, have started to spend the winter in the British Isles, particularly in the warmer south west.

Left: Both male and female herring gull build the nest of seaweed and lichen in a solitary spot along the edge of the cliff. The female lays two or three blotched and spotty eggs which vary in colour from greenish-blue to umber-brown.

Right: Herring gull chicks depend entirely on their parents for food and protection against predators. In their early stages all gulls are difficult to tell apart — most having a bold mottled down pattern.

Below: Lesser black-backed gulls — one of the fiercest species — fight over territory rights. They nest well back from the cliff tops; here they are on a rocky surface with shrubs in the background.

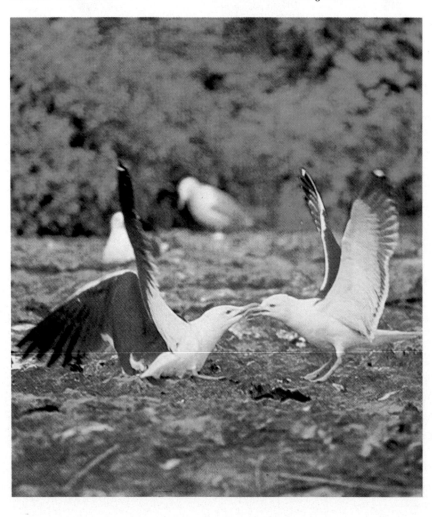

Great black-backed gulls, as big as geese, are the largest of our four gulls. Juveniles in their first year are darkly mottled; their plumage patterns in subsequent years are similar to those of the lesser black-backed and herring gulls.

They are birds of the north Atlantic, with a steadily increasing range and population. They have colonized the east coast of Scotland since 1960 and are found all around Ireland. Elsewhere in the British Isles, nesting is confined to western and northern coasts and there are few nests from the Forth to the Isle of Wight.

Great black-backed gulls tend to nest singly, on the top of outcrops, stacks and on small offshore islands as well as in lakes. The same pair may occupy a site for years. There is a colony of 1800 pairs on North Rona, but this is exceptional.

The nest and eggs of great black-backed gulls are proportionately larger than those of lesser black-backed gulls. The female lays her eggs on alternate days, and both adults share in the 26-28 day incubation. Both also feed the young, for about 50 days; after this the young can fly and look after themselves. The juveniles' plumage is paler than that of young herring and lesser black-backed gulls, and the underparts are whitish. Great black-backed gulls breed in their fourth year — earlier than the other two birds mentioned so far.

early autumn the population is increased by the many immigrants from northwest Europe and Iceland. These birds fly north again in March or April and are joined by others who have wintered further south. Non-breeding immature birds spend the summer all round our coasts.

Common gulls breed all round the northern hemisphere, but their name is ill-chosen in England and Ireland. The greatest numbers are in the Scottish Highlands and northwest Ireland. They are as much birds of inland waters as coastal species. No census of these birds exists in Britain because so much of the terrain is hard to cover. However, isolated pairs have nested at Dungeness, Anglesey and in the Pennines.

Common gulls are the smallest of this group of gulls – markedly smaller than herring gulls. They are best distinguished by the lack of a red blob on the tip of the lower beak, which also makes their head look rather pointed. During the breeding season common gulls are so rowdy that the noise can be unbearable. Both sexes take up a non-stop, shrill, rapid chorus of 'keeya-keeya-keeya', passing it on from group to group. As with other gulls, their vocabulary is extensive, but they hardly call at all in winter.

The nest, clutch and incubation are much the same for the herring gull. The young hatch on consecutive days, and take food from their parents until they can fly at five weeks old. Young common gulls have a whitish base to the tail with a black terminal band as well as a black bill and brown legs.

Common gull numbers are supplemented in winter by migrants from Europe. Huge flocks roost in winter on reservoirs (over 40,000 on Gladhouse in Midlothian). They are abundant in this season all down the east coast. In spring they return abruptly to their breeding places, leaving immature gulls to spend the summer in East Anglia. These young gulls breed in their fourth year.

The call of great black-backed gulls is much like that of herring gulls and lesser black-backed gulls, but is deeper and more resonant.

Great black-backed gulls are omnivorous, taking any kind of carrion, as well as killing weak lambs. They are also fierce, attacking puffins in daytime and any Manx shearwaters which land too far from their burrows on moonlit nights. They kill their prey, then turn it inside out to eat the tender flesh and avoid the tough skin and feathers.

The number of great black-backed gulls is rising, and the Operation Seafarer census in 1969-70 counted 22,000 breeding pairs, 16,000 of which were in Scotland. In the

Above: A great black-backed gull preens her feathers, while incubating her eggs. The common gull (right) concentrates more on just protecting her eggs. Her slender bill, with no red spot, distinguishes this gull from other species. The eggs are a pale blotchy olive in colour.

Common and Arctic terns

The Arctic tern is one of the world's greatest travellers, and the common tern is not far behind it; these two maritime birds, both notable for their graceful flight and endurance, well deserve their popular name of 'sea swallows'.

Below: Common terns calling. Despite their propensity for long-distance travel, common terns can be seen from spring until mid-autumn, feeding close inshore near many coastal resorts.

Terns have aptly been given the popular name 'sea-swallows', for they are perhaps the most graceful and elegant of our seabirds. Silver-grey and white, with darker wing-tips and black cap, and long tail streamers, they are smaller and much slimmer than any of the gulls. All are migrants, travelling to fish in the oceans of the southern hemisphere during our winter, and returning to our coasts to breed in the summer.

The two species most often seen off British coasts during the summer months are the common tern and the Arctic tern. Both fit the general description above, and are so similar in size, shape and plumage that they may often be very difficult to identify with certainty. Because of this, birdwatchers have coined the jargon term 'comic terns' for those whose identity has not positively been confirmed.

Telling them apart If a really close view can be obtained in good light, then you can see some plumage differences which distinguish the two. In a mixed group (and on passage mixtures of the two are often seen) standing on a beach, Arctic terns are noticeably shorter in the leg than common terns: they are so short-legged in fact, as to seem to be sitting rather than standing. Especially during the height of the breeding season, Arctic terns have a totally blood-red beak, while common terns have black tips to their orange-red beaks, often extending to half the beak's length.

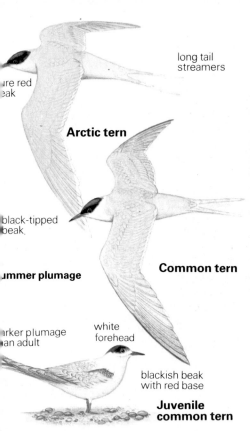

long tail
streamers

Arctic tern

ᵤre red
ᵉak

black-tipped
beak

Common tern

ᵤmmer plumage

ᵃrker plumage
ᵗan adult

white
forehead

blackish beak
with red base

**Juvenile
common tern**

Towards the end of the summer, as the adults
moult into winter plumage, beak colours
become drabber and this feature is less
reliable. Both species acquire white foreheads
in the autumn. Young birds have blackish
beaks and so cannot be separated by this
feature. Again, with the birds seen at rest, the
tail streamers of the Arctic tern (part of the
origin of the term 'sea swallow') extend for a
couple of inches or more beyond the folded
wing tips, while the common tern's streamers
and wings are about the same length.

Perhaps the best separation feature of all
is the wing pattern, seen when the birds are in
flight. The primaries, or flight feathers, of the
Arctic tern appear slightly translucent in the
light, giving the impression of an almost
luminous white patch in the outer section of
the wing. This noticeably bright area has only
a very narrow grey-black border along the
leading edge of the outermost feather and
along the trailing edge of the outer part of the
wing. In contrast, the common tern has a pale
smoky-grey outer half to its wing, above and
below, and its grey-black feather margins are
more extensive, especially on the upper wing
surface.

Listen to the call There are also slight
differences in the calls of the two species, but
these require a great deal of experience
before they can be successfully used as an
identification feature. Both have a long-
drawn-out 'keeee-yaaaah' call. In the common tern, the emphasis is strongly placed on
the first syllable, which forms the longer part
of the call, while in the Arctic tern the two
syllables have roughly the same length and
emphasis. On migration, the common tern
uses a 'kik-kik-kik' call which can sometimes
be distinguished from the higher pitched,
whistling 'kee, kee' of the Arctic tern.

Terns in spring During the breeding season,
terns fish close inshore, 'flickering' along
lazily in the air a few feet above the waves
before suddenly turning and plunging headlong into the sea. Often these dives result in an
audible 'plop' and a considerable splash, but
the bird penetrates only a few inches rather
than submerges deeply.

Arctic terns are colonial breeders, and the
colonies may be thousands strong. They are
birds of the Arctic, as their name suggests,
nesting on barren beaches and tundra. The
nest is a shallow scrape, lined with fragments
of shell and sometimes vegetation, and containing one, two or three eggs which are
incubated for about a month. The young
wander about soon after hatching, and fly
four or five weeks later. In Britain and
Ireland, not surprisingly, they are birds of
remote islands and beaches in the north and
west.

Generally, Arctic terns shun areas disturbed by man, but at one of their more
southerly breeding colonies, on the Farne
Islands, they have become accustomed to the
regular but well-managed parties of visitors
that are allowed to pay brief visits to their

Above: An Arctic tern brings
food to the nest after a
fishing flight close inshore.
The prey is usually small fish
or shrimps, and the fish are
caught one at a time, not in
a beakful as with puffins.
Early in the season the male
feeds his mate, an activity
known as courtship feeding.

Arctic tern (*Sterna
paradisea*); summer visiting
seabird, almost entirely
coastal. Breeding range
more northerly than that of
common tern, wintering
grounds more southerly.
Length 36cm (14in).

Common tern (*Sterna
hirundo*); summer visiting
seabird, mainly coastal but
sometimes nesting inland;
length 36cm (14in).

Below: A common tern
alights at its simple nest.

common tern
arctic tern

Above: Arctic terns breed on islands and beaches in the north and west; common terns breed further south and inland.

Above: A pair of common terns feed their young.

Left: Arctic tern eggs and young alike are perfectly camouflaged: a mixture of greys, fawns, blacks and whites that makes them almost invisible against a background of sand flecked with fragments of seaweed, vegetation and shells. Because of this, it is imperative that a birdwatcher coming across a tern colony should exercise extreme care in moving around: it is far better to sit and watch the goings-on from a distance.

Below: Arctic terns roosting on a reef.

coast and then on south to spend the winter in the Antarctic Ocean, often as far south as the edge of the ice shelf. Here, of course, it is again summer, and the Arctic terns have the benefit of an immense supply of small fish and plankton. One ringed bird, that lived for 20 years and travelled almost from pole to pole twice a year, must have had an unthinkably high lifetime mileage: certainly several million miles!

Apart from their differences in distribution and nesting habitat, common and Arctic terns are as alike in habits as they are in plumage. As most common terns migrate south to winter off West Africa, it would be easy to suggest that they had a much less extensive range than their Arctic cousins. That is not always true, for ringed common terns have been recovered in Australia, on the opposite side of the world from their British breeding grounds.

colonies. Indeed, they can be extremely aggressive to intruders, be they predatory birds or mammals such as foxes, weasels or stoats, and will often press home their vociferous dive-bombing attacks to the point of physical contact.

Although many common terns nest in the north of Britain and Ireland, others nest all around our coasts on isolated sandy beaches and shingle peninsulas, or on grassy islands among the mudflats of sheltered estuaries. Additionally, an increasing number are nesting inland, sometimes on natural islands in rivers but, more often, on man-made islands in flooded gravel pits and similar waters. Conservationists now even make large gravel-covered floating rafts, and moor them out in extensive areas of water, finding it relatively easy to tempt a few pairs of common terns to breed on them.

Global travellers Arctic terns probably see more hours of daylight each year than any other bird. Breeding in northern Britain and north into the Arctic Circle, they experience a virtually nightless summer. Having raised their young, they migrate southwards, crossing the equator and passing down the African

Razorbill

Razorbills breed in their thousands on our precipitous western and northern cliffs but spend the rest of the year over the sea. They are poor flyers, their wings actually being used as much for swimming as flying.

The razorbill is notable for its distinctive stance, elongated silhouette and striking black and white summer plumage. The stance of this bird on its breeding cliffs is usually upright, whereas on the water it appears low-lying and short-necked and about the size of a teal, but with the rather long, pointed tail usually held up at an angle.

Summer and winter appearance In summer the razorbill's underparts are pure white, while the tail, back, wings, neck and head are jet black, relieved only by a white vertical mark near the tip of the black beak, by a white line of 'furry' feathers stretching from the 'bridge of the nose' to the eye, and by a bold white wing bar. In flight this wing bar forms a conspicuous trailing edge on the inner half of the wing, visible both from above and below, and more striking than the wing bar of the otherwise confusingly similar guillemot. (At close range, confusion between the two is less likely since the slender, more dagger-shaped beak of the guillemot can be seen contrasting with the deeper, stouter beak of the razorbill. The guillemot is also chocolate-brown rather than black.)

The purpose of the white lines on the bill and head is not properly understood. It may be that they are simply plumage features that play a part in the razorbill's courtship: certainly display involves much preening and nibbling of the partner's head and neck. An alternative proposal—as yet untested—suggests that the marks may be of use when the razorbill is fishing under water, acting almost as the sights on a rifle.

In winter, when some of our razorbills remain well offshore in British waters, confusion with guillemots is even more likely.

Above: A razorbill in the typical upright stance. The white wing bar and beak stripe are particularly conspicuous. The beak is smaller in winter, the summer beak having been shed at the autumn moult.

Below: A group of razorbills —the wings are noticeably flipper-like in appearance.

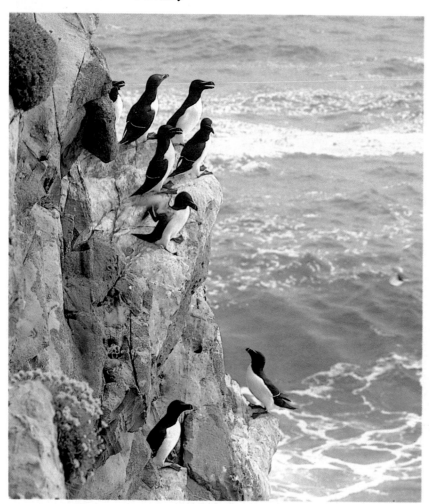

razorbills nest on open ledges, but many prefer cavities in the cliff face or seek similar shelter from such predators as the great black-backed gull deep beneath the rocks in the screes at the top or foot of the cliffs.

Most razorbill colonies are relatively small and interspersed with those of other auks; few colonies reach 10,000 pairs and only one, on Horn Head in County Donegal, is of any great size, perhaps exceeding 45,000 pairs. *Operation Seafarer*, a survey of our seabirds conducted in 1969-70, suggested an estimated 144,000 pairs as our grand total, and sample censuses since then would indicate little change, or perhaps a slight increase, in the last decade.

Courtship and breeding Razorbills may visit their breeding cliffs in fine weather almost any time after the New Year, but attendance becomes much more regular from March onwards. On the cliffs, pairs indulge in mutual neck-nibbling, but the sky is full of pairs involved in the 'butterfly' display. In this, the wing-beats are slowed right down and are exaggeratedly deep—hence the name.

The single massive egg is laid in mid-May and incubated in turn by both parents. As might be expected from the protected nature of the nest site, the razorbill egg is of normal chicken-like shape, not pointed and top-shaped like that of the exposed ledge-nesting guillemot. However, the spots and squiggles of dark markings, and the background colour

Both birds moult to a nondescript grey above, with smudgy margins, while the dark head is replaced by a pale greyish neck and face. As many are seen at long range, identification is often uncertain and only birds close enough to see the longer tail of the razorbill, or its square-ended beak, can be positively named.

Coastal distribution The results of ringing studies of British and Irish razorbills show that, in general, they travel further than guillemots, many reaching Mediterranean waters by mid-winter. In common with some other birds (gannets and gulls for example) razorbills, as they become older, tend to travel shorter distances during the winter, rarely moving further than the North Sea or the Bay of Biscay. Ringing recoveries also show that man plays a large part in causing the death of these birds: about half of those found dead are reported killed either by oiling, by being shot by Continental sportsmen, or by being drowned in fishing nets.

As much as 70% of the world razorbill population breed in Britain and Ireland. What makes our islands so special in this respect? Compared with much of Europe, our western and northern coasts, and the off-shore islands, are girt with precipitous cliffs. They form natural reserves, protected by treacherous and often rough seas. The rock of these cliffs, too, is often of just the type needed by the razorbills, cracking and fracturing to provide appropriate ledges and crevices. Some

Above: A staggering 70% of the world population of razorbills breed in Britain and Ireland, finding security on the inaccessible cliffs of our coasts.

Right: Only one large egg is laid each year by the razorbill; it is incubated by both parents.

Below: At the age of two or three weeks the razorbill chick must make its way down the cliffs to the sea, where it is safer from the predations of gulls.

of the shell, are just as varied as those on the guillemot egg, and presumably help the returning bird to identify its own egg among many others. During the nesting season the pair communicate with each other and with their neighbours using a variety of sepulchral, grumbling, low-pitched groans, but at other times they are totally silent.

The egg hatches about a month later, in mid-June, and is then fed by both parents. Like puffins, razorbills return to the nest carrying a beakful of several small fishes held crosswise. The approach to the nest is often difficult in the winds blowing about the cliff face. Razorbills, being heavy-bodied, with short, stiff wings, are not very manoeuvrable and may have to make several approaches before achieving a good landing.

Taking to the sea The razorbill chick remains on the nesting cliffs for only two or three weeks. Then, usually under cover of darkness to protect it from gull predation, it jumps from the cliff down into the sea. At this stage it is only half-grown, its wings little more than stubs and certainly incapable of sustaining flight for any length of time. Nonetheless, most chicks seem to survive perfectly well, protected by their down and fat from injury on the rocks on the way down. The chick then sets off for the open sea, accompanied by at least one of its parents. Whatever the apparent hazards, it would seem that this is less risky than staying on the cliffs to be persecuted by the gulls. While they are still at sea caring for the flightless chick, the adults moult all their flight feathers at once, thus themselves becoming flightless.

Diving and swimming The chicks can swim and dive well by the time they take to the sea, and beneath the water the birds are fast and expert swimmers, using both feet and wings for propulsion and steering.

Razorbill recognition features

The juvenile razorbill (below) looks much like the adult in shape, but has a shorter, blunter bill with no white stripe. In colour it resembles the adult in winter plumage, having greyish-white cheeks and throat patches. Male and female razorbills have similar plumage, both in summer and in winter.

black upperparts
white eye stripe
adult in breeding plumage
white bar on beak
white wing bar

juvenile

white throat and cheek patches

The body skeleton is better suited to life beneath the water than to flight, being a robust 'box girder' structure. A stout, inflexible backbone is joined to a strong breastbone by thick ribs, each with a backward-pointing projection overlapping the rib behind for additional strength. Within this rigid box the body organs are protected from the pressure of water during dives often many metres below the surface. The razorbill's prey includes sand eels, small sprats and the fry of a wide range of fishes and also some shellfishes and shrimps.

Above: Razorbills, like the other auks, have a whirring style of flight. The wings are used as much to propel the bird through the water as the air, while the large webbed feet (which act rather like the flaps on aircraft wings) are often used to steady and control the bird while landing— they are held in a 'straddled' position away from the body. The narrow, stiff wings and heavy body combine to make the razorbill somewhat clumsy in the air.

black guillemot **puffin** **razorbill** **guillemot**

Above: Four members of the auk family occur in Britain and Ireland: the puffin, razorbill, guillemot and black guillemot. They are all black and white birds characterised by an upright stance and the fact that they are expert divers and underwater swimmers. (Another member of the family, the great auk, became extinct in 1844 because of the depredations of egg collectors.) The puffin is the smallest of the four at 30cm (12in) long; the next smallest is the black guillemot (34cm/13½in), while the razorbill and guillemot are much the same size (41cm/16in long).

Razorbill (*Alca torda*). Resident seabird in British and Irish waters, breeding on precipitous cliffs on western and northern coasts and offshore islands; sea-going for rest of year. Length 41cm (16in).

Left: On the water razorbills appear low-lying and rather short-necked.

Puffin

The puffin, with its clown-like face, multi-coloured beak and quizzical expression, seems designed to attract our sympathy–and well it might. With the sharp decline in distribution and numbers, as well as the ability of some bird predators to kill them in mid-air, puffins need protection.

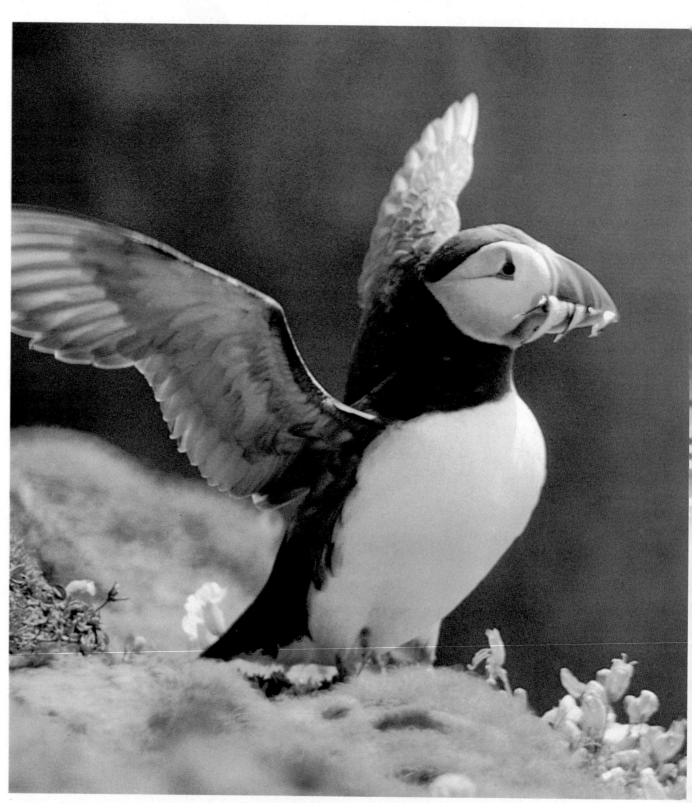

The puffin, in its 'dinner-jacket' of black and white feathers and colourful banded beak, is one of our most charming birds. It belongs to a family of seabirds–auks–which includes guillemots and razorbills. All auks characteristically hunt fish beneath the sea surface, and remain at sea outside the breeding season.

The puffin is a difficult bird to study in detail; comings and goings about the puffinry (as a colony of puffins is called) are notoriously erratic, and it nests in a burrow too deep and dark to permit eggs or young to be seen.

Distribution and dispersal For most of the year puffins live on our remote, almost inaccessible, northern coasts–particularly around uninhabited islands in the Orkneys and Shetlands. They once flourished along the Channel coast, but have now virtually disappeared from this region. In the east only suitable cliffs from Flamborough Head northwards support colonies. There are more puffinries on the western, generally rocky shoreline of Britain and Ireland. Here, the population increases towards the north.

In winter, puffins disperse widely from their breeding colonies, remaining at sea in ones or twos, not in the large groups (rafts) favoured by other auks. Some puffins stay in the North Sea or in the Bay of Biscay, while a few move south into the Mediterranean .

Puffins remain further out to sea than guillemots or razorbills, and most spend the winter scattered over the north Atlantic, feeding mainly on plankton. Even juvenile birds range far and wide: two nestlings ringed one year on St Kilda, off the Outer Hebrides, were recovered the following winter over the Newfoundland Banks.

Once a puffin moves away from its breeding site in winter, its brightly coloured beak turns a dull grey. The crisp margins of the black plumage also become blurred and the white areas of the face, breast and belly turn greyish. The puffin sheds the odd patch of wrinkled yellow skin at the corners of the mouth, as well as the horny red and grey triangles round the eyes.

Breeding sites The puffins return to their puffinries at varying times in spring. Many of

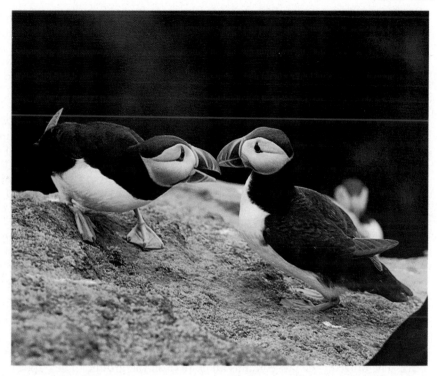

these sites are large, and some, with tens or even hundreds of thousands of pairs, are enormous. The Farne Islands are a good place to see puffins, on the National Trust reserve, but there are also large colonies on the Scilly Isles, Bempton Cliffs in Yorkshire and Skomer off the Pembrokeshire coast. Puffins are sensitive to the presence of humans, so all the best places to see them are inaccessible.

Some puffins live in holes in sea cliffs, while others choose the extensive screes and tumbled boulders at the head and foot of the cliffs. Most puffins, however, nest in grassland burrows, usually close to the cliff top. Here they either dig burrows themselves, making use of the long sharp claws on their strong feet,,or they take over a disused rabbit hole or Manx shearwater burrow.

The grassy slopes favoured by puffins are usually covered in pink thrift, white sea-campion, and often harebells–all flourishing on the guano deposited by the seabirds. This forms an attractive back-drop to the puffins' social gatherings at burrow entrances,

Above: Although puffins do not have an elaborate courtship display, the male and female bow to each other in a 'courtly' manner, and nibble one another round the back of the neck.

Opposite: As their young grows, the adults visit the burrow regularly with sand eels or similar fish held cross-wise in the beak.

Puffin (Fratercula arctica); about 25cm (10in) high. Distribution on coastal, rocky shores, particularly western Britain, Ireland and northern offshore islands.

Beak-full of colour

The huge, comical-looking, parrot-like beak of the puffin, is only coloured with red, blue and yellow bands for display in the summer breeding season. The adult sheds the horny outer sheath at the end of summer. It then grows a much smaller, slimmer and strictly functional grey winter beak — much the same size as that of the youngsters. This beak change is accompanied by plumage colour changes.

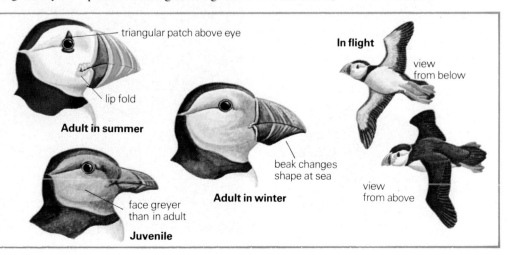

triangular patch above eye

lip fold

Adult in summer

face greyer than in adult

Juvenile

Adult in winter

beak changes shape at sea

In flight

view from below

view from above

and to the communal fly-pasts that are so much a part of the puffin's life.

These fly-pasts are a spectacular sight. The Kearton brothers, (pioneer Victorian natural history photographers) who visited St Kilda late in the 19th century, complained that the vast numbers of wheeling birds overhead seriously interfered with the light for photography. They also described a pattering 'like rain' which forced them to put up umbrellas for shelter; this was not, as you might imagine, from droppings, but from thousands of small feather parasites falling from the puffins above.

Beakfuls of fish The puffin catches fish by diving straight into the water. Its beak has enormous carrying capacity. Usually the bird catches only a dozen or so small fish and fry crosswise in its beak, in each expedition. But up to 60 small fry in one beakful have been recorded.

Ornithologists still do not fully understand how the puffin manages to catch more fish without dropping those it already holds in its beak. The hinge of the jaw contains an extra small bone, so the two halves of the beak open with the edges parallel. The edges are very sharp, allowing a good grip, but too tight a grip would just chop the fish into three. The roof of the mouth has many backward-pointing sharp projections. This must help the puffin as it sweeps through a shoal of fish, snapping first to one side, then the other, to secure its meal. In rough weather, when the sea is murky, the puffin concentrates on larger prey, up to 15cm (6in) long, but on calm days with clear water much of the catch is smaller.

Danger from the air On land the puffin waddles on its bright orange webbed feet. This may appear comical to us, but its clumsiness makes the bird vulnerable to predators, such as great black-backed gulls. These may pounce on puffins standing at their burrow entrance, or on a hungry well-grown chick peering out of the nest hole to see whether the next meal is on the way. The gulls sometimes chase and fly down an unfortunate puffin in mid-air, occasionally eating it while it is still alive. More often, they land and kill the puffin with heavy stabbing blows from the beak, before turning it inside-out to get at the flesh. Great skuas also attack puffins, especially on the water.

Crash-landings Puffins are not skilful fliers, and cannot easily escape the predators which attack them in mid-air. But they also have difficulty in landing in strong crosswinds. Their hesitant approach is exploited by some herring gulls. The gulls harass the puffins on their return runs to the burrow, and cause them to crash-land and drop their beakload of fish, which the gulls then gobble up. Although puffins are better adapted to marine life, landing on sea seems as precarious as landing on the ground. They appear to stop flying a few inches above the surface and land with a splash—rather like a thrown brick.

Once on or under the water the puffin is in its element. Short, stiff wings (similar to those of the penguin, but not so highly developed) and powerful legs provide propulsion, steering and levelling. The puffin's vertebrae are fused together, and the breastbone is very strong; the two are joined by sturdy ribs, each with an overlapping flange, so that the whole skeleton provides a rigid box girder structure, capable of protecting the vital organs from the pressure of deep dives.

Pressure on puffinries Sudden declines seem to be a feature of the puffin's history: some

Nest and young

The parents inspect a likely burrow (right) to prepare for the rearing of the chick. In the depths of the hole, the female lays her single, dirty white egg. By June the egg has hatched into a plump ball of sooty black, fluffy down (below) with a small triangular beak and dark eyes. Inside the dingy, dark hole the chick makes strange grumbling and groaning moans which may serve to guide the parents to the right hole. The chick is tended by both parents for about 40 days, after which it fends for itself.

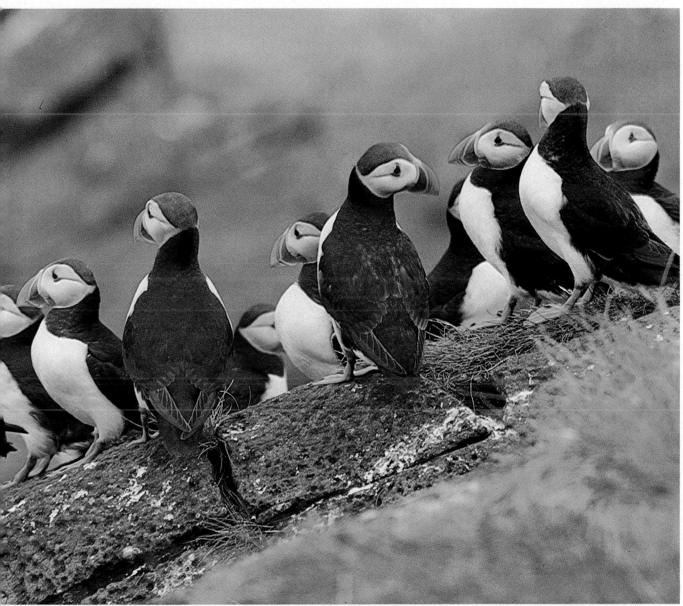

are due perhaps to chemical or oil pollution, or to the accidental introduction of the predatory brown rat, as on Lundy – which was formerly known as the 'Isle of Puffins'.

There was also a huge puffinry on Grass-holm, off the Pembrokeshire coast, until over-intensive burrowing by the puffins made the thin soil layer friable, so that erosion by wind and water left only bedrock. The puffins declined but an enormous gannetry then developed on the island. The problem is increased by the puffins' liking for grassy slopes on which sheep feed through the summer months. The sheep may easily trample in the burrow roof.

Local declines and increases are to be expected in any bird population, but the enormous decline in puffin numbers on islands like St Kilda in recent years is alarming. With the evacuation of the last islanders from St Kilda 50 years ago, the puffins might have been expected to expand in this remote stronghold. But *Operation Seafarer*, a seabird census taken in 1969-70, put the entire puffin population at just under 500,000 pairs – less than the number of birds

found on several individual colonies only 20 years earlier.

Harvested for food Against the background of this decline, it is difficult to understand the past stability of puffinries on remote islands including St Kilda, where for centuries the puffin was hunted and eaten. Each year many thousands, sometimes as many as 100,000, were slaughtered for food. Some were eaten immediately while others were split open and salted or dried for consumption during the winter when protein-rich food was scarce.

There were no long-term drops in puffin numbers. It seems that the good husbandry of the islanders, who took a strictly rationed 'crop' that they knew the population could sustain, ensured this. Even today, in the Faroe Islands and elsewhere, puffins are snared or netted for food. Their natural inquisitiveness leads them to venture too near the fowler and his traps.

The most pressing conservation concern today is the proximity of so many major puffin colonies and feeding areas to the expanding oilfields of the North Sea.

Above: Puffins breed in colonies, and communal gatherings around the burrow entrances are a common sight during the breeding season. Puffins, however, are sensitive to human disturbance. This is unfortunate for them, as more leisure time and modern transport now allow many more people to look for puffins than in the past. The moral is simple: always keep your distance and preferably look for puffins on established bird reserves, where disturbance is minimal and the birds are used to visitors. You can see puffins on the National Trust reserve on the Farne Islands, or at the RSPB reserve on Bempton Cliffs, Yorkshire, or from organised boat trips around the Scilly Isles.

Songbirds and garden birds

Many of our most familiar, everyday birds are included in this chapter, as are many of the most popular: their popularity largely due to the richness and variety of their song.

It is well worth considering the origins of this group of birds. Some 2000 years ago, much of Europe was covered in forest. Oak, ash and lime grew in the lowlands, beech grew on the chalky soils, conifers grew on the sands and in the uplands, and water-loving species like alder and willow grew in the substantial wetland areas which existed in river valleys in the days before land drainage. Man was of course present then, but in very small numbers. As the human population grew, so did the need for a more sophisticated farming system to produce food. To raise crops and stock, it was necessary to make clearings in the woodland cover.

Most of these clearings would naturally be near to centres of population, and these in turn would have been located in the most hospitable areas—mostly in the milder, drier lowlands. Hence most of today's remaining forests are in the remote and wet northern and western uplands. In the last 500 years these clearings for farming have expanded more rapidly, both to feed a fast-growing population, and to provide a surplus for export, for building houses and ships, and for fuel. Now we are left with only a residual pattern of cover which varies from the still predominantly wooded northern areas to the 'prairie farming' expanses of some fertile lowlands—a matrix of fields and woods with an interlinking network of hedges and spinneys.

Overall, this process has probably been extremely beneficial to birds. While it is true that some larger forest-loving birds (like the honey buzzard) will have suffered, continuous, dense mature woodland is a relatively poor habitat for birds, and therefore not particularly rewarding for birdwatchers. Creating farmland has vastly increased the woodland 'edge'—the area most preferred by birds in that it provides shelter, some food and nest sites, but also allows access to other food sources in the fields.

Thus it is this matrix that supports throughout the year large numbers of our wide range of resident seed and fruit-eating birds—each well supplied because of the variety of plants that grow *outside* the mature wood—and which holds many of our summer visitors (such as the warblers), that are primarily insectivorous, because on such a varied habitat a wide variety of insects naturally flourish.

Of these farmland and hedgerow birds, a considerable number have proved adaptable enough to consider our gardens as an extension of their preferred habitat: blackbirds, robins and blue tits are typical examples. Some—the feral pigeon and the house sparrow come to mind—have even adapted well to the apparently stark conditions of the hearts of our cities. Yet others have been encouraged to change their lifestyle. The blackcap is one such bird: a migrant, and largely insectivorous, it is now wintering regularly in northern Europe where its natural food is augmented by garden bird-feeding tables.

Opposite: A great spotted woodpecker swoops from its nest hole in the trunk of an oak.

Woodpigeon, collared and turtle doves

Pigeons and doves vary in size and colour but all have a plump body, small head and slender beak. They have succeeded in adapting to Man's urban sprawl, and have withstood the threat of the shotgun by rapid flight and consistent breeding.

Below: Turtle doves are thinly distributed on farmland south of a line between Durham and Lancashire (they are scarcer in west Wales and Cornwall). Their main food plant, which grows here, is fumitory.

There are about 300 species of pigeons and doves in the world, five of which occur in the British Isles. Whether you call them 'pigeon' or 'dove' is a matter of personal preference –though generally pigeons are large birds with short, square tails, and doves are more slightly built with long, rounded tails.

Cliff cousins Multicoloured town pigeons are a common sight in urban areas on buildings, statues and railway stations as well as in gardens. They are domesticated descendants of the rock doves, which now live only on remote sea cliffs in north and west Scotland and the Atlantic coast of Ireland. These 'true' rock doves also occur around the Mediterranean, on coasts and near inland cliffs. In Britain, however, it is their town cousins that thrive, with buildings for nest sites, ample supplies of bread and other scraps for food and an extraordinary tolerance of Man's proximity.

In the early days of agriculture, most farms had a dove-coat, containing free-flying, domesticated rock doves, which were bred for their different colours and racing abilities. The domestic birds look quite different from the cliff-dwelling ones, but extensive interbreeding between the two has 'contaminated' all but the most remote rock dove colonies. However, breeding feral populations tend to revert after a few years to the 'blue' coloration

...ion found in true rock doves.

Stock doves are easily confused with rock doves. Both have iridescent-green neck patches which they use in courtship display, but stock doves are less gregarious, more inconspicuous birds and lack the bold markings of their relatives. Once found only in south and east England, they have spread throughout Britain with the increase in agriculture.

Woodpigeons have also increased dramatically in number and range, and are even colonising the Outer Hebrides and Shetland Isles. They are unusually tame birds in urban areas where their numbers are increasing. A broad, white crescent bisects each wing. It is concealed when the wings are folded; in flight, however, it is obvious and recognised by other pigeons as a hazard-warning signal. Woodpigeons are larger than other British pigeons and have proportionately longer tails than stock doves. A good way to identify woodpigeons is by their bold white neck patch or ring–hence their other name 'ring' dove.

Collared doves take their name from the incomplete, white-bordered but otherwise black neck collar. The smallest of our resident species, they spread from the Continent and have colonised most of the British Isles in the last 25 years with a dramatic population explosion. Associating closely with Man and his cereal grain, collared doves are now common birds in villages and suburban areas.

Turtle doves are even smaller than collared doves, with a shorter, more rounded tail. They fly in a dashing manner, with quick flicking wing-beats, and when overhead the white belly appears outlined by darker wings and tail. Turtle doves spend the winter in Africa, and return in late April to May.

Cooing songs Pigeons and doves have a characteristic, monotonous call which they use to establish territories. The establishment of territories helps to separate nests and reduce the dangers from predators. Wood-

Above: Unlike most birds, a woodpigeon does not need to lift its head to allow water to drain down the throat with each gulp.

1 **Rock dove /feral pigeon**
(Columba livia)
2 **Stock dove**
(Columba oenas)
3 **Turtle dove**
(Streptopelia turtur)
4 **Collared dove**
(Streptopelia decaocto)
5 **Woodpigeon**
(Columba palumbus)

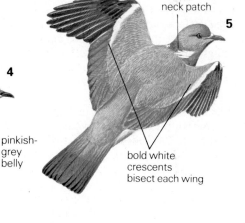

longer tail

4

white belly

pinkish-grey belly

long tail

bold white neck patch

5

bold white crescents bisect each wing

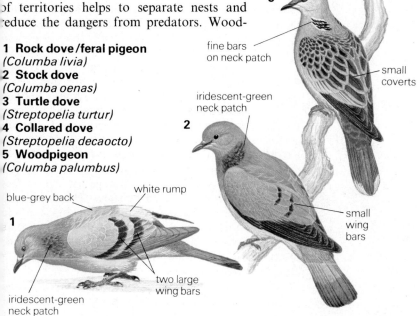

fine bars on neck patch

small coverts

iridescent-green neck patch

2

blue-grey back

white rump

1

two large wing bars

small wing bars

iridescent-green neck patch

pigeons, collared doves and stock doves have five, three and two-note rhythms respectively; they repeat each phase several times in succession. Male collared doves also have a nasal-sounding song which is often mistaken for the call of the cuckoo. The cooing of domestic and feral pigeons is well-known and seems not to have changed from that of rock doves. The turtle doves' soothing purr, which they sing hidden in deep cover, can easily go undetected.

Display flights Pigeons and doves also advertise their territory by flying in display positions. Rock and stock doves glide with wings held stiffly in a 'V'. Turtle and collared doves fly up and then parachute down with tail fanned and wings held below horizontal level. Woodpigeons have an undulating display-flight; they fly up, stall and 'clap' their wings two or three times, and then glide down before repeating the process. The claps, made on the downstroke of the wing-beat, are similar to the crack of a whip–contact between the wings is not important.

Nests Pigeons usually build their nests in trees, but also in holes, on ledges, and even on the surface of the ground. Sometimes you may see the conspicuous white eggs visible through the flimsy platforms of twigs. However as females incubate the eggs at night, and males take over during the day, the eggs are rarely left uncovered.

Pigeons lay only two eggs in each nest; but breeding continues until September or later and the parents raise at least two broods. Sometimes they make the second nest and the female lays her eggs even before the first brood has left. Pigeons and doves produce protein-rich pigeon milk–a cheesy curd that sloughs off from the lining of part of the crop;

Above: A special feature of pigeons and doves is their powder down feathers— small feathers of a crumbly material that breaks up into a dust to help in preening other feathers. If a bird flies into a window, this dust is shaken loose, leaving a remarkably detailed 'dust-shadow'.

Below: The stock dove has pale-grey feathers and hardly any noticeable white-coloured areas.

this is initially all the nestlings need. Later at feeding times, the parents regurgitate seeds which they have gathered and stored in the crop. Each parent eventually feeds the young only twice a day, in the morning and evening.

Feral pigeons, particularly the dark-coloured types, may nest throughout the year and, on average, raise five broods. Turtle doves cut their breeding season short to migrate in August or September. Other species have their greatest breeding success in high summer, when there is plenty of food, such as cereal grain.

Crop-eaters Pigeons eat a wide variety of natural foods; woodpigeons, for example, eat weeds, acorns, tree flowers, ivy and beech-nuts. British pigeons, however, largely depend on agriculture–stock and turtle doves either eat the weeds that grow beneath the crops or take the crops themselves. Resident pigeons and doves eat freshly sown grain and leftovers on stubble.

Woodpigeons even take unripe corn, using their weight to drag the grain to ground level. They are equipped with a strong, hooked beak, ideal for tearing leaves, and to some have become Britain's worst pest. Four million breeding pairs and their offspring cause over £1 million damage every year. Woodpigeons perhaps create the greatest devastation when they cannot get at clover leys which are covered by snow. Then they turn to the taller, but less nutritious brassicas. In short winter days they swallow more than their stomachs can cope with, and store the excess in their swollen-out crop to digest it after dark.

Woodpigeons previously fed on leaves and seeds of woodland weeds and now exploit the bigger, better sources provided by farmers. Attempts to eradicate them have failed.

Cuckoo

The cuckoo, whose call is so familiar in early summer, comes here to breed, but it neither builds a nest nor cares for its young – other birds do that for it!

The cuckoo is frequently heard but, being a shy bird, is seldom seen. The one British breeding species is extremely vocal from the moment it arrives here from Africa in mid-April. It sometimes calls on the wing, but usually waits until it alights before uttering the familiar, far-carrying 'cu-coo'. Occasionally the cry is 'cu-cu-coo' which, with other

variants (and contrary to popular belief), can be heard at the start of the season as well as near the end. A much lesser known call is a comparatively subdued liquid bubbling sound. It is likely that most of the 'cu-cooing' comes from the male and most of the bubbling from the female, but both sexes can make these calls. Both also use a deep 'grow-ow-ow' sound. Strangely enough, cuckoos often seem to call with their beaks closed.

The only view you're likely to have of a cuckoo is as it hastens by on a direct, level course, its rapidly beating wings held mainly below the body, or as it glides the last few yards to a perch. It is a long-tailed, hawk-like grey bird with barred underparts and bright yellow eyes, and often perches horizontally with wings drooping. Cuckoos' feet, which have two toes pointing forwards and two pointing backwards, like those of a parrot, are adapted to make perching and scrambling about in branches easy, but it makes the birds clumsy waddlers on the ground.

The cuckoo is insectivorous, feeding on the

Above: A young cuckoo about two weeks old. Juveniles are often reddish in colour and can be further distinguished by a pale patch on the nape. Occasionally, when two cuckoo eggs have been laid in the same nest, the foster parents find they have two chicks to rear because neither has succeeded in evicting the other.

♂

Left: A cuckoo perching in typical horizontal, wing-drooping posture. Right: A female taking an egg.

♀

Below: A cuckoo egg in a willow warbler's nest. Sometimes a cuckoo will lay eggs which very closely resemble the eggs of its host; for example, blue eggs which match those of the dunnock, a frequent host species.

caterpillars of magpie moths and the larvae of sawflies and other insects; it is also unusual in being an avid devourer of hairy caterpillars and brightly coloured ones which warn of an unpalatable taste—insects normally avoided by birds.

Take-over bid The breeding season begins as soon as the cuckoos arrive in Britain. The males display excitedly, sometimes several of them together: calling loudly, they sway from side to side, bobbing up and down and even spinning round, their large, decorative tails raised and fanned out.

While the males display, the female cuckoo keenly defends her own territory, at the same time observing possible host species—birds smaller than herself such as willow warblers, meadow pipits, dunnocks or even robins. Her aim is to find out where they are building and when they start laying their first eggs. After days of careful watching, the female chooses a nest with an incomplete clutch of eggs—usually with just one egg—where incubation has not yet started. Between mid-afternoon and eight in the evening—a time when her victims are likely to be away feeding (because their eggs were laid in the morning)—the female cuckoo flies straight to the nest, ignoring any small birds which mob her in mistake for a hawk. She takes an egg out of the nest and holds it in her beak while she quickly lays one of her own in its place. Finally, she eats or discards the egg.

Cuckoos' eggs have been found in the nests of over 50 different British birds. Some of these nests—such as the hole type—seem rather unsuitable. Where the nest is in a hole too small for the cuckoo to enter, she clings with outspread wings and tail against the opening and ejects her egg into the nest. If this fails and her egg rolls aside she abandons it, making no attempt to pick it up.

Most small birds lay an egg a day, but the cuckoo lays every second day, presumably to give herself time to find all the nests she needs, for she may lay a dozen or more eggs. When her final egg is laid the female cuckoo's task is over, and she takes no further part or interest in her progeny's future. Nor does the male. He stops singing by the end of June and then he, and all other adult cuckoos, are free to fly back to Africa. They leave in July, the earliest of our summer birds to go.

Fooling foster parents An intriguing feature of the story is the foster parents' generally willing acceptance of the cuckoo's egg. Occasionally the put-upon fosterers react by burying the alien egg under a fresh layer of nesting material; a very few species, such as the blackcap and the spotted flycatcher, seem to have become cuckoo-resistant, readily deserting the nest if a cuckoo lays her egg in it. Most cuckoos avoid the nests of these species. The female cuckoo's biggest risk is that her egg may be rejected. Perhaps her main reason for removing an egg before depositing her own is to minimize suspicion in the fosterer's mind. Sometimes two or even three cuckoo eggs are found in one nest, but they are almost invariably laid by different birds—something which is easy to check since the eggs of each cuckoo are individually marked and can be recognised from year to year.

Whenever possible a female cuckoo, all her life, lays in the nest of only one kind of host species. The females are grouped into various clans—such as the meadow pipit cuckoos (probably the commonest clan in Britain), hedge sparrow cuckoos (mainly in woodlands and hedgerows) and reed warbler cuckoos (in aquatic habitats). Such fixations seem to go back to the cuckoo's earliest days: a meadow pipit cuckoo is one which was born in a

Above: A newly hatched chick ousting the host's egg from a nest. The instinct to do this is very powerful and lasts for about four days.

Migration route
Adult cuckoos leave in late July, flying through Italy and across to Africa. The young follow in late August, finding their solitary way by instinct only.

breeding area
wintering area
route

meadow pipit's nest and becomes permanently imprinted to pipits. It is thought, however, that male cuckoos do not become imprinted.

Room for one only The cuckoo's egg is incubated with the host's eggs and hatches about the same time, or even earlier. The cuckoo chick is immediately faced with an acute problem of survival: to grow into a much larger bird than its foster parents it needs far greater quantities of food than would be given to each of the bona fide young. It must therefore eliminate all competition. So, when it is about eight hours old, the chick is seized by a powerful urge (lasting about four days) to get rid of any eggs or young sharing the nest with it. To do this–though tiny, blind and naked–it crawls beneath the eggs or nestlings one at a time, manoeuvres them into a hollow in its back and, using its legs and featherless wings, climbs up the side of the nest and heaves them out.

The parent birds take no steps to prevent this, nor to retrieve ejected eggs or feed any young that are thrown out. Eventually the cuckoo has the nest to itself and the entire attention of the foster parents. These birds feed the cuckoo as if it were their own, never abandoning it as long as it goes on begging for food and no matter how huge it becomes.

The rapidly growing cuckoo frequently utters a wheezy hunger cry–'chi-chi-chi'–and this persuades not only its foster parents but sometimes other birds (occasionally even a passing cuckoo) to drop food into its gaping mouth. At about four weeks old the young cuckoo reaches independence, and in August or September it flies off to find its solitary way to Africa for the winter.

Nest parasitism The large output of eggs– ensuring that a fair number are likely to survive–is the chief advantage of the cuckoo's remarkable life style. It is difficult to say how nest parasitism evolved. Only some of the world's many cuckoo species have become parasites. Of these, perhaps the most significant is the American yellow-billed cuckoo which does build a nest and rears its own young: the nest is usually only a very flimsy structure and the eggs often fall out of it, so the female frequently usurps the nests of other birds and uses them to bring up her family. Occasionally she leaves her eggs to be incubated in the nests of other birds. The yellow-billed cuckoo may therefore be a species hesitating on the brink of nest parasitism.

It seems likely that nest parasitism may have originated in birds which first got into the habit of appropriating the nests of other species for their own use. The sight of the eggs in the usurped nest might well have stimulated the newcomer to add another to the clutch. Eventually, the laying of eggs in other birds' nests could have become habitual. One mystery not yet fully understood is why the host species have not become more resistant to such victimisation. The survival value of a bird being a nest parasite is also questionable–it seems very risky for a species to entrust all its eggs to foster parents. However, it is a life style that is very successful: the cuckoo is a numerous bird with a breeding range that spreads across Europe and Asia.

Cuckoo (*Cuculus canorus*); 33cm (13in) from beak to tail; distribution widespread in woodland, heaths, commons, marshes, fields with hedgerows and coastal dunes; a summer visitor.

Below: A young cuckoo develops rapidly; in three weeks it is far larger than its foster parents and has usually outgrown its nest; so it has to perch nearby to be fed. When it begins to fly a little, the fosterers accompany it and continue to stuff its insatiable beak with insects.

Swallow

Every spring, swallows make an astounding journey from their winter quarters in South Africa. They travel nearly 5000 miles in one month, arriving here in early April to nest and breed and take advantage of our plentiful supply of insects.

Above: Young swallows about to receive a few welcome morsels of food from an assiduous parent. In their nest high up in the corner of an outbuilding, the young are generally fairly safe from predators; the adults warn of the presence of an inquisitive cat (or human) with a series of loud, sharp alarm calls, but use a longer, shriller and more penetrating cry if a bird predator—such as a hobby—appears.

According to the proverb, one swallow doesn't make a summer, but to many people the return of this bird each year is a sure sign that winter is at an end and summer just round the corner. As the weather gradually warms up in spring the flight paths swallows take on their migration journey north from South Africa can be mapped right across Europe. The first swallows appear in southern Britain on or around April 10, but the north of Scotland may have to wait until early May before the breeding birds arrive.

Food supply is the vital factor controlling both arrivals and departures. Swallows feed by catching insects on the wing, and in good weather you can often see them flying low over water meadows or skimming along a river, above a hayfield or even the local cricket pitch. In cold, wet or windy weather they gather in large flocks to concentrate on places where insect food remains available, often down-wind of large bodies of water where insects may be hatching, or in the lee of a wood or hedge where there is shelter. In temperate northern areas such as Britain where the birds breed, the summer supply of food is very good and is fully exploited by the migrants arriving from the south. In winter however there are few if any flying insects and any swallows rash enough to remain would soon starve to death.

A question of identity There are four species of fork-tailed, aerial-feeding birds which come to Britain for the summer months and which, at first glance, may be confused with each other. One, the sooty-black swift with its sickle-shaped wings, is not closely related to the swallow. The other two, the house martin and the sand martin, are members of the same family group as the swallow—the hirundines. The house martin has a patch of white on the back at the base of the tail while the sand martin can be distinguished by its dark brown upper parts and small size. The swallow has a longer and much more deeply forked tail than the other species, and the sleek, burnished blue of its head, collar and back, rusty red chin and pale pinky-brown undersides make it unmistakable.

Left: The angle between rafters in a barn or shed is a favourite nesting place for the swallow, providing a firm base for the cup of mud reinforced with dried grass. A lining of hair and feathers makes a soft bed for eggs.

Swallow (*Hirundo rustica*), also known as the barn swallow; 19cm (7½in) from beak to tip of tail; distribution widespread throughout the British Isles from spring to autumn.

Raising a family The first swallows to arrive–the males–are quick to establish their nesting sites; females arrive soon after. Pairs are formed with aerial display flights, mutual preening and exploration of the chosen site. Swallows show a very positive preference for buildings as breeding places, choosing a variety of barns, sheds, garages and porches. The main body of the nest is made with pellets of wet mud cemented together and is lined with hair and feathers and sometimes dried grasses.

The first clutch of four or five white eggs with reddish markings, laid fairly quickly, is incubated by the female and hatches after 14 or 15 days. The youngsters are fed by both parents for about three weeks, until they fledge, and then for a few days more while they fly around the nest site. After that, the young birds disperse and the adults set about raising a second brood. Some assiduous pairs manage to rear three broods successfully.

The birds you see gathering in flocks on the telephone wires for the autumn migration are generally young individuals. These birds do not have the pressing family responsibilities of the adults and spend their time gener-

ally making themselves familiar with the area to which, if they survive, they will return the following year to breed. Young birds are also the main occupants of the massive autumn roosts that form in reed beds throughout the country.

Migrating millions For centuries it was believed that swallows hid themselves in mud at the bottom of ponds throughout winter. People found it difficult to account for the sudden disappearance of the species every year in any other way. Even Gilbert White, the 18th century Hampshire naturalist famous for the accuracy of his observations, did not dismiss this idea completely. By the end of the 19th century, however, the migration of birds was established as fact, proved conclusively by the tracing of ringed birds. The 10,000 miles that swallows fly on migration to South Africa and back each year is a fact every bit as astonishing and marvellous as the supposed six month hibernation period under water.

Migration starts as early as the end of July in some years, and is in full swing from mid-August to the end of September. An early cold snap in October may catch lingering

How to tell adults from young

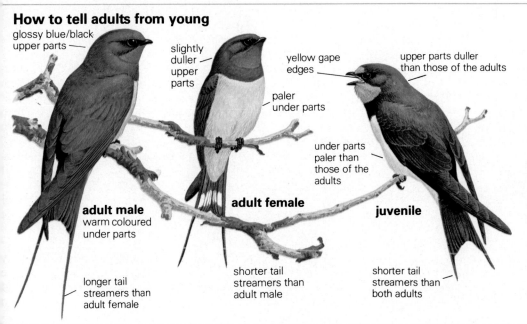

glossy blue/black upper parts

adult male
warm coloured under parts

longer tail streamers than adult female

slightly duller upper parts

paler under parts

adult female

shorter tail streamers than adult male

yellow gape edges

under parts paler than those of the adults

juvenile

upper parts duller than those of the adults

shorter tail streamers than both adults

At first glance, male and female swallows look very similar. But the male has much longer, thinner-tipped outer tail feathers than the female; also the male's chestnut or rust-red forehead and chin is often richer and darker than the female's. Both sexes share the glossy, deep blue upper parts, pinky-brown underside and white spots on the inner tail feathers. You can distinguish the juvenile in autumn by the short, blunt outer tail feathers and very pale forehead and chin.

Above: The route taken by swallows on migration to South Africa is a direct one, passing over western France, the east coast of Spain and Gibraltar. British swallows are joined en route by birds from Russia.

Below: Swallow drinking on the wing. The low, skimming flight over land or water is characteristic of this bird, which flies nearer the ground than any other in its search for insects.

swallows unawares and inflict heavy casualties. In such circumstances thousands of weak and torpid birds have sometimes been gathered up from north of the Alps and flown in a plane further south where they have revived in the warmer conditions and continued their journey. This is a worthwhile gesture, but not one on which the European population of swallows relies for its continued existence – there are probably as many as ten million individuals migrating south each autumn from Britain alone.

The swallows' passage south is generally fairly leisurely – taking up to two months; the northward spring trip is much faster, often being accomplished in just one month. The birds travel by day in large flocks, feeding as they go so they do not have to put on a great deal of fat before the journey to use as fuel. At sunset the flocks settle for the night in roosts – usually in marshy reed beds where there is adequate shelter. Young birds find their way south by instinct; they do not have to be taught which route to follow by their parents.

Hazards en route The greatest barrier the swallows face on their journey is the Sahara desert. They can rely on favourable winds to assist them on the autumn crossing but they must nevertheless be in good condition, and with reserves of fat, before they can set out across the Sahara with any hope of survival. On the return trip in spring the winds are not always favourable, and the area to the north may itself not be very hospitable. This part of the northward journey is therefore particularly risky and in some years there are mass fatalities in the desert and on its northern edge. Totally exhausted – and doomed – birds have been found still alive but weighing as little as 10g ($\frac{1}{3}$oz); their normal weight is about 20-22g ($\frac{3}{4}$oz).

Winter in the sun Swallows find an abundance of food and warmth in South Africa to keep them in good condition throughout the winter. The British population has shifted its wintering area at least once in the last 20 years. Up to 1961, only one British ringed swallow had been found in the south-western area of South Africa, but since then about a third of all records have come from there. Different populations of European and Eurasian swallows wintering in South Africa are quite well segregated. For example, German birds are generally found over 1000 miles north of the British birds, spending their winters in the Congo basin.

A few of our swallows are tempted to stay in South Africa all year round to nest and breed; but since there are 15 other native species to compete with for food, the majority undertake the incredible journey northwards each year to rear their chicks on the summer bounty of British insects.

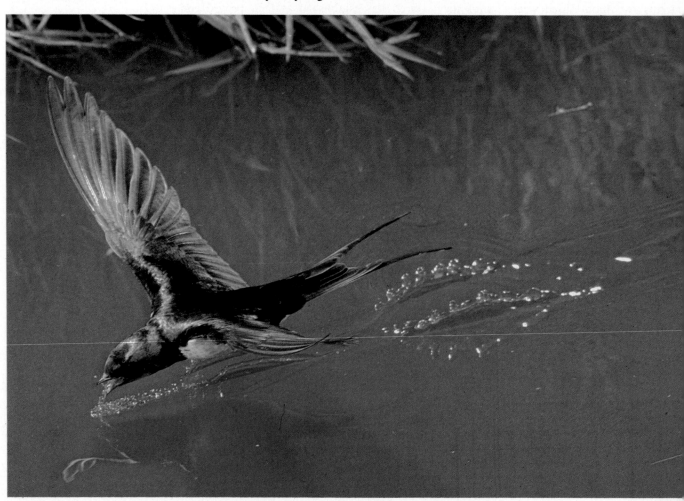

Swift

Swifts spend their lives in the air – feeding, sleeping and even mating on the wing. Once fledged, they do not set foot on the ground – not even on a perch – for two years or even more.

The swift is the most aerial of our birds. Every aspect of its anatomy and biology underlines its commitment to this mode of life. The swift rarely breeds until it is at least two years old, and entering its nest hole is its first contact with anything solid since it fledged. If a swift is accidentally grounded, its legs are so short and its wings so long, that the bird has little chance of getting airborne again.

Wing design The most obvious outward indication of specialisation is the wings – slender, sickle-shaped and extremely long. Much of this length comes from the unusually long primary feathers – the outer section of the wing.

The primary feathers provide the forward power for flight and – in most birds – are roughly equal in length to the secondary feathers which produce aerodynamic lift. But the swift's extra long primaries give greater power and make it one of the fastest birds, capable of speeds of over 60mph and perhaps even twice this in dives or if pursued by a falcon such as hobby.

Aerodynamics The streamlined body is shaped like a torpedo, with a blunt, rounded head and a body gradually tapering to a short, forked, tail. You might expect the bird to have a slender pointed head which would penetrate the air better, instead of the blunt front that appears to act as a buffer against the wind current. But the swift's shape is actually in perfect agreement with the engineering principles involved. The tapered rear end reduces the turbulent eddies of air *behind* the bird which would otherwise create a partial vacuum, or 'drag', and so slow the swift down.

The swift has few body projections interfering with airflow: the feet are tiny, and tucked into the feathers; the visible part of the beak is pointed, and extremely small; and the eyes, though large, are deep-set in slots – similar to the headlights of a sports car which are recessed in the smooth fibreglass body shell. The swift's body feathers serve a similar function in producing an unimpeded airflow over the body.

High-flyers In flight, swifts are capable of climbing up to 3000m (10,000ft). At these great heights they seem to spiral on set wing positions, certainly for long enough to obtain the necessary 'catnaps' of sleep. Sometimes swifts ascend to such altitudes in pursuit of their insect prey. They are highly specialised feeders, taking only flying insects and spiders drifting on gossamer-thin threads.

Behind the minute beak lies an enormous gape: the mouth literally opens from ear to ear, and when wide open occupies a large proportion of the front of the bird. The swift is ideally adapted to effective feeding on the wing, sweeping back and forth through the air, with its mouth gaping open, collecting small insects ('aerial plankton'), in much the way a whale scoops plankton from the sea.

Above: The swift grips on to brickwork, aided by four needle-sharp claws (below) which all point forwards. Its legs and feet, though small in proportion to the rest of its body, are very muscular.

Where to watch them One of the best places to watch swifts is over reservoirs in early summer as they feed on insects. Another good viewing site is marshland – here, using high speed passes, the swift catches the myriad midges that dance in smoke-like columns. In summer, insect abundance is controlled by the weather. In long, cool, rainy periods flying insects can become scarce, and in fine spells they may be at a great height, often accumulating at the junction of cold and warm air fronts.

Radar tracking Mobile and speedy, swifts may travel hundreds of kilometres daily in search of food. Striking evidence of this is provided by some remarkable film (taken by Marconi Ltd) of a radar screen in south east England. Many birds, swifts included, are large enough to leave a blip or 'echo' on modern radar; this spectacular film – covering a summer afternoon and the following night – shows the radar screen covered by a mass of blips caused by London swifts rising high into the sky at dusk. The blips show a rapid movement north to the Wash, where the birds congregated. Here they fed on the insects massing at a cold/warm front junction over the North Sea, before returning to their nests in the city.

Acclimatised young Nestling swifts are as well-adapted as their parents to the vagaries of the British summer which affect their food supply. Since their food is so specialised, they are more vulnerable than most young birds to shortages which may last several days. The young swifts have a survival mechanism that allows them to go gradually into a torpor – a sort of short-term hibernation.

Their body temperature falls, pulse and breathing rates are reduced to a minimum and growth ceases. The nestlings survive on a tick-over metabolism (using as energy their stored body fat), in a way not possible in

long primary feathers

sickle-shaped wi

short forked ta

Above: With long slender wings and body built to much the same design as high-speed, high altitude reconnaissance aircraft, swifts have difficulty manoeuvring in confined spaces. You can distinguish swifts from martins and swallows which have much lighter bellies when viewed from below.
Right: In common with many other birds that nest in dark cavities, the swift's eggs are white and rather spherical. In a new site the nest may be composed of no more than a few bits of mortar arranged in rough circle.
Below: Occasionally both adults roost in the nest hole, sharing the cramped quarters with the eggs or, more uncomfortably, with well grown young.

other birds. With the return of better weather, and a restoration of food supplies, the body temperature rises again, the nestlings become active and normal growth is resumed.

Mid-air mating 'Screaming parties' of adult swifts are a common sight in many towns and villages throughout the summer. Gangs of birds, all uttering their high-pitched call, whistle through the air on rapidly flickering wings. They seem to have narrow escapes with traffic and overhead wires, but in reality they are well in control of their manoeuvres. Following such mass displays, you may see the birds mating – the male alighting gently on the female's back while both are in mid-air. The birds may glide briefly on wings upheld in a narrow 'V' while actually mating. The pair then break apart and resume normal flight.

Nest sites In the British Isles swifts now nest under the eaves of houses in the older parts of towns and cities. In the past they may have depended on natural cavities in cliffs and caves, perhaps even trees. Related species in other parts of the world still nest in trees.

Swifts have benefitted from the expansion of human populations which have provided more nesting sites. But this must be set against the adverse effects of aerial pollution – particularly sulphur dioxide – on their food supply. Moreover, modern houses and blocks of flats have smoother outlines which are not suitable for nest holes or for the swift's

method of getting in and out. The bird approaches its nest entrance from below, landing briefly on the rim and scuttling in, and leaves by simply dropping out of the entrance and flying off. The nest hole usually faces downwards.

The nest itself is a spartan affair inside the roof of the building. As the birds cannot gather nesting material from the ground or trees, they rely on bits and pieces scattered about on roofs. They shuffle these loosely together using liberal quantities of droppings. They may even line the nest with a few feathers caught in mid-air.

There are usually one or two (sometimes three or four) dull white and rather rounded eggs. The parents share a 20-day incubation period and the young take five to eight weeks to fledge, depending on the weather. The short stay of the swift in Britain allows no time for more than one brood.

Travelling abroad Most swifts leave the British Isles in August for their winter quarters in the central regions of Africa. They do not return until mid-May. Despite their highly specialised and apparently risky lifestyle, the results of intensive ringing studies show that swifts are successful birds. Many may live for ten years or more – unusually long for a small bird. At a rough calculation, the oldest swift on record, at 16 years, may have exceeded four million flying miles in its lifetime.

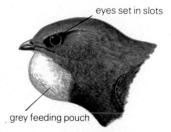

eyes set in slots

grey feeding pouch

Above: The adults catch food for their young by gathering 'aerial plankton' which they hold in their throats. This creates a 'food ball' that often exceeds 1cm ($\frac{1}{2}$in) in diameter, and produces a conspicuous, bulging grey patch – the only relief to the swift's sooty plumage.

Swift (*Apus apus*), 16.5cm ($6\frac{1}{2}$in) from beak to tail. Distribution throughout the British Isles, though scarcer the further north they go. Summer visitor.

Flight silhouettes

Flight silhouettes are useful indicators of a bird's way of life, and a great help when it comes to identifying unfamiliar birds in the countryside.

Swift, hobby The swift's silhouette shows an adaptation to fast flight. Though unrelated to the swift, the swallow, sand and house martins have similar silhouettes. This is due to 'parallel evolution', by which two unrelated groups arrive at the same evolutionary solution to their problem. The best example of design for speed is the hobby, a falcon that can outfly even these birds, and in fact specialises in feeding on them.

Hoopoe, grey partridge At the other end of the scale from speed is manoeuvrability. This makes opposing demands on wing design, and the hoopoe, with broad rounded wings with 'fingered' ends, is an excellent example of an agile bird able to twist in and out of the trees. The partridge has a similar pattern to give high lifting power, and an instant take-off to escape predators.

Greenfinch Most small birds, such as the greenfinch, fly between these two scales – not exceptionally fast nor exceptionally mobile, but just as successful in their less specialised habits.

Razorbill Other specialists include those seabirds – particularly the auks – that spend a lot of time hunting fish beneath the sea surface. Their short, stiffened wings give poor flying ability, but excellent underwater propulsion – like a penguin's flipper.

Buzzard, Manx shearwater You can see energy-saving designs in the buzzard soaring at high altitudes on thermal upcurrents, using broad wings and a broad rounded tail. In contrast the Manx shearwater uses its long, narrow, rigidly held wings to glide swiftly at low level. Shearwaters are adept at exploiting sea winds and upcurrents close to the waves.

Partridge

Hoopoe

Greenfinch

Razorbill

Shearwater

Buzzard

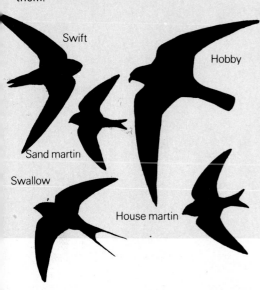

Swift

Hobby

Sand martin

Swallow

House martin

House martin

House martins, among the most aerial of all our birds, feed and even roost on the wing, coming down to earth only to collect mud for their nests.

The house martin is a familiar summer visitor to nearly all parts of Britain and Ireland. It is an almost entirely aerial species and is often confused with its close relative, the swallow. However, house martins' tails are more shallowly forked than those of swallows, and house martins also lack the chestnut colour seen on swallows. The crucial field mark of the house martin is the white patch on the rump, which is very prominent when the bird is flying. The sand martin, our third member of the hirundine family, is brown, in contrast to the metallic blue of the house martin. (The swift, though superficially similar to the hirundines, is much larger and lacks the white rump: also, it has an even smoother, narrower 'sickle' shape in flight than any of the hirundines.)

Both the swallow and the house martin build nests of mud, plastered on to the walls of buildings or the ends of rafters. The structure of these two birds' nests is quite different, however. The swallow's nest is a simple cup, generally placed inside a building rather than on the outside. The house martin produces a rather more elaborate structure, generally on the outside of a building: when complete, this forms an almost complete quarter globe with a narrow slit entrance on the outside top edge.

Spring arrival The first sightings of house martins each spring generally occur in early April, but most birds do not arrive until the end of this month, or early May. Stragglers continue to appear until the end of May and even during June. They are therefore later in arriving than both sand martins and swallows, but a little earlier, on average, than swifts. The first migrants search out areas where food is in good supply, and often congregate around the shores of lakes or reservoirs, for there they are able to find newly hatched insects.

The house martin's flight is not as acrobatic as that of the swallow, nor as direct and speedy as that of the swift. House martins are frequently seen hawking very high in the sky, but if the weather is cold they fly very low in the shelter of a hedge or bank. Because of their startling white rumps they are often much more conspicuous under such circumstances than the other hirundines and the swifts, all of which often feed together with them. A wide variety of aerial insects are taken, as are many species of gossamer spiders floating about in the air on threads of silk.

Mud collectors In order to build their nests, house martins must abandon their aerial life temporarily and come down to the ground to collect mud. Here they are not very agile, and walk with a pronounced 'waddle'. The mud may be gathered from the fringes of a pond, a muddy gateway or, most often, from a

Above: House martins start their nests about 7cm (3in) below the eaves and build steadily upwards. A nail in the wall is a useful keying point from which to start.

Opposite page: A multitude of house martins roosting on telephone wires before migration. They are smaller than swallows, with whiter undersides.

House martin distribution

Left: House martins are not timid and often allow a close approach, particularly if you are in a car and they are collecting mud from a roadside puddle. Seeing them at close quarters, you can appreciate the fascinating tiny white feathers that cover their legs. If dry weather removes the supply of mud, some people do the house martins a kindness by leaving out a bowl full of a mixture of earth and water.

Above: A crowd of young house martins on telephone wires: their plumage is more mottled than that of adults. Being aerial birds, their instinctive reaction to any approaching danger is to escape into the open sky, where their speed and endurance serve them best. The wires are a perfect aerial perch, giving them a clear view all round and an easy launch into fast flight.

Left: The nest, made of many hundreds of beakfuls of mud, forms a neat quarter globe. The entrance is a slit at the top.

Bottom right: This cliff colony of house martins is one of the few instances where the birds manage to nest successfully without resorting to house walls. The birds here are sunning themselves; their nests are in holes within the cliff.

Below: House martins waddle on very short legs when walking on the ground to collect mud.

roadside puddle. In really dry weather nest building may be held up for weeks through lack of mud, and birds may have to fly long distances to fetch it.

Observations of nest-building house martins have shown that it takes the birds roughly a fortnight to complete a nest. Many blobs of mud tend to be lost at the very start, in the process of keying the nest to the wall. Often the birds use a nail in the wall, a gutter bracket or a window hinge as a support. The complete nest may contain roughly 500cc (30 cu in) of mud, comprising more than 2500 beakfuls. The bare mud is then lined with feathers, grasses and straw. Much of the lining material is caught in the air, but some is picked up off the ground.

The brood in the nest The female lays a clutch of four or five white eggs, which are incubated, with the help of the male, for about two weeks. The young are fed in the nest, by both parents, for 18 or 19 days before they fledge. Most pairs are able to rear two broods, and three broods are not uncommon. The young from the first clutch often help their parents to feed later young, and the whole of this extended family may live crammed into one nest. There have been records of 13 birds living together in this way. Alternatively, a new nest may be constructed as a dormitory for the fledged young.

Man's dependant? In recent years, house martins have been recorded breeding much nearer the centres of many British cities than before. This is a measure of the success which the various Clean Air Acts have been able to achieve. Earlier this century, so much smoke was emitted that there were few if any of the insects needed by house martins in inner city areas.

Going back further in the history of the species, it is interesting to speculate how many (or how few) pairs of house martins there may have been in Britain and Ireland before man built dwellings on a large scale. There are certainly a handful of natural house martin colonies on coastal cliffs, in quarries and along river banks, but over 99% of all British breeding pairs now nest on buildings.

Feeding flocks of house martins

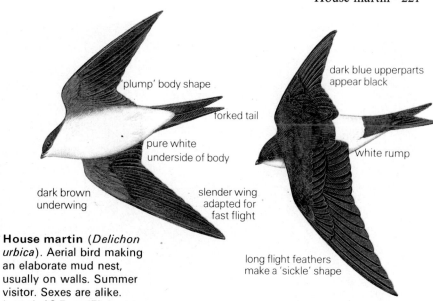

'plump' body shape

forked tail

pure white
underside of body

dark brown
underwing

slender wing
adapted for
fast flight

dark blue upperparts
appear black

white rump

long flight feathers
make a 'sickle' shape

House martin (*Delichon urbica*). Aerial bird making an elaborate mud nest, usually on walls. Summer visitor. Sexes are alike. Length 12.5cm (5in).

insects hovering over water

insects carried by wind

reservoir

birds fly back and forth catching insects

insects caught in circulating air currents

hedge

n cold weather birds very often hunt for insects near water. If there is a fairly strong wind, the newly hatched insects are blown downwind and, if there is a convenient patch of relatively still air, their numbers become concentrated. Here the birds can feed much more efficiently than they can in the open. Insect numbers in the sheltered air beside the hedge are augmented by those blown off the reservoir. Here house martins (as well as swifts and swallows) often feed.

Quite apart from nesting sites on the walls of houses, man provides the birds with two useful kinds of perches. Telephone wires are an ideal perch for such a truly aerial species, for they allow a good look-out in all directions, and also an unimpeded take-off. Small song birds react to a predator's arrival by dashing for cover, but the house martin needs the freedom of the sky.

The other man-made luxury is provided by houses whose roofs face both south-east and towards the rising sun. They absorb the early morning heat and, thus warmed, attract hundreds of sunning house martins.

Autumn departure Like other aerial feeders, house martins are forced to migrate from Britain and Ireland by the cold weather of the winter, which denies them sufficient insect food. The first movement of autumn passage birds through Britain is seen in August. Some roost in unoccupied nests at colonies which they pass, but it is almost certain that most of them roost on the wing–while their flight muscles are active, much of the rest of the bird is at rest. By September, large gatherings of house martins are seen on telephone wires and south-facing tile roofs. These continue to form until October in mild years, for some adults are still able to raise and feed late broods even in autumn.

Rather little is known about the house martins' migration routes, for few have been found abroad with rings from Britain or Ireland. The early stage of the journey, through Europe, is routed through France and (in general) Spain, later reaching North Africa. There are no records of British house martins south of the Sahara, but Continental birds reach tropical West Africa and may possibly fly even further south. In their wintering habitat, not being dependent on houses for nesting, the birds are less frequently in contact with man than in the breeding season. This is the principal reason for our lack of knowledge about this stage of the house martin's life.

Great and lesser spotted woodpeckers

You can tell a spotted woodpecker by its frenzied activity even before you come close enough to recognise its brilliant colouring. Its persistent drumming against wood to attract a mate and proclaim territory is unique among British birds.

A male great spotted woodpecker removing wood excavated from its nest. In northern Britain nests are made in birch or pine, but in the south in hardwoods.

The great spotted woodpecker is both the most numerous and widespread of our woodpeckers, occurring in almost all areas where there are suitable trees. Strangely enough, the great spotted shares with its relatives a complete, unexpected, difficult-to-

explain absence from the whole of Ireland even though there is abundant suitable woodland. There have been occasional sitings in Ireland, but these seem to be of Continental migrants blown off-course in autumn, and none has stayed to breed. The lesser spotted woodpecker is much less common than the great. It does, however, share many characteristics of the great, and has all the same adaptations, though they are reduced in scale.

Woodland bird The great spotted woodpecker prefers stands of timber where at least some of the trees are mature, usually with a few dead or dying branches. It lives in both deciduous and coniferous woodlands or a mixture of the two, but is scarcer in closely planted coniferous plantations without old or decaying trees. Where good hedgerows are still common, it penetrates deep into agricultural land, feeding and nesting in the tall trees of the hedge, or in spinneys and copses linked by the hedgerow network. It is unusual to find great spotted woodpeckers i isolated clumps of trees.

The magnificent old trees of parkland offer an ideal habitat, and through parks the great spotted woodpecker sometimes penetrates into urban areas. It is a common species of large old gardens, with big trees, that meet the surrounding countryside.

Striking colouring With its pied plumage and scarlet patches, the great spotted woodpecker is a conspicuous bird. Its normal year-round call, a harsh and far-carrying 'tchack', or its staccato breeding-season drumming, quickly draw attention to its presence. Its deeply undulating method of flight, too, is conspicuous and characteristic, consisting of a few flaps of the rounded wings, followed by a deep swooping glide, before the next series of flaps helps it gain height again.

The wings are boldly barred black and white, with a striking white oval patch on each wing near the body–a feature lacking in the lesser spotted woodpecker. The back is plain black (again, different from the lesser spotted, where the white bars cross the back as well), and the underparts are white save for a bright scarlet patch beneath the tail of both sexes. In addition, the male has a small block of scarlet feathers on the nape of his otherwise black crown.

Woodpeckers perch, or rather cling, to the sides of tree trunks and branches in a characteristic head-up position developed in the course of evolution as the tail feathers have become specially strengthened and inflexible, serving as a third leg, or prop, to use in climbing in much the same way as we balance on a shooting-stick. This adaptation assists a particularly powerful grip. Woodpecker legs are short but muscular, with strong toes tipped with long, sharp claws which give an effective hold even on the smoothest-barked trees such as beech.

Unusually for a bird, the toes are arranged with two pointing forwards and two back, (a condition called zygodactyly), which gives optimum performance on a vertical surface. Thus woodpeckers move vertically or often in a spiral up the trunk, and occasionally laterally. When they have finished searching for food on one tree, they swoop off to the base of another tree or branch and begin to ascend once again.

Woodpecker headaches? The most obvious wood-pecking adaptation is, of course, the beak. In the great spotted woodpecker this is relatively short, stout and sharp, with a squared-off end like a small chisel–an appropriate simile: rather than bludgeoning its way into the wood by sheer power, the woodpecker uses its beak as a combination of hammer and chisel, inserting the tip into the crack it has made and using its powerful neck muscles to twist the beak and prize off flakes of wood.

One obvious question relating to wood-peckers is: why don't they get splitting head-aches? The answer lies partly in the robust

scarlet nape-patch

white shoulder patch

plain black back

Great spotted woodpecker

scarlet
under-tail coverts

nest chamber

Below: A female great spotted woodpecker can be distinguished because it does not have a red nape patch like the male. Note the red under-tail covert.

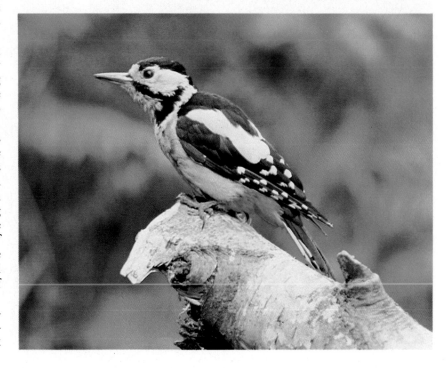

bone structure of the skull, especially in front of the brain, and partly in a layer of shock-absorbing cartilaginous material that forms a cushion between the bones within the beak and the rest of the skull.

Long-tongued feeder The diet of the great spotted woodpecker is varied, and includes seeds, fruit and nuts. Nuts are often removed to a well-used cleft in a favourite piece of bark, and hammered open while they are held in position in this natural vice. Insect and larvae are another important food item. During winter these are often found sheltering under easily lifted flakes of bark; the great spotted woodpecker is also a specialist at extracting wood-boring larvae that have tunnelled into trees. The bird senses the approximate location of the grub, perhaps hearing minute sounds of movement or chewing. After a few swift pecks an opening is hacked into the tunnel, and then the woodpecker's enormously long tongue comes into play. In the case of the great spotted, the tongue can be extended for a couple of inches up the tunnel. The luckless grub is harpooned by the sharp, barbed horny tip of the bird's tongue, and dragged out to be eaten.

At rest the phenomenally long tongue is far too bulky to lie in the floor of the bird's mouth: a thickened tube runs out of the lower jaw, backwards beneath the hidden ears and then up the back of the head to the top of the skull. It is here that the tongue is retracted when it is not in use.

The natural all-year-round diet is augmented at various times by rather surprising items. The great spotted woodpecker has a marked taste for the nestlings of other birds, and is adept at catching them. As they grow, the nestlings of most hole-nesting birds, such as tits, alerted by the shadow of their parent falling across the hole, jump up to the nest hole entrance. Woodpeckers have capitalised on this: as their shadow falls across the hole a young tit jumps up to be the first to be fed, and the woodpecker reaches in and grabs it, dragging it out to hack up and eat on a more suitable perch. Sometimes woodpeckers learn to associate this food supply with nestboxes put up for tits, and they chisel their way through the back of the box to get at the eggs or young.

In rural and suburban areas from late summer through the winter great spotted woodpeckers are regular visitors to garden bird tables. They come particularly for fat, suet and peanuts. Even if the peanuts (or the fat) are suspended on a string, the woodpecker quickly cuts through it with its sharp beak, dropping the food to the ground where it is easier to eat.

Excavated nests Great spotted woodpeckers excavate their nesting chambers in the trunk or a stout branch of a tree. The nest is usually at least 3m (10ft) above ground. The entrance hole is circular and about 6cm (2½in) in dia-

Great spotted woodpecker *(Dendrocopos major)*; 23cm (9in) from beak to tail. Common in both coniferous and deciduous woods in England, Wales, Scotland. Resident.

Lesser spotted woodpecker *(Dendrocopos minor)*; 14·5cm (5¾in) from beak to tail. Found in parks, orchards, gardens, copses, in England. Uncommon, but numbers have increased slightly in recent years. Resident.

scarlet cap in male

♂

Left: A male great spotted woodpecker at the nest of its young. Nests are made at least 3m (10ft) above the ground. The young birds have a red cap, like the adult male lesser spotted woodpecker.

Right: A cone cache collected by a great spotted woodpecker. The seeds form part of the bird's varied diet.

meter – slightly smaller and less oval with the green woodpecker and rather larger with the lesser spotted. A short horizontal tunnel leads to the pear-shaped nest shaft which is 25-30cm (10-12in) deep.

Each clutch is generally six, or fewer, beautifully spherical white eggs that are incubated by both parents in turns for 16-17 days. When they hatch, the youngsters are naked and noisy, and particularly ugly and reptilian-looking for small birds. They fledge in about three weeks, depending on the weather. There is normally one brood each summer.

Drumming for a mate The male advertises for a mate and later indicates the boundaries of his territory by drumming on an appropriately resonant, often dead, piece of branch. On occasion woodpeckers seek special effects by drumming on a corrugated iron roof. For many years controversy raged over how the noise was produced. Many skilled ornithologists argued that they could see that it was made vocally, much as we can 'roll rs'

Above right: A great spotted woodpecker feeding its young on another fledgling. It also eats insects and their larvae, fruit and nuts.

barred back
noticeable in flight

juvenile

juvenile lacks
any trace of red

**Lesser spotted
woodpecker**

with our tongues curled. The issue was only settled in the 1930s by embedding microphones in regularly drummed branches, which showed that a rapid succession of physical taps by the beak against the tree caused the noise.

Compared with the short and powerful bursts of drumming of the great spotted, the lesser spotted woodpecker drums at a noticeably higher pitch and in drum-rolls lasting twice as long.

The lesser spotted woodpecker shares the pied, barred plumage of the great, although it lacks the scarlet beneath the tail. It is the smallest European woodpecker. The circular nest hole is only about 4cm (1½in) wide and the nest is usually situated on the underside of the dead branch. There are normally four to six white eggs, and incubation and fledging take much the same time as in the larger bird. The eggs are incubated by both the male and the female parent, and both birds also feed the nestlings.

The lesser lives in similar habitats to the great spotted, although it penetrates less into agricultural and urban surroundings other than in old orchards which it particularly favours. It is nowhere very numerous. Old county reports and Victorian bird books, however, indicate that in the latter half of the last century the lesser spotted was the commoner, the greater spotted the rarer woodpecker. It would be fascinating to know the reasons for the change. Perhaps they are similar to the causes of the current increase in lesser spotted woodpecker numbers. For some reason they seem to have profited particularly from the Dutch elm disease outbreak, feeding off the numerous insects that live beneath the dead bark and nesting in the rotting wood: at least some small benefit from the disease.

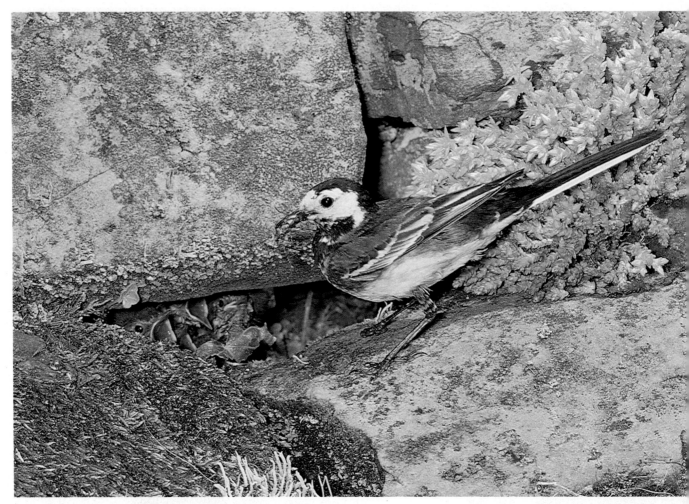

Pied and white wagtails

Pied wagtails are far commoner than the two other species of wagtails in Britain and Ireland. On almost any area of turf, shingle or rock, in towns or in the countryside, they can be seen hunting insects, with quick dashes, swerves and dramatic leaps into the air.

Above: A female pied wagtail at the entrance to her nest in a rock crevice. Unaided by the male, she builds the nest of mosses, grasses and dead leaves, and lines it with feathers or wool. Her clutch normally consists of five or six eggs, which are greyish-white and freckled with black or brown. She also undertakes most of the incubation, which lasts for two weeks; but she hands over responsibility for feeding the young to her mate when the time comes for her to lay again.

The pied wagtail is a familiar, lively and popular neighbour of man. Its bold black and white plumage, conspicuous habits and loud, distinctive 'chis-ick' call are easy to recognise and help to make it so well-known. It is surprisingly widespread, too: as widely distributed as any British bird, it breeds throughout our islands (but only occasionally on the Shetlands) and is thoroughly at home in city centres and on riversides, meadows, farms and seashore—in fact, almost anywhere except the open mountains and in woodland. One of its commonest vernacular names, water wagtail, is not as applicable as it might be, for it is not as closely associated with water as its relative, the grey wagtail. It is predominantly a bird of moist places, but not necessarily the very margins of open water.

The pied wagtail is a truly British and Irish species, for its breeding range is virtually confined to these islands. It is replaced on the Continent, and as far north as Iceland, by the grey wagtail race referred to—somewhat confusingly—as the white wagtail. Birds belonging to this Continental race migrate through Britain in spring and autumn to and from their northern breeding areas, which are in northern Scandinavia and Iceland. Some occasionally stay to breed in Scotland and on the northern and western islands. These birds are noticeably whiter than our pied wagtail, and in spring it is easy to distinguish them from the British race. In autumn the task is much more difficult, as the young of both races are very similar.

Chasing after a mate As April arrives each year, the wagtails prepare for another breeding season. Males begin to establish territories, and several of them may pursue a single female in erratic and excited chases, each displaying to her when on the ground by throwing back his head and displaying his bold black gorget (throat patch). The competition of courtship eventually results in successful pairing; then the newly paired birds spend some days together strengthening the bond between them, and establishing their breeding territory and nesting site.

Pied wagtails nest in a wide variety of sites

wherever an adequate crevice will conceal the nest. As well as choosing holes in banks, ivy-covered trees or cliffs, they often favour man-made objects: farm machinery, outbuildings or woodstacks are common sites.

A partial migrant All wagtails are insect-eating birds, but only the yellow wagtail migrates completely to warmer latitudes when the British winter reduces the abundance of its food. The pied wagtail demonstrates an interesting half-way stage between migration and year-round residence.

The appearance of increasing numbers of pied wagtails on school playing fields, in town parks and sewage farms in August and September is evidence of the fact that at least part of the population is migratory. In the south of Britain young birds predominate among those that migrate, but from further north there is a greater percentage of adults. All these birds flying south from Britain are bound for south-west France and Iberia, as is shown by the recovery of ringed birds. Birds from the south of England tend to travel further than those of more northerly origin; some of the southern birds fly as far as Morocco.

The other part of the population remains in Britain, one of the few species of insectivorous birds to gamble on finding an adequate supply of insects through the winter months as an alternative to facing the hazards of a long two-way migration. Through the British winter, the pied wagtail's secret lies in the ever-replenishing supply of insects to be found at the edge of water. Individual birds establish themselves in a winter territory along a river bank (sometimes a lake or other stretch of water) and defend it resolutely against others of their kind.

They feed along a fixed route near the water edge, returning each time to the starting point by the time the waters of the river or lake have delivered another supply of tiny insects and other invertebrates. To share the territory with another bird would be self-defeating for

grey back
of head
♀

White wagtail

black cap   light grey back

grey back
may have an
olive tinge

♂

whitish grey
flanks

♀

Pied wagtail

black
throat

black crown
and back

lower breast
white

smoky grey
flanks

♂

Pied wagtail (*Motacilla alba yarrelli*); the British and Irish subspecies. Some individuals are resident and others are summer visitors. Length 18cm (7in).

White wagtail (*Motacilla alba alba*); the Continental subspecies, seen in Britain occasionally as a passage migrant.

Right: The white wagtail is similar in appearance to the female of the pied wagtail, but its back is a lighter shade of grey.

Below: A female pied wagtail stands on a log in a typical jaunty attitude. Pied wagtails forage energetically, running jerkily on short turf, shingle or rock. With tails flicking non-stop, they make rapid dashes and swerves to catch their insect prey. Sometimes they leap into the air in dancing flight, to catch insects on the wing.

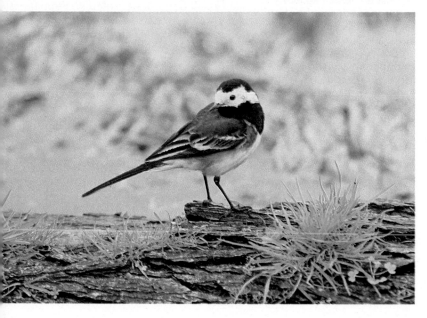

both, and would tip the balance between survival and failure. Defence of the territory is therefore crucially important.

Communal roosts At most times of the year outside the breeding season (except when winter is at its severest), pied wagtails roost communally, normally choosing reedbeds, scrub or bushes. An interesting development of this has been an increasingly common adaptation to the urban environment – roosting on buildings and trees in city centres. Here the winter temperature can be a little higher than in the open countryside.

In a further adaptation to man's presence, they have been recorded as roosting in commercial glasshouses, sometimes in large numbers. Heated glasshouses obviously have enhanced survival value for them in cold winter months, and may also be thought of as giving security from predators. On the other hand, however, little owls and cats have sometimes discovered these roosts, and as there is small chance of escape the results can be disastrous.

Grey wagtail

The grey wagtail is similar to the yellow wagtail, except for its blue-grey upperparts. This difference is 'clinched' by the habitat – the grey wagtail lives beside rocky streams, while the yellow wagtail prefers damp meadows and marshes.

The grey wagtail is somewhat confusingly named: although it is true that the upperparts of the bird are a bluish grey, the feature that most often catches the eye is the brilliant patch of lemon yellow on the under-tail coverts and on the belly. In summer this yellow colouring often extends up on to the breast. It is at all times conspicuous, even in birds seen flying overhead. Thus it would seem sensible to call this the 'yellow wagtail'. However, the true yellow wagtail has yellow upperparts as well as underparts; besides its difference in colour, the yellow wagtail is distinguished from the grey by the habitat in which it is seen, for it is a bird of damp meadows and marshes, only occasionally being seen on arable farmland, while the typical habitat of the grey wagtail is beside fast-flowing water.

Changing with the seasons Unlike yellow wagtails, which are migrants visiting us in summer from Africa, most grey wagtails remain in Britain or Ireland throughout the year. Their plumages, however, change with the seasons. In summer, the male grey wagtail

Above: The grey wagtail's nest is built by the female (shown here). She performs the bulk of the work of incubation, which takes 13 to 14 days. However, both sexes feed the young. In many lowland areas, two broods are raised, and the season usually starts early. Most pairs produce their first eggs in the second half of April. Natural nest sites include cavities between exposed roots, wall crevices (as shown here), and holes in the banks of streams.

Right: A grey wagtail nest with 5 eggs. Apart from this rather unusual nest site, other man-made sites used by grey wagtails include mills, bridges and weirs. Indeed, a good way to find the birds is to seek out old mills, which are favoured haunts.

has a conspicuous white stripe above and below the eye, and a large black 'bib', while the female's throat is whitish. In winter, the sexes are difficult to separate, both having buffish-white throats and pale buff breasts, with the yellow restricted to the vivid patch below the base of the tail. Young birds are grey-green above and dirty white below, with some dark marks round the throat.

Beside rivers and streams The map of the grey wagtail's breeding distribution shows a uniform coverage of Ireland, much of Scotland, Wales and western England. The only 'blank areas' are in East Anglia, the easternmost Midlands and Lincolnshire. In the western part of its range, the grey wagtail is typically a bird of shallow, fast-flowing rivers and streams, preferring to feed along the waterside or where the water is broken up by pebble banks.

Metallic call Often the first indication of the presence of grey wagtails, if they are not seen flying in an undulating path low over the water, is their frequently uttered call. This is considerably higher-pitched and more metallic than that of the pied wagtail. The grey wagtail's 'tzi-tzi', although formed of two distinct syllables, lacks the harsh emphasis of the pied wagtail's 'chiz-zick' call.

In mild winters, the song starts soon after Christmas. It is often said that the bird sings infrequently and even stops singing early in spring, but this may be because the sound is difficult to hear well against the background noise of fast-flowing, tumbling water. The song, in fact, sounds like a squeaky version of the descending trill of a blue tit's song, or perhaps a treecreeper's song without the terminal flourish. This is so different from the song of other wagtails that if the singing bird cannot be seen, the sound can cause moments of uncertainty even for the experienced ear.

Varied diet The grey wagtail's food consists of small animals – insects for example that the bird gathers as it dashes nimbly among the pebbles and boulders, or runs across floating water plants. Sometimes a grey wagtail seems to tiptoe along the brink of a weir, risking being swept away by the rushing water. At other times (particularly

Grey wagtails in summer

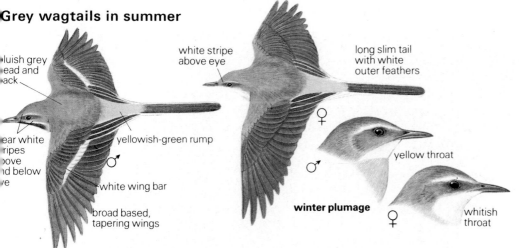

bluish grey head and back

near white stripes above and below eye

white stripe above eye

yellowish-green rump

white wing bar

broad based, tapering wings

long slim tail with white outer feathers

♀

♂

winter plumage

yellow throat

whitish throat

♂

♀

Grey wagtail distribution

when columns of midges are 'dancing' in their mating flight) grey wagtails fly out over the water and hover, as flycatchers do, to snap insects from the air. Besides aquatic and terrestrial insects, the birds take a wide variety of small animals, including worms, leeches, flatworms and small freshwater shrimps.

Surviving winter Because their habitat is along the waterside, where a cold winter freeze either kills or covers in ice any animals that the birds need for food, grey wagtails tend to suffer considerable losses in winters with extended and severely cold spells. Upland birds can 'migrate' to lower altitudes in winter without difficulty, but once the lowland streams and lakes freeze, only those birds that can reach a suitable stretch of unfrozen coast can survive. This may help to explain the distribution pattern, with more birds in the west, for the slow-moving streams in the generally colder east freeze quicker, and for longer, than the faster running streams of the west. This makes it rather difficult to

estimate the grey wagtail population: numbers are subject to sweeping variations caused by cold-winter mortality every few years. In 1967, following two severe winters, the population was estimated to be below 10,000 pairs, which is probably the lowest level to which it ever falls. Another estimate, of 25,000-30,000 pairs in 1974, reflects healthier circumstances.

Periods of bad weather provoke long-distance winter flights (better called cold weather movements), and ringed birds have been recovered in France, Spain and Portugal. Most flights are shorter, however. Many birds leave their home stretch of water during the period of moult in late summer, and at this time there are records of ringed birds being recovered up to 160km (100 miles) away from their nesting territories. For much of the year, most grey wagtail pairs stay in their territories and defend them: often both sexes defend their territory from a neighbouring pair, with vigorous posturing and mock combat.

Above: Numbers of grey wagtails are considerably lower in eastern England, where the streams are generally more sluggish and offer few suitable habitats.

Above left: The grey wagtail is distinguished by its combination of blue-grey upperparts and yellow underparts. The extent of the yellow is greater in summer than in winter, and in older birds compared to younger ones.

Grey wagtail (*Motacilla cinerea*). Resident bird living beside fast-flowing streams. Moves south in autumn. Length 18cm (7in).

Right: A male grey wagtail lives up to its name—the wagging of the tail neatly recorded by a blurred stripe on the photograph. There has been a considerable amount of debate concerning the reasons for the tail wagging in the wagtail family, with no certain conclusion. However, one theory that is at least plausible is that against the sparkling, ever-changing background of broken water, the continuously moving, white-edged tail helps to break up the silhouette of the bird and give a good camouflage effect.

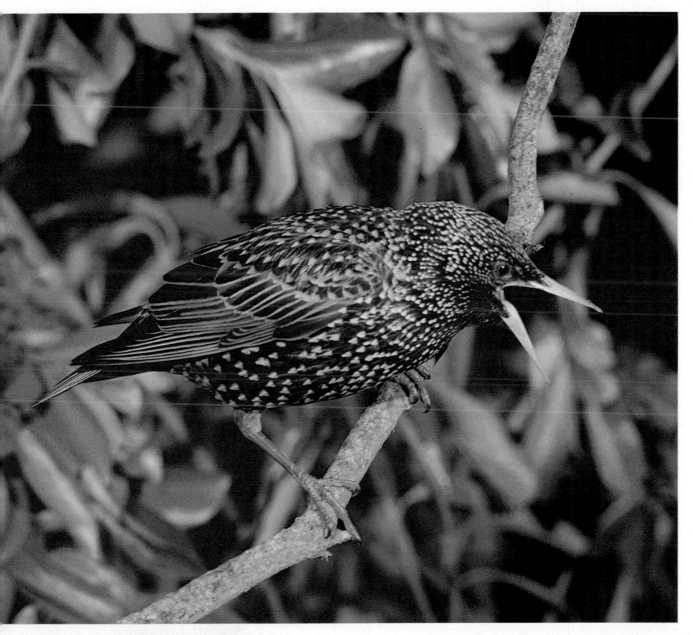

Starling

In both town and country the starling (above and opposite) is so familiar that birdwatchers all too often ignore it. Yet, if it were as rare today as it used to be, its superb iridescent plumage would rank it as one of the most beautiful of British birds.

Starling (*Sturnus vulgaris*). Resident; numbers swell in winter with the arrival of Continental migrants. Very common in both rural and urban areas, forming large flocks. Length 22cm (8½in).

The starling is one of our most common birds. More than four million pairs breed in Britain every year, and in the winter they are joined by at least 30 million more individuals that migrate here from northern and eastern Europe. Yet, up until the middle of the last century, the starling was relatively uncommon in Britain. The rise in the British population is part of a general pattern throughout Europe in which starlings have increased in numbers and spread westwards.

Omnivorous eaters The reasons for this population increase are not completely understood but an important factor is the bird's ability to live on a wide variety of foods. Fruits, seeds, flying insects, caterpillars, grubs, earthworms and household waste are all eaten, although the amounts taken of these different foods vary with the season. In spring the starling's diet consists mainly of insects and their larvae; in summer fruits become important; by winter these are replaced with seeds. Throughout the year, however, animal foods remain an important source of protein.

Another reason for the starling's success is that, during the last century or so, large areas of Europe's indigenous forests have been cleared to create grassland for farming. Close-cropped grassland is the starling's favourite habitat and you can often see them probing

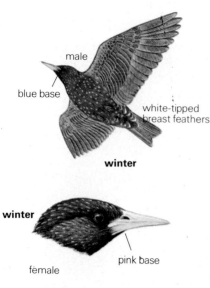

male
blue base
white-tipped
breast feathers

summer

winter

winter

female

pink base

iridescent
plumage

male

juvenile

Above: Starlings are so familiar that their beautiful iridescent plumage is too often overlooked. In autumn they develop white-tipped feathers on the breast; these remain until spring when they grow new feathers. Males and females can be distinguished by their eyes—female eyes have a distinctive brown ring—and, during winter and spring, by the colour at the base of their bills.

Right: Juveniles are grey-brown with white chins until summer, when they develop adult white-tipped plumage.

grass roots for invertebrates such as caterpillars, earthworms and leatherjackets (the larva of craneflies and a serious agricultural pest).

During the breeding season starlings spend most of their feeding time in grassland but at other times of the year they spread out into new habitats—a necessity if they are to take full advantage of their omnivorous nature. Bushes, hedgerows and trees are visited by starlings for fruits such as cherries, elderberries and sloes; they also search stubble fields, newly sown cereal fields and farmyards for seeds.

Forming flocks People often ask how starlings gather so quickly and in such numbers when food is put out into a garden. Starlings have an excellent memory, especially when it comes to remembering places where food appears regularly and in abundance. These places are always under observation by at least one bird. When food appears, one starling flies down to investigate. If it begins to peck, then all the other starlings nearby recognise this as a sign of food and fly down to join in. Within a very short time a feeding flock has formed.

The formation of a flock for feeding is advantageous for the flock members in that they can feed much faster than when they are on their own. There are many more eyes on the look-out for predators such as cats and sparrowhawks. Against this, however, is

Right: A flock of starlings searching for food. The starling's remarkable increase in numbers during the last century is, in part, the result of its omnivorous habits. Its diet ranges from seeds and fruits to insects, grubs and earthworms, and includes household waste as well.

the problem that a flock can grow too big for the food source, with the result that bickering and fighting ensue.

The starlings' omnivorous diet means that depending on what they are eating, a large flock can either inflict great damage or be of great benefit. The starlings' consumption of large numbers of leatherjackets is an obvious boon to the farmer but, on the other hand, they can devastate cherry orchards that are in fruit.

Roosting by the million As well as feeding in flocks, starlings also roost in flocks. Sometimes more than a million birds gather together in night roosts, attracting large numbers of predators. In places such as Trafalgar Square in London, huge flocks can be seen wheeling around and darkening the sky at dusk.

Quite why starlings roost in such numbers is not yet known, but the advantages must be considerable since they outweigh the attentions of predators. It may be that roosting presents a good opportunity for poorly fed birds to learn from their better-fed neighbours the location of good food supplies.

Nesting in letter boxes The starling's choice of nesting site shows again how well it takes advantage of opportunities presented by man. Its most typical nest site is a natural hole, usually in a tree but also in a cliff. However, any hole of the right size and situation will do: cavities in the roofs of houses and farm

Mimicry in birds

The starling's song is not particularly musical but it is remarkable for its mimicry. Sometimes it mimics phrases from the songs of neighbouring starlings, but it can also mimic the calls of other birds, including bullfinches, curlews, tawny owls and green woodpeckers. It can even imitate mammal noises—as well as inanimate sounds, such as telephones ringing.

Ornithologists have discovered that, with some species, if a male possesses a wide repertoire of songs it has a better chance of breeding successfully. This explains why starlings make such a variety of noises but not why they mimic 'foreign' sounds rather than create their own distinct sounds. That remains a mystery.

Starlings are closely related to those master-mimics, the mynah birds. Unlike the mynahs, however, starlings cannot imitate human speech.

Mimicry is not confined to the starling family: parrots and jackdaws reproduce words, and many species imitate other birds.

buildings are especially popular, and on occasions it even nests in letter boxes.

The breeding season begins in April. The male chooses his nest site and starts to build the nest–a bulky affair of dried grasses decorated with fresh green vegetation and the petals of spring flowers. The breeding season is the only time of year when starlings are territorial. The male defends a small territory around his nest site, but other breeding pairs are tolerated only a few yards away.

Once the male has built his nest he tries to attract a female by flying inside the nest hole and singing. Once the male has a mate, she completes the nest, lining the cup with material that can range from fine grasses and feathers to string and cellophane.

Eggs and young Between three and six eggs may be laid, though the usual clutch is five. The eggs are small, about 3cm (1¼in) long, and clear pale blue or blue-green with no markings. Incubation is carried out mostly by the female and takes about 11 days.

At first the young chicks are blind and without any feathering, save for a few tufts of down. But the chicks grow quickly since they are fed by both parents on a protein-rich diet of invetebrates; in the first 12 days their weight increases from 5g (⅙oz) to 60g (2oz). After the twelfth day they virtually cease to add weight, but their feathers begin to develop rapidly and by the time the chicks are 21 days old they are ready to leave the nest.

In most years the parents begin a second clutch of eggs. Between the first and second broods starlings often swap partners, the females moving on to join males at other nests, and the situation is further complicated by the fact that a few male starlings are polygamous, having two females occupying nearby nests.

Above: Large flocks of starlings gathering together to roost is a common sight in both the city and the countryside. Flocks can contain as many as a million individuals.

Right: A starling feeding its young. The chicks grow very quickly and leave the nest when they are about three weeks old, though they continue to follow the parents and beg food from them for a while afterwards.

Below: A typical clutch of starling eggs is five. Incubation takes about 11 days and is carried out mainly by the female. Starlings usually manage to raise two broods in a season.

Above: A waxwing in winter. Note the yellow tail band.

Waxwing (*Bombycilla garrulus*). Irregular winter visitor from Scandinavia and northern Russia, appearing in 'irruptions'. Length 18cm (7in). Sexes alike.

Waxwing

The waxwing does not breed in Britain, for its home lies in Scandinavia and the north of Russia. It visits us only in winter, but even then its appearances are unpredictable.

One morning in early December 1970 a roadside bank in Aberdeen was suddenly transformed from brilliant scarlet to a subtle pinkish-brown. The scarlet had been an almost total cover of cotoneaster berries, upon which had settled a flock of over 400 waxwings, colourful and bizarre immigrants from Scandinavia which had just completed

their crossing of the North Sea. They were busily replenishing the energy stores used on the journey by devouring the cotoneaster berries.

A handsome visitor The waxwing is a strikingly handsome bird, about the size and build of a starling. Its flight silhouette is in fact very similar to that of a starling, with long pointed wings and a short square-ended tail. If a waxwing flies low overhead, you can see that its bill is noticeably shorter than that of the commoner bird, while the tip of its tail carries a bright yellow band. Although it does not often call, the waxwing's voice can also betray its identity, for its usual note is a thin, high-pitched trill (its Russian name–'sviristel' –means 'reedpipe bird').

When seen perched or feeding, the waxwing is unmistakable. The general colour of the head, breast and belly is pinkish-brown, but the back is a darker brown. The rump and tail are grey, the latter shading into black with a conspicuous yellow tip, while the under-tail is a rich, dark chestnut. The chin is black and a black line extends round and behind the eye. The forehead is chestnut, shading into pinkish-brown on the top of the head, where the feathers are elongated into a remarkably long crest.

The flight feathers are mainly black but carry white markings. The bird's name is derived from the red tips to the inner flight feathers (secondaries); the webs of the feather tip are fused to the shaft, resembling bright red sealing-wax.

Britain invaded Despite this conspicuous appearance and the bird's tendency to form flocks (sometimes large, like the one in Aberdeen), the waxwing is unfamiliar to most people because it is an irregular visitor, whose arrival follows irruptions from its breeding areas (Scandinavia and northern Russia) in the manner of crossbills and the much rarer nutcracker and Pallas' sandgrouse. These irruptive species visit our shores infrequently, but when they do arrive, they tend to occur in substantial numbers.

A flock of over 1000 waxwings was seen near Louth in Lincolnshire during the early days of an invasion in the autumn of 1965.

Waxwing irruptions

When Britain plays host to these northern invaders, many other European countries– normally far south of the birds' range–also receive wandering birds. During large irruptions waxwings may range as far south as Italy, Spain and Portugal (shown on our map in a dotted line), but in most years they are able to spend the winter on their northern nesting areas. The solid lines on the map indicate the main advances of the birds in an irruption year.

September
October
November
December
January-February

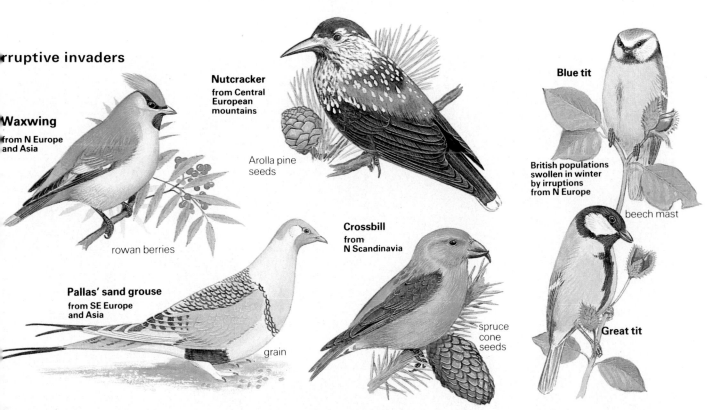

rruptive invaders

Waxwing
from N Europe
and Asia

rowan berries

Nutcracker
from Central
European
mountains

Arolla pine
seeds

Pallas' sand grouse
from SE Europe
and Asia

grain

Crossbill
from
N Scandinavia

spruce
cone
seeds

Blue tit

British populations
swollen in winter
by irruptions
from N Europe

beech mast

Great tit

Such large flocks are typical of the early arrivals and therefore tend to occur along the east coast. As the birds move further into the country, these large flocks break up so that later in the winter, and the further west one goes, the smaller the flocks tend to become. Nevertheless, flocks of a hundred or more do occur occasionally in Ireland.

The number of birds that arrive in Britain during an invasion can vary widely from a few tens to several thousands. Equally variable is their time of arrival. In 1965 the earliest birds appeared in September, while in the much smaller invasion of the 1956-7 winter waxwings were not seen until February.

Once an invasion of Britain occurs, they move from their initial landing places on the east coast and spread to other parts of the country, but the extent to which more westerly areas receive visitors depends to a certain extent on the size of the irruption. When numbers are small, the waxwings may remain near the east coast, but after a large immigration, as in the 1965-6 winter, the westward spread during the early part of the invasion is followed in the spring by a return to the east of the country as the birds that have survived our winter prepare to return to their breeding grounds. Most waxwings have left Britain by the end of April.

Population and food supplies This unpredictability over the waxwing's arrival in Britain and southern Europe is ultimately related to the bird's diet. In spring and summer waxwings do in fact eat insects, but at other times of the year they are vegetarians. In fact they are among the relatively few species that can, if necessary, survive on a diet consisting solely of plant material. Within the vegetable realm, however, waxwings prefer berries and it is this specialisation which forces them to vacate their breeding areas periodically.

Most fruiting trees do not produce large crops every year, rather they crop heavily every second year, but even this heavy crop can be quite variable. In the vicinity of the breeding areas rowan, hawthorn and juniper are the waxwing's main autumn and winter foods. If a series of good breeding seasons coincides with reasonable winter berry crops, the waxwing breeding population increases over successive years and may extend the breeding area southwards. Once a high population level has been attained, a failure of the berry crop will force these birds to emigrate in search of sufficient berries to survive the winter.

Above: Besides the waxwing, other bird species arrive suddenly in Britain from time to time. When their populations have become large—this coinciding with a failure of the fruits or seeds upon which they depend—they leave their normal areas in search of food to keep them alive over winter. This is called an 'irruption'.

Below: Cotoneaster berries, and also those of rowan, hawthorn and juniper, provide the waxwing's main food in the winter.

Jay

Jays are our most handsome and distinctive crows.
They are shy birds, and you never find them far away
from trees. In autumn they are busy collecting acorns
for their larder—in one wood 30 jays stored an
estimated 200,000 acorns in just four weeks!

The jay belongs to the crow family, but it has much brighter plumage than its relatives. At close range it looks quite exotic. Its crest, delicately spotted with white and black on the forehead, is raised when it is displaying to other birds. It has pale blue eyes and a broad black moustachial streak; most of the body is pale pinkish-brown. The flight feathers are black and grey, with a conspicuous patch of white, and the wing coverts are beautifully barred with pale blue and black.

Elusive bird Jays are shy and restless birds, and you may find it hard to get a good view. Most often you just see them flying away, when the large, white patch just above the black tail is very noticeable. They have broad, rounded wings and their flight often looks weak and laboured. At a distance, jays can be mistaken for hoopoes, an unrelated bird found in Europe which is fairly similar in size and shape and also has black, white and pink plumage.

Oak woodland is the jay's preferred habitat and you rarely find them far from trees. Unlike our other crows–magpies, carrion crows, rooks and jackdaws–jays seldom venture out into open fields. When they are searching for food in the trees or on the ground, they tend to hop and leap about, rather than walk or run.

Jays are often quite noisy, so you may hear them before you see them. The main call can be heard from far off. It is a loud, often twice-repeated, rasping shriek of alarm which they make when disturbed. People have also heard jays make a variety of chuckling and chirruping calls, a buzzard-like mew and even a low, warbling song.

Like their relatives, jays are intelligent, opportunist birds, and adapt to various diets. Usually they feed on the woodland floor, eating tree nuts such as beechnuts, sweet chestnuts, hazel nuts, pine seeds and especially acorns. They also eat fruits such as pears, plums, cherries and other soft fruits. In the summer they search for eggs and nestlings of other woodland birds, and they have been seen eating mice, slugs, worms, insects, woodlice, spiders, bread, fish and even bees. In gardens some jays have learnt to eat peanuts by tipping the holder upside down and shaking the nuts to the ground. Unlike crows and rooks, they rarely eat carrion or grain, and they have little effect on agriculture.

Acorn hoarders The jay's favourite food is acorns. In September and October when the acorns ripen you can see jays searching methodically for them in and beneath oak trees. However, instead of eating only what they require and leaving the rest to fall to the ground where all kinds of animals and birds would find them, jays hoard them. By making their own private larder, they can be sure of enough food to last throughout the year.

Jays can hold up to nine acorns at once in their specially large oesophagus, but more usually they take just three or four. They

crest

wing coverts

white rump and black tail conspicuous in flight

flight feathers

Opposite: The blue and black wing coverts and pinkish breast make the jay one of the most attractive of woodland birds.

Above and below: The favourite food of jays is acorns. Each jay's larder consists of several thousand acorns collected over about two months. A storing trip takes only a few minutes, and in autumn you may see jays flying back and forth all day.

Above: An adult jay about to drink water. Jays thrive in most types of woodland, particularly oakwoods, but you occasionally see them in suburban areas and city parks where there are plenty of trees. Note the distinctive blue and black barring on the wing. You can sometimes find one or two of these blue feathers dropped by a jay as it flies over woodland.

The acorns are often 'planted' in suitable sites for growing and, when there is a surplus, those that are not retrieved grow into trees and provide food for future generations of jays. So the jay's storing habit ensures the survival of both the jay and the oak. It is probably also the most important method by which oaks spread uphill.

When eating an acorn, a jay usually holds it still against a branch or on the ground with its inner toes. Then with its strong, slightly hooked beak, it levers and tears off the shell to reach the nutritious core.

Jay 'marriages' In spring you may find gatherings of jays known as jay 'marriages'. These are probably courting birds trying to find mates. On some occasions up to 30 jays are present displaying and calling in great excitement.

Jays prefer to nest fairly low down in thick undergrowth – in bushes and small trees, and in evergreens such as ivy, or suckers next to a tree trunk. Occasionally they choose the outer branches of a large tree. Both male and female help to build the well-concealed, robust nest. They use numerous small sticks and twigs and a little earth, and then line the nest with a thick layer of fine roots.

The female usually lays four to six eggs at the end of April or in May, and does most of the incubation. She is very difficult to spot because she crouches very low in the nest, only leaving when her mate comes to feed her and can stay on guard.

The eggs hatch after 16 days but the female still has to brood her family for the first week or so, because the tiny, featherless chicks soon chill if left uncovered for long. At this time the male finds all the food they need. To start with, the chicks look all beak and belly – because they are eating as much

take each acorn to a separate place, usually within half a mile but sometimes up to 2 miles away from where they found it. Favourite hiding places are under leaves or roots, in small holes or amongst moss. Sometimes the jay actually makes a hole in the ground with its beak so the acorn is properly concealed.

Jays appear to have excellent memories, because they know every detail of their local wood and they remember where most acorns are hidden. Even when snow covers the ground, they know exactly where to dig. In the summer many uneaten acorns begin to germinate, but jays can also recognise the fresh oak seedlings and dig them up to find acorn remains below.

Anting: feather-care

Most birds replace their feathers once or twice a year, but without daily servicing the feathers quickly lose their warmth and waterproofing, and flight becomes inefficient. So birds regularly bathe, preen, dust and oil their feathers even – or especially – in winter when days are short and the water cold. Passerines (perching birds) have developed an additional feather-care technique – anting. In this country it is the jays, rooks, thrushes and starlings that most often do this. The anting bird crouches in a mass of ants, holding its wings out to the ground so the ants crawl over its plumage. Often it picks ants up in its beak and puts or rubs them on the feathers.

There are over 40 species of ants in Britain and most produce toxic chemicals to defend their colony, attack others or immobilise prey. Such poisons are effective against other insects and, while various explanations of anting have been suggested, it is now thought that the birds' behaviour encourages ants to release their 'insecticidal shampoo' on to their feathers, so reducing populations of parasitic insects living within the plumage. Subsequent bathing and preening removes the dead insects. Interestingly, birds never use ants that sting, even though these are common.

food as possible and growing quickly. By the time they are two weeks old, they are big and fat, and all the feathers are sprouting except perhaps the tail which is last to appear. When they leave the nest the young jays already have their adult plumage.

The jay parents collect a special diet for their nestlings. Mostly they choose leaf-eating caterpillars from nearby trees and bushes, storing them in their throats until they have enough to give each nestling a good mouthful. The chicks wait silently for a parent to land beside the nest, and then reach up and open their beaks wide. The parent carefully puts food down the bright orange-pink gape of each chick in turn. If one gets too much to swallow, some is taken away and given to another.

Nesting adult jays are secretive, and the nestlings are also fairly quiet, even when being fed—you may hear a few squeaks and squawks if you are close. Even the egg-thieving jay has to keep its nest-site secret from crows, magpies, squirrels and even other jays who rob the nest if they get the chance.

Just as small birds mob jays, so for the same reason jays mob their enemies.

Jays spend about three weeks in the nest but are not independent for another two months, so only one brood is raised each year. They can live for several years and some have been known to reach the age of 14. Throughout their lives jays tend to stay in one area, and most fly no more than four miles from their birth place. Very occasionally the British Isles is invaded by hundreds of jays from the Continent if food supplies there fail to support the jay population.

In the past, when Britain was covered in forest, jays were probably numerous and widespread. However, they were persecuted because of their egg-thieving habit, and many trees have been cut down to make way for agriculture, so jays became quite scarce early in this century. Since then they have benefited from being unmolested, and from afforestation. Some have spread into suburban areas and city parks, especially those with a good collection of trees such as oak, beech or sweet chestnut, and shrubs.

Above: A pair of jays with their young in a rhododendron bush. Jay nests are small compared with the size of the well grown young, but they are well behaved and accidents are few.

Jay (*Garrulus glandarius*) about 34cm (13½in) from beak to tail; distribution widespread in woodlands of all types, particularly oakwoods, throughout the British Isles apart from northern Scotland. Resident.

Crow, rook and jackdaw

The rook, crow and jackdaw all co-exist on farmland without competing for food.

The crow, rook and jackdaw are all outwardly similar members of the crow family–so similar, in fact, that many people refer to them all simply as 'crows'. They are all common species on agricultural land, but they are able to share this habitat because each exploits it in a different way, so that they do not compete with one another for the necessities of life–food, nest sites and living space.

Three black birds Although they are superficially just black birds, these three 'crows' do differ in appearance. The most distinct is the jackdaw, which is the smallest of the three at about 32cm (13in) long. It is mainly black, but its chief distinguishing feature is the colour of the cheeks and nape, which are a silvery grey.

At close range you can see that the black feathers of the crown, wings and tail are glossed with blues and greens, and that the eye is a conspicuous bluish silver. In flight, the fast wing beats and the call of the jackdaw are also characteristic. The most usual call is a short, high-pitched 'chack'.

The rook and crow are similar in size, about 45cm (18in) long, and at a distance both appear uniformly dark. The adult rook, however, is glossy bluish black or purplish black all over, while the crow is generally a duller black with little gloss. The bills of both species are much longer than that of the jackdaw, but while that of the crow is black, with bristly feathers around its base, the bill of

Above: Rooks at a rookery near Selborne in Hampshire. Rooks build their nests in the upper branches of tall trees, while crows nest in the fork of a branch.

Below: For people who live in northern Scotland and the northern half of Ireland, separation of the rook and crow is a much simpler matter than in the south. In these places there is a different variant of the crow called the hooded crow or grey crow. Its back, belly and breast are grey.

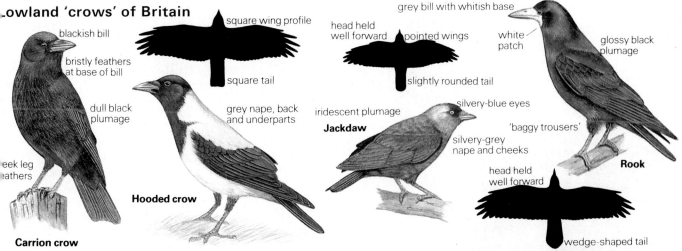

Lowland 'crows' of Britain

Carrion crow
- blackish bill
- bristly feathers at base of bill
- dull black plumage
- sleek leg feathers

Hooded crow
- square wing profile
- square tail
- grey nape, back and underparts

Jackdaw
- head held well forward
- pointed wings
- slightly rounded tail
- iridescent plumage
- silvery-blue eyes
- silvery-grey nape and cheeks
- head held well forward

Rook
- grey bill with whitish base
- white patch
- glossy black plumage
- 'baggy trousers'
- wedge-shaped tail

...the adult rook is grey, tending to white at the unfeathered base.

Social or solitary Differences in the appearance of our three lowland crows are rather subtle, but other aspects of their lives show more marked variation–particularly regarding their degree of sociality. Crows are generally solitary creatures, spending their time alone or in pairs, although family parties can of course be seen for a few weeks after the young leave the nest. Rooks and jackdaws, on the other hand, live in flocks which can number from a dozen or so to several hundred, and sometimes over a thousand birds.

For most of the year rooks and jackdaws live in mixed flocks, and often these flocks are joined by other birds such as starlings, lapwings and gulls. However, the country adage 'one rook is a crow; a flock of crows are rooks' is not absolutely true, for occasionally rooks, especially juveniles, do feed alone and crows, especially youngsters, do form flocks.

Differences in sociality tend to be stricter during the breeding season, when pairs of crows invariably defend the territories in which they feed and build their nests. Rooks and jackdaws are generally colonial, and solitary nests are something of a rarity. The rook's nesting colonies are the familiar rookeries which can number from a few nests to over a thousand, but these really large rookeries occur only in Scotland. Both the rook and crow build their nests in trees, using twigs, earth and grasses. They usually select tall trees, but while the crow builds its nest in a fork, the rook chooses the slender upper branches.

Apart from their noisiness, jackdaw colonies are less obvious than rookeries because the nests are built in holes. The most frequently used holes are those in buildings (especially derelict buildings, but also the chimneys of inhabited premises) cliffs and trees, but other sites, such as rabbit burrows, are sometimes used. In large holes, vast quantities of sticks and grasses are used to construct a base for the nest, which is lined with wool and grass; in smaller holes the nest consists of little more than the lining.

Carrion crow (*Corvus corone corone*). Resident bird of farmland and gardens. Plumage is uniformly dull black. Length 45cm (18in).

Hooded crow (*Corvus corone cornix*). Northern subspecies of carrion crow with grey plumage on back and underparts. 47cm (18½in).

Rook (*Corvus frugilegus*). Resident farmland bird with glossy black plumage. Length 45cm (18in).

Jackdaw (*Corvus monedula*). Resident on farmland. Small crow with grey patch on nape and cheeks. 32cm (13in).

Right: Jackdaws nest in holes, usually in colonies.

Below: The crow is a solitary feeder and nester.

rapid growth. Fresh animal material also has another vital resource–it contains about 90% water and constitutes the only water source available for the chicks.

For adults, and for all birds at other times of the year, food selection is less exacting and the diets of all three species encompass a wide range of foods. Furthermore, the diets of the three crows show considerable overlap.

The items the birds eat in common are earthworms, grubs, snails, wild seeds, cultivated cereals, fruit and the wide variety of offal found on rubbish tips. In some parts of Britain, notably in oakwoods, they also take defoliating caterpillars in the early summer– for this purpose they feed in the trees. In general, however, there is a tendency for the jackdaw to take more food items from the soil surface than the rook, which is more adept, with its longer bill, at digging for worms and

Taking turns The egg-laying seasons of the three species differ: the rook is one of our earliest nesting birds, laying its eggs in March. The crow lays mainly in mid-April, and the jackdaw between mid-April and the end of May. The eggs, 3-5 laid by the rook, 4-5 by the crow and 4-6 by the jackdaw, are variable in colour but are generally greenish, with blackish or brownish spots and blotches. In all species, only the female incubates, and while she is sitting she is fed by the male. The hen broods the young chicks, and at this stage the entire family is provisioned by the male, but as the chicks grow the female leaves them to take her share in feeding them.

Overlapping food requirements All three species are catholic in their tastes for food, eating both animal and plant items. Most of this is taken from the ground. During the feeding of the young, animal foods–mainly earthworms and insect larvae–predominate in the food brought back to the nest since the chicks need animal protein to sustain their

Above: Rooks at a rookery with nestling young. The most useful distinguishing feature of the rook is its grey bill. It is also slimmer than the crow, and has loose feathers on the thighs, giving a 'baggy trousers' appearance.

Below: Inside view of a jackdaw nest, after partly removing the boards that form the 'roof'. Clutches vary between 4 and 6 eggs, which are generally greenish with dark spots and blotches.

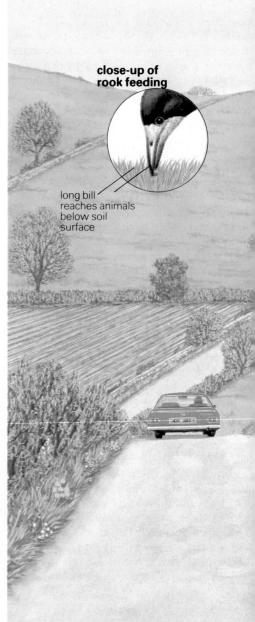

close-up of rook feeding

long bill reaches animals below soil surface

grubs in the top 7cm (3in) of the soil. The crow takes more carrion, often in the form of birds and mammals killed on the road, than the other two species.

Unfriendly reception There is no doubt that the three crows all take insects that are pests, and that they feed on weed seeds and leftovers from cereal harvests that might otherwise germinate and become weeds. Whether by doing this the birds confer any benefit to the farmer is an open question. At times, however, they all incur the wrath of the farmer or gamekeeper.

In sheep-rearing areas, crows are often blamed for killing or maiming lambs, but good evidence indicates that the vast majority of lambs taken are dead or very close to death, often through starvation, before the crows attack them. Crows are also renowned for their partiality to eggs, especially those of game birds.

Eggs also form a minor part of the diet of some rooks, but this species is of more serious concern for its consumption of several crops: germinating maize; sown, germinating and ripening wheat, barley and oats; potatoes; peas; and the foods laid in the open for cattle, sheep and pigs. Feeding in company with rooks, jackdaws also eat cereals and animal fodder.

Plentiful numbers Recent estimates suggest that there may be around half a million pairs of jackdaws and a million pairs each of the crow and rook in the British Isles. The three crows of lowland farming country are very similar in appearance and life-styles, but clearly their differences are sufficient to allow large populations to live side by side, forming an integral part of our country life throughout all four seasons of the year.

Rook, crow and jackdaw: how they share the farm

rooks—colonial nesters
nests are always
in upper branches

close-up of jackdaw feeding

jackdaws— colonial nesters
colony in disused building

short bill picks animals from soil surface

quarry— potential site for a jackdaw colony

crow—a solitary nester

nest is in a tree fork

rooks and jackdaws feed in a mixed flock

flocks prefer feeding on grazed land

close-up of crow feeding

crow—a solitary feeder

crow eating carrion (rabbit)

strong bill for carrion and live prey

crow eating beetle in turf

Magpie

The magpie is notorious for its habit of stealing other birds' eggs and chicks. You are most likely to catch it in the act in summer—at other times it eats almost anything.

Magpies are members of the crow family and are easily distinguished from their relatives—indeed from all other British birds—by their distinctive black and white colouring. Whether young or old, male or female, all have the same boldly patterned plumage which, at a distance, is only black and white, without any other colours or even shades of grey. The black head, back, wings and tail contrast with the pure white underparts and shoulder patch. Apart from the coloration, you can identify magpies easily by their long,

wedge-shaped tail—half the bird's total length—and by their short, rounded wings.

Nest predators Like others of the crow family, magpies will often plunder eggs and nestlings of less aggressive neighbours—particularly in farmland. Searching methodically for a suitable nest-worthy habitat, such as a thick, overgrown hedge, a single magpie may find several nests in quick succession. When a small bird sitting on a nest sees a magpie, it may 'freeze' until the last possible moment—hoping to be missed. Once the magpie

Opposite: Typical magpie country.

Above and opposite inset: with their striking black and white plumage, magpies are unmistakable.

Magpie (*Pica pica*), 45cm (18in) from beak to tip of tail. Resident. Distribution—see map below.

Magpie distribution
Magpies are probably capable of living anywhere in the British Isles, but the present breeding distribution is distinctly patchy in northern England and Scotland. Here persecution from gamekeepers—who rear grouse on the moors and pheasants in the valleys and dislike the magpie's habit of stealing eggs—is still common. Built-up areas with less keepering around cities such as Glasgow and Aberdeen act as refuges and support expanding populations. Gaps in eastern England may reflect changing agricultural practices.

discovers it however, the other bird must retreat hastily, and magpies have even been seen catching small birds in flight.

Like birds of prey, magpies are mobbed by smaller birds that must have no difficulty in recognising this particular enemy. Large birds are generally better off against magpies; their nests are only robbed when left unguarded, so the parents sit tight regardless.

When there is plenty of food, the nest of a bird such as the woodpigeon (in which both sexes incubate the eggs) is only uncovered during the changeovers, so the magpie may make several visits before it gets a meal. In some other species where only the female bird incubates the eggs, she must feed and return to the nest as soon as possible, especially if the eggs are not well hidden from view. In only a few seconds a magpie can force its way to a nest and eat or carry off the eggs or nestlings–leaving only a few fragments of eggshell. The magpie's job is relatively easy early in the summer when nesting cover is thin and food shortage forces many birds to spend more time feeding and less time incubating. Fortunately most birds can lay another clutch of eggs.

Wide-ranging diet Apart from this form of plundering–which is really a summer sideline–magpies mainly eat insects and larvae such as ground-dwelling beetles and moth caterpillars. However, magpies are opportunists and take whatever food they find. They eat small mammals such as voles and mice and also carrion. Magpies also feed on the more nutritious parts of plant matter such as fruits, nuts, berries and cereal grains, as well as on some invertebrates–slugs snails and worms–and a range of household scraps. Occasionally you may see magpies perching on the backs of farm animals where they eat fly larvae and parasitic ticks, as well as

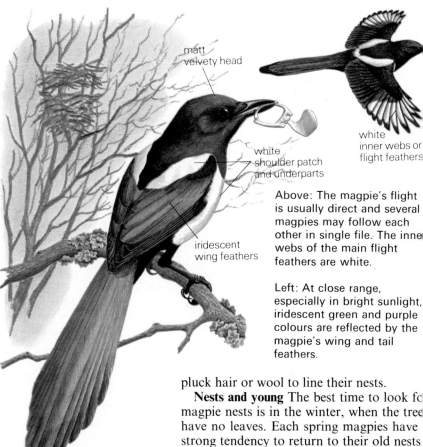

matt velvety head

white shoulder patch and underparts

iridescent wing feathers

long wedge-shaped iridescent tail

white inner webs of flight feathers

Above: The magpie's flight is usually direct and several magpies may follow each other in single file. The inner webs of the main flight feathers are white.

Left: At close range, especially in bright sunlight, iridescent green and purple colours are reflected by the magpie's wing and tail feathers.

Below: Magpies find much of their food on the ground, such as this dead rabbit. They walk or hop along the surface with the tail held a little elevated.

pluck hair or wool to line their nests.

Nests and young The best time to look for magpie nests is in the winter, when the trees have no leaves. Each spring magpies have a strong tendency to return to their old nests, adding to them or building on top of them. The nests may be renovated but still stand empty for two months before the female lays her eggs.

Magpie nest sites range from the top of tall isolated trees to thick, thorny hedges or thickets at the edge of a wood, and even on sea-cliffs. Though easy to see, the nests are rarely easy to reach.

The nest is constructed of sticks, and is thickly lined with mud and a layer of grass roots. Most magpies also build a dome of thorny twigs above the nest, leaving only a single, inconspicuous entrance at the side. The parents, which are said to pair for life, participate in building.

The female lays her eggs in April and has only one brood per year. The number of eggs varies from five to eight, though up to ten have been recorded. Only the female incubates the eggs, which take about 17 days to hatch. After this both parents feed the nestlings for three to four weeks. You can see family parties of magpies throughout the late summer and autumn; and you may spot the young jumping around using their short tails to help them balance each time they land.

Decline and rise Magpies are more widely distributed in the world than any other crow except the raven. In the British Isles, however, their distribution has been affected by many years of persecution. Shooting, poisoned bait and traps have reduced the magpie population throughout Scotland and parts of England. In some game-rearing areas it was eliminated altogether. Though many are still shot and hung from the gamekeeper's gibbet, a substantial recovery has been recorded this century. The introduction of laws prohibiting the use of poison and traps, and a decrease in game rearing has encouraged increases in the magpie's numbers and range, particularly during the last 40 years.

Moreover, magpies show an ability to survive changing conditions in a variety of habitats. They have colonised built-up areas as well as open country—a trend that is still continuing. In Scotland, where there are still large gaps in their distribution, the magpie has strongholds around cities such as Aberdeen, Glasgow and Edinburgh. In Ireland, magpies now breed in every county—as they do in England and Wales. Recently the only noticeable declines have been in country areas of England, particularly in East Anglia where the grubbing up of woodland and hedgerows and use of pesticides are thought to be the cause.

Distribution The spread of the magpies' distribution from the natural habitat of woodland edge, grassland and farmland to the man-made habitat of towns and cities reflects the species' adaptability. From the parks and large gardens of suburban London, they have spread in the last ten years to such places as Hyde Park and Buckingham Palace Gardens. Magpies are not fussy about their choice of food, habitat or company, and seem well fitted to life with man—if man allows it.

Bold and inquisitive It is worth watching magpies closely. They are constantly inquisitive and are known to hoard bright objects. Often they seem 'visibly intelligent'—soaking dry bread in a fishpond, for example, to make it easier to eat; then hiding the excess in a crevice in the rockery, carefully covering it with moss and grass pulled from the lawn.

Frequent raucous chattering makes magpies within earshot difficult to miss, and they often strut about in open grassy fields, or perch conspicuously on the top of fences and trees. It appears that their robust and intelligent nature, coupled with a large, sharp beak, is sufficient to deter most natural predators, so that secrecy and camouflage are of limited value.

Magpies are always alert, and city birds are quick to give warning of approaching cats, and they are becoming increasingly bold and some regularly visit bird tables. Of course they are not always welcome, especially as they thieve from the nests of garden birds. Magpies have even been seen drinking milk from the bottle like tits, and in Manchester they now take advantage of the eggs left in the cartons alongside the milk.

Telling the future Magpies have an important place in British folklore. Most people know of the good or bad luck that is supposed to follow if one or more magpies crosses their path. Your fortune or fate depends on the number you see, what the magpies are doing and where in the country you are.

Are birds 'intelligent'—or do they just imitate?

Magpies and other members of the crow family are often classed as the most intelligent of all birds. They are able to learn complex behaviour patterns and can be taught to 'talk' and count up to three or four. They survive heavy persecution and adapt to changing environments. Tits are also placed high on the intelligence scale—they are good at finding peanuts, and experiments have shown that they can be taught to obtain food from trick peanut-holders. The rapid spread of the habit of opening milk bottle tops clearly illustrates that they can both imitate others and discover for themselves. However, it is difficult to equate our anthropomorphic view of intelligence with the natural 'intelligence' of all birds.

Magpies are naturally inquisitive, and can handle a variety of foods in the countryside, so observations of 'intelligent' behaviour in built-up areas are not surprising. Similarly, the ability of tits to find and use man-made food is an extension of their natural feeding techniques. They need to be skilful at finding food in their natural woodland habitat; so they explore every possible nook and cranny, tearing and chipping bark away from holes where insects might hide. As they move into the suburban environment, these birds will find peanuts and milk, and treat them in the same way as normal foods.

Perhaps the 'intelligence' test should be related to birds' innate ability to build nests, migrate or even feed. How many people could build even an ordinary nest like that of a blackbird, or navigate like the migrating swallow, or collect 10,000 caterpillars in 18 days to feed a brood of blue tits?

Right: The female lays five to eight eggs in a nest that can be up to one metre (3ft) in diameter. The eggs, which are pale green with grey and brown spots or blotches, are about 3·5cm (1¼in) long.

Below: The young magpies leave the nest in June or July, and are distinguished by their stubby, incomplete tails.

Wren

The perky, diminutive wren – the smallest British bird apart from the goldcrest – is ideally suited to its foraging life in the undergrowth of woodland and hedgerow and, with ten million breeding pairs, is our most numerous species.

Opposite: Typical hedgerow habitat of a wren. Inset: A wren at its nest.

Below: The plumages of both sexes are identical.

In legend the familiar brown wren is condemned to live a skulking life of shame for cheating in the great election to find the king of the birds. The story goes that the birds decided to choose as their king the one which could fly the highest. Hoping to win the contest, the cheeky wren concealed himself in the plumage of the mighty eagle and hitched

a ride for most of the way, only emerging to outfly the eagle when it finally tired. The strength of this legend, which appears in many countries and cultures, testifies to Man's ancient association with and fondness for the perky little bird.

Tiny troglodyte The wren prefers to frequent holes and corners in cliff overhangs, derelict buildings, outhouses, tree roots and piles of boulders. Its scientific name means 'the cave-dweller' – a name not to be taken too literally, but nevertheless apt since the bird is one of the few able to exploit such recesses and cavities. It is an active little bird, full of verve and familiar in town and country.

The rounded, dumpy body, short whirring wings and cocked tail may look ungainly, but in fact the wren is superbly equipped for its ground-foraging way of life. It creeps about in the undergrowth in a characteristic crouched posture – very much like a small rodent – negotiating its way efficiently through narrow openings and working energetically through tangled vegetation, tree roots and brambles. On a branch, its tail-cocked perching position is unmistakable.

Year-long songster The sexes are indistinguishable in plumage, but only the cock sings. For the size of the bird's body, the volume and carrying power of the song is remarkable. The male sings consistently throughout the year and song is important in his life. He uses one type of call—a vehement, rattling warble usually lasting a few seconds—for a variety of purposes: territorial warning and defence, courtship, attracting others to roost and communicating with partners. In the excitement of courtship and nesting, he will even sing with his beak crammed full of building materials!

Wren (*Troglodytes troglodytes*); 10cm (3¾in) from beak to tail; distribution widespread; resident.

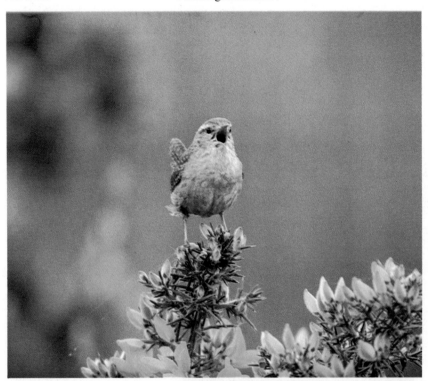

Above: A male wren singing to proclaim his territory. Apart from a series of loud warbling calls, the wren's repertoire includes cheery trills and a scolding 'tit-tit-tit' sound.

Right: The wren's domed nest, made of moss, dry grass and bracken and lined with feathers, makes a secure, snug home for the young. Some wrens prefer to nest in close proximity to Man and choose odd sites to build—such as in an old cap hung in a shed.

Numerous nests The wren's breeding season starts from the second half of April onwards. It is catholic and often quaint in its choice of nesting sites, frequently ignoring natural recesses in hedge bottom, ivy bank or upturned tree root in favour of man-made places such as outhouses or the corners of gardens.

The cock builds several nests—outsize, domed structures of moss, dry grass, bracken or leaves—to tempt his mate. The hen selects the one of her choice, lines it with feathers, then lays from five to twelve eggs and incubates them by herself for 14 or 15 days. The glossy white eggs are often speckled with minute black or red-brown spots at the large end. When the young hatch, the male leaves the female to do all the feeding. The hen usually rears two broods a season, especially in more vegetated areas where food is plentiful. The male bird—not the most diligent of parents—may install several females in succession in different nests.

Success story The wren is a successful and adaptable bird—something that is particularly noteworthy since it is the only Eurasian representative of an extensive family of otherwise exclusively New World birds. Not only is the wren one of the most widespread of all our birds, it is also extremely numerous. Densities of up to 100 pairs per square kilometre have been recorded. At the same time, the wren is vulnerable in hard winters when numbers may fall dramatically. However, the rate of recovery can be equally dramatic: after the cold winter of 1962-63 the wren recovered numbers faster than any other common bird.

The wren is almost entirely insectivorous. Its diet is composed mainly of the larvae of small moths, flies, beetles and other insects, as well as spiders, mites and a limited variety of small soft-bodied invertebrates—all probed, extracted or caught with the bird's fine, slender, slightly curved bill. It is little wonder that protracted hard weather—which decimates insects—spells disaster for the wren. Unfortunately, it is our one garden visitor that is not drawn to bird tables, so it is no use putting out extra food in the hope of saving it from starvation. In times of plenty, however, there are probably up to ten million breeding pairs of wrens in existence.

Quite a crowd One oddity of wren behaviour is communal roosting which sometimes occurs in particularly severe weather. Wrens are usually solitary at night, but large numbers are sometimes found roosting in very confined spaces, the birds huddled together in a feathery mass with tails pointing outwards. As many as 30 or 40 individuals have been found in one nest box, in tier on stifling tier. Obviously, the insulation obtained by this crowding has a high survival value in hard weather. It helps the birds retain the precious body heat they have gained from hard-won insect food foraged during the short winter daytime. After the young have fledged in summer, but before they have become independent, parent birds can sometimes be seen shepherding their families to the safety of a communal roost.

Island races Wrens are not only found in woodland, farmland, river banks and suburban gardens—where we are most familiar with them; they also occur on sea cliffs and mountainsides. They even inhabit some of our furthest–flung islands, particularly Shetland, St Kilda and the Hebrides. On these islands the species has been isolated for 6000 years or more and has produced distinctive, clearly separated local races. The island birds tend to be larger and greyer in colour and have heavier chestnut-coloured barring on the back than their mainland relatives.

The wren hunt The wren frequents the dwellings of Man more than any other bird, and it is not surprising that legends about it abound. One curious and ancient custom— the wren hunt–which originated over 1000 years ago took place (in various forms) in

many parts of England, and was particularly popular in Ireland, parts of Wales and the Isle of Man. The hunt was specially associated with St Stephen's Day (26th December). Wrens were hunted along hedgerows, and through woods with sticks, stones, bows and arrows or birch rods; any found were killed– often ritually. They were then borne through the town on an elaborate bier or specially constructed wren house by grotesquely dressed 'wren boys'–all to the accompaniment of traditional wren-hunt songs. In many ceremonies, money was solicited by the wren boys for 'the burying of the wren'. The hunt persisted until very recent times, and in Ireland is still practised. Its origins go far back into history: it is said that a wren hopping on a drum awakened the Danes and foiled a stealthy Irish attack.

Fortunately for the wren, it has outlived the barbarous hunt; now, though we no longer have the farthing coin which carried the wren emblem and testified to its popularity, the bird is fully protected by the law.

Above: A parent wren bringing a beakful of insects to its young in the nest. Its short wings make the wren's flight rapid and whirring. Note the characteristic white eye stripe.

Polygamy in birds

Most birds have only one mate; the advantage is that both parents help to rear young. Some birds, however, practise polygamy—having more than one mate. Male wrens often do this, especially where food is plentiful and the hen can feed the young on her own.

There are two types of polygamy. Simultaneous pairing can take place with two or more females (as with corn buntings). With successive polygamy, the male initiates consecutive broods with different females. Male wrens do both. The advantage is that the largest possible number of broods can be produced without the male increasing the size of his territory; also the female may have the opportunity to select more vigorous, active males—to the benefit of the species.

Well-adapted for creeping about in the undergrowth, the wren has an unmistakable bobbing, jerky method of feeding on the ground.

Blackcap and garden warbler

These two warblers nest in thickets and open woodland. It is hard to get a good enough view to tell which is which; if you succeed in coming close up to them, you may notice that one has a 'cap' – but the other has no distinctive markings at all!

Above: A garden warbler tidies its nest. The nest is more substantial than that of the blackcap, but both species use similar materials.

Opposite: A female blackcap at the nest.

Birdwatchers have a habit of referring irreverently to some groups of birds as 'little brown jobs'. On account of their rather drab plumage, the similarity between species, and the consequent difficulty in identifying them, many of the warblers fit nicely into this category of birds. In fact, the garden warbler is so featureless that it has been said that its best field character is its lack of distinguishing marks!

In addition to looking rather alike, warblers also have similar life-styles. All but one (the Dartford warbler) of the British warblers are summer visitors; they all eat insects, and most have fairly melodious songs. When we look closely at the biology of similar-looking and closely-related warblers however, we find that there are important ecological and behavioural differences between them. It is, in fact, these differences that enable such outwardly similar species to live in the same district without severely competing with one another.

The blackcap and garden warbler are two species that illustrate this point well. They are closely related, both being members of the genus *Sylvia*. They are both typical warblers, with fine bills, bristles round the base of the bill and fairly short, rounded wings; and both feed by gleaning insects from foliage and catching other insects in flight. They are about the same size, being 14cm (5½in) long and weighing around 20g (¾oz).

Look-alikes of the thicket

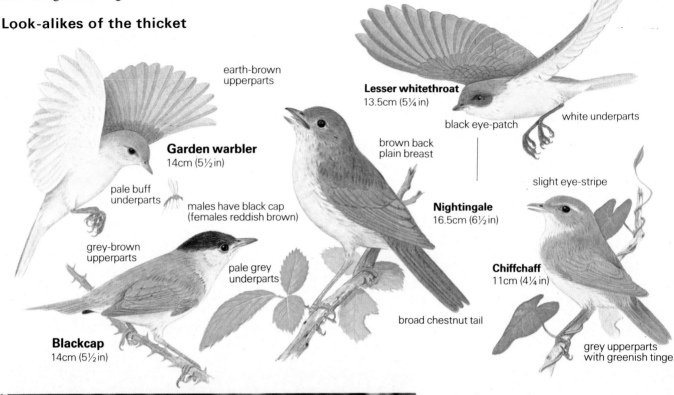

Garden warbler
14cm (5½ in)

earth-brown
upperparts

pale buff
underparts

males have black cap
(females reddish brown)

grey-brown
upperparts

pale grey
underparts

Blackcap
14cm (5½ in)

brown back
plain breast

Nightingale
16.5cm (6½ in)

broad chestnut tail

Lesser whitethroat
13.5cm (5¼ in)

black eye-patch

white underparts

slight eye-stripe

Chiffchaff
11cm (4¼ in)

grey upperparts
with greenish tinge

Above: The female blackcap
does have a 'cap', but it
is an attractive reddish-
brown instead of black.

Right: A blackcap nest with
eggs. The eggs of both
species have white, yellowish
or greenish backgrounds,
blotched and spotted with
brown or grey. Garden
warbler eggs tend to be
slightly larger and glossier,
and often number only four
compared to the blackcap's
usual five.

Even their songs are so similar that most
people are unable to distinguish them. The
experienced ear, however, recognises that the
rich warbling song of the blackcap consists
of more varied notes than does the warbling
of the garden warbler, and that the latter
sings in longer phrases.

Hide and watch them Song is certainly not
a good identification feature, however, and
for most people the only way to decide between the two species is to obtain good views.
Then, the birds are more readily distinguished.

The garden warbler is pale buff below and
earth-brown above. It has no eye stripe or
other head marking, or indeed any other
patterning that can be regarded as a distinguishing feature. Fortunately for the birdwatcher, however, it is the only warbler in
Britain and Ireland to lack such markings.
The blackcap is a greyer bird, being grey-
brown above and a paler ashy grey below,
but its best field character is the colour of the
forehead and crown. In the male, these parts
are glossy black, while in the female this 'cap'
is reddish-brown. Young males in the autumn
can look slightly strange, with both black and
brown feathers in the cap.

Once you have determined that the bird is
either a blackcap or a garden warbler, some
other slight differences between the two
species become apparent. Although the songs
are very similar, the two birds tend to sing in
different places: the garden warbler sings low
down in thick undergrowth, where the songster is well hidden, and the blackcap sings
on favoured perches in bushes or tree-tops
although again usually hidden by the foliage.

Different habitats This difference in singing
position may seem trivial but it is, of course,
related to the habitats that the two species

Opposite: A garden warbler feeds its young. These fledge when about ten days old. This rapid growth is very important for their survival, keeping to a minimum their time of greatest danger, for nests low down in the bushes are well within the reach of foxes, weasels and other denizens of the thicket. Each year, about half of the nests of both blackcaps and garden warblers are plundered by these predators, which find it easier to locate a nest containing calling chicks than one on which an adult bird is silently incubating. The shorter the time the chicks remain in the nest, the greater their chances of survival.

prefer. Again, there are close similarities, and blackcaps can be found breeding alongside garden warblers. Both species inhabit open woodland and copses with thick undergrowth, often of brambles, in which the birds nest. Large gardens, too, may play host to one or both of the warblers. But while garden warblers often nest in thickets where there are no trees, blackcaps seem to require that tall trees should be a feature of the habitat. Blackcaps are also more likely to nest in areas of evergreens than are garden warblers.

Both species build their nests in dense thickets, especially of brambles, but once again slight differences occur in the actual positioning of the nest. Once you know the bird must be either of these two species, the height can often be a helpful guide. Nests between 30 and 60cm (1 and 2ft) above the ground could belong to either species; but a nest below 30cm (1ft) is likely to belong to a garden warbler, and one above 60cm (2ft) is probably that of a blackcap.

Blackcaps arrive first The general lifestyles of the blackcap and garden warbler are there-

Male garden warblers arrive a week or so in advance of the females and similarly devote their time to establishing territories and singing. Garden warblers, however, do not begin to appear until late April, and their arrival continues through May. They are consequently unable to breed as early as blackcaps, and the peak of nest-building and egg-laying for garden warblers does not occur until the middle of May.

Migration patterns Why should there be this difference in the time of arrival, and hence of breeding? For the answer to this question we have to look beyond our shores. The garden warbler has a far longer migration: its wintering grounds range from tropical western Africa (Guinea and Nigeria) to Kenya, and from there to southern Africa. Blackcaps, too, travel to Africa, but their wintering range generally lies north of that of the garden warbler. Some blackcaps winter around the Mediterranean, and a few even stay in southern England. This species therefore travels a much shorter distance on its migration and this, together with its greater ability to utilise winter foods such as the berries of holly, privet and ivy, means that it can undertake its relatively brief and rapid migration early, permitting an early spring arrival in the breeding area.

Above: A garden warbler surveys its territory. This is the only bird in our countryside to have such an utterly bland appearance: indeed, the absence of any stripes, contrasting colours or white marks is the best way to recognise the species.

Garden warbler (*Sylvia borin*); summer visitor; warbler typical of thickets and large gardens; sings from low down in bushes. Length 14cm (5½in).

Blackcap (*Sylvia atricapilla*); mainly summer visitor, with small numbers overwintering; warbler nesting in thickets with tall trees; sings from tree-tops or bushes. Length 14cm (5½in).

fore very similar, although differences in song, habitat and nest position can be noted. These may appear minor to us, but they are undoubtedly very real to the birds. Much greater differences, however, become apparent between the two species when we look at the timing of events in their life cycles.

Blackcaps make their presence felt by singing from March onwards. Those that sing in early March are probably birds that have spent the winter in Britain – for although the species is overwhelmingly a summer visiting one, small numbers do stay for the winter in Britain and Ireland. In late March, the returning migrants begin to swell the numbers; this arrival continues during April. Males arrive first, and quickly establish territories and start to sing, so that when the females arrive a week or two later, pairing can occur without delay. Nest-building and egg-laying take place in late April and early May. This early breeding, and the rapid development of the young, enable some pairs of blackcaps to rear two broods each year.

Not only do garden warblers arrive later, but they must also depart earlier for their autumn journey to Africa, and they make their preparations for this (by feeding to store fat) well in advance of blackcaps; and so the featureless warbler of our scrubby woodlands has a hectic summer season. Could it be that this hectic life and all the dangers of the long journeys contribute to its scarcity, compared with its close relative? Blackcaps are three times as abundant in Britain.

Dartford warbler

The Dartford warbler is the only British bird that lives exclusively on heathland. This fact alone places it among our most endangered species.

Much has been written in recent years of the disappearance of our southern lowland heathland, its specialist reptile inhabitants – the smooth snake and the sand lizard – and its one specialist bird, the Dartford warbler. The Dartford warbler is a true specialist, entirely dependent on these low heaths dominated by gorse and a mixture of heathers (usually ling and bell heather or sometimes cross-leaved heath). It is the dense cover provided by these plant species, as well as the unique invertebrate fauna of the heaths, that the bird needs for its survival.

Other bird species occur as close neighbours of the Dartford warbler on the heaths, including the stonechat, the grasshopper warbler, the whitethroat, the hobby and the nightjar, but apart from the resident stonechat all these others are annual visitors coming from the south to breed in the warmth and plenty of our temperate summer. These birds thrive on the shrinking heathland but, unlike the Dartford warbler, each can also prosper in other habitats. If the heathlands disappear completely or become too fragmented, the Dartford warbler must inevitably vanish with them.

The first recorded description of the Dartford warbler was based on two individual birds shot in 1733 on Bexley Heath (now known as Bexleyheath, and a far cry from heathland for it is today a populated suburban district) near Dartford in Kent. At that time similar heathlands spread extensively across lowland England, and the warbler had a range extending from Cornwall to Norfolk and from the Isle of Wight as far north as Shropshire and Staffordshire. Today, only a residual population exists on remnant heathland in Hampshire and Dorset, with unsteady outposts in Devon, the Isle of Wight, Surrey and Sussex.

Hard winters It seems clear that the Dartford warbler has always been subject to fluctuations in its fortunes, certainly so far as total numbers are concerned, even in times when its heathland home was far more extensive than it is now. Hard winters, in particular, take a heavy toll on this small insectivorous bird: after the severe and protracted winter of 1962-63 the population crashed from about 460 pairs to a mere 11. Its powers of recovery, however, are shown by the fact that by 1970 the numbers had picked up again to about 70 pairs, and then climbed to 560 pairs by 1974. Then the hard winter of 1981-82 reduced the numbers again, to perhaps half the previous summer's total.

On individual heaths, the density of Dartford warblers is inconsistent and often erratic; frequently the bird is numerous in one area, but scarce in another that was previously favoured and held good numbers. Uncontrolled fire is a serious factor in reducing the population, as in the dry summer of 1976 when severe heath fires destroyed many hundreds of acres of deep, mature gorse and heather; the damage was temporary in some areas, but permanent in others where reclamation of the ground for agriculture followed the burning.

A hidden bird The Dartford warbler is a shy and elusive bird, in many respects the archetypal skulking warbler, moving through thick cover with utmost ease and all too easily avoiding detection. On bright days it may show itself more readily, giving quick glimpses of its distinctive cock-tailed form before diving again into thick cover. Its appearances in the open are fleeting, and any obligatory movement from thicket to thicket involves only low darting crossings of open areas.

When glimpsed in the open there is no con-

Above: The upperparts are grey-brown, more slate-grey on the head, and the underparts a dull pinkish chestnut. Brightest among the bird's features is the reddish-orange eye ring, which gives the eye an unusual impression of size and a quality of penetrating brightness.

Below: In Britain the Dartford warbler is at the northern edge of its world range, which reaches south to the Mediterranean and North Africa.

Dartford warbler distribution

using this diminutive bird with any other on the British list. Its small body size is equalled by the exceptionally long tail, which makes up half the total 12.5cm (5in) length. It weighs a mere 9-10 grams ($\frac{3}{8}$oz). The tail, characteristically cocked and frequently flicked, gives the bird much of its unmistakable outline, the remaining impression being of a dark coloured bird with small, rounded body, fine bill and a high forehead and crown. Its large reddish eye ring is immediately noticeable.

Displaying in April For a short period in early April, the cock birds are briefly conspicuous as they advertise their territory and sing. They have a lively dancing display flight in which the male bird rises above the dense canopy of gorse or heather and flutters down on vibrating wings. This display is reminiscent of that of a whitethroat, although it is neither as elevated nor as abandoned. The short, musical song also is similar to that of the whitethroat, but more mellow and liquid. The song is delivered from deep inside the gorse, or in a brief excursion to the topmost swaying twigs of a bush. Sometimes it is performed as an accompaniment to the dancing song flight.

Dartford warblers, sedentary throughout their range wherever they occur, are thus on site when the breeding season arrives and are among the early breeders. By mid April in a warm spring the first nests are built in the rank heather and gorse. The nest, although built by such a small bird, is remarkably robust, outlined first with twigs of heather and grasses and then shaped with finer grasses, rootlets and hairs, often woven with a little thistledown, wool or spiders' threads and individual feathers.

Three or four eggs are normally laid, dirty white in colour and finely spotted with lavender brown. The cock bird plays a small part in the incubation, which is chiefly carried out by the hen. The eggs hatch within a fortnight of the start of incubation.

Winter's shortage Very few species of wholly insectivorous small birds have evolved a sufficiently sound strategy to survive the vagaries of a British winter with reliability. The Dartford warbler faces no serious hardships in spring and summer, when the heathlands throb with the volume of insect life and the birds find an easy living. They have a ready harvest of small beetles, spiders, midges, small butterflies and moths, caterpillars and other larvae.

In winter, however, the choice narrows dramatically. The critical factor is the depth of cover provided by the heather and gorse. Deep under this canopy, even when it is covered with a thick layer of snow, the tangle of branches still provides a subsistence diet. Here the small warblers forage for heathland spiders, hibernating insects and the depleted stock of other invertebrates. In the hardest winters of all, shortages of these bring heavy losses to the Dartford warbler.

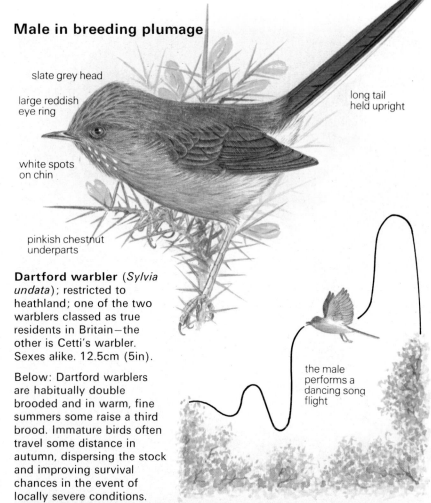

Male in breeding plumage

slate grey head

large reddish eye ring

white spots on chin

pinkish chestnut underparts

long tail held upright

Dartford warbler (*Sylvia undata*); restricted to heathland; one of the two warblers classed as true residents in Britain—the other is Cetti's warbler. Sexes alike. 12.5cm (5in).

Below: Dartford warblers are habitually double brooded and in warm, fine summers some raise a third brood. Immature birds often travel some distance in autumn, dispersing the stock and improving survival chances in the event of locally severe conditions.

the male performs a dancing song flight

Chiffchaff, willow warbler and wood warbler

Our warblers are grouped according to whether they are birds of reed-beds, scrub or leafy treetops. Here we look at the 'leaf explorers'.

Britain's three species.

The chiffchaff This, the dingiest of the three, has olive-brown upperparts and yellowish-buff underparts, an indistinct eye stripe and, usually, black legs. In keeping with its plumage and its name, its song is the least varied, alternating between two monotonous squeaky notes – 'chiff' and 'chaff'. Sometimes one note predominates as the bird 'misses' the other.

The chiffchaff is the earliest of our summer migrants: the harbinger of spring. The first birds arrive in early March, the last in April or May. However, this pattern is complicated by the tendency of an increasing number of chiffchaffs to overwinter in southern England. Although these hardy individuals may fly north to Scandinavia and beyond to breed, they are usually still here when the British breeders arrive.

The chiffchaff requires both bushy undergrowth for its nest, and tall trees as songposts and feeding sites. While it can therefore live in well-grown deciduous and coniferous woodland, it is excluded from many areas where tall trees are uncommon, particularly parts of northern England and Scotland.

The willow warbler This bird is greener above, and more yellow below, than the chiffchaff; it has a stronger eye-stripe and, usually, pale legs. The overall impression it gives is of clearer colours and a 'cleaner' appearance.

The first willow warblers to arrive, usually in mid or late March, signal that the spring influx of visiting birds is under way. Their song is one of the most welcome country sounds, especially as it typically rings out from the heart of a colourful pussy willow tree on a bright sunlit morning. Starting quietly, the musical warbling gains volume and pitch and then descends back down the scale to a deliberate final flourish.

In its choice of habitat, the willow warbler is the least fussy of the three leaf warblers. Almost any wooded or open bushy area is suitable, provided the canopy is not too dense. Ideal habitats range from damp areas with willows (as its name suggests) to young conifer plantations and small copses. The

Above: A willow warbler sings amid the opening buds. Besides the warbling song, the bird has a faint 'hoo-eet' call. The chiffchaff also has a similar call, sung slightly faster.

Right: Plentiful down surrounds the eggs in a willow warbler's nest. All three leaf warbler species usually lay 6 or 7. Only the females incubate, and this takes 13 days. The young fledge within 2 weeks, so sometimes there is time for a second brood.

Three species of leaf warbler are found in Britain and Ireland: the willow warbler, the chiffchaff and the wood warbler. Many people find warblers of any kind difficult to identify because they are invariably well camouflaged, retiring birds. Leaf warblers provide additional problems because they look so similar to one another. A leaf warbler can generally be described as a small, greenish-brown, lightly built bird with a fine, insect-eating bill, a pale stripe above the eye and yellowish underparts, flitting about in the canopy of a tree. This description applies to virtually all the *Phylloscopus* (leaf warbler) species that occur in the Old World (there are about 30 of them). It certainly applies to willow warbler is the commonest and most widespread of all our summer visitors, breeding throughout Britain and Ireland, even in sites close to built-up areas.

The wood warbler Of the three leaf warblers, this is the most brightly coloured, having yellowish-green upperparts, a sulphur-yellow throat and breast, a white belly, a noticeable yellow eye stripe and pale legs. At 12.5cm (5in) long, it is also noticeably larger than the other two leaf warbler species, for they each measure only 11cm ($4\frac{1}{4}$in) in length.

The wood warbler is the last of the three leaf warblers to arrive, mainly between mid-April and mid-May. Full appreciation of its song is certainly only achieved when you can both see and hear the bird in action. Starting with a steady 'stip, stip, stip', it accelerates to a marvellous, far-carrying trill which sets the whole bird quivering with the effort involved. The wood warbler also has a second, less well-known though equally distinctive song: a piping 'piu' repeated several times in quick succession.

The wood warbler is very particular in its choice of habitat: it prefers mature oak, birch, beech and chestnut woodland with little or no undergrowth. The sessile oak-woods of the valleys of western Britain are ideal, but this type of habitat is not common elsewhere. Consequently this species is the least widespread, being scarce or absent from wide tracts of England and Scotland. For every one of our breeding wood warblers, there are about ten chiffchaffs and a hundred willow warblers.

The breeding season Males of all three species typically arrive to set up territories a week or two earlier than their mates, often in the same area in which they were raised. Their beautiful, domed nests, almost spherical with the entrance at the side, are solely the work of the females. Leaves, grass, stalks, moss and perhaps bracken comprise the main structure, but whereas the wood warbler lines its nest with fine grass and hair, the other two use feathers. Each species hides its nest among low-growing plants and bushes. The chiffchaff builds its nest a foot or two above the ground in most cases, while the others make

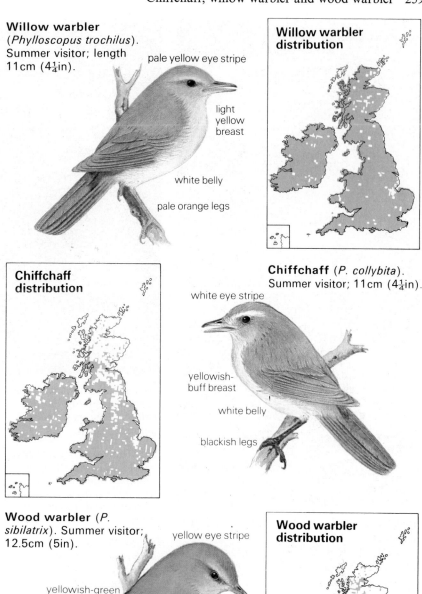

Willow warbler (*Phylloscopus trochilus*). Summer visitor; length 11cm ($4\frac{1}{4}$in).

pale yellow eye stripe

light yellow breast

white belly

pale orange legs

Willow warbler distribution

Chiffchaff distribution

Chiffchaff (*P. collybita*). Summer visitor; 11cm ($4\frac{1}{4}$in).

white eye stripe

yellowish-buff breast

white belly

blackish legs

Wood warbler (*P. sibilatrix*). Summer visitor; 12.5cm (5in).

yellow eye stripe

yellowish-green upperparts

bright yellow throat and breast

white belly

brown legs

Wood warbler distribution

Wing formulae

Wing formulae are a series of measurements made to prove the identity of a bird such as a leaf warbler. In some cases, the first measurement alone is sufficient, but in others as many as four are necessary:

A How long is the wing?
B Which primaries (or primary) are longest?
C Which primaries have the same (or nearly the same) length as the second?
D Which primaries have an emargination?

SAMPLE WING

wing length measured from 'shoulder' to wing tip (A)

secondaries   primaries

1 (small first primary)

emarginations (D)

3 longest primary (B)

5th primary is closest in length to 2nd (C)

Willow warbler

wing length 53–68mm

emarginations on 3,4,5

Wood warbler

wing length 69–81mm

emarginations on 3,4

wing length 59–72mm

emarginations on 3,4,5,6

Chiffchaff

• emarginated primaries
Nos 1–10 = primary feathers
------ line showing relative length of 2nd primary

theirs at ground level among grass and dead leaves.

Moult strategy One of the most distinct differences between our three leaf warblers, though perhaps the least obvious to the casual observer, is the timing of their feather moults. The only feature they share is that the young birds of all three species undergo a partial moult in autumn before they leave this country. (A partial moult is when the birds replace their body feathers, but not their wing or tail feathers.)

After this stage, chiffchaffs undergo a partial moult each winter and a complete moult each autumn; wood warblers undergo a complete moult each winter and a partial moult each autumn; and willow warblers undergo two complete moults, one in winter and one in autumn. To moult the entire plumage twice in each year is highly unusual, and so the willow warbler is in a class of its own in this particular respect. Curiously, there seems to be no obvious advantage in this behaviour, for all three strategies are demonstrably successful.

End of the season Late summer is the time when each individual bird must find extra food to fatten itself. This facilitates the growth of new feathers after the moult, and then fuels the bird's migration journey south. Leaf warblers are quick and agile birds, hopping to and fro to pick up tiny insects and caterpillars from twigs and leaves, hovering

Above: The chiffchaff is the least colourful of the three leaf warblers: its upperparts are olive brown.

Left: The wood warbler has brighter plumage than the other two species. Its nest is made at ground level and is domed, with the entrance at the side.

Below: The chiffchaff's nest is normally sited above ground level in the shrub layer; the bird is dependent on bushy undergrowth for nest sites.

to catch those out of reach or darting out to intercept them in flight. At this time of year, berries provide additional variety, and those chiffchaffs that stay for the winter occasionally visit bird tables for fat, meat, bread and other household scraps.

It is remarkable that such tiny birds, weighing some 10g ($\frac{1}{3}$oz), are able to fly to winter quarters as far away as Africa. Migration begins as early as the end of July. The first to leave are willow warblers, which migrate to tropical west Africa, some even crossing the equator. Most wood warblers migrate up the Nile valley to southern Sudan. The last to leave are the chiffchaffs, many of which fly no further than the Mediterranean.

Goldcrest and firecrest

Contrary to popular belief, Britain's smallest bird is not the wren; it is just pipped at the post by the goldcrest and its less common relative, the firecrest.

The goldcrest and firecrest are not just the smallest birds in Britain; they are also the smallest in the whole of Europe. At just 9cm (3½in) long, they are 5mm (¼in) shorter than the wren. Both birds are also extremely light, weighing no more than 5g.

By far the more common of the two species, the goldcrest can be seen in most parts of Britain, whereas the firecrest has only recently begun to breed here and is still confined to southern and eastern England.

The goldcrest The most noticeable feature of the goldcrest is the lemon-yellow stripe, bordered by a black line, on its crown–this is the crest after which it is named. During display, or in winter when a competitor for food comes too close, the bird's feathers become erect and the stripe widens. In the male, the raised feathers reveal that the crest has a deep orange centre.

The rest of the goldcrest's plumage is much drabber since it was developed not for display but to provide camouflage in conifer woods. The upperparts of the body and tail are olive-green and the underparts buff. The wings are greenish-black with feather margins tinged yellow, and there are two distinct white wing-bars close to where the wing meets the body. The eye of a goldcrest is large and dark, and is surrounded by a broad

Above: Coniferous forests and woodland are the most common habitats for the goldcrest, though it is becoming a familiar bird in gardens having conifer trees or hedges. Goldcrests also inhabit deciduous woods, but usually in small numbers. Only after a mild winter, when the goldcrest population tends to 'explode', do they become common in deciduous woods.

Goldcrest (*Regulus regulus*). Resident; length 9cm (3½in), which makes it, jointly with the firecrest, Britain's smallest bird. Between 5 and 13 extremely small white eggs flecked with brown are laid between March and August.

Goldcrest

male

female

yellow and orange crest

juvenile

Goldcrest distribution

pale ring of feathers that give the bird a look of permanent surprise.

Nationwide distribution The goldcrest is widely distributed in the British Isles, being absent only from the fens of East Anglia and the Scottish Highlands, though it is rare in the Hebrides, Orkneys and Shetlands.

Its favourite habitat is coniferous forests and woodlands. As more and more conifer plantations become established, so the gold-crest has spread out and increased in numbers, and it is now also beginning to colonize garden conifers.

Despite being so common in coniferous habitats, the goldcrest can be extremely difficult to observe since it spends much of its time high up in trees. A good way of detecting a goldcrest is to listen for its song: a pulsating series of 'zee-zee-zee' squeaks, breaking into a 'deedly-deedly-deeee' and ending with a flourish. The song is extremely high-pitched; one of the signs of increasing age in a bird-watcher comes when he or she visits a conifer wood in spring and does *not* hear a goldcrest (the frequency range detected by the human ear decreases as people age).

Coniferous woodland is the most im-portant habitat for the goldcrest, but it can also be found in deciduous woods, though usually in far fewer numbers. However, after a succession of mild winters, the goldcrest population can multiply dramatically, the birds inhabiting even lowland oakwoods in large numbers.

Just as mild winters lead to a population explosion, so a severe winter can lead equally dramatically to a population crash; the heat loss from such a tiny body during a long winter's night can be too great for the bird to survive. During the exceptionally severe winter of 1962-3 about 60% of our goldcrests

Above: and right: Male and female adult goldcrests differ most noticeably in the colour of their crests, the male's (see right) being more orange than the female's. The juvenile goldcrest lacks any crest. Goldcrests are found in most parts of Britain.

Below: A goldcrest feeds its young, a task shared by both parents. The chicks fledge after about three weeks which, in most seasons, leaves plenty of time for a second brood.

died. But, in the decade that followed, a run of mild winters allowed the population to increase tenfold from the low point of 1963.

The breeding season Nest-building begins in March. The nest consists of a basket of mosses, held together by woven cobwebs and suspended hammock-like in the fork of two twigs. Most are built in thick foliage towards the end of a branch, though less often in ivy or honeysuckle close to a tree trunk; or a prickly bush such as gorse, may be chosen. Both sexes help in the construction.

A typical clutch of eggs is between seven and ten, though it can range from five to thirteen; the eggs are incubated by the female alone. The young brood is fed by both parents on the typical goldcrest diet of insects, mites, spiders and their eggs and larvae. The young fledge after about 20-23 days. In most seasons the parents can easily manage to rear two broods—such a high reproductive cap-acity helps the population to recover from severe winters.

Once they have fledged, the young gold-crests usually join up with other woodland colonized.

This colonization is paralleled by an increase in the firecrest's Continental range and in the number of firecrests seen in spring and autumn at the regular migration-watching spots. Ornithologists do not yet know why this is happening, though it is possible that, in the past, firecrests were simply overlooked by birdwatchers and so their numbers were thought to be lower than they actually were.

Similarities to goldcrest The firecrest breeds in similar habitats to those of the goldcrest, and its way of life and food are also similar. On the Continent, however, the firecrest tends to be a bird of open, usually deciduous woodland, whereas the goldcrest usually inhabits conifers. So, in Britain, the goldcrest occupies both its own habitat and the firecrest's as well. Yet, when the firecrest started to colonize Britain it chose to settle mainly in dense conifers–the stronghold of the goldcrest. Not surprisingly, there have been reports of territorial fights between the two.

As with the goldcrest, the best way to locate breeding firecrests is by their song. This is very similar to that of the goldcrest but, with practice, the two can be told apart. The firecrest's song consists of a harsh and repetitive 'zit-zit, zit-zit . . .' that accelerates towards the end but lacks a terminal flourish. The best time to hear it is in late May and June; firecrests rarely sing later in the season than that.

birds, such as tits, wrens and warblers, to form large foraging parties. As autumn progresses, our resident goldcrest population is joined by often considerable numbers of Continental migrants. Since the Continental winter is so much more severe than ours, this migration obviously has survival value; nevertheless, it is remarkable that so small a bird routinely makes such a hazardous journey– often crossing the North Sea at the height of the autumn gales.

The firecrest In appearance, the firecrest is similar to its commoner relative, but its plumage is much brighter. Its upperparts are greenish-gold with a mantle of delicate bronze over the shoulders. The underparts are paler and more silvery than those of the goldcrest. The most striking difference, however, is on the head. The eye has a black stripe running through it; below this is a short white stripe, and above a bolder, long, white stripe which offsets the black-bordered crest. Both sexes of firecrest have an orange-yellow crest, though on the male it is much deeper and richer in colour.

Once rare migrant Not so many years ago, the firecrest was a rare passing migrant and much sought after by birdwatchers. Each spring, a few arrived at isolated spots along the south and east coasts of England as far north as Norfolk. A few birds were also sighted each autumn on their way southwards. This migration still takes place, but small numbers of firecrest are now beginning to settle in Britain, instead of just passing through. The first sighting was in 1962, when some recently fledged chicks were seen in the New Forest. A small but regularly breeding population has become established at several sites in that area, and other counties in southern and eastern England have also been

Above: Until about 20 years ago, the firecrest was seen only as a passing migrant but it has now settled in the same habitat as the goldcrest. On the Continent, however, it tends to be a bird of deciduous woodland.

Firecrest

orange crest

female

Firecrest (*Regulus ignicapillus*). Resident; length 9cm (3½in). Distinguished from the goldcrest particularly by its black eye-stripe. The eggs are similar but laid in May-July.

Below left: Breeding firecrests are confined to southern and eastern England.

Firecrest distribution

male

black eye-stripe

Whinchat and stonechat

Chats are delightfully extrovert in their behaviour, posing obligingly in full view while they sing from the top of a bush or tuft of grass. Our two species are the stonechat, which is a resident bird, and the whinchat, a summer visitor.

Above: A male stonechat perches on a prominent tuft of grass to sing and survey his territory. This scene is in county Galway in the west of Ireland, where the climate is a little milder than elsewhere. The stonechat's combination of a sedentary existence and demonstrative habits makes it an easy bird to observe.

Opposite right: A male whinchat, with a freshly caught small heath butterfly.

Both the stonechat and the whinchat are plump, colourful, upstanding birds, characteristic of open habitats with few trees. Both species are small, measuring only 13cm (5in) from beak to tail. Their English names are for the most part appropriate, since their alarm calls sound just like two pebbles being knocked together–hence 'chat' in imitation of the sound. Whin is another name for gorse, so you might expect the whinchat to be more common in gorse than the stonechat–but this is not the case.

Easy to recognise Both stonechats and whinchats are easy to identify. The male stonechat is an elegant bird, with a black or dark brown back, head and throat, highlighted by a pure white, though incomplete, collar. His chest is conspicuously reddish, fading to white on the belly, and when he flies, or as he flicks his wings while perched, you see white marks on the wings and a pale rump. Females and young birds are similar but much less striking, being more brown than black and having relatively little white.

The male whinchat is also elegant. He has

a broad and conspicuous white eyestripe, blackish crown and cheeks and a richly chequered and speckled back. His chest is a beautiful buff colour – not reddish like that of a stonechat. Flying whinchats show more white on the wings than stonechats, and white at the base of the tail on either side.

Two important differences between the two chats affect their behaviour, breeding biology and distributions. First, whereas stonechats are mainly sedentary, whinchats are migrants. Secondly, the two species choose slightly different habitats.

Staying through winter The stonechat is a resident species in Britain and Ireland, even though it is difficult for such a small, insect-eating bird to keep warm and well fed in winter. In the past, hard winters have spelt near disaster for British stonechats, with local populations being wiped out on a number of occasions. The coastal areas of south and west Britain and Ireland have the mildest winters in these islands, and consequently that is where stonechats are most numerous. After a particularly bad winter, few can be found in any other areas. Only after a run of mild winters do they spread north and east.

Stonechat habitat Ideal country for stone-chats consists of open, fairly close-cropped grassland (for feeding) with scattered gorse and bramble bushes (for nesting). Bracken or heather is often present, but uninterrupted moorland or scrub are of little use to the birds. Such habitat is characteristic of coastal headlands and valleys of the south and west, where sheep, rabbits and the wind keep the grass short and where conditions are unsuit-able for arable farming. Inland, this habitat is found on heaths, commons and vacant areas such as railway cuttings.

At the turn of the century stonechats were common in every county of Britain, but many counties have now been deserted by them. This long-term reduction in the population is mainly due to the destruction of their habitat. Curiously, neglect of land is sometimes as serious for the stonechat as modern agricul-ture since, unless traditional farming methods are maintained – including sheep grazing and periodic controlled burning of gorse – heath-land quickly changes to scrub and then wood-land. Because of the spread of myxomatosis in recent decades, rabbits have become much less numerous and many areas have become overgrown as a result.

Whinchat habitat Whinchats seem to make use of a wider variety of habitats than stone-chats, but their numbers have also decreased this century. Rough, tussocky grassland with some bushes is probably most suitable, but they seem more tolerant of long grass and moorland and frequent, for example, lowland marshes, scrub, arable land and upland pastures more often than stonechats. Their tolerance of, or even preference for, uplands is clearly reflected in their British distribution: the most dense populations are in Wales,

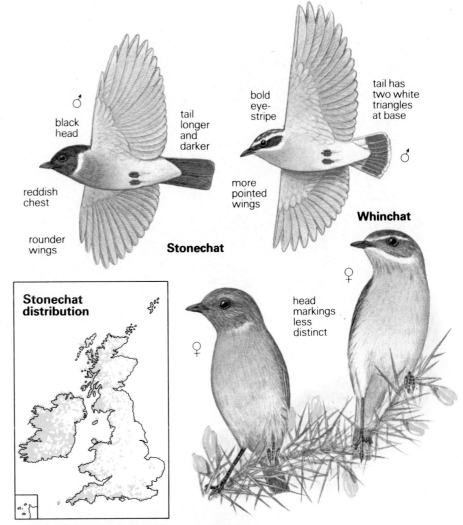

Stonechat
black head
tail longer and darker
reddish chest
rounder wings

Whinchat
bold eye-stripe
tail has two white triangles at base
more pointed wings
head markings less distinct

Stonechat distribution

Whinchat distribution

Left: A male whinchat with its insect prey. Since the habitat and food requirements of whinchats and stonechats overlap, competition is fierce.

Stonechat (*Saxicola torquata*). Resident in heathland and open lowland landscapes. 13cm (5in).

Whinchat (*Saxicola rubetra*). Summer visitor, breeding in heathland, on higher ground and in young conifer plantations. Length 13cm (5in).

northern England and Scotland.

Stonechat breeding Stonechats hold territories all the year round and the boundaries –marked by such features as streams, fences or boulders–often remain the same over several generations. In spring and summer the males defend the territories from other stonechats by singing–a tuneful dunnock-like jingle–from a prominent perch or in a high, hovering song flight.

While some stonechats may keep the same mate for life, there seems to be a tendency for considerable reorganisation each spring. This is well illustrated by a study in Jersey in 1955, in which eight pairs of stonechats were under close observation. All the birds had apparently been quite content with their mates throughout the winter months. Then, within four days at the very end of March, two males and one female found new mates from outside the study area, two adjacent pairs exchanged mates, one male found a second mate, one

Above: The nest of a whinchat. This is normally extremely well hidden– here the sheltering layer of grass and foliage has been removed temporarily for photographing. While the female incubates, the male stands by looking out for danger, ready to call the alarm if necessary. When leaving the nest–either because of an intruder or in order to feed–the female does so with great caution. On the 13th or 14th day the chicks hatch, their greyish-white down drying to provide insulation within a few hours. Both parents feed the young. The usual technique is to find a perch and watch the ground for insects.

pair changed its territory and only one pair remained unchanged!

The nest is made inside a clump of grass or in the shelter of a bush, and up to six eggs are laid, one a day. After they have hatched, the chicks are fed on such insects as moths, butterflies and small flies, as well as on larvae.

Whinchat breeding The breeding season of the whinchat is quite different. Most whinchats lay their first clutch in May–a full two months later than most stonechats. Indeed, whinchats usually arrive in this country in late April or early May, just as the stonechat broods are leaving their nests. Most stonechats raise two or three broods, the last clutch of eggs being laid in July or early August, whereas whinchats can raise only one or two broods, the second clutch being laid by mid-July.

When they first arrive at their breeding sites, male whinchats stake out territories as soon as possible, so that when the females arrive a few days later, breeding can start immediately. Their song is very variable and often includes mimicry of neighbouring bird species. Like the stonechat's, it is delivered from an exposed perch and initially there is considerable rivalry between males.

Whinchats lay, on average, one more egg than stonechats, but this does not make up for the smaller number of broods. In addition, studies have shown that whinchats' nests are more vulnerable to predation and other losses than those of stonechats, and it has been calculated that stonechats may fledge almost three times as many young in a season as whinchats. As a result of this you might expect stonechats to be much the commoner of the two. However, the winter survival of whinchats is comparatively high and this restores the balance between these attractive and closely related species.

Right: A female stonechat with four chicks. The nest is well concealed amid the grass: often it is placed inside a clump of grass, with a tunnel or shaft up to 25cm (10in) long for access. Sometimes the nest is built inside a bush. Fledging takes about two weeks: it can be delayed by adverse weather or precipitated by the appearance of a predator near the nest. After this period the chicks can fly, though their wings are not yet fully grown. Both parents remain in attendance for about 5 days; the male then continues to feed the brood while the female starts building a second nest. In normal conditions the second clutch is complete only 46 days after the first.

Common and black redstarts

The redstart is an elegant summer visitor that breeds in mature, open woodland over much of England, Wales and Scotland. It has a town-dwelling cousin, the black redstart, which can sometimes be seen in industrial or derelict sites – places that are not often visited by birdwatchers.

Above: Redstarts are forever active birds, restlessly flitting about among the twigs or down on to the ground to seize some insect or caterpillar. In autumn they augment their diet with ripening berries.

Below: Redstarts are more common in the north and west, but almost absent from Ireland. Black redstarts, on the other hand, favour the south and east.

The distinctive feature of redstarts of either sex and any age is the orange-chestnut tail, with its slightly darker and browner central stripe. Redstarts' tails are constantly on the move, with a perpetual up-and-down quivering, unlike the tails of robins or stonechats which have a precise, flicking motion. Their very name is derived from this distinctive tail: the 'red' is obvious, but the 'start' is derived from the Anglo-Saxon word *staert* which means a tail.

In the male, this conspicuous tail is enhanced by a chestnut belly (fading to buff around the vent), a chestnut rump, and by a back, mantle (the back of the neck) and crown of an elegant dove grey. His forehead is white, his face and throat jet black. Altogether, this must be one of the most beautiful of British birds, strikingly so during his display flights, when he flits rapidly between the trees. The females and young birds are altogether drabber, having grey-brown and orange-buff plumage.

Life in the woods Although its original habitat in Britain may well have been sandy heathland with large pine trees (now found only in the south), the redstart is today more typical of northern and western Britain, and, rather strangely, it is almost absent from Ireland. It seems to have adapted well to the loss of much of its ancestral habitat, and has become a bird of old deciduous woodland

☐ redstart

● black redstart

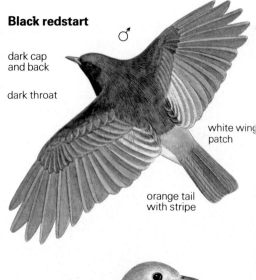

Black redstart

♂

dark cap and back

dark throat

white wing patch

orange tail with stripe

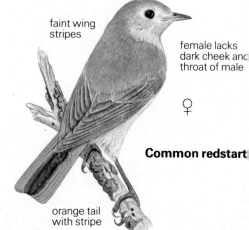

faint wing stripes

female lacks dark cheek and throat of male

♀

Common redstart

orange tail with stripe

(particularly sessile oak); parkland with well spaced, stately but ageing trees; and meadows with pollarded willows along their margins. In northern Scotland, open pinewoods and large birches remain its favoured habitat.

Nests in southern England are usually in holes in branches or tree stumps, but in dry areas they may occasionally be at the end of short burrows. In the north, nests in crevices in rock faces and stone walls are more common. Redstarts readily take advantage of nest boxes, provided the entrance hole is large enough—larger than that needed by tits at 3.6-4.8cm (1½-2in) in diameter.

During nesting or afterwards, as they move about in the bushes and trees, redstarts very much resemble slim robins in carriage and behaviour. They have a plaintive 'whoo-eet' call, easily mistaken for that of the willow warblers that are usually plentiful nearby. They also have a soft 'twick' of alarm, and a brief but nonetheless melodious little jingle of a song, again with much of the quality of the robin about it.

African migrants Ringing recoveries indicate that our redstarts winter in West Africa, and a series of declines in the British redstart population has been linked to periods of drought in their winter quarters, in much the same way as the drought in the Sahel region adversely affected the whitethroat.

An unusual relative Although at first sight it may seem far drabber than its woodland cousin, the male black redstart—especially when fully mature at three or four years old—has, on close inspection, particularly fine plumage. The tail is typical of the redstarts, being a rich chestnut-red, but there is no trace of orange or buff on the underparts. The head, mantle and back and the throat, breast and belly are all dark grey, becoming black with successive moults as the bird gets

Above: A female black redstart with her nest in a deserted shed. The clutch usually contains four to six shining white eggs, occasionally with a faint peppering of fine brown spots. They are incubated by the female for just under a fortnight, and fledge about 16 days after hatching.

Right: Common redstarts make a neater nest, in which they usually lay five or six eggs; these are usually blue, occasionally with a greenish tinge or freckled with brown. Incubation again is just under a fortnight, and the young fledge after about 14 days. Both species usually have two broods each summer.

Below: A male redstart stands guard over the brood.

older. The wings, too, are black, with a striking white patch in mature birds. Females and young birds are far more difficult to tell from redstarts unless a good view is obtained, but black redstart underparts are always grey, and never buff or orange as in the common redstart.

Across much of Europe and Asia, the natural habitat of black redstarts is rocky mountainsides, where they feed on a wide variety of insects caught on the ground or on the wing, and nest in crevices between boulders. Black redstarts also form an attractive component of the bird life of many European towns and cities, usually associated with large old buildings where crumbling masonry has provided suitable nest-sites. In their association with man they are probably most typical of the whitewashed walls, geraniums in hanging baskets and colourful tiled roofs of Mediterranean cities, towns and villages. Particularly numerous in southern France and Germany, they range as far north as Denmark and Latvia to breed. They are short-haul migrants; the more northerly birds winter in the Mediterranean basin, while some populations rarely migrate at all.

In consequence, it comes as something of a surprise to find that a bird so numerous, homely and widespread on the Continent should be so scarce in Britain. Perhaps one hundred pairs breed in England in an average year, mostly in the south and east. It is also

Above: Redstarts are hole-nesters, and it is often argued that keen competition for the nest holes (from tits, pied flycatchers, nuthatches and others) is the only restriction on the growth of the redstart population.

Above: A young black redstart perches on scrap metal. Besides derelict factories and yards, the birds also favour some active sites—docks, warehouses, gasworks and power stations.

Redstart (*Phoenicurus phoenicurus*); summer visitor to mature, open woodland; 14cm (5½in).

Black redstart (*Phoenicurus ochruros*); small breeding population in towns; 14cm (5½in).

surprising to discover that only in the middle years of the present century did they become firmly established here as breeding birds.

Wartime arrival The story of their colonization is an intriguing one. Apart from a few isolated records, the first substantial breeding reports were published in the earliest days of World War II. In May 1939 a male was found singing in Bloomsbury—in most illustrious circumstances—from the towers of the University of London and the nearby British Museum. Bombing had begun in real earnest when breeding was proved in the summer of 1940, in Inner London and again illustriously, this time in the shadow of Westminster Abbey. Although breeding was reported in

other southern counties, London remained the stronghold of the British breeding population as it increased over the wartime years. Many of the breeding pairs were in the City of London, and took advantage of the devastated buildings and piles of rubble (doubtless reminiscent of mountain screes) in the blitzed areas to feed and to conceal their nests.

The many reports and articles on black redstarts that were published during the war rarely gave any detail of the habitat, probably for reasons of security so that the enemy did not gain too clear a picture of the extent of the damage. By the end of the war, the black redstart population, though still with its stronghold in London, was spread over at least 11 counties and had reached about 50 pairs.

At that stage, startling fresh information was released. In 1944, the journal *British Birds* published retrospective information on breeding, described as 'one of the most remarkable discoveries of recent years in British ornithology'. A caretaker at the Wembley Palace of Engineering (which housed the great Empire Exhibition of 1925) told the authors of the article that during the years 1926-41—since the closing of the exhibition—three pairs of black redstarts (and once four) had nested there every year.

After the war, the breeding black redstart population fluctuated, sometimes reaching 60 recorded pairs, sometimes falling as low as 20. In the early 1970s there was a continuing rise in the number of nests reported, and the present-day level of around 100 pairs was established. About one third of the breeding population is in the London area, the remainder largely in the south-east and East Anglia, with a scattering of records in the Midlands and the most northerly in Yorkshire and Cheshire. In a 1977 survey, 98% of sites described were man-made.

Robin

The robin (below and opposite) is a particular favourite among bird lovers; everyone enjoys the attentions of this familiar redbreast in the garden during winter. But despite all the efforts made to feed this bird in the harsh weather, thousands perish each year.

The robin enjoys a popularity with man un-rivalled by any other species. A familiar visitor at the bird-table in winter and constant gardening companion, even nesting in the toolshed, it is a year-round bird. This close association with man is a special feature of the robin's relationship with the British. Robins of exactly the same species nest over most of Europe, but a tendency on the con-tinent to shoot and eat small birds has made robins there generally shy and retiring wood-land birds.

The bird's popularity in Britain has built up over the years and legends about the bad luck incurred by anyone harming a robin go back to the 16th century. A Christian link has been

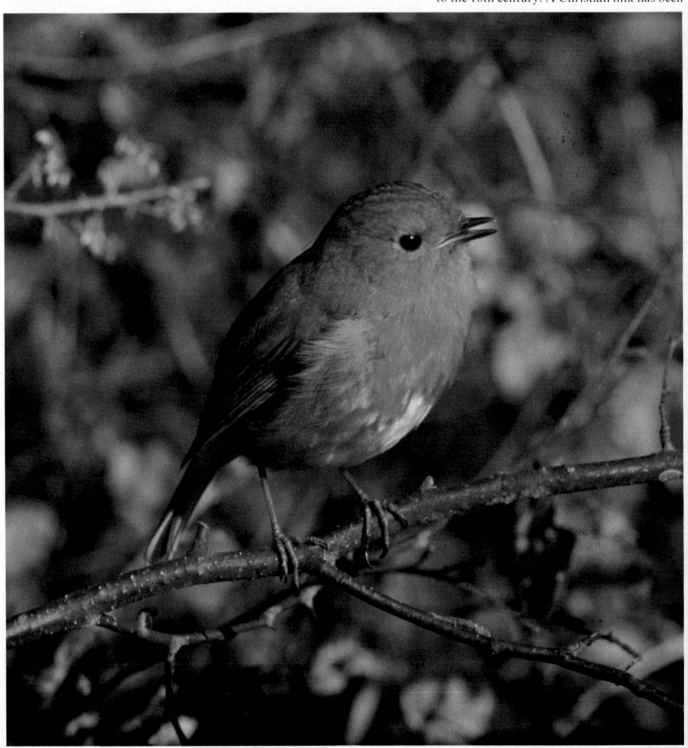

attached to the legend because the robin's red breast was supposedly stained by blood after the bird had been pricked by Christ's crown of thorns. This is why the robin features prominently on the earliest Christmas cards.

Pairing and nesting The adults get together as pairs in early January. As they look exactly alike, the sexes can only recognise each other by display and posture. An unmated male singing loudly in his territory will, at first, behave aggressively to any intruding robin. If the intruder is a male it either retreats or tries to oust the occupier. If the new bird is a female seeking a mate, she persists in approaching the resident male, apparently unimpressed by his threats. Over a period of some hours, sometimes as much as two days, the bond between the two is built up so that they accept each other.

In many species this pair-bonding is directly followed by nest-building and egg-laying. With the robin, pairing is accomplished weeks or even months before any nesting attempt is made. During this time the birds occupy the same territory and recognise each other as mates but do not pay much attention to each other. As the weather improves the hen bird starts to build her nest, using moss and dead leaves and lining it with hair. In the natural state she may choose a rocky crevice or hollow of a tree, most often, a bank or an ivy-covered tree—usually well concealed and difficult to find.

However some robins select the most unlikely sites. One nest was found in a chest of drawers in a toolshed. The drawer was half-closed and the nest at the back was only discovered when the drawer was opened.

When she begins to build the nest the female also starts to receive food from the male. This so-called 'courtship-feeding' was initially thought to be a ritual designed to reinforce the pair-bond between male and female. In fact it is an important source of food for the female—one that she almost completely relies upon during incubation.

The clutch of white eggs with pale reddish freckling is laid, one egg each day, and the complete clutch is generally five or six eggs, although up to nine have been recorded. The

Robin (*Erithacus rubecula*). Also called redbreast; 14cm (5in) from beak to tip of tail; 5-9cm (2-4in) high. Distribution nationwide.

Below: Hungry fledglings wait to be fed in their nest, which is usually made up of twigs, grass and moss. Robins are well known for making their nests in such unlikely places as kettles, old buckets—even the pockets of jackets left in garden sheds.

incubating female loses the feathers from her breast and belly and the blood vessels just under the skin enlarge greatly. The bare skin and increased blood supply allow her to transfer heat more efficiently to the eggs.

Greedy chicks After two weeks the eggs hatch out and the blind chicks, covered in thin dark down, increasingly dominate the parents' lives with their enormous appetites. Both adult and young robins feed on insects, spiders and worms. They do not generally eat seeds or berries. About 15 days after hatching these young robins, now weighing more than their parents, leave the nest.

Two particularly attentive parents were reported by naturalist David Lack. They

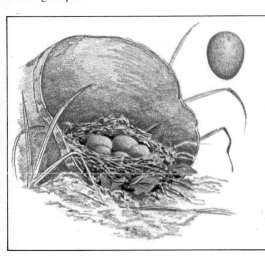

Five or six eggs—12mm (½in) long—are laid and incubated for two weeks. Eggs generally have a whitish background and orange/brown freckles.

Nests vary in size. They are made of dead leaves, grass, moss and hairs; very few feathers are used as lining.

built their nest in a cart which had to go on a 200-mile round trip just after the young hatched. Undaunted, the adult birds accompanied their offspring, feeding them on the way.

When the young birds leave the nest they face two or three days of great danger since they cannot yet fly well. At this stage they have a soft speckled brown plumage with no trace of their parents' red breast. By the beginning of June they start to lose their body feathers and to develop their red breasts —growing from the bottom upwards. The wings do not moult but continue to develop until July of the next year when they reach their full size.

Second brood Once the young are fledged the adults build a new nest within the same territory and, unless they are prevented for any reason (disturbance by a cat, flooding of the nest in bad weather or thoughtless hedge-cutting), will raise another brood in May. During the summer for a period of five weeks, the adult robins replace their old feathers with new ones. They stay in the same area, but make themselves less obvious and less active, concealed in shrubberies and thickets. During this moult the adult robins also fall silent—the only time of the year when the robin song is not a feature of the British countryside.

As the second brood of young birds acquires its red plumage and the adult birds their replacement plumage, the autumn song starts up. The rich and fruity spring song of the males gives way to the thinner, more piping song of young and old, cock and hen, as each claims its own territory; this is kept, with a few local alterations, through the winter until pairing takes place. In times of real food shortage, territoriality breaks down as all the birds concentrate on feeding.

Population control Although some British robins migrate each autumn, most stay within a mile or two of their birthplace. So what happens to all these robins? If each pair of adults raises two broods with five or six young in each, there are six times as many robins at the end of the breeding season as at the start. A single pair would become almost ten million pairs at the end of ten years—about twice the total British population of robins. In fact the majority of them die. As many as a million robins may be killed by cats; while owls, cars, plate glass windows and harsh winters also take their toll. Sadly, but naturally, of the original pair and their offspring, on average only one adult and one youngster survive to breed the following year. Harsh winter weather often provides the greatest danger; so millions of people who feed birds leave out all sorts of titbits—even mince meat and grated cheese—to ensure that 'their' robins are the ones to survive. This feeding also encourages the robins to stay in backyards and gardens.

Left: A spotty juvenile robin, speckled brown and with no hint of a red breast which develops later in the summer. In its first year, the robin has a one-in-six chance of survival.

Below: Proudly displaying its red breast and singing its rich spring song, this robin lays claim to its territory and warns off other birds.

Competing for space

Almost all birds are territorial. It is generally during the breeding season that each bird defends a home area, and will not tolerate any bird of the same species apart from its mate within its territory. Robins are no exception, and like other song birds (such as blackbirds and song thrushes) they stake out quite large claims by their presence at strategic songposts. Other birds restrict themselves to much smaller areas—gannets, for instance, only defend the immediate nest area.

The blackbird singing on your television aerial may seem full of the joys of spring but, much more important to itself and other blackbirds, it is saying: 'This is part of my territory—keep off'. If the message is not understood it may still have to chase off the encroaching birds—a sight often seen when disputing birds dart at each other along a lawn or hedgerow without actually making contact. It is both these aggressive flutterings and song patterns that prevent actual fighting—unless large numbers of birds are competing for a very small territory.

Nightingale

The nightingale is justly praised for its tuneful singing, but it cannot excel in all things: despite its wonderfully varied musical performance, it is an unobtrusive, dull brown bird, here for a short breeding season spent hiding in the thickets.

The nightingale combines the extremes of delightfully melodious singing and a generally uniform, unremarkable plumage. It is about half way in size between the robin and the song thrush, two fellow members of the thrush family. In its general posture the nightingale is comparable to these two birds. Its plumage, however, is considerably less colourful than that of other members of the thrush family, being chestnut-brown all over the upperparts and paling to a rufous fawn beneath. The most interesting feature is the tail, which is frequently flicked while the bird is perching, sometimes catching the light and revealing a rich rufous quality.

Like the robin's, the nightingale's eye is large and dark; but the legs are stouter than those of the robin. Young birds, before the autumn moult of their first year, have scaly, pale fawn fringes to many of their feathers, and unless you catch a glimpse of the tail you might easily mistake them for young robins.

Thicket dweller According to one country saying, the distribution of the nightingale, the cowslip and the hop have much in common in England; and this is indeed broadly true. Most nightingales breed to the south of a line between the Severn and the Humber, preferring habitats with a well-developed and dense undergrowth. Thus most are found in woodland areas, usually of deciduous trees and very often of oak, with the mature trees widely spaced. Towards the north-western fringe of this breeding range, the wooded slopes of river valleys are particularly favoured.

Over the last few centuries, the distribution of the nightingale right across Europe has contracted considerably. Possibly this is partly due to wholesale trapping (particularly on the Continent) of nightingales for caging as song birds or, even more unpleasantly, for

Above: The nightingale has three main adaptations to its life in the thickets. The beak is suited for taking large and small invertebrates as well as berries. The legs are strong enough for ground foraging, and the large eye enables it to see well in the dense undergrowth.

Previous page: The rich tone of the plumage is seen on the rump and tail.

Below: The nightingale is restricted to the south and south-east of England.

Nightingale distribution

Right: The nest is either low down in the vegetation— frequently bramble or nettles —or actually on the ground. It is always in an overgrown and inaccessible spot. In many cases nightingale pairs return to exactly the same spot each year.

sale in delicatessens. Though this does still occur, it seems more likely that the major factor in the decline is the loss of the appropriate type of deciduous woodland. This is due both to modern farming, with its demands for full land usage and increased field sizes, and to modern forestry practice, in which broad-leaved woodland is replaced by dense plantations of conifers.

Watching for nightingales Generally, nightingales are shy, rarely venturing into the open, so for many of us this is a bird far more often heard than seen. Considerable patience, and quiet watching from semi-concealment in an area with several nightingale pairs—and preferably with some paths to provide open ground—is required to obtain even fleeting glimpses. If you are lucky, a male nightingale may choose to sing from a perch in your line of sight, head thrown slightly back, throat bulging, giving you a chance to see the performance as well as hear it.

More often, apart from the song, much of what you hear in the undergrowth is the surprisingly varied repertoire of 'chack' and 'churr' noises with which the nightingale deters intruders from approaching its place of concealment. You may also hear the soft 'weet' call that the pair use to keep in contact.

Our best night singer The voice of the nightingale, heard solo at dead of night, comes through the clear, warm early summer air as one of the most delightful bird songs in the world. The song period is, however, short, generally spanning the second half of May and the month of June, but rarely continuing as late as July.

For quality, range and versatility the nightingale's voice cannot be matched, even among British birds with their exceptionally rich songs. Part of the enjoyment stems from the sheer variety—from throaty chuckles to far-carrying whistles—and part from the quality of the tonal range, from rich, deep phrases to the purest of treble-like trills and flourishes.

Special adaptations In the shelter of its habitat of thick undergrowth, the nightingale spends much of its time concealed from view. It is one of the more terrestrial birds in the thrush family. Strong legs and large eyes are adaptations to this mode of life, as also is the beak. Though not so stout as the conical beaks of the finches, nor so fine as that of insect-eaters such as the pied wagtail, the well pointed but strong beak of the nightingale allows it to tackle most soil and litter-dwelling invertebrates. These range from tiny insects and spiders to caterpillars and worms. The beak is also suited to feeding on berries as they become available later in the month. At this time they are invaluable as a sugar-rich resource to help the nightingale put on fat as a fuel reserve for the long migration south.

The breeding season Nightingales perform a pairing display which is rarely seen because of the dense cover in which it takes place. It involves much ritualised posturing, with wings drooping and fluttering, and with tail fanned. After the display, the nest is built low in the vegetation or, quite commonly, on the ground. It is always well concealed from disturbance by humans and large predatory mammals or birds, although it is not safe from such predators as weasels or mice. The nest is basically constructed of dead leaves, usually those found lying nearby. Those found in England are most often held together by fine twigs or stout grasses. The lining of the cup is of fine grasses and hair, and the normal clutch is four or five (occasionally six). The eggs are brown, so densely speckled as to

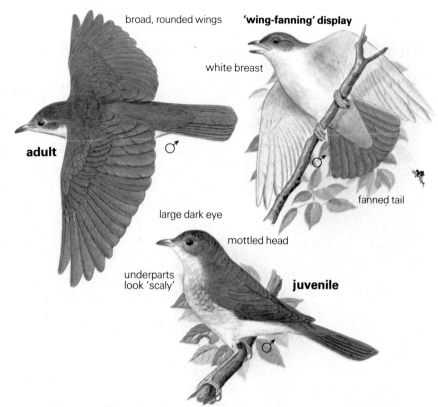

broad, rounded wings

'wing-fanning' display

white breast

adult

♂

large dark eye

underparts look 'scaly'

mottled head

fanned tail

juvenile

♂

appear almost uniformly coloured. Because of their early departure on migration, there is normally time for just a single brood each season.

Long-distance migrants Nightingales desert their breeding woods from late July onwards. Ringing results indicate that most nightingales cross the Mediterranean in autumn and fly over the western margins of the Sahara Desert. Their wintering areas are in tropical West Africa. As with many other migrants, individual breeding birds often return to precisely the same patch of dense cover in successive years, for unless the site has been cleared by man, nightingales keep to their traditional nesting grounds.

Nightingale (*Luscinia megarhynchos*). Summer visitor breeding in thickets. Splendid song audible at night. 16.5cm (6½in).

Below: After an incubation period of about a fortnight, the brood hatches. In their earliest days, nightingale chicks have the same speckled appearance as young robins—a resemblance which continues into the juvenile stage. The season is too short for more than one brood.

Night singing birds

It is interesting to note that nightingales sing a great deal during the day as well as the night, but in the daytime their song tends to be drowned by the richness of other birdsong heard at this time. However, *why* they sing so much at night is intriguing, and by no means well understood. Few other songbirds sing at night, but two that do, the grasshopper and the reed warblers, are both birds of dense cover, like the nightingale. Also like the nightingale, they are summer visitors to this country, migrating by night to and from wintering areas in Africa.
One theory is based on the observation that males usually migrate some days in advance of the females. On arrival, they set up territories and defend them by song, and then it is thought that they sing to the night skies to attract the females as they pass over. Although plausible in this context, the theory leaves unexplained the fact that all these species continue their nocturnal singing until well into the breeding season.

Song and mistle thrushes

The clear, musical, flute-like notes of the thrush
family are justly famous. On most days of the year
from the first light of dawn to late dusk you can hear
the vigorous, repetitive phrases of the song thrush,
and the more leisurely song of the mistle thrush
which continues even in the rain.

Apart from the Shetland Islands, there are few places in the British Isles where you will not find a song thrush; they are a familiar part of our daily lives, and one of the first birds children learn to recognise. The mistle thrush, however, is slightly less widespread and is absent from Shetland and Orkney, and decidedly scarce in the outer Scottish islands.

People sometimes think the two species are difficult to separate. Both are immediately recognisable as thrushes, with medium length, fairly stout bills, speckled underparts, brownish upperparts, long legs and rather large eyes. The mistle thrush is slightly longer than the song thrush but there are other differences as well. The upperparts of the song thrush are a warm brown, and those of the mistle thrush a distinctly greyer brown. You can see these features quite clearly when the birds are in flight. As the birds pass overhead, look at the axillaries (the feathers covering the 'armpits'): they are a flaming orange-yellow in the song thrush and white in the mistle thrush. The tail of the song thrush is a uniform brown but the mistle thrush has whitish tips to the outer tail feathers. The underparts differ as well: both birds have dark brown breast spots on a pale background, but the spots of the mistle thrush are bigger, more rounded, and altogether bolder, on a paler background.

Rich song All members of the thrush family sing loud, clear, musical flute-like notes. The special qualities of the song thrush are its vigour and repetition. The bird sings the same notes two, three, even five or six times – sometimes you could swear that it is practising a choice phrase. The song thrush uses favourite note sequences time and time again, interspersed with numerous other notes and phrases, many of them mimicking other birds. Some species, such as the chaffinch, sing rather poorly at the start of the season and their performance steadily becomes more polished, but the song thrush sings well right from the start, and some people think its performance is enriched with age.

The mistle thrush has a more limited song – a sequence of a few notes in permutation. It is loud, clear, full, rich and leisurely, and could be monotonous if it were not for its fine quality.

Aerial song posts Members of the thrush family like to sing from high song posts, and song thrushes and blackbirds have been quick to commandeer television aerials. The mistle thrush prefers to sing from the topmost branch of a tall tree, and its readiness to do so even in heavy rain has led to its widely used folk name, stormcock. In most

Right: Song thrushes excel in cracking snail shells and extracting the flesh, thus providing themselves with a valuable source of food when drought drives the worms deeper. They beat the victim against a stone or hard surface ('anvil') to break it.

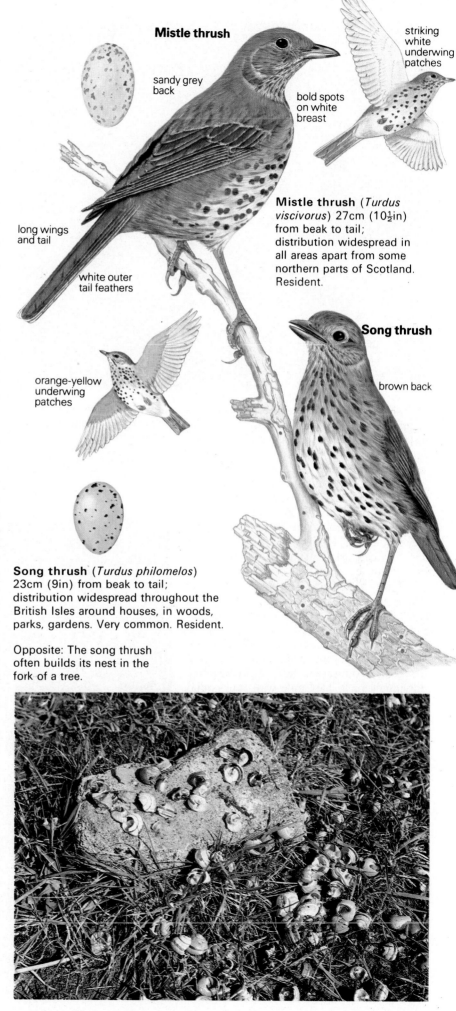

Mistle thrush

sandy grey back

striking white underwing patches

bold spots on white breast

long wings and tail

white outer tail feathers

Mistle thrush (*Turdus viscivorus*) 27cm (10½in) from beak to tail; distribution widespread in all areas apart from some northern parts of Scotland. Resident.

orange-yellow underwing patches

Song thrush

brown back

Song thrush (*Turdus philomelos*) 23cm (9in) from beak to tail; distribution widespread throughout the British Isles around houses, in woods, parks, gardens. Very common. Resident.

Opposite: The song thrush often builds its nest in the fork of a tree.

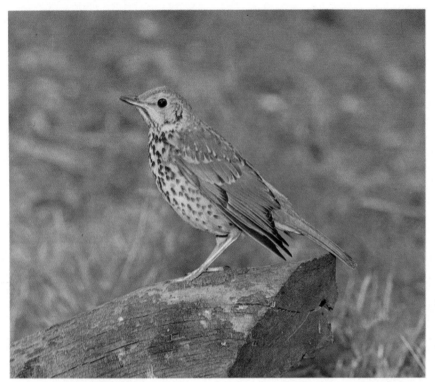

years song thrushes start to sing in November –even October– and do not stop until July or later. The mistle thrush does not start singing until the turn of the year and usually ends at the beginning of June.

The call notes of the two species are quite different. An alarmed song thrush says 'tchouk tchouk . . .', the notes coming faster and closer together when the bird is particularly anxious. The mistle thrush has a loud, vigorous call which sounds rather like a football rattle.

Habitat preferences Although the two species are frequently found in the same acre of ground, they have different habitat preferences. Song thrushes are at home in gardens and shrubberies, and you will probably see more nesting around houses than in farmland. You might hear eight or nine individuals on a half mile walk on a mild November morning, which suggests a density of one bird every hundred yards or so.

Mistle thrushes are always more thinly distributed and seem to require much larger territories. They too penetrate urban areas, but they tend to favour parks, cemeteries, and playing fields rather than gardens. Large mature gardens and parklands, on the other hand, are typical habitats for them. In the breeding season you may find them in woodlands and even conifer plantations, so long as there are grassy rides or adjacent grasslands for spring feeding.

Song thrushes tend to favour the same type of habitat in winter and summer, although the higher ground is vacated before the cold winter weather sets in, and a proportion of the population migrates. In northern Britain the migration is chiefly to Ireland, but those individuals that migrate from the south make chiefly for Iberia. In harsh

Above: A juvenile song thrush can be distinguished from an adult by its speckled back plumage. Song thrushes nearly always sing from an elevated song perch.

winters, non-migrating song thrushes may suffer so severely that they are obliged to carry out a cold-weather movement–an emergency migration. The small proportion of song thrushes that migrate usually go to France.

Song thrushes are solitary and flock together only on migration. Mistle thrushes, on the other hand, tend to move about in family parties at the end of the breeding season; the parties later amalgamate to form loose flocks of up to 100 birds which roam the countryside together, penetrating even wild upland country in their search for food. During midwinter the flocks split up and the birds occupy their territories for the start of a new breeding season.

Superbly structured nests Mistle thrushes tend to start breeding two or three weeks earlier than song thrushes, work on the nest often starting before February is out. In both species the hen alone builds the nest, which is well-engineered and incorporates grasses and mud for bonding. The nest of the song thrush is especially beautiful– smooth, symmetrical, and rather like the inside of a coconut shell.

The song thrush is versatile and adaptable in its choice of nest sites, hiding–or sometimes failing to hide–its nest in bushes and shrubs. Its willingness to live so close to man enables it to exploit such unlikely sites as the top of the cistern in an outside lavatory, although

Left: An egg and some chicks of a song thrush. This species is unique among European birds for its habit of plastering the inside of its nest. The plaster is made from dung or rotten wood mixed with saliva.

Below: A song thrush removing a faecal sac from its young. The parent does this to keep the nest clean, depositing the sac some distance from the nest.

natural sites greatly predominate.

The mistle thrush normally builds its nest in the fork of a tree, perhaps 7-9m (20-30ft) up, and remarkably well hidden. From this vantage point the incubating female keeps a watchful eye, crouching low if she suspects she is being observed. Mistle thrushes are fearless in the defence of their nests and young, and do not hestitate to tackle birds much larger than themselves. Apart from egg-stealing members of the crow family, their chief avian predator, and the song thrush's as well, is the sparrow-hawk. Peregrines occasionally eat them.

There are four or five song thrush eggs in a clutch, each a beautiful blue thinly speckled with black. They are incubated by the hen alone, and take 13-14 days to hatch and a similar period to fledge. A second brood is often followed by a third. The mistle thrush may lay three to six eggs, though four is normal. Their background colour varies from cream to pale greeny-blue, and they are dramatically blotched and speckled with sepia. The incubation period is the same as for the song thrush, but the young may take a day or two longer to fledge. The juveniles develop speckled back plumage which they lose when they become fully mature by the following spring.

Feeding habits Thrushes feed on fruit for much of the year; the rest of the time they rely on worms, insects and other invertebrates.

You often see them feeding on lawns: a quick hop forward to focus more accurately, using monocular vision, (not to listen); a few vigorous pecks, and the worm is dragged out. Song thrushes crack snails on their 'anvils' (stones), and during snow cover they ferret about for food in hedge bottoms and even among the marram grass along the coast. Mistle thrushes are more reliant on worms and insects, often feeding in the centre of fields. In a sense the feeding habits sum up the temperaments of the two species: the mistle thrush bold but wary, even self assert-ive; the song thrush more retiring, and often unobtrusive.

Above: A mistle thrush feeding its young. Fruit is an important part of the diet of both species, but particularly of the mistle thrush which favours mistletoe berries—hence its name. In northern Britain rowan provides tasty berries and even isolated trees far up on the fellsides may be visited and stripped bare. Holly, yew, hawthorn and, later in the winter, rose hips and ivy berries are also eaten by both species.

Identifying songbirds

Redwing

Song thrush

Blackbird ♀

Fieldfare

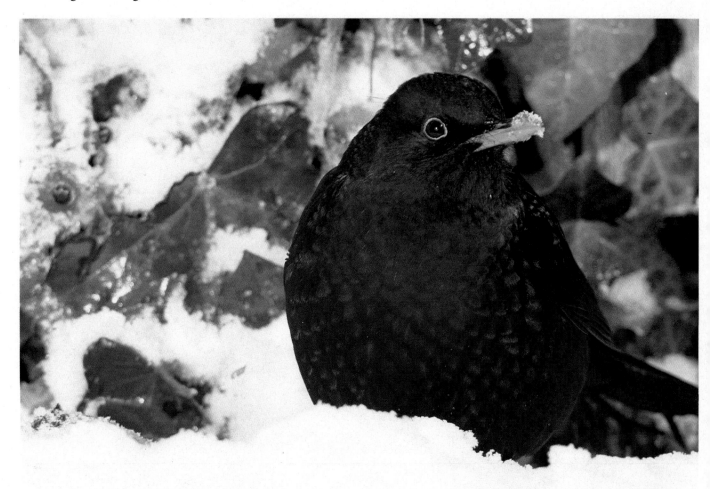

Blackbird

The blackbird – one of the most familiar and best loved of our garden birds – is often regarded as uninteresting because of its very familiarity. In fact, because it is so easy to study, more is known of its life-style than of almost any other bird.

Above: A male blackbird with jet black plumage and bright orange bill. This bird is easily recognisable by its jaunty, hopping gait and also by its habit of standing with head cocked to one side, listening for worms.

Opposite: Although blackbirds are so often seen in our gardens and parks, they are predominantly woodland birds. Beech woods such as these provide food for blackbirds among the leaf litter.

The blackbird, a bird familiar to everyone, is a successful and adaptable species whose natural habitats, before man started to make his mark on the British countryside several thousand years ago, were woodland edges and natural clearings. Now it not only frequents gardens in town and countryside but also most of the hedges over the millions of acres of British farmland.

The blackbird's very numbers allow it to be studied in much greater detail than most species; thousands are ringed each year and nest-recorders are able to find and record nests in great quantities.

Male, female and juvenile The adult male is quite literally a 'black bird', with a wholly black plumage relieved only by a bright orange bill and an orange eye-ring. The younger males, hatched the previous summer, retain their old flight feathers and some wing coverts, giving their wings a peculiar 'patch-work' effect where the old brown juvenile feathers contrast with the newer ones grown during the post-juvenile moult in their first autumn. The females are much browner, with a pale throat and speckling on the breast. Juvenile birds of both sexes have rich brown centres to many of their body feathers, but these are retained only for a month or two.

Territorial song and combat The blackbird's year, in Britain, may be said to start in February when the singing males begin to define their territories for the coming breeding season. This is not only accomplished through the exceptionally melodious medium of their song – used by the birds to announce their presence and continuing occupation of their territories – but also by physical displays.

These displays are particularly visible on a lawn, where two males may posture at each other for periods of ten or twenty minutes at a time. Often they never come to within a metre of each other but, just occasionally, physical warfare breaks out. Later in the season, when the adjacent males are both paired, such posturing (and even fights) may have extra protagonists – three or even four territories may meet on a lawn and the females may join in.

A long breeding season It often seems as if the blackbird breeding season extends from early April through to the end of May. This is indeed the time when they are at their most conspicuous, but many pairs already have a nest with eggs in the middle of March (or even earlier), and may continue with breeding attempts right through to July or even early August, provided the weather is suitable. Early broods are often quite successful for the predators, such as cats, jays, magpies and crows, which take such a toll on nests, are not yet active.

During April, when most species have started to nest, the blackbird's success is at its lowest (although clutch size is then at its highest); success is higher in May and June when there is plenty of cover for the birds to nest in.

The clutch of three to five (sometimes six) eggs is laid in a nest which, although it contains a layer of mud, is lined with grasses. The blackbird's eggs are a dull blue-green with reddish-brown speckling.

Incubation, carried out mainly by the female bird, lasts for about a fortnight from the laying of the penultimate egg, and the young are then fed–on worms and other animal food–at increasingly frequent intervals by both parents for two weeks before they fledge. This is their most vulnerable period for they are still unable to fly for up to 36 hours after fledging and are at the mercy of cats or any other predator able to withstand the brave and noisy attentions of the parent birds. The youngsters may be fed by their parents for a further three weeks–first by both and then later only by the male, as the female will already be sitting on her next clutch.

The annual moult At the end of the breeding season–which may be as early as mid-June in a dry year when the blackbirds are unable to find their food easily, or as late as mid-August in a wet summer–the adults undergo a complete moult to replace all their feathers. At the same time the partial moult of the juveniles takes place and, for a few weeks, the blackbirds, although still present, are not at all easy to see.

However, a little later they become much more conspicuous, particularly to anyone with an orchard and windfall apples or with ornamental shrubs bearing a good crop of berries. Although worms are readily taken at all times of the year, most of their food during the autumn and winter is fruit (where bird-table food is not being exploited).

Urban versus country populations Our own breeding blackbirds are mostly fairly sedentary, although ringing has shown some movement, particularly from northern and upland areas in winter. Indeed, it is certain that the majority of blackbirds hatched in Britain move no more than a kilometre or two from their natal territory throughout the whole of their lives. This has enabled detailed research to unravel the different pressures on different

Identifying the blackbird family

orange eye-ring

orange bill

♂

jet black plumage

brown bill

speckled breast

♀

brown plumage

juvenile

plumage similar to that of female but more spotted

Blackbird (*Turdus merula*). Resident in town and country gardens, hedgerows, woodland edges throughout the British Isles. 25cm (10in).

Right: An albino blackbird. This species seems to be prone to albinism, as many records show. The birds may be partially albino, with just a few white feathers here and there, or pure white, as here.

Below: A female blackbird sunbathing, with wings spread wide. Note the speckling on the breast. Blackbirds are one of the most common bird species of British gardens, on a par with the robin and the acrobatic blue tit.

Above: A juvenile blackbird
—the body feathers of the
young birds often have
rich brown centres.

Left: A blackbird's nest
(close to the ground) and
the eggs. Unlike the nest
of the song thrush (a close
relative of the blackbird),
which is just made of bare
mud, this nest is lined
with grasses. A clutch of
three to five eggs is usual.

Below: A young blackbird
in first-year plumage, with
brown primary feathers.

populations of blackbirds.

In urban habitats it appears that adult blackbirds survive very well indeed—the food provided for them on bird-tables keeps them fit and healthy through even the coldest weather, and the experience of their first few years of life teaches them, as it does most urban birds, to avoid cats and cars. Their nests and eggs are, however, much more likely to be preyed upon or fail for other reasons and the few young that they raise have a difficult time surviving all the hazards of city life.

In the country, on the other hand, more young are produced by each breeding pair and they are able to survive better—which is just as well, for the overall adult mortality is higher in the country than it is in urban areas. This seems to be due largely to shortages of food during the winter—urban birds, which have access to more food, put on a greater amount of fat in hard weather to keep them going.

Since they are easy to observe, blackbirds are among the best species to keep notes on. For instance, if the birds in your garden are territorial, or possess distinguishing features, it is possible to list the feeding preferences of particular individuals.

Communal roosts During the winter, in particular, blackbirds spend their nights together in communal roosts. These are often at traditional sites and it has been shown that they chose areas which offer them shelter and safety from predators. The shelter enables them to conserve heat most efficiently, and gathering together in one roost may even serve the birds as an information exchange, so that those with sub-standard feeding sites are able to follow out those who know of the best feeding areas.

These roosting birds are not just the home-grown British population, for vast numbers of blackbirds from Germany, Denmark, Norway, Sweden, Poland and Finland come to Britain for the winter and join our own birds. Many British birds stay in their own home territories but, although some remain territorial, many tolerate visits from the foreign migrants. In the spring, when our own birds are just starting to breed and have already acquired their bright orange beaks, many of the migrants still sport their dull brown winter beak colour.

Albino blackbirds One feature of the blackbird species is that it is prone to albinism. There have been many records of pure white male blackbirds which still show the orange (or yellow) beak and eye-ring (and, in the albino, legs). Often the birds just show a few white feathers flecking the plumage, but this is sometimes neatly symmetrical and progressive—becoming more and more apparent year after year. The whiteness does not seem to put the birds at such a disadvantage that they get caught by cats or other predators, however. In some areas the albinism is transmitted genetically within the population, and pockets of partially albino birds persist for several years.

A gallery of beaks and bills

The blackbird has a general-purpose beak but other birds have beaks which are specialised for eating different types of food. This chart illustrates the diversity of beak types possessed by various British species. They are arranged in random order because no really comprehensive categories exist.
Note: The terms beak and bill are interchangeable.

Hawfinch: A unique and powerfull bill for a bird that is a nut and seed-eating specialist.

Robin: A generalised insectivore, hunting on the ground, in trees and also in the air.

Great spotted woodpecker: A strong hammer-and-chisel bill for cutting into both hard and soft wood.

Merganser: A fish-eating duck which is equipped with a saw-toothed bill for holding prey.

Peregrine: Like all the raptors, its bill is specially shaped for tearing prey.

Blackbird: General-purpose beak for eating worms, fruit, seeds, bread, spiders, insects and larvae.

Black-headed gull: A bill like a pair of shears, useful for scavenging almost anywhere.

Heron: Strikes suddenly to stab through the body of a fish, frog, large insect or even a dabchick.

Swift: Its bill is used in the manner of a sweep-net to collect insects while flying.

Partridge: General-purpose bill for various foods from leaves and buds to insects and seeds, including grain.

Treecreeper: Like a pair of tweezers, its fine beak is used to pick up insects from fissures in bark.

Shoveler: An unusual shape of bill, containing a sieve for filtering plankton from the water.

Wigeon: With the tip of its bill it cuts blades of grass, its main form of food, throughout the year.

Snipe: It probes under the turf with its long bill, which is able to feel for worms.

Puffin: This bird is our best example of the use of a colourful bill for courtship display.

Blue and great tits

Blue and great tits (a great tit is shown below),
delightful to watch as they peck away at food in the
most awkward of positions, survive in spite of intense
competition for nest sites, devastating predator
attacks and near starvation in winter.

Blue and great tits, both colloquially known as tomtits, are popular garden birds which visit bird tables regularly in winter. Both are widespread throughout the British Isles and you'll see them in deciduous woodland, scrubland, hedgerows and farmland everywhere. The blue tit is an agile, aggressive, always excitedly active little bird which specialises in hanging at awkward angles to feed, while the great tit, larger than the blue and twice as heavy, often prefers to feed on the ground like a finch. Male and female blue tits are very similar in appearance. Among great tits a distinguishing feature between male and female is the black line which runs down the centre of their primrose-yellow breasts. This is faint in the female but very bold and wide in the male.

Seasonal foraging In summer blue tits feed mainly on insects, searching for them at the tips of twigs and shoots. In winter this diet is supplemented with occasional nuts and seeds. Since insects are neither active nor easily visible in winter, blue tits have to spend considerable time peering and probing round buds and under flakes of bark to find hibernating adults and larvae. If you observe the apparently aimless acrobatics of a blue tit through binoculars, you'll see that it is in fact purposefully searching every potentially rewarding nook and cranny.

In the garden the boldness and agility of blue tits as they attack peanuts hung in a plastic mesh sock is a delight to watch. They feed on almost everything put out on a bird table except bird seed, but above all they prefer nuts and fat.

Great tits eat much the same food as the blue, but take more vegetable food in winter –particularly seeds and nuts which have fallen to the ground. In fact, great tits are so fond of nuts that 'intelligence tests' have been devised where they demonstrate their inquisitiveness and learning ability by pulling up threads with a nut on the end, or prising open matchboxes to get at the nuts concealed inside.

Attacking milk bottles Sporadic outbreaks of tits pecking open the cardboard tops of milk bottles to drink the cream were first reported in the early 1930s. The habit rapidly spread to become nationwide–an excellent example of how quickly newly learnt skills can spread throughout a population. The post-war transition from cardboard to aluminium foil tops presented the tits with no problems, and in many rural areas milk bottles now have to be protected as a matter of routine.

Feeding for breeding The breeding season for great tits begins in late March and for blue tits in early April. To get into peak condition for egg laying as early as possible–earlier broods tend to be larger and healthier than later ones–the female must eat prodigiously. In the three weeks before laying begins, she puts on weight at an extraordinary rate, increasing her normal weight by at least a half and sometimes more. Then, over 10 or 12 days, she produces almost her own weight in eggs, laying one each day. This remarkable feat cannot be achieved by the female unaided; the male must feed her. You may well see a pair of tits side by side on a branch, the male offering his mate a beakful of caterpillars which she accepts with rapidly fluttering wings. This behaviour–called courtship feeding–may be essential if breeding is to be successful.

The female tit does all the nest-building, choosing a hole or crevice in a wall, tree or garden nestbox. The nest–a cup of moss, grass, wool, leaves, roots and spiders' webs–is lined with hair or feathers.

All eggs in one basket In summer, in deciduous woodland, both great and blue tits often rely heavily on just one species of insect as food for themselves and their young. In oak woods this is the winter moth which frequently produces huge numbers of caterpillars. The parent birds need to synchronise the maximum food demands of their young with the single, short-lived peak in the caterpillar food supply. They therefore produce a single large brood each year. This is unlike most other small birds which rear two or even three broods a year and thus have two or three chances if anything goes wrong. It is almost literally a case of the tits putting all their eggs in one basket!

great tit

Great tit
(Parus major);
14cm (5½in);
widespread;
resident.

blue tit

blue tit

Blue tit
(Parus caeruleus);
11cm (4½in);
widespread;
resident.

Left: A blue tit in flight carrying food for its chicks.

Left: Tit attacks on milk bottles, first reported as isolated incidents in the 1930s, are now common all over the British Isles.

Above: Peanuts, which have high nutrional value, are a favourite food of garden-visiting tits.

Left: The aggressive little blue tit raises its cobalt blue crest and droops its wings in characteristic gestures that are both courtship and threat display.

One in ten survive In spring each breeding pair of tits is generally composed of one adult bird which bred the year before and is at least 21 months old, and one young bird which is about nine months old and breeding for the first time. One half of each breeding pair dies each year. For the population to remain steady, only one youngster would need to be reared per pair to replace the dead adult. On average, however, ten youngsters leave each nest in summer. This means that nine die by the following spring – a staggering 90% mortality rate. Gruesome though it sounds, this is an insurance against catastrophe and is quite usual in the bird world. Indeed, if one extra youngster per brood were to survive each year, the whole countryside would soon be overrun by hordes of tits eating up all available resources and precipitating a disastrous drop in the population.

Plenty of predators The high mortality rate is largely the result of natural causes, especially starvation, since inexperienced young birds have difficulty finding enough food in winter. Also, at the start of the season, competition for nesting holes is fierce. Larger birds such as the starling may oust tits from the bigger holes, and tit may oust tit from smaller ones. The larger great tit does not always succeed in evicting the smaller but more aggressive blue. Tree sparrows can squeeze through an entrance apparently only

Above: A parent blue tit bringing a caterpillar to its young. The nest is only relatively secure from predators. Weasels and woodpeckers take a large toll of eggs and young chicks every year.

Left: A clutch of great tit eggs. The blue tit's eggs are slightly smaller but very similar in colour. In both species the female incubates the eggs by herself for 12-16 days, often fed by the male while she is sitting on the nest.

Right: A brood of blue tit chicks in their down and feather-lined nest. The youngsters are fed by both parents and fledge in about 15-23 days.

just large enough for a blue tit, and often build their untidy nest on top of a clutch of tit eggs or, as tree sparrows are late nesters, even on top of a flourishing brood of chicks.

Predators also play a significant part in the high mortality rate, and may account for a third or more of the deaths. Great spotted woodpeckers have a taste for tit eggs and young and can easily open up a nest hole with their strong beak. Woodpeckers capitalize on the fact that well-grown tit chicks are alerted by a shadow falling across their nest hole and jump up to the entrance to grab the expected food from a returning parent. As soon as the unfortunate chicks appear, the woodpecker catches them. In the early days after fledging, the inexperienced youngsters may fall easy victims to hunting sparrowhawks.

Strangely enough, wood mice and sometimes voles climb trees readily and enjoy any eggs they happen to find. The prime predatory mammal, however, is the weasel, which can squeeze through the nest hole without much difficulty. Often the weasel will gorge on young birds to such an extent that it has to sleep off the meal until it slims down enough to squeeze out again. Weasel predation is particularly high in summers when the weather is poor and the young tits are underfed. The hungry chicks squeak noisily for more food and are heard by patrolling weasels on the look-out for prey.

Irruptions The general trend in tit numbers is more or less steady, but there are some fluctuations from year to year. Often, after a series of good summers and mild winters (especially on the Continent), mortality is lower than usual and consequently tit numbers far higher than average. In this situation, the sudden onset of a severe winter, or a shortage of natural food, produces a massive westward movement–called an irruption– as hungry birds move about in search of food. When these hordes cross the Channel, autumn numbers in the eastern counties of England reach spectacular levels. Strange reports sometimes appear of tits eating the putty round window frames and even entering houses and tearing strips of wallpaper off

Mixed flocking

Anyone walking in deciduous woods between August and March is likely to encounter a tit flock. These roving bands of birds operate from ground level to the top of the tree canopy, probing for food and flying from perch to perch. In late summer young willow warblers and chiffchaffs, fattening up before migration, may join the tits. Later goldcrests, nuthatches and chaffinches also turn up, as well as wrens and treecreepers. Wrens tend to search the ground for food, while treecreepers probe the tree trunk for concealed insects. The small coal and blue tits favour the ends of twigs high in the canopy, as do the even smaller warblers which hover in front of the twigs, picking off insects. Lower, on branches and trunk, you'll see great tits and nuthatches whose greater weight excludes them from the canopy. Great tits often feed with chaffinches on the woodland floor, picking up seeds and nuts. One advantage of mixed flocking is that a large group of birds has many eyes to watch for predators and give the alarm quickly. Another is that the trees are exploited for food on every level.

the walls. Irruptions occur irregularly, perhaps only once a decade.

Ringing results show that most of the birds in an irruption are of Continental origin, coming from as far away as eastern Poland. Winters in mainland Europe are generally more severe than in much of Britain and Ireland, so Continental blue and great tits migrate south and west in autumn to escape climatic hardship and to find easier feeding. British birds, on the other hand, tend to stay close to home, and, although they may roam around several parishes, rarely make journeys of more than 30 miles. Many establish a circuit of known good feeding spots and visit each in turn.

Nuthatch

Nuthatches look like small woodpeckers but, unlike
them, can walk down trees head first, and instead of
chiselling out grubs, they split open nuts,
or hunt for insects.

Although superficially similar to our wood-peckers in its choice of habitat and in its behaviour, the nuthatch is generally thought to be more closely related to the tits and tree-creepers. True, it climbs with great ease even on the trunk of the smoothest-barked beech tree, but the nuthatch's toes are arranged three forward, one back, as in the other families of birds within the passerine order, not two forward, two back as in the wood-peckers. It is also true that the nuthatch has a large, dagger-shaped beak just like a wood-pecker's, but this is the result of 'parallel evolution' (in other words it has evolved over the ages to do the same sort of work, but in a totally different bird), and the nuthatch lacks the extremely long tongue that the wood-peckers use to extract their insect food.

There are other, subtler differences. Wood-peckers always move head-up on a tree-trunk, leaning back on their stout tail feathers as if these were a shooting stick. But nuthatches can move with similar ease head-up, head-down, or horizontally across a trunk. Their tails are short, and the tail feathers are of normal shape, flexibility and toughness: only rarely do they come into contact with the bark at all, and nuthatches are able to rely on their strong claws alone to maintain their position on the trunk.

Nuthatches are attractive woodland birds, slightly more than sparrow-sized, neat but not gaudy. They are dove-grey above, white on the throat and the sides of the face, and a rich, cinnamon-tinged fawn on the belly. On each flank, and extending up under the wing, is a rich chestnut patch, considerably more extensive in area and darker in colour in the male than in the female, so with a little practice it is possible to separate the two sexes. The effective-looking beak leads to a striking long narrow black patch, running through the eye and backwards on to the nape.

Wing display When a nuthatch flies directly overhead, its underwing pattern becomes visible: the underwing is silvery white and grey, with a black blob beneath the carpal joint (equivalent to the wrist). In much the same way as kingfishers, nuthatches flick their wings open and shut while perched during display. The other feature of display is the song: a loud, clear and ringing trill in rapid tempo. Most other nuthatch calls are loud and clear, too, particularly the often-used metallic 'chwit-chwit' and piping 'twee'. They are at their noisiest in late winter and early spring, but once breeding gets under way they are much quieter, so much so that you might suspect that they had left the area.

Nuthatch distribution This is rarely the case, for nuthatches are among the most sedentary of our birds, rarely moving more than a mile or two from the area of their birth. Their distribution is an interesting one: over an area roughly south of a line from the Wirral to the Wash they are widespread – except in a few lowland areas, principally in Cambridge-

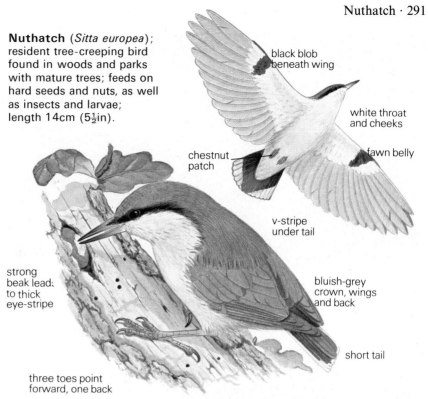

Nuthatch (*Sitta europea*); resident tree-creeping bird found in woods and parks with mature trees; feeds on hard seeds and nuts, as well as insects and larvae; length 14cm (5½in).

black blob beneath wing

white throat and cheeks

fawn belly

chestnut patch

v-stripe under tail

bluish-grey crown, wings and back

strong beak leads to thick eye-stripe

short tail

three toes point forward, one back

Above: The larger and harder nuts, such as acorns, beechmast, hazel cobs and chestnuts, are often carried in the nuthatch's beak and wedged in a crevice in the bark of a tree, or perhaps in a wall. The nut is then hammered and split open with the beak (right).

Opposite: At nest hole.

Below: The nuthatch's toes are arranged three forward, one back, unlike those of a woodpecker, two of which face forward, and two back shire, which is probably because there are few suitable woodlands. North of this line, there is an outlying area, mostly in Yorkshire, where they occur, but very few other breeding records.

Their range seems to have contracted southwards, as the birds left their northern English haunts, during the 19th century, and at the same time it was noted that they had deserted the parks of central London and some other large urban areas. One suggestion is that this might have been due to increasing atmospheric pollution in industrial areas, reducing the insect food supply. This is borne out by the gap between the present-day Yorkshire outpost and the main area of distribution, this gap corresponding with the location of much of south Yorkshire's heavy industry. Other species sensitive to industrial pollution—such as the kingfisher—are also missing from this area.

Though well-distributed in Wales, the nuthatch is another of those birds (such as the tawny owl and the woodpeckers) whose complete absence from Ireland seems so puzzling. One possible explanation is that being sedentary birds, and having poor powers of long-distance flight, nuthatches were unable to reach Ireland during the re-colonization period that followed the last Ice Age, before the rising seas formed what is now the Irish Sea and created an insuperable barrier.

Nuthatches are birds of mature, or even old, deciduous woodland; they sometimes occur in mixed deciduous and coniferous areas, but rarely in woodland that is predominantly coniferous. They particularly favour areas where beech, oak, sweet chestnut, hazel and hornbeam occur, for these provide winter food. Open parkland and, in many parts of England and Wales, large gardens with very old trees, also appear to be attractive to them.

Although the species is widespread within its area of distribution, the nuthatch is not a numerous bird in Britain. There are many sites that seem highly suitable, but where there are no nuthatches at all. Recent estimates put the number of pairs between

Above: Nuthatch eggs, resting on a bed of yew bark flakes. The usual clutch is of six to nine white eggs, heavily spotted with dark reddish brown. Occasional clutches of as many as 13 eggs may well be the product of more than one female.

Below: Both parents share in feeding the young, which fledge after about three weeks or rather longer if the weather at the time is poor. Like the tits, nuthatches produce only one brood.

10,000 and 20,000, which compares unfavourably with ten times that number of coal tits, but is roughly equal to the breeding population of the lesser spotted woodpecker and the long-eared owl.

Patient plasterwork The nest is built in a natural cavity, usually in a decaying broad-leaved tree but sometimes in a little-used or deserted building. Most are within a few metres of the ground, but nests at least 20m (60ft) high are on record. Nuthatches take readily to nestboxes, but other, more extraordinary sites include disused woodpecker and sand martin holes, an old magpie nest and even a series (reported from Sussex) in haystacks. Neither the size of the cavity nor that of the entrance hole seem to influence their choice, and nuthatches have a habit—unique among British birds—of cementing up the entrance with mud until the hole is of the right size. When using nestboxes, they also plaster round the lid, from the inside.

Inside the cavity, the nest itself is also of a unique type. The eggs are laid on the floor of the cavity, on top of a layer of flakes of bark (especially of yew or larch if this is available), or of oak or other leaves. When the incubating bird (always the female) departs to feed or drink, she covers the eggs with similar debris, so on a superficial inspection the occupied nest looks like the long-deserted winter lodging of a field-mouse or dormouse.

Bullfinch

The bullfinch, one of our most beautiful garden birds, has a darker side, having earned a reputation as a wanton destroyer of buds on a variety of fruit trees.

The bullfinch is one of our most colourful garden birds, the male's rose-red breast contrasting strikingly with its blue-black chin, cap, wings and tail. In spite of all this colour, however, it is easy to miss a group of feeding bullfinches. Usually all you'll see is a brief glimpse of a white rump flitting along a hedgerow or darting off into the thick cover of scrub or woodland.

Efficient foragers Woodland, especially coniferous forest, is the bullfinch's preferred habitat, but it is a versatile bird both in choice of habitat and in the food it eats. Only the most open land, lacking in bushes and hedgerows, seems to be too bare. A bullfinch rarely moves more than a few miles from

Below: Both male and female birds feed the young. The nest—a platform of interwoven twigs—is easily recognisable, but take care not to visit it too often as you may alert eager predators.

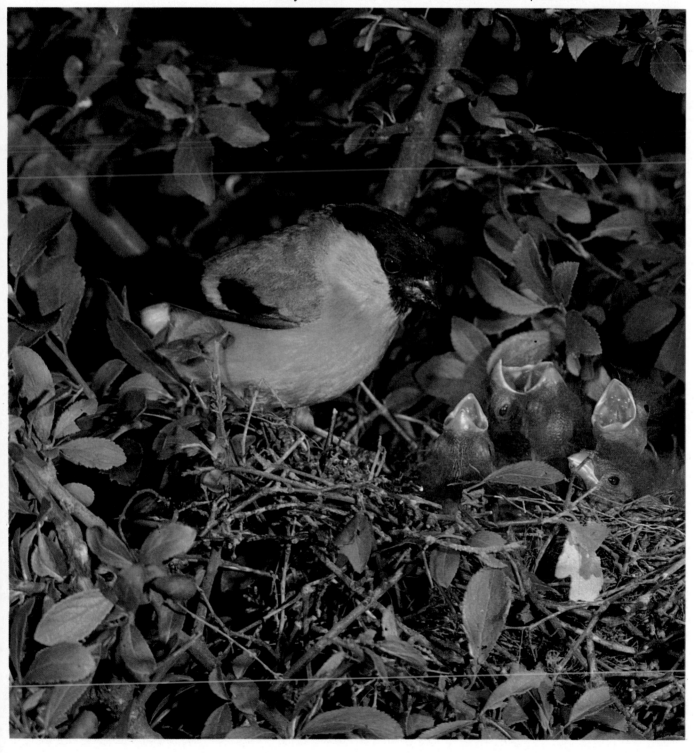

home territory and is expert at seeking out the best food available in its local patch–even to the extent of choosing between different varieties of fruit trees. In gardens and orchards it eats the buds of numerous bushes and trees, especially those of forsythia, apple, pear and plum. The short, stubby bill is ideally suited to this food; it can strip the hard outer husks off seeds and buds with very little trouble.

Adult bullfinches are vegetarians, though they feed their nestlings on large quantities of insects and spiders, which are predigested and then regurgitated for the chicks. As the young grow, the parents start to include seeds in their diet, increasing the amount gradually,

Half-a-tree-a-bird-a-day

Bullfinches eat buds at a horrifying rate. Calculations on fruit farms show that one bird can eat half the buds of a pear tree in a single day. In fact, this only takes about $1\frac{1}{2}$ hours' feeding at a comfortable pace. Rates of 10 to 30 buds per minute are common, depending on the size and type of bud. Fortunately, most bullfinches depend on the seeds and buds of wild plants and only turn to fruit buds as the best alternative when wild supplies have failed.

At present there is no effective bullfinch deterrent which is economically viable. Assessing the cost of bullfinch damage is difficult, even when it is confined to single trees. Damage to plums and damsons is long-term, affecting the growth of the tree and, in subsequent years, the crop. Other fruit trees, notably pears and apples, can withstand substantial bud loss without loss of crop and, though damaged, often produce larger fruit.

The male offers his mate a beakful of twigs as part of the courtship display; bill caressing is another part of their ritual.

until by the time the young leave the nest they are fed almost entirely on seeds. Throughout the summer and until late autumn bullfinches eat a huge variety of seeds–anything from minute grass seeds to the ash keys which hang in inviting bunches and are one of the bullfinch's favourite food.

From December onwards bullfinches eat tree and shrub buds; these contain next year's leaf and flower growth and are very nutritious. Unlike other finches, bullfinches don't have to search ground covered by leaves or snow to find fallen seeds or berries. They husk buds on the tree, leaving a scattering of litter which leads some people to think that they are vandals–destroying but not eating the buds. Many garden plants and commercially grown trees and bushes, cultivated for their early flowering or fruiting capacity, produce large flower buds that swell early in the year when the wild equivalents–hawthorn and blackthorn–are much smaller. Because of the damage done to orchards in southern England, the bullfinch has been removed from the protected bird list in some counties and many are now trapped or shot.

Busy breeding season The bullfinch is one of the many birds which overproduce young each summer to ensure that some survive winter to breed the following year. This is perhaps one of the main reasons why trapping and shooting, even on a large scale, does not seem to have affected the British population.

Above: The juvenile bird does not have the glossy black cap of the adult, nor the rose-red breast. By the end of the year, however, this bird's pale bill will have darkened and it will have a thick, waterproof coat of feathers to protect it through the winter.

Left: Male bullfinch in all the glory of full spring breeding plumage.

Bullfinch (*Pyrrhula pyrrhula*); length from beak to tail 15cm (5¾in); distribution widespread in woodland, plantations, hedgerows and gardens; absent from Isle of Man. Resident.

Most pairs of bullfinches rear two broods of about four nestlings a season; some pairs even manage to fit three broods into a nesting season lasting from late April to August or even September, despite the fact that over half the broods started do not survive. Efficient predators such as jays, magpies, stoats, weasels and cats often find even the best concealed nests and eat the eggs or nestlings. For this reason the bullfinch builds its nest – a distinctive platform of twigs bearing a cup of fine roots lined with hair – in a thick, prickly, inaccessible bush or hedge. The pale blue eggs, dotted with reddish spots at the blunt end, are conspicuous. However, the hen bullfinch with body feathers in a combination of pink, grey, buff and brown, is well camouflaged for sitting on the nest.

Only the hen builds the nest and incubates the eggs. Incubation starts in earnest when the last egg is laid so that they all hatch together – usually on the thirteenth day. Both parents feed the young. While the nestlings are being fed, visits to the nest are kept to a minimum. The parents develop special cheek pouches in the summer and cram them with food to bring back to the young. They sneak silently into the bush together so predators don't follow them to the hidden nest. Because the cheek pouches hold so much food, the youngsters need feeding only every half-hour or so. The young spend 12-18 days in the nest. After this the adults abandon them

and start a new nest.

At this stage you can identify the young bullfinches by the absence of black on the head but from July onwards each bird moults, replacing all its fluffy juvenile body feathers.

Serenades and songs Bullfinches sing most often during the breeding season. Not many people have heard the song because it is very quiet – a soft, pleasant mixture of short, clear piping notes and hoarse wheezes which the cock seems to reserve for his mate. With feathers fluffed, head bobbing up and down and tail cocked to one side, he serenades her to secure the firm pair-bond necessary for successful breeding. More frequently you can hear the short, plaintive, carrying whistle which is used to contact others of the same species. This happens particularly in winter, when several birds – possibly a family party – may flock together where food is to be found. The call has many variations and is sometimes repeated three or four times as a second type of song. The finely tuned ear of the bullfinch can almost certainly recognise individuals by their particular accent – something which must be particularly useful when recently fledged young are still being cared for by their parents. From March onwards, except when the hens are incubating their clutch of eggs, you can often see bullfinches in pairs. It seems from the evidence of ringing that some pairs may well mate for life.

Chaffinch and brambling

The chaffinch, our commonest finch, has a breeding population in the millions. Its close relative, the brambling, visits our woodlands for the winter.

The chaffinch is the most widespread and numerous British finch, and one of the most numerous of all British and Irish birds, especially in winter when our resident chaffinches are augmented by extra millions of European birds. Estimates of our breeding population made during the last 40 years have ranged between four and seven million pairs. The species is ubiquitous throughout the British and Irish mainlands, but uncommon in the Hebridean Islands, the Orkneys and Shetland.

White wing bars The summer plumage of the male chaffinch is unmistakable: a deep wine-pink breast contrasts with a dove-grey crown and nape and a black forehead, a russet mantle and dark blackish-brown wings and tail. White feathers are visible at each side of the tail, even when it is tightly closed; but perhaps the most conspicuous recognition feature of all is the double white wing bar. The two bars are as clearly visible on the perched bird as in flight. The foremost white bar covers the 'shoulder' (the wrist in human terms) of the closed wing in a broad white patch; behind this, the greater coverts carry a more slender stripe.

These striking wing markings are also seen on the female, which is otherwise clad in a mixture of browns and beiges for camouflage. In winter, the male too is more sombre in

Above: Chaffinches usually raise only one brood each year, and begin their nesting activities in late April or early May. The nest is one of the most neatly constructed, and well concealed, of all our birds' nests. The basic structure is of moss, with a framework of grass and rootlets. The outside of the nest is usually ornamented with lichen or flakes of white bark taken from birch trees, if the nest happens to be in or near one of these.

Right: The cup is lined with soft hair or feathers, and usually contains 4 or 5 eggs, but occasionally nests with as many as 8 are found. The eggs are whitish blue, marked with dark purplish-brown spots and squiggles.

plumage, when subtle camouflage among the stubble is more important than the bright colours of display. At all times of year, both sexes have a grass-green rump patch, which is particularly noticeable when you see the birds taking off.

Chaffinch song Chaffinches start to sing early in the year: from February onwards in the south (later in the north) their boisterous song can be heard in almost any part of the countryside. It consists of a long descending trill with a final swashbuckling flourish. One of the most intriguing questions of bird song is how such complicated and often beautifully melodious phrases are passed on from one generation to the next.

Recent research at Cambridge University has gone some way towards unravelling this mystery in the case of the chaffinch. The Cambridge experiments suggest that the basic framework of the song is inherited, for it is produced 'automatically' even by a young male chaffinch reared in total isolation. In the wild a young male, possessing these instinctive foundations of song, listens to his elders and gradually develops the quality, and the trills and flourishes, of his full song. In such a way, local 'dialects' develop: West Country chaffinches, for example, sound as different as their human counterparts do to a visitor from, say, London.

Woodland bird Chaffinches are essentially woodland birds, but they inhabit a wide range of different types of woodland. The densest populations are normally found in mature broadleaved woodland, especially oak with wide glades, but most other types of woodland (including the darkest and densest Norway spruce) support chaffinches, as do scrubland, farmland, parks and gardens. In remote areas in the north and west, it seems that even a clump of weatherbeaten trees or

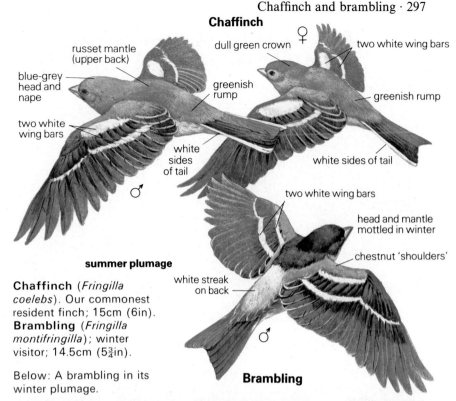

Chaffinch

russet mantle (upper back)

blue-grey head and nape

two white wing bars

dull green crown

greenish rump

♀

two white wing bars

greenish rump

white sides of tail

white sides of tail

♂

summer plumage

two white wing bars

head and mantle mottled in winter

chestnut 'shoulders'

white streak on back

♂

Brambling

Chaffinch (*Fringilla coelebs*). Our commonest resident finch; 15cm (6in).
Brambling (*Fringilla montifringilla*); winter visitor; 14.5cm (5¾in).

Below: A brambling in its winter plumage.

bushes is sufficient to encourage a chaffinch pair to take up residence. In winter, many forsake woodland and join other finches, sparrows and buntings on farmland, especially where plenty of cereal or weed seeds are available.

Varied diet In summer the diet is very varied, not having such a high seed content as that of most finches. It includes small snails and worms, various fruits and seeds, and often aphids gathered high in the woodland canopy. For the first few days after the young have hatched, chaffinches feed their brood mostly on insects, and their beaks, relatively long-pointed and slender for finches, are suitable both for this and for the small seeds that they also tend to select. In winter, foraging is done more often on the ground than in the treetops, and seeds tend to predominate.

The brambling Bramblings breed from northern Scandinavia eastwards into Siberia. Their chief breeding habitats are birch woodland and the mixed woodland fringes of large expanses of coniferous forest. In winter they migrate south to the Mediterranean and west to Britain and Ireland.

Like the chaffinch, the brambling has white wing bars: these are much less bold than those of the chaffinch, and are not always visible when the bird is on the ground, though they can be seen clearly when it is in flight. When flying, the brambling shows a more mottled upper surface than the chaffinch, with a conspicuous white patch on the rump, which is its best identification feature. It contrasts strongly with the green rump of the chaffinch.

On the ground in winter, the mottled plumage is good for camouflage, but a close view reveals the orange breast of both male and female, the all-brown or blackish-brown heads, and the orange-buff shoulder patch of the male, all of which help to separate the brambling from the chaffinch. As winter progresses into spring, the mottled blackish

Above: A female chaffinch. At all times of year, in flight or on the ground, the common chaffinch call is 'pink, pink' – the basis of the Dutch name for the species, 'fink', and indeed the English word finch. This same call, more stridently produced, is used as an alarm, to warn, for example, of the approach of a jay or the presence of a roosting owl.

Left: A male chaffinch in the snow, towards the end of winter. In winter, his plumage is less vivid than in summer. After the autumn moult, most of the newly grown body feathers have broad buff fringes. As winter proceeds into spring, the fringes wear off, revealing the beauty of his plumage beneath – in time for the spring display. In this bird, the fringes are almost worn away, but still dull the full brilliance of the plumage.

brown head and mantle of the male brambling become glossy black as the paler feather fringes wear away, and he comes into his breeding plumage, which we are only rarely lucky enough to see.

The male's plumage is much more striking than his song, which is a metallic, poorly formed jumble of 'dwee' calls and chirrups. Bramblings have several flight calls – a low-pitched 'chuck-chuck-chuck' and, more characteristically, a hoarse 'zweek' and a metallic 'dwee' which rises in inflection as it ends.

An irregular visitor As a winter visitor, the brambling is irregular in the extreme. In most years there are a few bramblings scattered throughout Britain, but occasionally (and normally in years when there has been a very heavy crop of beech mast) numbers are much higher. The erratic nature of brambling migration is largely responsible for this. Instead of adopting a routine pattern of autumn and spring migrations to and from regularly used wintering areas, bramblings move to wherever their food is easily found.

This means that birds wintering in Britain one year may be found (say) in northern Italy or Yugoslavia the next. Most arriving migrants reach our east coast – often in company with Continental chaffinches – in October and early November; in years of low numbers they may not even reach the West Country. The return journey usually starts during March.

Beech mast is an important component of the winter diet, which also includes a few late berries and many seeds. Bramblings are usually seen foraging on the ground under a large area of mature, widely spaced and heavily cropping beeches; otherwise they can be found with other finches and buntings in weed-grown fields, stubbles, and around feeding places for farm livestock, where seeds have dropped from hay and straw.

The only positive British breeding record of bramblings was in 1920 in northern Scotland, but recently there have been several instances indicative of breeding elsewhere in Britain. These suggest that the brambling may follow two other Scandinavian birds, the fieldfare and the redwing, and establish regular breeding colonies.

Which are our commonest breeding birds?

The most reliable guide at the moment is the B.T.O.'s survey of 1968-72. Although this is now over a decade old, the populations of the birds referred to here happen to be generally stable ones, which means that the overall picture still applies today. Another point to remember is that populations of some of the species mentioned here rise in winter. The highest breeding population of all is that of the wren, estimated at 10 million pairs or more. After this the picture is a little confusing, for estimates can only be rough and include guesswork, however well informed. The blackbird probably takes second place, with a firm estimate of seven million pairs. However, the chaffinch population is estimated at between four and seven million pairs, as is that of the starling. Coming in the middle of this range are the less vague figures of around five million pairs each of robins, dunnocks and blue tits. The house sparrow's possible range of three and a half to seven million pairs may place it among the highest populations.

Goldfinch

With a broad yellow band stretching across its wings, the goldfinch lives up to its name. Parents and young birds feed in family groups attractively called 'charms'.

It is not just the yellowy gold patch along the wings that makes the goldfinch instantly recognisable. The red, white and black striped head pattern is also unmistakable. The tail and rest of the wings are black, with delicate white markings. In spring look for the white tips to each wing feather–by the end of the summer when the feathers are nearly a year old they have often worn away. In flight you can see the goldfinch's whitish rump, similar to that of a bullfinch or brambling. A warm buff-coloured back and flank feathers complete the bird's neat and tidy appearance.

Seed-eaters Thistles are the goldfinch's most important food plant. It eats the seeds from mid-summer through to autumn, and even in winter if they are still available. Often the goldfinch prefers the easy pickings of seed heads that have fallen to the ground, and leaves the seeds that remain on the plants. These then provide a useful reserve of food when snow covers the ground.

During the summer months, the goldfinch's diet includes a variety of other seeds as they ripen, though it prefers those from plants in the daisy family, for example groundsel, dandelion, ragwort and sowthistle early in the summer, hardheads in August, and later still burdock which is an important winter food. The goldfinch is the only bird able to reach the seeds buried in the depths of teasel flower heads; in fact, these seeds are eaten mainly by the male goldfinch which has a slightly longer beak than the female.

Above: Most finches have wing bars, but none are as large and striking as those of the goldfinch. The bright yellow patch is obvious even on perched birds. The goldfinch's scientific name comes from *carduelis* the latin for thistle. The seeds of this plant are the bird's favourite food.

Goldfinch *(Carduelis carduelis),* 18cm (7in) from beak to tip of tail. The two sexes are almost identical in colour and size, and there is no distinct winter or summer plumage. Although not thought of as migratory, about three-quarters of British goldfinches leave here usually in October.

There is, however, a risk factor: sadly, goldfinches occasionally get trapped by the powerful hooked seed heads of these plants, and die.

Versatile feet The goldfinch uses its feet to hold food while it eats – something that few other birds can do. From a firm perch, the feeding bird pulls a thin seed-bearing stem with its beak and places it under its feet to hold the stem steady while eating the seeds.

A trick commonly taught to goldfinches in the sixteenth century – caught and caged for their colourful plumage and song – involved a repetition of this pull and hold procedure. The birds could only get food and water by pulling the strings of a cart, without letting go, and drawing the cart up a slope.

Song-flights The goldfinch has a pleasant, canary-like, twittering song. You can hear the song throughout the year, but the bird sings most regularly from March to July, either from a perch or in flight. In a display above his territory, the male has a rather hesitant song-flight with deep, slow wing-beats and spread tail. Like other finches, the normal flight is undulating; during this flight the goldfinch often repeats a characteristic 'stickelitt' call.

Building a nest Goldfinch territories are usually small, and several pairs may nest together in a loose colony. The swaying outer branches of large trees, bushes and tall

Above: Goldfinches have long, narrow tweezer-like beaks that can prise open prickly seed heads to extract seeds that other birds cannot reach. Equipped with relatively short, stout legs, goldfinches are acrobatic birds, clinging to swaying plants like tits.

Left: Both parents feed the nestlings on regurgitated seeds and a few insects, often collected some distance away. The mother normally produces two broods a season. The earliest chicks leave the nest in June. In years when the summer is warm and dry and food is abundant, breeding continues into August or even September, enabling a third brood to be raised.

hedges might seem precarious for a nest, but the goldfinches favours such sites. In a garden the bird often chooses a fruit tree for a nest site, but there are no hard and fast rules—anything from a full-grown horse chestnut to ivy on a wall will do.

The nest, immaculately neat and compact, and deep enough to retain the eggs and chicks in windy conditions, is bound firmly to branches with spiders' webs. Rootlets, dead grass, hair and wool are the usual nesting materials, while wool and fluff from ripe seeds, especially sallow catkins, are used to make a soft, warm lining. The goldfinch may attach moss and lichen to the outside of the nest. Occasionally these birds make use of unusual nesting materials. A few years ago, at East Malling Research Station in Kent, one pair of goldfinches carefully untied plastic labels from trees, and used them to decorate their nest.

Both adults fly to and fro together during construction of the nest, but only the female builds—the male watches her. The female lays about five or six eggs and does all the incubating. The male has the task of collecting food for himself and his mate at this time so the female need leave the nest only to stretch her legs, to drink or to preen. The eggs take nearly two weeks to hatch, and the young can fly in two to three weeks.

Safety in numbers Like other finches, goldfinches are gregarious; breeding pairs and family parties flock together in places where food is plentiful, in groups given the attractive name 'charms'. This enables young birds to learn where to find food, and offers some protection by virtue of the group's large numbers—many pairs of eyes spot danger more easily than one.

Many parents and young birds leave Britain, migrating to their wintering grounds in Holland, Belgium, western France, Spain and Portugal. Until the end of the nineteenth century, many were trapped on the south coast of England as they migrated. Trappers used a cage with an automatic trap door called a *chardonneret*—from the French for goldfinch.

World-wide distribution The absence of goldfinches from much of Scotland and their scarcity in northern England, despite the presence of suitable habitats, suggests that the climate in these areas is unfavourable to the birds. Their natural range extends throughout much of Europe, to western Asia and North Africa, but not much further north than southern Sweden.

Attempts to introduce the species to several states in North America have failed, perhaps because of competition from the native American goldfinch. Nevertheless, it was successfully introduced to Bermuda, Australia, Tasmania and New Zealand—perhaps too successfully in the latter case, where it has become something of a pest on strawberry farms, nipping seeds from the ripe fruits.

Above: Until they moult in the autumn, the young goldfinches have pale heads without the red and white pattern of their parents. The young birds also have streaks on their back and flanks, and have the same wing-bars as the adults.

Right: The smooth, finely spotted eggs are laid in nests usually 4-15m (13-50ft) above ground. Despite these often dangerous heights, the deep nest provides ample security.

Fitting the bill

The **greenfinch (1)** with its 'general purpose' seed-eating bill tackles small seeds like those of chickweed and groundsel, or larger seeds such as bramble, sunflower and corn.

A long, thin tweezer-like bill enables the **goldfinch (2)** to delve into the prickly seed heads of thistles and teasels.

The short, round bill of the **bullfinch (3)** is sharp at the edges—ideal for nipping off and then peeling buds.

Only the **hawfinch (4)** with its strong skull and jaw muscles can crack open the large hard seeds of cherries and damsons. These are held between special pads in the massive bill, and crushed slowly—the beak exerts over 45kg (100lb) of pressure.

The upper and lower parts of the **crossbill's (5)** beak twist and cross. This is effective for prising open the scales of spruce and pine cones—the bird then uses its long tongue to scoop out the seeds.

1

sunflower seeds   corn

2

thistle   burdock

3

fruit tree bud   redcurrant

4

cherry
rose hip

5

spruce cone and seed

Hawfinch

The hawfinch–a large species of finch–is equipped with a disproportionately large bill which can exert as much power as can a man with a pair of pliers. Cautiously concealing its movements in the foliage of tall trees, it presents a unique challenge to the most patient of birdwatchers.

Below left: A female hawfinch–less colourful than the male–on a low garden wall. The habitat of this species ranges from mature deciduous woodland, which is its commonest haunt, to mixed woodland, large parks, and gardens with trees. Hawfinches can even occupy scrubland areas that have a few trees. In winter and spring they frequent cherry, plum and damson orchards.

Hawfinch distribution

Above: Our hawfinch population is estimated at about 10,000 pairs. Most of them are in central and south-east England, where woods with hornbeam trees are plentiful.

Below: The normal hawfinch clutch is of 4-6 eggs, buff or blue in ground colour with various darker blobs and squiggles adorning them. Most clutches are laid in May, and incubated by the female alone for 11-13 days. Both parents feed the youngsters after hatching, and they fledge a fortnight later.

To see the hawfinch, our largest and most spectacular species of finch, is regarded by ornithologists as a considerable achievement. Despite its size, this bird is extremely secretive and normally very quiet, betraying its presence in the neighbourhood only by a series of 'tick' calls–sounding a little like those of the robin.

It feeds both on the ground (where you are most likely to get a chance to see it) and in the trees, but if disturbed on the ground it flies up into dense cover, often being so wary that half an hour may pass before the first individuals drop down from the branches and cautiously begin to feed again.

Stocky outline Slightly smaller than a song thrush, the hawfinch is a stocky bird. In flight it has a characteristic heavy-headed, short-tailed appearance. Its flight path is steeply undulating, with a brief burst of wing-flaps followed by a glide rather like the flight of a woodpecker. Also reminiscent of a woodpecker are the conspicuous broad white wing-bars, clearly visible from above or below. The white flashes on either side of the stumpy tail

are very noticeable in flight.

On the ground, the first feature that catches the eye is the enormous head and beak, which seem out of proportion to the rest of the bird. The head is pale chestnut in the male, drab brown in the female–in both cases set off from the rich rufous-brown back by a grey or fawn collar. Both sexes have a black

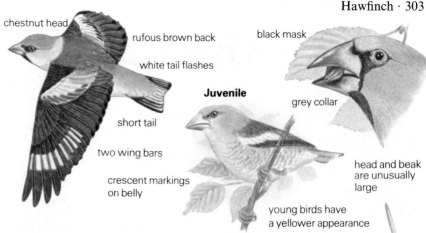

chestnut head

rufous brown back

white tail flashes

black mask

Juvenile

grey collar

short tail

two wing bars

crescent markings
on belly

head and beak
are unusually
large

young birds have
a yellower appearance

'mask' round the base of the beak and a large black bib. The massive beak, slightly larger in the male than the female, is silver-grey with black edges and a black tip. Shaped like a triangular pyramid, it may be as much as 18mm (¾in) long, wide and deep.

The belly and flanks are rich buff, and against them the wings appear dark, almost black. A close view reveals that the outer flight feathers are grey-brown, but they are largely concealed by the inner feathers that overlie them. These have a rich purplish sheen and peculiar splayed ends, almost like old-fashioned curled moustaches. They are thought to play a part during courtship display. The white wingbar is clearly visible on the folded wing, shaded with brown or chestnut. The legs are pale yellowish-brown, and the eyes have a most unusual marbled pink iris surrounding the dark pupil, particularly in the male.

Young birds are altogether drabber, with a yellow-washed appearance and speckled slightly on the belly and flanks. After they moult in August and September of their first year, they become difficult to distinguish from the adults.

Calls and songs By far the best way to spot hawfinches regularly is to become familiar with their call. This is the sound the birds make at all times of year for such purposes as maintaining contact or warning of approaching danger.

The hawfinch makes its call both in flight and when perched, so it is advisable to look both up *and* around. Although the call has much in common with that of a robin or song thrush, the 'tick' or 'tchick' is rather more abrupt and clicking than in either of the other two species. A good way of learning to make the distinction without error is to gain access to a recording. Several of these are available through specialist shops or the main ornithological societies such as the RSPB or the British Trust for Ornithology.

The song, however, is an entirely different matter. This sound, usually more musical or attractive than the call, is made at a specific time of year – the breeding season – and its purpose is to advertise territory and attract a mate. There are few, if any, good recordings of the hawfinch song, partly because the birds are so shy and difficult to approach, and partly because it is so quietly uttered. Produced from March to May, it is a hesitant but tuneful jangle, perhaps most reminiscent of the song of the goldfinch.

A widespread bird Despite these difficulties in seeing hawfinches, recent surveys on a county and national scale have shown them to be quite widespread across England and southern Scotland. The major concentrations, perhaps associated with the distribution of one of their favourite foods – hornbeam seeds – are in central and south-east England, while the records fall off rapidly in Wales and the West Country. There are few records from

Ireland and none breed there today, though one pair did nest in County Kildare in 1902.

Recent estimates suggest that the population may amount to about 10,000 pairs. From such historical records as there are – mostly associated with hawfinch attacks on cherry crops – it appears that they were restricted to the south-east until the middle of the 19th century, when an expansion phase began to give hawfinches their present-day distribution pattern.

Feeding hawfinches The presence of feeding hawfinches in an orchard is given away in winter by large numbers of neatly split fruit stones on the ground. During the summer, look for shredded pea pods, another favourite food. As with several other finches, insects feature considerably in the diet of the nestlings, but at other times they eat a wide variety of seeds, ripe and unripe, from herbaceous plants, shrubs and trees. Like bullfinches, hawfinches also turn to buds of both wild and orchard trees.

Among the seeds they eat are the kernels of wild and orchard cherries, sloes, damsons and other plums, and beech and hornbeam

A hawfinch secondary or inner-wing flight feather. At the tip, one corner protrudes in a triangle and the other is cut away in a neat curve. The feather has a blue-green sheen.

Hawfinch (*Coccothraustes coccothraustes*). Our largest finch species. Resident in woodland, especially in fruit-growing areas. Length 16.5cm (6½in).

Below: Hawfinches often visit puddles to bathe and drink.

Above: A male hawfinch on the ground. The head is a pale chestnut colour, the collar is grey and the back a rich rufous brown. Here you can see the purplish, splayed inner flight feathers—the four inner primaries and the secondaries. These feathers, the unusual shape of which does not impair flight efficiency, are thought to be used in courtship. No other British bird has splayed feathers like this.

Right: Like some other finches, hawfinches often breed socially—not in densely packed colonies like rooks or herons, but in a scattering of up to half-a-dozen pairs in an acre or two. Whether in a loose colony or singly, the hawfinch pair feeds well away from the nest, thus attracting less attention to the nest and making it harder for predators to locate. The nest itself is like a large version of the bullfinch's nest, with a platform of twigs supporting a shallow cup lined with rootlets and fine grasses. Usually it is built high up, over 3m (10ft) and up to 27m (70ft) above the ground, and often at the end of a long horizontal branch for extra security.

Opposite: A pair of hawfinches feeding their young at the nest.

mast. All of these are extracted from very robust shells–and it is here that the formidable beak comes into its own. Not only is the beak huge, but the mouth is equipped with sharp ridges, as are the jaws of a vice, to hold seeds while they are crushed.

One reason that the hawfinch's head is so large is that its jaws are worked by extremely powerful and thus bulky muscles, capable, it has been calculated, of exerting a peak pressure of 200 pounds per square inch. Certainly, any bird ringer handling a hawfinch who is careless enough to let a finger come within reach of that massive beak can testify to a nip at least as painful as catching the finger between a hammer and nail!

A social species Hawfinches display social behaviour at all times of the year–both in and out of the breeding season. Colonies are small groups, loosely scattered over a communal territory of an acre or two. During the winter, particularly in orchards where plenty of fallen fruit from the previous summer has ensured a lasting food supply, they will join with other finches and thrushes to feed on the orchard floor, often in some numbers.

On winter nights there are several reports of large roosts (more than a hundred birds) gathering high in dense trees. This occurs in coniferous trees as their evergreen foliage provides dense cover. One site, for example, is in the Bedgebury Pinetum in Kent, where the roost has frequently contained up to 100 hawfinches.

Such roosts must draw in birds from a considerable area, and it is interesting to speculate on their function. Is it just that these roosts are the best shelter available for miles around, or is there some communal purpose– perhaps to convey in some way the location of good feeding areas?

Apart from movements of a few miles within their home range to feed or roost, ringing recoveries show that hawfinches in the British Isles are relatively sedentary birds compared with their Continental counterparts, which migrate south regularly to escape severe winter weather. There is very little evidence that Continental birds reach our woodland areas for the winter months.

The range of the hawfinch outside the British Isles is fairly extensive. It can be found from North Africa right across Europe, and through central Siberia to Manchuria and Japan. The furthest north it reaches is southern Sweden. Throughout this range its powerful bill allows it to maintain a monopoly of certain food items–cherry and plum kernels, for example–that other finches are unable to utilise. Only the bullfinch–with a bill roughly half as big as that of the hawfinch–can compete at all.

Greenfinch

The greenfinch is the largest of a trio of British finches with partly green plumage (the others are the siskin and the rare serin). It is one of our more numerous birds, being well suited to our lowland countryside with its mosaic-like pattern of woods, farmland, hedgerows, thickets and gardens.

Above: A pair of greenfinches (the male is on the right) with four young. In the past, these birds were often caught and caged— such birds used to be called 'green linnets'.

Below: A male greenfinch (right) with a juvenile (left) at water. The juveniles are much less highly coloured than the adults. Many have brown streaks on their plumage, like sparrows.

The greenfinch is one of the most widespread and abundant visitors to bird-tables in Britain and Ireland. It is sometimes disparaged by birdwatchers who are captivated by the acrobatic feats of the blue and great tits as they hang on to strings of nuts. The greenfinch, being a relatively large finch, is not a particularly acrobatic feeder although, in many areas, it has learned to feed on hanging nuts. Some people actually overlook its presence since it is similar in size to the ubiquitous house sparrow, and many greenfinches have rather little yellow or green on their plumage, which strengthens the resemblance.

The adult male greenfinch is a handsome bird, with brilliant yellow flashes on the wings and tail–most obvious when in flight–and washes of green and greenish yellow over the rest of the plumage. The females, and the young of either sex, are less highly coloured, with much brown streaked plumage–like a sparrow's. (In recent years another much smaller finch, the siskin, has also taken to feeding in gardens, mostly at the end of winter, but there is little chance of the two being confused.)

Habitat and range As with many of our garden and farmland bird species, greenfinches are naturally birds of the woodland edge, finding hedges in arable land, and shrubberies in parks and gardens, ideal places for breeding. They can be found over most of Europe, spreading into Asia in the east and to north Africa in the south, but they are absent from the far northern parts of Europe and Asia, which lack trees or shrubs. Many areas in Britain have reported recent spreads in the breeding range and local increases in numbers.

Seed eaters Greenfinches feed on seeds for almost all their lives. In the autumn the flocks of young birds, which are soon joined by the adults, may become very numerous, with some numbering in the thousands. These large flocks are sometimes seen feeding on ripening corn, gleaning the stubbles or feasting on weed seeds in root crops or on waste ground. Their weight generally precludes feeding from seeds still held on the plants, but they are adept at finding seeds on the ground. They can live well on open ploughed land, finding dormant seeds which may, in some cases, be several years old.

The weeds particularly favoured include charlock, persicaria, groundsel, chickweed and fat hen. When a large flock has found a good feeding site, it is quite possible to hear the birds from thirty or forty yards away – not from their calls but from the cracking of seeds in their bills. All the food is first manoeuvred in the bird's beak to remove the husk, for greenfinches only eat the central nutritious part.

Autumn and winter The autumn flocks frequently contain other finch species, but during the evening the greenfinches tend to roost on their own. The roosting site is often a clump of rhododendrons, laurels or an old hedge with plenty of holly or ivy. The birds prefer roosting sites which are not particularly high, but have plenty of thick cover. Ringing results have shown that the birds move regularly from roost to roost and that, in general, they are a mobile and 'nomadic' species. There are not many indications of movements over 200 or 300km (120-180 miles) within the British population, but many birds from the northern part of the European range travel 1000km (600 miles) or more each autumn and spring.

Cold winter weather is not a serious threat to survival – provided that the feeding grounds are clear of snow. If the weather is very cold and the day-length is very short, they may find it difficult to take in sufficient food to see them through the night. In such circumstance, and during snowy weather, many more may join the flocks feeding in gardens.

Human help Greenfinches visiting gardens take almost any sort of seed. Hemp, peanuts (loose on the ground or hanging) and par-

ticularly sunflower seeds are favourites. As with many species observed at feeding stations, the numbers seen at any instant in a garden are a tiny proportion of all the individual birds using the site through the whole winter.

As many garden bird feeders know, the number of greenfinches seen in gardens reaches a peak in March and April, and many are still present in early May. Ringing returns show that this is the period when more greenfinches die in the wild than at any other time of year. This is easily explained, for the birds have been exploiting a stock of seeds which has not been replenished naturally since the autumn. The food supply has thus

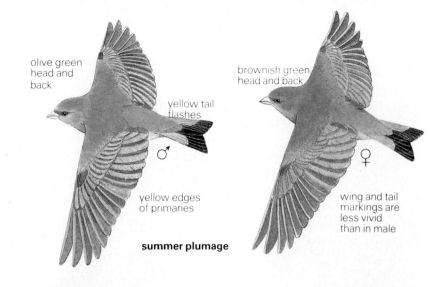

olive green head and back

yellow tail flashes

♂

yellow edges of primaries

summer plumage

brownish green head and back

♀

wing and tail markings are less vivid than in male

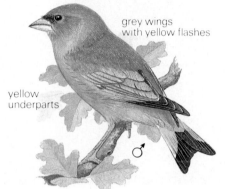

grey wings with yellow flashes

yellow underparts

♂

The song flight

conspicuously beating wings

The spring display of the greenfinch includes an interesting song flight. The male performs a circular flight over his territory, flapping his wings in an exaggerated and noticeable manner.

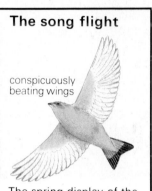

Greenfinch distribution

Greenfinch (*Carduelis chloris*). Resident in Britain and Ireland; partial migrant on the Continent. Habitats include woodland edges, gardens, shrubberies and farmland. 14.5cm (5¾in).

Left: Nesting begins in late April or early May. With six eggs, this is a good clutch for greenfinches; many have only four.

Above: A male greenfinch in flight. The two flight (and contact) calls are 'chup, chup, chup' and 'chit-chit-chit-chit-chit'. When the bird is seen in flight the yellow wing patches and tail edges are conspicuous.

Below: A greenfinch bathing in a stream. Note the stout body (even allowing for the fluffed-out feathers) and the clear pink beak.

run out, and continued feeding – by people who put out food for birds in their gardens – is particularly important.

The breeding season During the spring, the males start to give their 'dreeeez' summer call. When displaying, they precede this by a rather weak, chattering song. Displaying males may sing and call from the top of a tree or bush, or may advertise their presence in a characteristic song-flight. In most cases several pairs take up territories close together, each male defending only a small area round the chosen nest site.

The nest is built of twigs, roots and moss in late April or early May, and is lined with fine grass, roots, hair, wool or feathers. Four to

six eggs are generally laid in each clutch and incubated for two weeks. The chicks are fed on insects for the first few days, but soon the diet is changed to regurgitated seeds. Two or three broods are often raised by a single pair, and young may sometimes be found in the nest as late as September.

Countless hazards In ideal conditions, the two or three broods raised by a single pair of greenfinches could be expected to produce a total of about 20 birds where there had been only two at the beginning. Nature is not in fact so profligate, for although a highly successful pair may be able to produce three large broods, the great majority of breeding attempts actually fail.

Failure arises in many ways – lack of food may cause starvation, one of the adults may die or be killed, or a predator may find the nest and eat the eggs or young. Apart from these dangers, the eggs might be infertile, the nest may be blown out of its bush or the bush may be destroyed during agricultural or gardening work.

In any case, the production of eggs and the successful fledging of young is not the end of the parents' responsibility, for they also have to look after the young birds, out of the nest, for a period of ten days or more, while they learn about the world and how to find food for themselves.

Resilient population Besides all the difficulties that they have to face at breeding time, greenfinches are affected by wide variations in winter weather conditions from year to year. Despite this, the British breeding population, as shown by the Common Birds Census index, has remained constant over the last 20 years. The two cold winters in 1961-62 and 1962-63 probably halved the population, but it had returned to an average level by 1966.

Since then it has varied by less than 10% either way, except in 1975 when it was rather higher than normal. These figures are based on observations made on farmland – probably the habitat holding the most stable populations. The figures relating to woodland are based on a smaller sample and show a rather greater fluctuation. The highest woodland population they indicated was in 1966.

The prospects for this attractive bird look excellent, with range expansions being reported during the present century. These have occurred in western areas, where the birds were formerly absent, and also in city centre areas. The most serious problem which they are likely to face arises from the increasing use of herbicides in cereal growing and other farming. If the trend continues, the range of species of weeds which are able to seed and thus produce natural winter feeding for the birds may be reduced. On current evidence, it seems likely that human bird-lovers will more than make up for the deficiency, with the plentiful supplies of seeds and peanuts that they put out for the birds in their gardens.

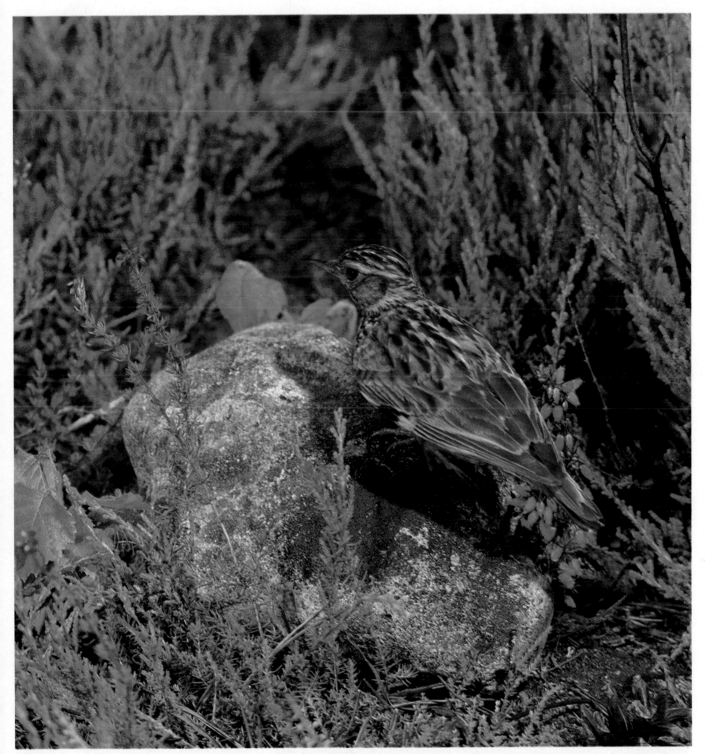

Skylark and woodlark

The skylark is recognisable for its sustained song as it flies in a broad sweep high over open ground. The rarer woodlark sings as it spirals upwards, its distinctive song a rich and beautiful melody.

The woodlark and skylark have very different distributions within the British Isles. To see a woodlark on any but a few lowland heaths in southern England is enough to turn an ordinary day's bird-watching into a red-letter day. On the other hand, the skylark is the characteristic bird of open country and, according to the BTO's field-work completed in 1972, it is undoubtedly the most widespread breeding bird in Britain and Ireland.

The skylark's brown plumage serves as a good camouflage for the bird when it is in the open ground it prefers. Unlike most birds, it sings on the wing, marking out its territory on the ground by circling and singing above it. Its song, which includes mimicry of the notes

Woodlarks are rare birds and the total British population may now number only 150-200 pairs. They are specially protected under the first schedule of the Bird Protection Acts; they only breed in dry areas of heathlands or downlands.

Woodlark (*Lullula arborea*), 15cm (6in) long from beak to tail. Migrant.

Bird song

The skylark (right) is famed for its habit of soaring high in the sky, rising and descending repeatedly, all the time pouring out a torrent of song. The woodlark (far right) has a circular song-flight and its song is mellow-toned. Both birds also sing from song-posts. A singing bird is advertising itself. It is proclaiming that it owns a territory and warning its neighbours that it is around. Birds also sing to find a mate. Females may be attracted to a particular type of songster and, with many species, the unpaired male sings a different song from the male with a mate. Winter song is rare in most birds as there are few species that defend their territories or pair up then.

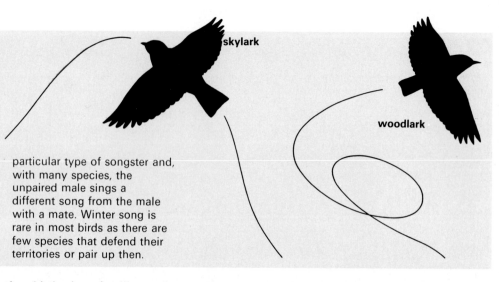

skylark

woodlark

Below: The eggs of the skylark hatch after 11 days incubation, and the young remain in the nest for 8-10 days. Then, although they are not yet able to fly, they leave it and move around in the grass. At this stage their bodies are well feathered, but their wings are not yet grown and they still retain some down.

of other birds, is a familiar and attractive feature of the countryside for much of the year. It is very loud, and a bird which seems to be singing overhead often turns out to be a mere speck in the sky. One singing bird stimulates another: as dawn breaks over an area of downland where there are no larks singing, all the birds start to sing within the space of one minute, producing a complete wall of sound. This habit of singing in flight is crucial to the skylark's ability to colonize truly open areas: other species of open ground are often unable to breed if there are no song-posts from which to sing and mark their territories.

The skylark can often be seen busily peck-ing at apparently bare earth. For most of the year it is mainly vegetarian, feeding on tiny weed seeds that lie dormant in the ground. At other times, particularly spring when the seeds are beginning to grow, it may feed on the nutritious growing points of the young plants. Because of modern agricultural techniques, this has turned the bird into a pest: in the past sugar-beet growers planted the seeds densely in rows, later thinning them. Today farmers have taken to sowing single encapsulated seeds exactly where they want the plants to grow. However, the skylarks may then peck the growing point from the young seedling and spoil the farmer's carefully planned harvest.

Three broods Skylark pairs form during early spring. You often see a singing bird at the end of its song-flight drop to the ground and display to another bird already standing there. The nest is always on the ground, often built into an existing depression such as the hoof-print of a cow. Indeed, some bird-watchers have encouraged skylarks to nest by forming hollows with their heels in firmly rolled grounds.

The nest cup is built of coarse grass and roots lined with fine grass and sometimes hair. The eggs, generally three or four to the clutch, are whitish and thickly speckled all over with olive or brownish markings. The young, which hatch after 11 days incubation, are able to fly at about three weeks old and start to behave more like their parents. They are still easily distinguishable from their parents because of their more blotched and softer brown plumage. A single pair may raise three broods during the breeding season from April to July.

New plumage The only period when skylark song is absent is during the moult in August and early September when young and old alike renew their plumage completely. The young birds lose their soft blotchy plumage and the adults the old, bleached and tattered feathers they have worn for the whole of the preceding year. When the moult is complete, juveniles and adults are indistinguishable. The sexes always look alike, at least to human eyes, but the males average about 6% bigger

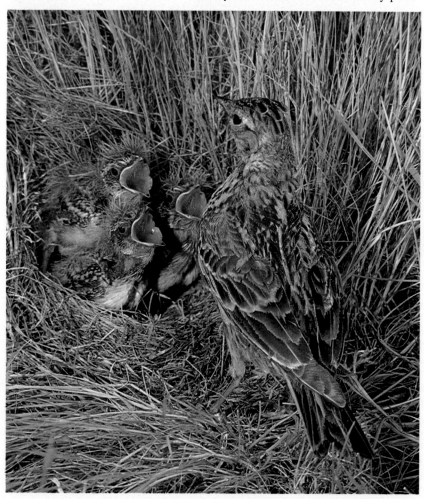

than the females.

During autumn and winter skylarks often join together in flocks which include young birds and immigrants from further afield. For much of the winter, territorial males can be heard singing in all but the bleakest areas. Only during the period of least daylight does song almost cease – presumably since the full hours of daylight are needed to find food.

Woodlark There is a marked contrast between the widely distributed and familiar skylark and the rare and local woodlark which is limited to southern Britain. Although the woodlark is now a rare bird it was common at the beginning of the 19th century. It suffered particularly during two cold winters in the early 1960s. During the 1970s there were many years when none was recorded but there may now be one or two territories occupied each year. Indeed, since the BTO's 1972 study the distribution of the species has contracted, with the outlying populations in parts of Wales and Lincolnshire in particular diminishing still further.

Woodlarks breed only in dry areas of heathland and downland. They need short grass areas for feeding, longer vegetation for nesting and some vantage points such as trees, bushes or even fence posts for song-posts. The woodlark's song is its most distinguished attribute – few birds have such a melodious and distinctive series of flowing notes which may continue, uninterrupted, for 15 or 20 minutes at a time.

The woodlark looks fairly similar to the skylark but it has a very short tail, (don't confuse it with the tailless, moulting skylark of late summer), a conspicuous dark brown and white mark on the leading edge of the closed wing, and a rather finer bill than the skylark.

One problem with such a rare species is that many inexperienced bird-watchers report tree pipits as woodlarks. Tree pipits inhabit a similar habitat and have a fairly pleasing song, although it is boring and repetitive when compared with a genuine woodlark. Their song flights are also quite similar for although the woodlark commonly sings from a song-post, it also sings during its looping display flight.

Breeding woodlarks are often found in traditional sites after intervals of several years. This may mean that breeding birds had been overlooked in the meantime, but it is much more likely to indicate that woodlarks look for a particular sort of area in which to breed.

The first clutch of eggs, usually three or four, is laid at the end of March or early April and there may be three broods a year. The young birds leave the nest before they can fly and hide singly in the vegetation whilst being cared for by their parents for a further 10-14 days. Both young and old birds moult in late summer and, in European areas where they are more common than in the British Isles,

Woodlark

Skylark

they can often be found in quite large loosely associated flocks on stubble. The song has ceased by this time, but their distinctive liquid call-note of three syllables – 'ti-loo-whit' – and their short tails identify them.

Skylark pie? With the great interest in bird-watching and bird protection in the 1980s it is amazing to record that less than 100 years ago there was a thriving export trade with France in dead skylarks. They were netted on the south downs and shipped across the Channel to be sold in French markets.

Skylark (*Alauda arvensis*), 18cm (7in) long from beak to tail. Distribution map opposite. Resident, winter migrants from northern Europe.

Below: Skylarks always make their nests on the ground. These nestlings are about two weeks old and are well camouflaged with their soft brown plumage.

House and tree sparrows

The house sparrow is a species closely associated with man, sharing his environment and sometimes even becoming a pest. Another less numerous species – the tree sparrow – leads a relatively hidden life in our woods and orchards.

The house sparrow is always seen in close association with man, his buildings and his livestock. It might be possible to describe such an association as 'commensal', except that this would imply some form of mutual benefit, or at least no detriment to either partner in the association. Short of enjoying its presence, we derive little benefit from the house sparrow. The bird, on the other hand, while gaining access to plenty of good nest sites (at no cost to us), oversteps the bounds of commensalism in its attacks on our garden plants. This becomes more serious when it attacks our cereal crops: the sparrow ceases to be commensal and becomes a competitor or, in plain terms, an agricultural pest.

House sparrows are not normally birds of open environments such as hillsides or moors. In the vicinity of farm buildings, however, especially those with livestock, a colony of house sparrows is likely to be present. The birds are also common bird-table visitors, eating almost everything that is put out for them. They even feed on scraps of meat, if it is ever available to them.

Above: The house sparrow's nest, made of coarse grass or straw, is roughly domed.

Below: The male house sparrow (right) can be distinguished from the female (left) by its black bib and grey crown.

Variations in plumage In spring, the male house sparrow is an attractive bird, with a grey crown bordered in rich chestnut brown. His back is a mixture of rich browns fringed with golden buff, his breast is greyish fawn and beneath the chin is a fan-shaped black bib. In winter he is drabber, since many of his body feathers have broad buff fringes which gradually wear away to expose the colours beneath in early spring. The upper plumage of the female (both in summer and winter) is a mixture of sandy or greyish fawns and pale browns, and she is greyish beneath. Until they moult in their first autumn, young birds of both sexes resemble the females.

If you travel about in Britain and Ireland, you may notice that house sparrows living far from towns have much brighter plumage than those living in the industrial conurbations, where the sparrows seem particularly dark. In such circumstances, some species of animals have adapted by changing colour to improve their camouflage. Best known is the peppered moth, normally white with a black peppering of spots. By the process of natural

Tree sparrow distribution

Distinguishing 'sparrows' in flight

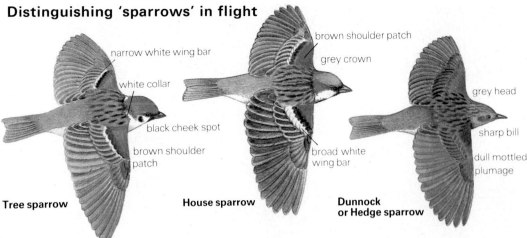

narrow white wing bar

white collar

black cheek spot

brown shoulder patch

Tree sparrow

brown shoulder patch

grey crown

broad white wing bar

House sparrow

grey head

sharp bill

dull mottled plumage

Dunnock or Hedge sparrow

selection, this moth has gradually evolved darker and darker colours, which improve its camouflage on the grimy trunks of city trees. Recently there was some debate as to whether house sparrows, too, were exhibiting this change (which is called 'industrial melanism'). Samples of sparrows of various shades were examined by experts. A strong superficial correlation was indeed found between darker plumages and more industrialised areas. Washing the feathers of all colour types with strong detergent, however, revealed that the darker ones had been contaminated with soot and other industrial grime, and thus their sombre shades were only 'skin deep'.

Feeding habits The house sparrow is an opportunist feeder, taking what food is easily available in greatest abundance at the time. The diet includes seeds, buds, leaves, shoots, flowers and a huge variety of human food waste and leftovers. Our sparrows are representatives of the largely African weaver-bird family, some members of which are as devastating to crops as plagues of locusts. It is not surprising, then, that our house sparrows flock into the corn at harvest time. Although each bird eats only a few grams of grain in a day, the house sparrow has an extremely wide distribution, and flocks often contain some hundreds of individual birds. The nationwide total of house sparrows is so high that the species is a serious pest, causing many millions of pounds worth of damage each year.

Many gardeners are incensed by house sparrow attacks on their flowering plants. We put out food for them, which they take greedily, only to start to tear apart the crocus and primula flowers when they appear. Although it may be of little comfort to the gardener, there is at least an explanation for this. Notice how often it is the yellow flowers that are attacked. Yellow coloration is associated with flowers that have a particularly strong attraction for pollinating insects, and tends to occur together with a rich supply of nectar. Yellow crocuses, for example, have far more nectar than purple ones. It is this nectar at the base of the flowers that the sparrows are seeking.

Formation of flocks Flocks are very much a part of sparrow life. They are an effective means of exploiting local abundance of food (as in cereal fields) and offer considerable protection from predators. They start to form in late summer, and are often composed largely of juvenile birds. These flocks roam over a distance of several miles. In winter, they join with other species, particularly finches and buntings, on stubble or weedy ground, or around places where livestock are fed.

From late summer onwards, roosting, too, is often communal. Sometimes the roosts are within buildings, and sometimes in the dense shelter provided by rhododendron, hawthorn

House sparrow (*Passer domesticus*). Resident near human habitations. Length 14.5cm (5¾in).

Tree sparrow (*Passer montanus*). Resident in many lowland rural areas. Length 14cm (5½in).

Below: A tree sparrow at its nest site on a cliff. Eggs are laid all through spring and summer, starting in March and continuing into August. Some pairs raise as many as three broods in a season.

or blackthorn thickets, or ivy-clad trees or buildings.

Nesting sparrows House sparrows can be seen around their nest sites in almost any month of the year, though attendance is at its lowest in late summer and early autumn. Attendance remains low through the winter, increasing as days lengthen and the temperature rises. Most nests are under the eaves of houses, or in some other cavity in a building. Some are in haystacks and more natural sites such as crevices in cliffs or in thorny or dense shrubs like hawthorn. Usually, several pairs build nests in a loose colony.

The song of a territorial male house sparrow is a monotonous, repetitive 'chirrup', a familiar noise to us all as he sits close to his chosen site, often adopting a squat, fluffed-up posture. Just as familiar is the sight of the female, perched on roof or guttering, wings drooped and shivering, soliciting the male's attentions. Sometimes there is a communal display, which becomes more and more excited, sometimes even out of hand, developing into a rough-and-tumble chase. Often a single female is the centre of attraction for several males.

Eggs are laid from March through to August, with each pair attempting two or three, sometimes four broods in a season. Their colours vary from off-white to dull brown, and all are flecked with rich brown. Four or five is the usual number, but clutch sizes range from two to seven. Incubation takes about 12 days, but the time is more variable than in most birds. The young fly after 11 to 18 days, depending on weather conditions and food supply.

The tree sparrow In many ways, the tree sparrow can be considered as the house sparrow's 'country cousin'. It is a slightly smaller, more muscular looking bird, about

Above: A male house sparrow in full breeding plumage.

Below: A tree sparrow in full summer plumage (the sexes are alike). It differs from the male house sparrow in having a brown cap and nape, and a black cheek spot.

two thirds the weight of its larger relative. The sexes are similar in plumage; the all-brown cap, the small black bib and the characteristic black spot in the centre of a white cheek distinguish them from the house sparrow. Their call, a rich, fruity chirrup, once heard and learned is an excellent way of separating the two species at a distance or in flight.

Tree sparrows are just as catholic in their food choice as house sparrows, but tend to shun the presence of man, usually feeding and nesting at a distance from human habitation.

The display pattern and the breeding season are closely similar to those of the house sparrow. The tree sparrow lays from two to eight eggs, usually about six, densely flecked with grey-brown. The nest is often in a hole in a building or a tree. In the latter case, the hole may be a natural one, or else the disused nest of a woodpecker. Tree sparrows readily occupy nestboxes, and are pugnacious in their tenancy of them, even evicting other birds such as blue or great tits, and building their own nests on top of those of the first occupiers. Incubation lasts 12 days, sometimes less, and the brood fledges after 10 days, or sometimes more.

Tree sparrows are nowhere as numerous as house sparrows, and have a much less widespread distribution in Ireland, northern and western Scotland, the Shetlands, Orkney and the Hebrides.

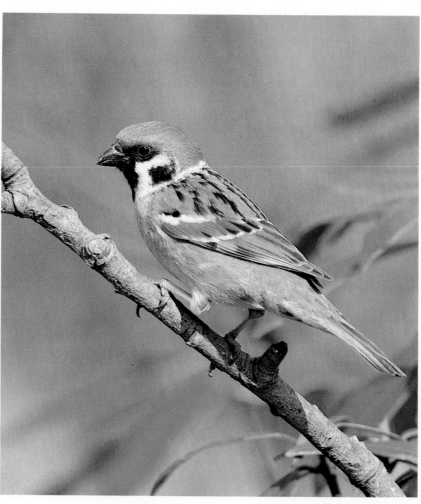

Yellowhammer and cirl bunting

Two of our smartest buntings are the yellowhammer and the cirl bunting. The yellowhammer is well suited to our climate, but the cirl bunting is really a Mediterranean species.

Buntings are slender songbirds that look similar to finches, with the same stocky seed-eating bills. However, they generally prefer more open country, feed mainly on the ground and have less musical or varied songs than finches. In all except the corn bunting, the male is brightly coloured–male yellowhammers and cirl buntings are particularly attractive–but females and young birds are drab and inconspicuous.

Vivid yellow The male yellowhammer is yellower than all other British birds except the yellow wagtail, and in summer his head is almost totally bright lemon yellow. His underside is also yellow, but with a brownish breast-band and a few brown streaks on the

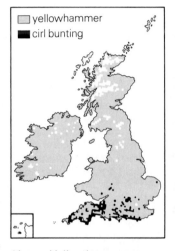

yellowhammer
cirl bunting

Above: Yellowhammers are widely distributed in Britain and Ireland, while cirl buntings are limited to southern England. Most birds of both species rarely travel more than a few miles in their lifetime.

Right: A male yellowhammer sits on a typical songpost. You can often hear the yellowhammer's jingling territorial song from late February to August or even September. Traditionally this familiar sound is verbalised as 'a-little-bit-of-bread-and-no-cheese'. A more accurate version might be 'chi-chi-chi-chi-chi-chi-chi-chi-chee'. At breeding time, his song warns other males where his territory is.

Right: Yellowhammers make their nests out of grass and a little moss, and line them with hair, fine grass and roots. Most choose a site within a couple of feet of the ground. Many actually nest on the ground, hidden among grass and other low plants. Some lay eggs as early as mid-April, but most start in May.

flanks. His upperparts are chestnut, and attractively marked with black and brown except for the rump, which is plain. The outer tail feathers are mostly white.

All yellowhammers, whatever their age or sex, have a chestnut-coloured rump–an important distinguishing mark. Young birds and females are much less yellow than males, particularly on the head. They are more heavily streaked and, apart from the rump, are easily confused with cirl buntings.

Active farmland life Yellowhammers are familiar farmland birds; in winter you find them feeding on stubble fields and ploughed land, mingling freely with larks and finches. Often the male's yellow head is the first thing

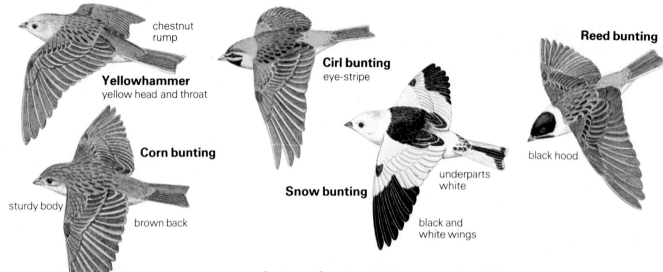

Yellowhammer
chestnut rump
yellow head and throat

Corn bunting
sturdy body
brown back

Cirl bunting
eye-stripe

Snow bunting
underparts white
black and white wings

Reed bunting
black hood

you see as he hops along in a low, crouched position. They often flock together at feeding places, and if disturbed fly into nearby trees for safety. In flight, yellowhammers have noticeably long, white-edged tails and a slightly bounding action. Often they call as they pass over—a sharp 'chip' or 'chillip'. Another characteristic call is a low 'dzee'.

They eat mainly seeds, especially leftover corn and the seeds of grass and weeds. They also eat wild fruits such as blackberries and, in summer, insect larvae, beetles, spiders, millipedes, and even slugs and earthworms.

Mixed habitat Yellowhammers nest in almost any country area. Ideally they need open ground for feeding, low scrub for nesting and taller bushes or trees as song-posts. Their favourite habitat is the edge of a young conifer plantation where brambles and other plants are still common; here they reach densities of up to 58 pairs in a square kilometre (150 per square mile). Most of our farmland has an excess of open ground and a

shortage of scrub and song-posts, but fields bordered by hedges with some tall trees are nevertheless quite suitable. Heaths and commons with clumps of hawthorn bushes have always been good yellowhammer sites, but in recent years the birds have spread into woodland.

During the cold winter of 1962-63, the whole yellowhammer population was severely reduced, but since then it has recovered well and there are signs that it was relatively unharmed by the cold snap in January 1982. Each year, the best breeding sites are occupied very early in spring, and late arrivals occupy whatever sites they can. However, now that the population is large again, farmland has become overcrowded, leading to an overspill into woodland rides and edges. Normally yellowhammers ignore these far-from-ideal sites, but since the only alternative is a tiny patch of farmland already filled to capacity, they have little choice.

Bird of many names In the past, the yellowhammer has been known by over 20 different names. Its bright plumage is mentioned in many of these. In Scotland, its local names

Above: left: There are five buntings that nest in Britain and Ireland, the most common and colourful being the yellowhammer. The cirl (pronounced serl) bunting has a very similar plumage but is quite rare. Two of the other species are common: the corn bunting—most frequent around cornfields—and the reed bunting, which favours wetlands. The snow bunting is a very rare British breeder; only a handful of pairs nest on mountains in Scotland, though many more visit us in winter.

Yellowhammer (*Emberiza citrina*); resident farmland bird, with yellow plumage, especially on head of male; 17cm (6½in).

Right: A female yellowhammer at her nest. The usual clutch is three or four eggs, but clutches tend to be smaller in conditions of overcrowding, in poor habitats, in northerly areas or very early or late in the breeding season; this is likely to be because there is not sufficient food for the parents to cope with large broods in these circumstances. As laying can continue until August, each pair has time for three successive broods, but egg-stealing magpies limit some to only two. Incubation takes 12-14 days and is largely the responsibility of the female, who is far better camouflaged than the male. The young fly at 12-13 days.

Above: The easiest way to find a cirl bunting is to listen for the male's rather simple, monotonous song. It sounds like a hurried yellowhammer's song (without the 'cheese'), but it can be hard to judge because yellowhammers themselves sometimes do not complete their song. The song is also often compared to the final rattle of the song of the lesser whitethroat–a warbler which sometimes nests close by. The cirl bunting's usual call is a weak, squeaky 'seep'.

Cirl bunting (*Emberiza cirlus*); resident in farmland in southern England; not unlike the yellowhammer but with black chin and eye-stripe, and olive colour on rump. 17cm (6½in).

include yellow bunting, yellow yorling, yellow yite and yellow yoit; and in some English counties it is known as the yellow amber, yellow yowlie and yellow ring. The lines on its eggs give rise to names such as writing master, scribbling or writing lark, scribblie and scribbler.

Cirl buntings These birds are stockier and slightly shorter-tailed than yellowhammers, but have very similar habits. Their food seems to be similar and you may see both species feeding together. Pairs are usually widely scattered, so that although family groups stay together in autumn and winter, they do not form large flocks.

An adult male cirl bunting is a handsome bird with very distinctive head pattern (although, as with the yellowhammer, breeding colours are subdued in winter). He has a black chin, a yellow-bordered black eye-stripe and a greyish streaked crown. Across the breast is a greyish-green band, and the flanks are chestnut coloured. The rest of the underparts, the tail and the back are similar to those of the yellowhammer except

for the rump, which is an inconspicuous olive colour and not chestnut.

As with yellowhammers, female and young cirl buntings are less distinctive, browner and more heavily streaked, but they still have the tell-tale olive-coloured rump. They lack the male's head markings, although the female has faint yellow stripes above and below the eye.

The song period, breeding season and choice of nest site are similar to those of the yellowhammer. Sometimes the cirl bunting nests in a large garden on the edge of a village, in which case the male may sing from a roof top or television aerial. The female both builds the nest and incubates the eggs, but is fed by her mate at this time. Even when she is feeding nestlings, he gives the food to her and she distributes it.

A more southern species England is currently the most northerly outpost of the cirl bunting; they were first discovered breeding in Devon in 1800. A century later they were common throughout England and Wales, and some bred as far north as Cumberland and Yorkshire. However, since then their range has contracted dramatically, and none now nest north of Worcestershire. At their peak, cirl buntings were more common than yellowhammers, but now you are lucky to find any –only 500 pairs are thought to survive here, compared with one million pairs of yellowhammers.

The cirl bunting is mainly a Mediterranean species, living in vineyards and orange groves, and on warm, bushy slopes. In these places they are still common, and yellowhammers have to nest in mountainous regions to avoid competition. As you might expect, in England cirl buntings only remain in the south and south-west–areas with relatively warm summers and mild winters.

Left: Female cirl bunting at her nest. Cirl buntings choose sheltered farmland habitats with tall hedges and trees, woodland edges, parkland and heaths, especially on south-facing slopes on chalk downland and in coastal valleys. The decline of the cirl bunting may be partly due to destruction of habitat, and also to disturbance; but the underlying factor is probably a change in the climate. The bird is a sedentary species and cannot escape bad weather; our cooler, wetter summers and occasional hard winters since the mid-century have not been to its liking. Outside this country, the cirl bunting is resident in south and west Europe and north-west Africa.

Index

Entries in italics indicate illustrations